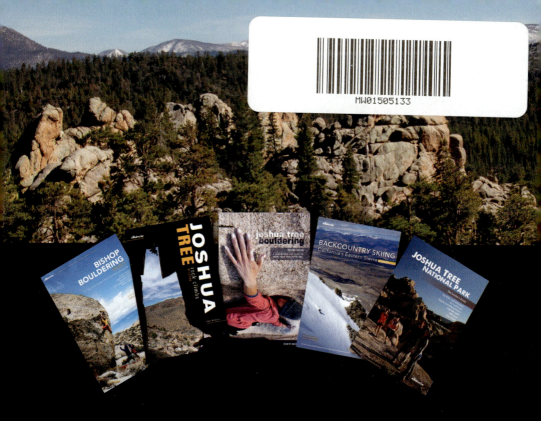

SoCal, so cool, all seasons

Wolverine

www.wolverinepublishing.com

WARNING

DO NOT USE THIS GUIDEBOOK UNLESS YOU READ AND AGREE TO THE FOLLOWING:

Climbing is a dangerous sport that can result in death, paralysis, or serious injury.

This book is intended as a reference tool for advanced/expert climbers. The activity and the terrain it describes can be or is extremely dangerous and requires a high degree of ability and experience to negotiate. This book is not intended for inexperienced or novice climbers, nor is it intended as an instructional manual. If you are unsure of your ability to handle any circumstances that may arise, employ the services of a professional instructor or guide.

This book relies upon information and opinions provided by others that may not be accurate. Opinions concerning the technical difficulties, ratings, and dangers of a climb, or lack thereof, are subjective and may differ from your and others' opinions. Ratings may differ from area to area, holds may break, fixed protection may fail, fall out, or be missing, and weather may deteriorate. These and other factors, such as rock fall, inadequate or faulty equipment, etc., may all increase the danger of a climb and may contribute to the climb being other than as described in the book. Furthermore, errors may be made during the editing, designing, proofing, and printing of this book. Thus, the information in this book is unverified, and the author and publisher cannot guarantee its accuracy. Numerous hazards exist that are not described in this book. Climbing on any terrain described in this book, regardless of its description or rating, may result in your death, paralysis, or injury.

Do not use this book unless you are a skilled and experienced climber who understands and accepts the risks of climbing. If you choose to use any information in this book to plan, attempt, or ascend a particular climb, you do so at your own risk. Please take all precautions and use your own ability, evaluation, and judgment to assess the risks of your chosen climb, rather than relying on the information in this book.

THE AUTHOR AND PUBLISHER MAKE NO REPRESENTATIONS OR WARRANTIES, EXPRESSED OR IMPLIED, OF ANY KIND REGARDING THE CONTENTS OF THIS BOOK, AND EXPRESSLY DISCLAIM ANY AND ALL REPRESENTATIONS OR WARRANTIES REGARDING THE CONTENTS OF THIS BOOK, INCLUDING, WITHOUT LIMITATION, THE ACCURACY OR RELIABILITY OF INFORMATION CONTAINED HEREIN. WARRANTIES OF FITNESS FOR A PARTICULAR PURPOSE AND/OR MERCHANTABILITY ARE EXPRESSLY DISCLAIMED.

THE USER ASSUMES ALL RISKS ASSOCIATED WITH THE USE OF THIS BOOK INCLUDING, WITHOUT LIMITATION, ALL RISKS ASSOCIATED WITH ROCK CLIMBING.

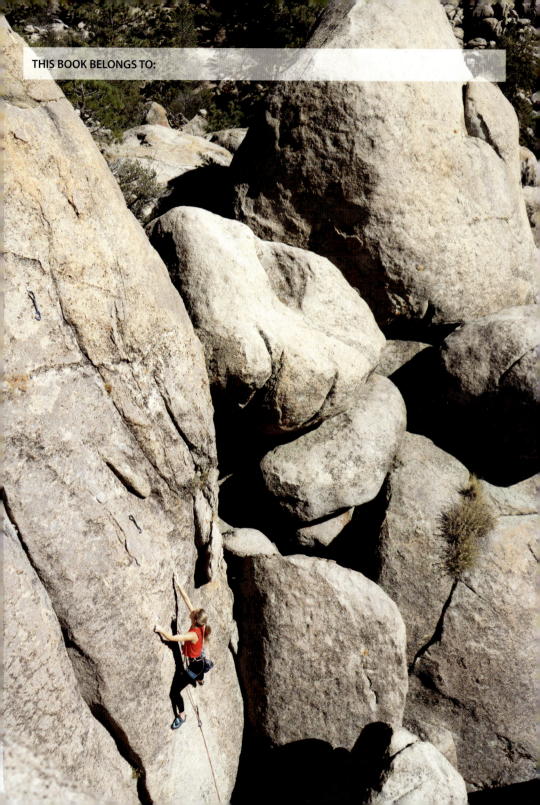

THIS BOOK BELONGS TO:

A CLIMBER'S GUIDE TO BIG BEAR LAKE AND HOLCOMB VALLEY PINNACLES

By Brandon Copp

Photographs: All uncredited photographs by the author

Design by Cardinal Innovative and Wolverine Publishing

Published and distributed by Wolverine Publishing, LLC

Cover: Brandon Copp on *Rapala,* Fisherman's Buttress, page 164. 📷 Jacqueline Copp

Back cover: Brad MacArthur at Microwave Towers, Grapevine Canyon, page 322. 📷 Brandon Copp

Title page: Helen Don Sing on *Heatseeker*, Holcomb Valley Pinnacles, page 100. 📷 Stephen Lê

International Standard Book Number: 978-1-938393-37-2

Library of Congress Catalog in Publication Data:
Library of Congress Control Number: 9781938393372

Wolverine Publishing is continually expanding its range of guidebooks. If you want to discuss a book idea, or would like to find out more about our company and publications, contact:

Wolverine Publishing, LLC.
PO Box 195
New Castle, CO 81647 USA
www.wolverinepublishing.com

Printed in South Korea

Brandon E. Copp

ACKNOWLEDGMENTS

First and foremost, I would like to thank my wonderful wife, Jackie. Thank you for pushing me to follow my dreams, for your unceasing patience throughout this entire project, and for spending countless late nights editing text with me. Without you, I would have never seen this book come to fruition. I would also like to thank my amazing family, for always believing in me and encouraging me to do this passion project. Your love and support mean the world to me.

A huge thanks to Ken Snyder, Thomas Laursen, Angela Hwangpo, and Matthew Janse for being the best climbing partners a guy could ask for. I appreciate all of the time you sacrificed to help me with this project, the endless days spent wandering to find obscure crags, the constant encouragement, and your invaluable review of my writing. Kenn Kenaga, I cannot begin to thank you enough for being one of my biggest supporters, putting me in touch with countless members of the climbing community, and becoming a dear friend. I want to thank Pat Brennan, Brian Elliott, Doug Odenthal, Eric Odenthal, Joe Sheehy, Dean Goolsby, Pete Paredes, Mike Rigney, Jim Voss, Reed Ames, and Brad Singer for providing valuable route information. This book wouldn't be what it is without all the contributions from the climbing community. Special thanks to Casey Ayotte & Joe De Luca for helping write the Little Tibet bouldering section, and also to Joe & Carey De Luca for all the work they put into the Holcomb Valley rebolting effort in the summer of 2019.

There have been so many people who have provided valuable assistance in some way, shape, or form along the way. Thank you to Brad MacArthur, Marina Amador, Derek Volcan, Landon Holman, Gene Yonemoto, Agustin Florido, Elliot Warden, Shehdad Khundmiri, Stephen Lê, the Rim of the World Climbing Club, and countless others who came out to lend a hand and contribute to this guidebook. I hope you all know how much you are appreciated. I also want to give a shoutout to Odub for his inspirational climbing music that pumped me up as I headed out to the crags each day.

Last, but certainly not least, I would like to thank Jeff and Amber and the team at Wolverine Publishing for their patience and assistance in making this dream become a reality. I couldn't have done it without you!

CONTENTS

GEAR COOP

SAVE 20%
ON GEAR TODAY!

CHECKOUT WITH CODE:

BIGBEAR20

TO GET 20% OFF YOUR PURCHASE

GEARCOOP.COM
#THRIVEOUTSIDE

NORMAN BIGAY ON "LONG ARM OF THE LAW", HOLCOMB VALLEY PINNACLES
PHOTO BY RYAN CHASE

COUPON VALID IN-STORE OR ONLINE. DISCOUNT MAY NOT BE COMBINED WITH OTHER OFFERS.

CONTENTS (CONTINUED)

FOREWORD

I received a phone call a few years back from Brandon telling me he was in the process of writing a new rock-climbing guidebook to the Big Bear Area and asking if I could help him with some information, history, and other specifics. Having written the past two guidebooks to the same area, I was a bit hesitant, as my territorial instinct kicked in. I thought, who is this guy, writing about our area and using my previously published material? However, I knew that I was not going to write another edition as the work involved amounted to huge time commitments, energy, and further research. Writing a rock-climbing guidebook to a one-dimensional geographical area is difficult enough. Writing the same for virtually dozens of crags spread over a large area can be overwhelming. What may start off as a hobby becomes an obsession and moreover, a labor of love. My desire was just not there.

Brandon has shown that desire and done a superb job. With persistent ground-work, dogged determination, and further research, he has produced an appealing, in-depth volume for any and all that seek fun and adventure rock climbing in the San Bernardino Mountains. With my nearly 40 years climbing experience in the area, I can appreciate the work that has gone into this edition.

With an ever growing population of climbers in Southern California and a limited amount of crags in which to climb, the San Bernardino Mountains, formerly a backwater in the climbing world, seem to have come into their own. Thanks to all the many first ascensionists who have made this happen, and namely to folks like Pat Brennan, Mike Rigney, Kenn Kenaga, Eric Tipton, Chris Miller, Eric Odenthal, Brian Elliott, and too many others to name who have opened up these areas to the next generation of climbers. But most of all, enjoy your time spent in these lovely settings and please treat the area as if it were your own backyard.

— *Brad Singer, Lake Arrowhead, 2020*

INTRODUCTION

Nestled in my sleeping-bag cocoon, I awake to the sounds of birds chirping and the quiet rustle of the breeze. I lie there for a long moment, enchanted by the harmonious music of the forest. Begrudgingly, I coax myself to get out of my cozy bed and soon the excitement for today registers in my brain. As I crawl out of my tent, I'm greeted by warm rays of sunlight streaking through the trees. The crisp fall air awakens my senses, and the smell of pine is heavenly. I gaze out at the spectacular granite spires rising in the distance, gleaming in front of a backdrop of majestic mountains. I can hardly contain my excitement at the prospect of another glorious day climbing at beautiful Big Bear Lake.

Over the last few years, I've begun countless days in exactly this way. I've been lucky to have the opportunity to spend my time in the picturesque San Bernardino Mountains, exploring the crags around Big Bear Lake for the sake of this guidebook project. The area is truly special, a haven above the clouds with a lifetime's worth of climbing tucked away in the trees, accessible only by dirt roads. Big Bear is a fantastic summer destination, with stunning scenery, endless rest-day activities, a laid-back mountain town, and a ridiculous number of climbing crags. Whether you want easy plate-pulling, spectacular views from atop a pinnacle, or a burn on a pumpy overhanging line at your limit, you're bound to discover what you're looking for at Big Bear Lake. Slabs, vertical faces, overhanging walls, monster offwidths, perfect hand cracks, thin seams, technical crimpers, big jugs, you name it! It doesn't matter if you are just learning to climb or sending your first 5.12s — once you experience what Big Bear has to offer, you'll be coming back again and again.

Many folks are destined to only visit Holcomb Valley Pinnacles, the most popular area in this book. While excellent classics exist there in high concentration, my goal is to open your eyes to many other amazing crags around the lake with equally good (if not better) routes. I hope to encourage you to lace up your hiking shoes and go have an adventure. Who knows?

You might just fall in love with the area and decide to join the clan of lucky climbers who call Big Bear Lake home. But whatever you choose, I really hope you enjoy your time here, and I look forward to seeing you at the crags.

— Brandon Copp, Huntington Beach, June 2020

HOW TO GET HERE

Main Route Via Highway 330/Highway 18:
From San Bernardino, exit from the 210 freeway onto Highway 330 in the city of Highland. Merge onto Highway 18 in Running Springs and continue east to Big Bear Lake.

The Back Way Via Highway 38: Take I-10 East to the Orange St. exit in Redlands. Continue straight for one block to the second stoplight at Orange St. Turn left. After 1 mile, turn right on Lugonia Ave./Highway 38. Follow Highway 38 to Big Bear City, situated on the east end of Big Bear Lake.

Alternative Route Via Highway 18: From the city of San Bernardino, exit from the 210 freeway onto Waterman Ave. North / Highway 18. Follow Highway 18 (Rim of the World Highway) as it passes near Lake Arrowhead and through Running Springs before heading to Big Bear Lake.

From the High Desert Via Highway 18: From Victorville, exit from the I-15 onto Bear Valley Rd. Head east toward Lucerne Valley. Turn right onto Highway 18, which bears right (south) in Lucerne Valley. Follow Highway 18 up the Cushenbury Grade to Big Bear Lake.

WHEN TO VISIT

The main climbing season is spring through fall, usually beginning in April and lasting until October. July to September is generally warmest with the most stable weather, but early and late-season climbing is often possible at lower elevation crags such as Grapevine Canyon or at south-facing walls like North Shore Boulders. Be advised that certain forest roads may be closed from November 1 to May 1, depending on weather conditions. A great resource for local Big Bear weather is www.bensweather.com.

VISITOR INFORMATION

Big Bear Lake is a tourism hub, and there's no shortage of information or activities. The following websites are great resources for planning your trip:

Big Bear Visitor Center: www.bigbear.com
Big Bear Discovery Center: www.mountainsfoundation.org

BIG BEAR DRIVING TIPS:

Conditions on the forest roads constantly change. For up-to-date information on road conditions and seasonal road closures, contact the local San Bernardino Forest Service office or check their website: www.fs.usda.gov/sbnf.

- Use turnouts to let others pass!
- Carry chains from November to April and be prepared to show them at checkpoints.
- In summer, turn off your air conditioner when heading up the mountain to prevent your car from overheating.
- Listen to FM 93.3 for road conditions.

EMERGENCY INFORMATION

FOR AN EMERGENCY DIAL 911

The nearest hospital, Bear Valley Community Hospital, is on Garstin Drive in the town of Big Bear Lake. It is a 40-minute drive from Holcomb Valley Pinnacles. Useful numbers:

- Bear Valley Community Hospital (909) 866-6501
- Big Bear Lake Fire Department (909) 866-7568 or (909) 866-4668
- Big Bear City and Sugarloaf Fire Department (909) 585-2362
- Fawnskin Fire Department (909) 866-4878
- Police non-emergency (909) 866-0100
- Big Bear Off-Road Recovery & Towing 24-hour service (909) 222-0265

HOW TO USE THIS BOOK

Crag Introductions. The sun and shade icons will help you determine the times of day you'll be able to find sun or shade. These are generalizations, since different facets of the same cliff will often have different aspects and sun/shade times. Hike times are estimates for a fit climber carrying a normal-sized pack and not lollygagging.

10 min

hike-time icon

Sun icons:

 All-day sun.

 All-day shade.

 Morning sun, afternoon shade.

 Morning shade, afternoon sun.

 Mixed sun and shade.

Color Coding. Both the route lines on cliff photos and the number bubbles in the photos and text are color coded with respect to how the route is protected:

BLUE denotes sport climbs. These are fully equipped — nothing but quickdraws, slings, and carabiners should be required. Protection is almost always from bolts, but occasionally optional gear placements can be found. Use your own judgment to evaluate what protection is adequate for your skill level. For some sport climbs, a stick clip may be recommended for high first bolts.

RED denotes traditional or mixed climbs. Cams, nuts, etc. are required for protection and often for anchors. Sections of bolt-protected climbing may or may not be found along the way.

GREEN denotes a toprope climb. Some of these have been, or could be, led, but are typically toproped through a fixed or gear anchor at the top.

ORANGE denotes a boulder problem. Some may have anchors and could be toproped, but most will have no protection and should be climbed with a bouldering pad.

Difficulty and Protection Ratings. This book uses the well-known Yosemite Decimal System, including the 3rd and 4th Class designations for scrambling, plus 5th Class difficulties from 5.0 to 5.15. Letters indicate subdivisions within the upper grades. Grades are subjective, derived from consensus whenever possible, but never perfectly applicable to everybody. Difficulties may vary with height, hand size, etc. Older climbs may hold their "historical" ratings even when newer climbs of similar difficulty are given higher grades. In short, there is no end to the reasons you may find a route's rating wrong, so use it as a general guide and be prepared for surprises.

In rare instances we have used "R" (dangerous) and "X" (very dangerous) grades to indicate routes with serious runouts or "ground-fall" potential. Note that runout sections well below the grade of the climb are generally not considered. Any lead can become X-rated if the leader overlooks protection placements, places pieces poorly, or wanders off route. Even perfectly protected climbs may have dangerous fall consequences if the leader becomes entangled in the rope or fails to protect against normal hazards such as sharp edges. Also, guidebook information is never complete; protection difficulties are not always known or indicated. You alone should always be the judge of a route's hazards. Be ready and able to back off if you find yourself exposed to an unacceptable risk.

Star Ratings. These describe the quality of climbs. Rock quality, aesthetics, quality of equipping, continuity and interest of the climbing movement, length of route, position, and historical significance are all taken into consideration. These ratings are relative to the area, and extremely subjective. If you don't like the kind of climbing — for example, offwidth crack or runout slab climbing — the stars will be meaningless. In other words, you personally may like, or hate, any given route regardless of the number of stars it's given in this book! That said, in general:

NO STARS: Not recommended. Might be chossy, dirty, poorly bolted, all of the above, or just too unknown to recommend.

★ 1 STAR: worth doing, but with some flaws.

★★ 2 STARS: a good climb.

★★★ 3 STARS: exceptionally good for the area.

★★★★ 4 STARS: one of the gems of the region for its grade.

(**NOTE:** Boulder problems are not star-rated.)

Pitch Lengths. These are approximate. Note that for some crags listed, 70-meter ropes are mandatory. In most areas, 60-meter ropes are fine. We have taken special care to note when a 60 or 70 is known to be barely long enough, or not long enough, for lowering or rappelling, but this information is not always complete. Tie knots in your rope ends!!

Bolt Counts. These are often given for sport climbs. Care has been taken to ensure bolt counts are accurate, but bolts may have been added since the count was taken, or the count may simply be wrong, so always bring a few extra quickdraws. The count does not include the anchors, so bring additional draws to account for those. Special consideration has been made to identify the anchor situation (no rap rings, shared anchors, etc.), as these can vary greatly from route to route.

Gear Recommendations. These are often given for trad climbs, but should always be taken with a grain of salt. Your gear needs may vary! The default recommendation of "standard rack" can be taken to mean a dozen or so nuts and a double set of cams from 1/2-inch to 3 inches, plus singles in the smaller TCU sizes and the larger cam sizes up to 4 inches. Eight full-length slings or quickdraws, one double-length sling, and a few free carabiners is also our trad "standard." We freely use the term "TCU" to indicate any small (1/2-inch or smaller) camming device, and use "wires" to mean small nuts. "RPs" is used to mean very small wired nuts or brassies.

Toproping. Routes that are commonly toproped (even though some may be led) are noted as such in this guide. Often there are bolts on top that can be used to set the toprope, although gear callouts have been made when

an anchor must by built. A few long slings or a section of short cord is helpful for extending the anchor over the lip to reduce rope drag. Please do not toprope directly off the anchors, as it prematurely wears the fixed gear! If you place a toprope on a route that is commonly led and leave it up for more than a short time, please be courteous, offering to share the rope or pull it to allow other climbers to lead the route. Totally dominating a rock or route with topropes, especially in the case of large groups, is extremely rude.

Map Legend. Scale of maps vary. Roads and trails are shown as follows:

interstate
improved road (paved or dirt)
4WD road
- - - - - - - - foot trail

Corrections & New Routes. Every attempt has been made to gather and verify the information in this book. If you do spot any errors, or have new routes to add to future editions, please contact the author by email at bigbearlakeclimbing@gmail.com. Thank you for helping to improve climbing at Big Bear Lake.

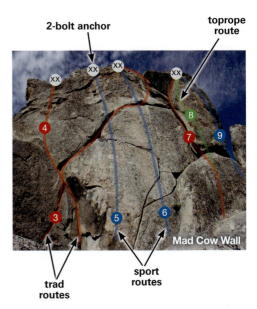

2-bolt anchor

toprope route

trad routes

sport routes

Mad Cow Wall

WHERE TO STAY

CAMPING

Camping options are plentiful in the Big Bear Lake region, with both developed and undeveloped sites near most of the crags. Please be smart and conscientious about human waste and fire, both of which are becoming an increasing problem in the area. Historically, the San Bernardino National Forest is one of the most wildfire-prone forests in the country, with a dry climate, flammable vegetation, steep slopes, and seasonal winds contributing to the danger. Know that campfires are only allowed in developed campgrounds and yellow post sites within designated fire rings, yet depending on current fire restrictions, will not always be appropriate or legal. Camp stoves will always require a permit for any location outside a developed campground. These permits are free, last a year, and are available at: www.readyforwildfire.org.

Holcomb Valley Campground. The closest campground to Holcomb Valley Pinnacles. $23/night. 19 first-come/first-serve tent sites. Vault toilets but no drinking water.

Serrano Campground. On the lake's north shore. $37/night. 100+ reservation campsites for tents and RVs with tables and campfire rings. Flush toilets, showers, and drinking water.

Pineknot Campground. Located next to Snow Summit Ski Area. $31/night. 47 reservation campsites for tents and trailers. Drinking water and flush toilets.

Big Pine Flat Campground. Northwest of Fawnskin. $25/night. 19 first-come, first-served tent sites with tables. Drinking water and vault toilets.

Hanna Flat Campground. Northwest of Fawnskin. $29/night. 88 campsites for tents and camping trailers, half reservation, half first-come, first-served. Drinking water and vault toilets.

Horse Springs Campground. Located in the Grapevine Canyon area. $10/night. 11 first-come/first-serve tent sites with tables. Vault toilets but no drinking water.

Oak Springs Ranch & Campground. Located nearby Grapevine Canyon. $15/night. Suitable for tents and RVs, with 2 cabins available. Drinking water, toilets, an outdoor kitchen, and horseback riding.

Bluff Mesa Group Campground. Located near Bluff Lake. $132/night. One large group campsite for tents and trailers that can accommodate 40 people. By reservation only. Picnic tables, grills, campfire circle, and a vault toilet, but no water.

Gray's Peak Group Campground. North of Fawnskin. $132/night. One large group

campsite for tents that can accommodate 40 people. By reservation only. Picnic tables, grills, campfire circle, and a vault toilet, but no water.

Yellow Post Sites. These sites are free, usually with picnic tables and fire rings but no other amenities. There are 33 designated first-come/first-serve sites in the Big Bear area, many shown on the maps in this book. Two-vehicle limit and 14-day maximum stay. For a complete map of locations, rules, and restrictions, visit the Big Bear Discovery Center.

Dispersed Camping. Dispersed, undeveloped campsites abound in the national forest. Before traveling, visit or call the nearest Ranger Station for current fire restrictions and area closures. General rules for dispersed camping include:

- Camp at least 200 feet from springs, water, meadows, trails, and main roads.
- Camp at least a quarter-mile from designated campgrounds, picnic areas, & trailheads.
- Camp at least a quarter-mile from state highways and private property.
- No wood or charcoal fires; chemical and propane stoves allowed with a California Campfire Permit.

HOSTELS
Big Bear Hostel – (909-866-8900) Located near the Village and the Big Bear Lake Brewing Company.

ITH Big Bear Hostel – (909-866-2532) Located near the Village in Big Bear Lake. They offer free hot breakfast and a home-cooked dinner.

HOTELS, MOTELS, BED & BREAKFAST
There is a wide variety of hotels, motels, and quaint bed & breakfasts in the area. You can find most of the big chains such as Best Western, Motel 6, Travelodge, and Holiday Inn. For a more historic stay, try the **Oak Knoll Lodge**, one of the oldest in Big Bear (circa 1920s) that's close to the south-shore climbing areas. In addition, the **Black Forest Lodge** is the epitome of Big Bear roots, owned and operated by the Wilson family since 1976. **Apples B&B** is known for its Victorian charm and is located near the Snow Summit Ski Resort. For more high-end comfort, **Robinhood Resort** is situated at the Village, within walking distance of the restaurants.

CABIN RENTALS
Many private options exist, including Airbnb. **SoCal Vacations** has a nice assortment of vacation rentals and a lodge in the Village. Use the code **BigBearLakeClimbing** for the climber discount!

Or, just rent a boat.

RESTAURANTS

FAWNSKIN

North Shore Café. The only place to eat in Fawnskin. They serve American dishes and it is definitely worth the stop for breakfast or dinner.

BIG BEAR LAKE

Big Bear has just about any type of food you might be craving. Listed below are a few of my favorites, but by no means is it a complete list. The Village is the place to visit for restaurants, a nice walk, and an ice cream for dessert.

Tropicali. A local favorite & highly recommended! Delicious Hawaiian-inspired bowls including poke, and everything is super fresh. Open for lunch and dinner.

Café Crêpe. Climber-owned — stop by and show some support! Authentic French crêpes (sweet or savory) and a good cup of coffee.

Fire Rock Burgers & Brews. The burgers here are amazing. Combine them with a great selection of tasty beers and you've got the perfect ending to your day.

Lumberjack Café. This cozy spot is locally owned and well worth the stop for any meal, but breakfast is best.

Whiskey Dave's. A "haunted" sports bar with live music and burgers.

Himalayan Restaurant. Wonderful Indian dishes in a great atmosphere.

Saucy Mama's Pizzeria. They'll make your pizza any way you want it and their dough is hand-tossed.

Big Bear Mountain Brewery. A great place to stop for a beer or grab a growler to go. Sandwiches, burgers, salads, and fries.

Big Bear Lake Brewing Company. Craft brewery centrally located in the Village.

Oakside. Casual dining, rustic-modern atmosphere. Large menu of quality food and a wide selection of wine, craft beers, & whiskey.

572 Social. This is a nice hangout spot with a chill ambiance and outdoor seating. American-style menu featuring steak, fish, burgers, and pizza.

Fast Food. There are plenty of fast food locations, including but not limited to: Domino's Pizza, Taco Bell, Jersey Mike's Subs, Subway, Jack in the Box, Carl's Jr., and McDonald's.

GROCERY STORES

Vons & Stater Bros. Both are located off Big Bear Blvd. on the east end of town.

CLIMBING STORE

Our local climbing store in the Big Bear area is **Bear Climbing Company**, located in the town of Fawnskin on the north shore of the lake, 3.2 miles east of the stoplight at the dam. They offer fair prices and the essentials to supply your climbing trip — chalk, carabiners, ropes, harnesses, helmets, quickdraws, and shoes. 5% of sales support the local climbing community.

OTHER ACTIVITIES

Big Bear Lake is a year-round playground for winter and summer sports enthusiasts, as well as a relaxing refuge. Its quaint mountain-town ambiance is a wonderful escape from city life. You'll find activities can be found for almost any interest: horseback riding, hiking, biking, camping, driving the Gold Fever Trail, pontoon-boat rentals, fishing, water skiing, jet skiing, kayaking, Big Bear pirate-ship rides, ziplining, bird watching, tours of the Big Bear Solar Observatory, picnicking at Boulder Bay, ski resorts (Bear Mountain & Snow Summit), Big Bear Alpine Zoo, escape rooms, horse-drawn carriage rides, helicopter rides — you get the idea. The Village also features unique shops and a great range of tasty cuisine. No matter your pace, there is bound to be something fun to do in Big Bear. For additional information, stop in at the visitor center at the base of the Village, your one-stop shop for all things Big Bear. Online, visit www.bigbear.com.

NEARBY CLIMBING AREAS

The San Bernardino Mountains offer a wealth of climbing, not all of which is included in this book. In addition to the Big Bear Lake area, other popular spots include Lake Arrowhead Pinnacles, Keller Peak, Snow Valley, and Frustration Creek. Check these resources for more information:

- *Climber's Guide to Frustration Creek and Surrounding Areas* by Louie Anderson (2020)
- *Boulderfest! The Snow Valley Bouldering Guide* by Matt Artz (2012)
- *Hidden Treasures: Rock Climbing in the San Bernardino Mountains* by Brad Singer (2002 — out of print)

The climbing options within a short drive of Big Bear Lake are almost limitless, but two of the more famous areas are:

- Joshua Tree National Park (1.5 hours)
- Tahquitz Rock (2 hours)

Climber's Guide to Frustration Creek and Surrounding Areas

by Louie Anderson

available from louieandersonclimbing.com

ETIQUETTE, ETC.

Please help preserve and secure access to climbing areas by joining the Access Fund. The majority of crags in this guidebook are located on National Forest Service land. Your behavior will help determine whether we retain the privilege to climb at these crags in the future. Please treat all climbing areas, private property, and old mining claims with sensitivity and respect. Obey signs, and follow any rules set forth by the Forest Service or landowner.

Please be respectful and considerate of others at the crags. The following are a few recommended guidelines.

- Use existing trails to protect plants and help prevent erosion.
- Park and camp in designated areas.
- Clean up after yourself (and unfortunately others).
- Toprope through your own quickdraws, rather than directly through lower-off anchors, to prevent unnecessary wear.
- Don't "claim" routes you aren't actively climbing by leaving topropes in place. In busy areas, share the resource!
- If you must retreat from a route, leave a bail biner, not a quicklink. Quicklinks soon become impossible to remove without a wrench, and often need to be cut off.
- Do not manufacture or enhance holds by chipping, drilling, or gluing. Rather, modify your ego.
- If you must bring your dog to the crags, be considerate of other climbers. You are responsible for maintaining a safe environment for others.
- Drones are loud and irritate other climbers; only launch if you're alone.
- Don't play loud music when others are nearby.

BOLTING AND HARDWARE

In the 1980s, when bolting began in the San Bernardino Mountains, routes were bolted from the ground up, on lead. Power drills were unknown, so developers used a hammer and hand drill, placing ¼-inch "buttonhead" bolts in most areas — the standard of the day, but now considered inadequate even when new. When places such as Holcomb Valley were developed in the 1990s, hardware improved slightly: 3/8-

inch expansion bolts became the norm, but stainless steel was still rare. In the 30-40 years since these bolts were placed, various chemical reactions have caused corrosion of the steel, with the bolts rusting away inside the rock.

Nowadays, there have been several changes to both ethics and hardware. Power drills have made it quick and easy to use larger bolts. Bolting on rappel has become common practice, allowing bolts to be placed wherever desired, rather than have locations dictated by natural stances or hook placements. Better awareness of corrosion has led to the widespread use of stainless steel, as now recommended by all climbing-industry sources. Part of the old ethic was a push to create bold, minimally protected climbs, with psychological challenge contributing to the difficulty. Today, the dominant ethic is to create safe and lasting climbs, with the challenge focused on the technical difficulty of the moves. Both styles can be found at Big Bear, with many shades of gray in between.

When assessing a possible new line, prospective developers should consider potential deal-breaker issues such as staging-area erosion problems, proximity to other routes, fragile rock features, sensitive plants, or potential for other resource damage. Please note that anchors, chains, quicklinks, hooks, etc. found at hardware stores are not reliable for climbing applications. For guidance about what to use on a route, please see the American Safe Climbing Association website: www.safeclimbing.org.

On less-trafficked crags you may encounter hanger-only anchors when a rappel is desirable. It is acceptable (and encouraged!) for anyone to add quicklinks and rap rings so that they and others may safely rappel off the route. It's a good idea to have a few such setups in your pack when you visit backcountry crags.

Climbing demands focus — but don't forget about everything else around you.
🄯 Stephen Lê

LEAVE NO TRACE PRINCIPLES

1. Plan Ahead and Prepare: Know the regulations of the area you're visiting. Call the local ranger station to find out current weather and trail conditions. Plan for the possibility of extreme weather, high water crossings, and other unexpected hazards. Bring a map and compass and know how to use them. Consider the physical condition, skills, experience, and expectations of all the members of your group when planning your trip.

2. Travel and Camp on Durable Surfaces: Please stay on the trail; cutting switchbacks causes erosion. If you have to hike off trail, avoid fragile areas such as meadows. Select a campsite on a hard, dry surface such as

GENERAL TIPS

If you are coming from down the hill, keep in mind that Big Bear Lake sits at an altitude of 6700 feet. Drink plenty of water, as your body needs extra to stay hydrated at this altitude!

Be aware of the local hunting seasons, especially if you're visiting more remote crags. Hunter-orange hats or clothing is highly advised — for dogs, too.

Limited cell phone reception is available at many crags, but do not assume your cell phone will always work. Some cell providers have better reception than others, but always have a backup plan and a first aid kit in case of an emergency.

Bolt counts, pitch lengths, and difficulty ratings will not always be correct, nor will notes regarding the amount, size, and safety of gear. Please rely on your personal assessment, take a few extra draws or cams, and check the reliability of all fixed hardware. Tie a knot in the end of your rope(s) whenever you rappel or lower.

If you are used to climbing in a gym or more "civilized" climbing areas, many of the crags in this book may take some getting used to. Some climbs have seen little traffic. Loose rock and lichen is not uncommon. Choose staging areas wisely and wear a belay helmet. On some crags, if you accidentally stray off route you may encounter very hazardous terrain. Be alert.

rock, sand, gravel, or pine-needle duff, not on vegetation or in meadows.

3. Dispose of Waste Properly: Pack out everything you pack in. Human food and trash are unhealthy for animals and leads to harmful habituation to human presence and food. Leave your campsite cleaner than you found it. Use toilet paper sparingly and pack it out.

4. Leave What You Find: Natural objects of beauty or interest, such as wildflowers, should be left for others to discover and enjoy. In all areas it is illegal to remove cultural artifacts such as arrowheads or pictographs.

5. Minimize Campfire Impacts: Where fires are permitted, use established fire rings. Consider using a portable gas camping stove instead. Always check fire restrictions before camping/hiking by calling the nearest ranger station.

6. Respect Wildlife: Never feed wild animals! This is for your own safety and the health of the wild animal. Habituation to human food leads to unhealthy interactions between wildlife and people. Pets must be kept under control and not allowed to harass wildlife, stock or other visitors.

7. Be Considerate of Other Visitors: Respect the solitude of others by avoiding boisterous behavior and loud noises, let nature's sounds prevail. Avoid the use of bright lights, cell phones, radios, electronic games, walkie-talkies and other intrusive devices. Use earphones instead of speakers. Keep noise down, especially at night or in remote places. Keep voices low.

ABOUT THE AREA

FLORA AND FAUNA

Big Bear Lake lies in a beautiful mountain valley with abundant wildlife, towering pines, and a plethora of flora. Fir, pine, cedar, juniper, willow, manzanita, mountain mahogany, lupine, sagebrush, buckwheat, buckthorn, and the rare Bear Valley sandwort are just a few of the species. Consider yourself lucky if you happen to see the unusual and rare red snow plant. There is also a diverse collection of wildlife, with over 200 species of fauna. Some of the more common you may encounter include the chipmunk, ground squirrel, lizard, Steller's jay, deer, redtail hawk, great horned owl, and various snakes. Less common are the black bears, bobcats, mountain lions, and gray foxes. Watch out for poison ivy and especially rattlesnakes.

In addition, Grays Peak in Big Bear is currently home to a pair of bald eagles, Jackie and Shadow, who have welcomed an egg to their nest in 2020 and will hopefully soon have a fledgling. The Forest Service has shut down public access to the surrounding area during nesting season. According to Friends of Big Bear Valley, this eagle nest has been actively used since the fall of 2013. With the public's continued support we are able to watch the local bald eagles thrive. More information can be found on the Friends of Big Bear Valley website: www.friendsofbigbearvalley.org/eagles.

Recently, the Forest Service has seen increased poaching of native wildflowers in Big Bear, some of which are endangered. We all share that impulse to pick wildflowers, but please help protect them in their natural habitats so that they can thrive and remain an enjoyment for future generations.

The Big Bear Discovery Center is a great place to learn about the local plants, wildlife, and the history of the area. They conduct 30-minute nature walks twice a day on weekends. These are free, and an excellent activity for a family. Find details at Big Bear Discovery Center's Guided Tours web page: www.mountainsfoundation.org.

GEOLOGY

The San Bernardino Mountains were uplifted by tectonic forces between the Pacific and North American plates along the San Andreas Fault. Rising high above the surrounding terrain, the mountains have experienced great amounts of erosion by intermittent streams that have carved numerous steep gorges. During the last ice age, the valley that is home to present-day Big Bear Lake was carved out by glaciers. As these glaciers receded, they left behind "pebble plains," fields of quartzite pebbles that became home to plant species not found anywhere else in the world. Because the mountains starkly contrast their surroundings, they have been deemed a "sky island" ecosystem.

The majority of the climbing at Big Bear Lake is on granite, with a few small crags of

Ken Snyder

quartzite. The granite ranges from smooth and featureless to coarse with visible crystals. The rock is generally well-featured, with positive edges, pockets, knobs, chickenheads, and interesting flakes that make for enjoyable climbing. The rock quality is generally good, best in spots like Holcomb Valley Pinnacles where years of traffic have cleaned off the loose rock, and more gritty at off-the-beaten-path crags.

BIG BEAR HISTORY

The first known inhabitants of Big Bear Valley were the Serrano people, Spanish for "mountain dwellers," or the Yuhaviat in their own language, meaning "People of the Pines." They occupied the Big Bear region for 2500 years until their lands were claimed by the Spanish in the late 1700s and early 1800s. The native population was decimated by smallpox and other European diseases during the first half of the 19th century. In 1821, the region became part of the new country of Mexico, until ceded to the United States in 1848.

In 1845, Benjamin Davis Wilson led a search party looking for outlaws who had been raiding ranches in Riverside. Their search took them deep into the San Bernardino Mountains, where they encountered a valley full of grizzly bears, which is how Big Bear earned its name.

The only "lake" there at the time was the seasonal marsh today known as Baldwin Lake, east of the large modern reservoir called Big Bear Lake.

In 1860, an Iowan named William Holcomb found gold in the Big Bear Valley. Holcomb was one of many thousands who had moved to northern California following the start of the gold rush of 1848, but with no luck there he decided to follow rumors of gold to the south. Along with many other prospectors, he made camp at Starvation Flats — located at the present-day intersection of Division Dr. & Big Bear Blvd. Holcomb was hired by other prospectors to hunt bear for food. One day, while tracking a large bear he had wounded, he discovered gold in a backcountry creek in what is now Holcomb Valley. The stream would yield some of the purest gold ever recovered in California. Soon, California's largest gold rush was ignited, and by July of 1860 the population of Holcomb Valley grew to 1500. This lasted until Barney and Charley Carter made the last major gold discovery in 1873 while they were on their way to the Rose Mine. Barney decided to explore the "shiny stuff" in the quartz ledge above their camp and found a mountain of gold ore. Elias J. "Lucky" Baldwin purchased "Carters' Quartz Hill" and set men to work the claim.

Today, a lone cabin sits in the meadow of Holcomb Valley at the site of the mining boomtown called Belleville. When prospectors discovered gold in the area, a town quickly sprung up that included saloons, gambling dens, hastily thrown-up miners' shacks, and

even a brewery. Most famous was the Octagon House, an eight-sided saloon and dance hall that had rooms where glitter girls entertained. For the town's first 4th of July celebration, the blacksmith's wife, Mrs. Jed Van Dusen, sewed together a flag made from dance girls' shiny skirts and the red and blue of miners' shirts. In honor of her patriotism, they named the town Belleville for her daughter Belle, the first child born to the settlement.

In 1883, a dam was built on Bear Creek to supply irrigation water to citrus farms in Redlands. This created the lake we all know and love today. Though smaller than the current lake, at the time it was the largest man-made lake in the world. As such, there were many skeptical engineers who claimed the dam wouldn't hold. When it did, it was called, "the Eighth Wonder of the World." In 1912, a new dam was completed 150 feet downstream and 20 feet taller than the original, submerging the old dam and nearly tripling the capacity of the lake. The Bear Valley Dam remains a tourist attraction to this day.

Getting to Big Bear Valley in the early days was a difficult trek, a two-day journey by horse-drawn stage from San Bernardino. In 1861, Jed Van Dusen opened a wagon trail — partly following the present-day route of Coxey Truck Trail in the Grapevine Canyon area — that was one of the first routes into Big Bear Valley from Hesperia. By May of 1892, the Bear Valley Wagon Road opened from Hunsaker Flat (Running Springs) to Fawnskin via Green Valley Lake. In 1899, Gus Knight and Hiram Clark built the Bear Valley and Redlands Toll Road that passed by Bluff Lake. These trips to Big Bear back then were quite the thrill. Daredevil drivers took dirt roads through pine forests and grizzly bear territory. Bear hunting was unregulated, however, and the entire grizzly population was soon killed off, with the last local grizzly bear seen in 1906.

As things progressed, so did the transportation to Big Bear. The early buses were known as White Stages. Kirk Philips opened the famous Mountain Auto Line in 1912, bringing passengers in by motor power, establishing the world's second-ever bus line. These buses carried 13 passengers and traveled via the Mill Creek Road past Bluff

Lake and emerged at the control gate opposite the historic Oak Knoll Lodge, which is still in business today.

Hollywood has long been drawn to Big Bear. Some of the movies filmed here include Rocky Mountain Mystery, Heidi, Gone With the Wind, North to Alaska, The Insider, Small Town Saturday Night, Doctor Dolittle, Old Yeller, and The Parent Trap; plus shots from TV shows including Bonanza, Lassie, General Hospital, The King of Queens, Grey's Anatomy, and The Bachelorette. The beautiful mountain landscape (and close proximity to LA) continues to draw in location scouts today.

As Big Bear continued to grow, a ski jump was installed in 1928 near what is now the Elk's Lodge, and a toboggan run installed behind the Village in 1938. These additions spurred the growth of winter sports in the Big Bear Area, leading more lodges and businesses to stay open year-round. The area's first ski

resort, Snow Forest, opened in 1949, followed three years later by Snow Summit Ski Resort. Artificial snowmaking began in 1961, allowing the resorts to operate all winter, and the area grew into a predominately winter destination compared to its earlier status as a summer attraction. Regardless of the season, Big Bear Lake is always a breath of fresh air and a beautiful retreat.

For more on Big Bear's colorful history, visit the Big Bear Historical Museum on Greenway Dr., which is open all summer.

CLIMBING HISTORY

Climbing in Big Bear likely dates back to at least the 1960s, evidenced by way of old pitons and pin scars at Castle Rock, one of the most obvious crags in the area to a passing climber. No records of these first ascents have been uncovered, however. Early pioneers Steve Untch and Aaron Barnes first explored Holcomb Valley in the early to mid 1980s. Focused on crack climbing, they did many of the obvious cracks — including *Bye Chimney* at Claim Jumper Wall and *Hootenanny* at Coyote Crag — before leaving the area in search of crags with more crack climbing. Typical of the era, their ethic was to lead everything without bolts and walk off afterwards, leaving no trace. While they were instrumental in putting the area on the map, not much is known about their early ascents. Although Big Bear's climbing history was not well recorded until later in the decade, another early ascent happened in 1982, when Dwain Warren, Rodger Gorss, and Roccko Spina climbed *Butt Crack* (AKA *Getting Small*) at Butt Rock with wedged 2x4s protecting the (now bolted) squeeze-chimney section!

As sport climbing took off in the late 1980s, Troy Mayr and his friends bolted numerous routes on Hungover Wall at nearby Keller

FA of *Canoe Slab*, Finger of God, 1990.
📷 Odenthal collection

Peak, just southwest of the crags covered in this guidebook, establishing Southern California's first summer sport crag. For a time, climbers flocked to this small spot in the San Bernardinos, and during its brief heyday it wasn't unusual to find more than 30 people there on any given weekend. Soon, with the large-scale development of Williamson Rock in the neighboring San Gabriel Mountains, Keller Peak settled back into obscurity.

Fueled by the sport-climbing boom that brought eager climbers to the San Bernardinos, exploration of Holcomb Valley began anew. While compelling crack climbs were rare, the rock's fantastic face features held much promise for this new breed of climbers. In 1989, Rick Shull established Holcomb Valley Pinnacles' first bolted route, *Cling Plus* (5.11c), a classic to this day. At the hands of Shull, Brad Henderson, Jim Hammerle, Bob Cable, Julia Cronk, Chris Miller, Tim Fearn, and Dave Masuo, early route development began in Holcomb Valley Pinnacles, known at the time as Big Bear Pinnacles or Coyote Crags.

While this was happening, Doug Odenthal discovered the potential for climbing in Grapevine Canyon. In mid-1989, he and his friends Joe Sheehy, Brian Elliott, and Cindy Elliott established some of the first climbs in this area, including *Committee Crack, Newtonian Mechanics, Nothing but the Blues, Wook'n Pa Nub*, and *Nuclear Meltdown*. Unlike the new breed, this team was focused on bold, ground-up ascents, hand-drilling bolts sparingly, as was done in nearby Joshua Tree. In 1990, the spectacular arête climb *Vector Analysis* was established on the pristine granite of Butt Rock (AKA Gnome Dome). While it was kept off of the radar for many years, Grapevine Canyon was actually one of the first locations to see significant development. In a few short years, Brian, Joe, Doug, and Cindy opened over 100 new routes before their dust settled in the mid 1990s.

The 1990s saw a surge in development around Big Bear Lake. Dean Goolsby and Craig Pearson began ticking off routes on the south shore near Bluff Lake, uncovering Castle Grey Skull and many other small formations on Kidd

Creek Road. They soon set their sights across the lake on the taller walls of the Coven, where they spent the next few years opening lines like *Sorcery, Alchemy,* and *Weave the Magic.* Concurrently, Bob Cockell established the majority of the routes at North Shore Boulders, located near his home, before moving out of state. At this same time, Chris Miller and company were putting up quality lines in the Central and South regions of Holcomb Valley Pinnacles. Gems such as *Lost Orbit, Road Crew,* and *The Incinerator* were all products of this time period. Grahm Doe and Brent Webster established a handful of lines there as well, including *Mighty Quinn,* one of the most popular 5.10s in Holcomb today, and *The Prowler,* an imposing and overhanging 5.12.

In 1994, W. Scott Hoffman created the area's first printed guide, titled *Climbing Routes of Southern California's Big Bear Valley.* It documented 95 routes and provided climbers with a valuable resource for the area. The next guide was published in 1995, adding new spots like Hanna Rocks and the Coven to the mix. *¡Oso Grande!* by Alan Bartlett and Chris Miller captured over 130 routes specifically on the north shore of the lake, and provided some of the first overview maps of these crags. In addition to these publications, topos of Big Bear crags ran as mini-guides in popular magazine publications in the '90s, including *Allez, mOthEr rOck,* and *Rock & Ice.*

During the late '90s and early 2000s, development continued in earnest. Chris Miller, Lisa Guindon, Pete Paredes, Chuck Scott, and Loren Scott were instrumental in the development of Holcomb's Central Pinnacles, bolting volumes of routes and establishing many of the well-known classics and modern-day testpieces. Along with them, other important players began breaking into the Big Bear Lake climbing scene. Brad Singer, Mike Rigney, Pat Brennan, and Kenn Kenaga were working their way east from Lake Arrowhead, exploring and prolifically developing routes throughout the entire region. John Cardmon, Eric Tipton, Rob Stauder, Jeff Brennan, and others added many other excellent lines at various crags. In addition, Eric Odenthal and David LePere were responsible for establishing many of the area's hardest climbs, including two 5.12d routes, *Screaming Trees* and *Silk.* The

Doug Odenthal, FA of *Bolting Begins at 40,* Physics Rock, 1989. ◻ Odenthal collection

climbing scene was growing rapidly.

This time period saw crags such as Black Bluff and Fisherman's Buttress emerge. The long, tall cracks at Arctic Temple were climbed, as were the short, sunny faces at Legoland and the Holcomb Creek Crags. More and more scattered formations saw ascents as Brad Singer, Pat Brennan, Kenn Kenaga, and members of the Rim of the World Climbing Club (ROWCC) continued to seek out new lines. Based in Lake Arrowhead, the ROWCC was becoming increasingly active, as its membership had been growing steadily since its formation in 1989. From 1996 to 1998, the ROWCC hosted the Snow Valley Boulderfest competition, with 40 people participating the first year on 80 different boulder problems. At its last iteration, over 130 climbers attended, and in that short time span, almost 500 problems had been established. Today, over 1000 established boulder problems for all abilities exist at Snow Valley, a testament to the dedication of this core group of climbers.

Brad Singer's 2002 publication of *Hidden Treasures: Rock Climbing in the San Bernardino Mountains* described nearly 1350 routes in the San Bernardinos, including the crags of Big Bear Lake and Holcomb Valley Pinnacles along with the Lake Arrowhead Pinnacles, Keller Peak, Green Valley Lake crags, and more. When Williamson Rock was closed in December of 2005 to protect the endangered Mountain Yellow-Legged Frog, Holcomb Valley Pinnacles became Southern California's new summer climbing destination. With the boost in popularity, Brad followed up his first guide with a second in 2008 — *Hidden Treasures East: Big Bear Basin* — focused entirely on the crags around Big Bear Lake.

2006 saw first ascents of some of the most difficult lines in the region. Butt Rock in Grapevine Canyon attracted Chris Righter, whose challenging arête *Losing My Edge* (5.13c/d) set the high bar for climbing in the San Bernardinos. That same year, Louie Anderson added his burly, overhanging *Analysis Paralysis* (5.13c) to the same wall. Combined with a few nearby 5.11s and 5.12s, this solidified Butt Rock as a crag to seek out for its high concentration of hard routes.

In the last decade, development has slowed since its peak in the late '90s and early 2000s, but folks are still filling in the gaps. Pat Brennan, Kenn Kenaga, and other members of the ROWCC have developed lesser-known crags such as John Bull's Box Canyon. Pete Paredes and Loren Scott have found new climbs in the outer reaches of Holcomb Valley. Chris Miller continues to put up numerous lines, alongside Reed Ames and other friends, while newcomers have begun to establish a few lines here and there. The popularity of the Big Bear area is continuing to grow — who knows what the future will bring?

Circa 1960s: *Castle Crack* (5.10c) – A prominent 100-foot crack, likely one of the routes done during early explorations at Castle Rock.

1982: FA *Butt Crack* AKA *Getting Small* (5.10b) by Dwain Warren, Rodger Gorss, and Roccko Spina. Spectacular dihedral at Butt Rock.

1989: FA *Cling Plus* (5.11c) by Rick Shull, at Parking Lot Rock in HVP – first bolted line in Holcomb Valley.

1989: *Committee Crack* (5.10c) – first of many Grapevine Canyon routes put up by Brian Elliott, Doug Odenthal, Joe Sheehy, and Cindy Elliott.

1989: Rim of the World Climbing Club formed.

1990: FA *Canoe Slab* (5.11a) at Cap Rock and *Vector Analysis* (5.11b) at Butt Rock, two of Grapevine Canyon's best, by the Elliott et al team.

Early 1990s: First 5.12s in the area, including *Armageddon*, a 5.12a splitter crack in Grapevine Canyon, by Troy Mayr. Also *Road Crew* by Steve Shobe and Chris Miller, and *The Incinerator* by Chuck Scott, both 5.12a sport routes in HVP.

Mid-1990s: FA *Sorcery* (5.12c) on Dragonlance Wall at the Coven, Dean Goolsby and Craig Pearson's hardest route and the toughest route in the area at the time.

1995: FA *Coyotes in the Henhouse* (5.10d) on Claim Jumper Wall by Sam Owings, Tony Egnozzi, Kevin Duck – one of the best routes in Holcomb Valley Pinnacles.

1997: FA *Trout Fishing in America* (5.11b) by Brad Singer and Rob Stauder, one Fisherman's Buttress' first sport routes.

1998: FA *Migs Over Moscow* (5.11b), a fine route at Hanna Rocks. This was David LePere's first new route in the Big Bear Lake area.

1999: *Aurora Borealis* (5.9) at Black Bluff by Eric Tipton and Pat Brennan, one of the best crack climbs in the region.

2002: FA *Screaming Trees* (5.12d) on Dragonlance Wall at the Coven, hardest climb in the area at the time and the toughest of the many that Eric Odenthal put up.

2003: FA *Silk* (5.12d) on Siberia Creek Tower. David LePere's hardest route.

2006: FA *Analysis Paralysis* (5.13c) by Louie Anderson, and *Losing My Edge* (5.13c/d) by Chris Righter – hardest routes in the region, both at Butt Rock in Grapevine Canyon.

2010: FA *Crematorium* (5.12d) at Incinerator Wall by Matt Hulet, one of Holcomb's hardest.

2011: FA *4-Star 5.9* (5.13b) by Joe De Luca, currently the hardest-rated line in HVP.

KENN KENAGA

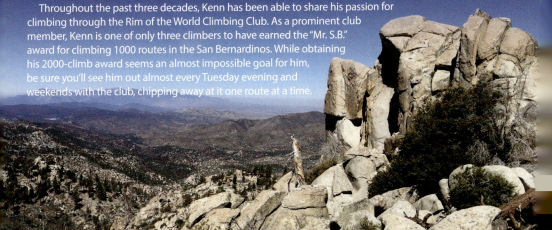

Kenn Kenaga has been a fixture of the Rim of the World Climbing Club since its founding in 1989. His insatiable desire to share his passion for climbing with others has resulted in many friendships over the years, and the classic lines he's established have helped make the San Bernardinos into the premier climbing destination it is today. Born in 1952, Kenn grew up in San Diego with six brothers and a sister. Always a mountain man, he plastered his wall with forestry maps, aspiring to one day become a lookout-tower ranger. At age 16, Kenn attended Camp Alpine in Lake Arrowhead with his church group. He instantly fell in love with the area and applied for the camp's summer staff the following season. In 1971, Kenn moved up to the mountains, where he and Susan, his wife of 43 years, have lived ever since.

In 1989, Kenn attended a slideshow given by local climber Steve Untch, where he met Pat Brennan, who quickly became his main climbing partner. At the time, Kenn aspired to climb the Keeler Needle after laying eyes on its spectacular face during a previous trip to Mount Whitney, and Pat promised to get him trained up. The pair's first outing was to Turtle Dome, where Pat informed Kenn that in order to climb Keeler Needle, he'd have to work the *Turtle Dome Crack* offwidth until he could do five laps up and down without touching the ground. From then on they trained relentlessly, climbing all the cracks they could get their hands on.

In order to get in shape for the routes in the Sierra, Kenn and Pat soon started putting up FAs near their homes in the San Bernardinos. In the early 1990s, they led bold crack lines and began bolting crags at Lake Arrowhead Pinnacles. When they had tapped out the obvious lines there, the duo set their sights on finding undone projects further east around Big Bear Lake. All of this "training" paid off, as Kenn went on to free many old Fred Beckey routes in the Sierra and climb the 28 14,000-foot summits on the West Coast.

Kenn is best known for his climbing tenacity, grit, and love of offwidths. The first ascents he's most proud of include two routes at Lake Arrowhead Pinnacles that have to be climbed feet-first while hanging upside-down — *11DD* at the Skull and *Soles to the Sun* on the upper tier at Rotten Rock Valley — as well as his multi-year project *Does Sue Know?* (5.12a), an impressive overhanging crack route at the Aztec Pond near Running Springs, California.

Outside of climbing, Kenn works in high-end custom cabinetry, and notably used his expertise to build the solar envelope home where he and his wife live. He is a devout Christian and is passionate about his relationship with Christ, one of the only things in his life more important than climbing. He has been a member of the Rim of the World Search and Rescue team since 1985. Over the years, Kenn has even applied his search & rescue and climbing skills to rescuing numerous local cats that became stuck in trees. To date, he's completed over 50 cat rescues, but a nasty fall that left him with nine broken ribs and multiple compressed vertebrae forced him to "retire" from duty.

Throughout the past three decades, Kenn has been able to share his passion for climbing through the Rim of the World Climbing Club. As a prominent club member, Kenn is one of only three climbers to have earned the "Mr. S.B." award for climbing 1000 routes in the San Bernardinos. While obtaining his 2000-climb award seems an almost impossible goal for him, be sure you'll see him out almost every Tuesday evening and weekends with the club, chipping away at it one route at a time.

HOLCOMB VALLEY PINNACLES

Brad MacArthur ascends *Claim Jumper*, 5.10a,
Claim Jumper Wall, page 67. 📷 David Aldama

HOLCOMB VALLEY
PINNACLES

Holcomb Valley Pinnacles is the central hub for rock climbing in the Big Bear Lake area. Nestled in picturesque mountains near 7500 feet in elevation, the Pinnacles experience perfect sending temps from spring through fall. This climber's mecca has become one of Southern California's premier summer climbing destinations. The heavily featured granite makes the area a moderate sport climber's paradise, home to the greatest concentration of routes (400+) in the San Bernardinos.

Moderate sport climbs may have put the area on the map, but with everything from easy plate-pulling to technical slab, strenuous overhanging lines to fist-eating cracks, there's something perfect for everyone! The majority of the routes range from 40 to 60 feet in length, with the Central Pinnacles area boasting the most classic and tallest lines. In addition to the well-traveled walls, Holcomb contains a plethora of smaller crags with a handful of routes apiece. These walls are perfect for escaping the weekend crowds and offering a change in scenery. If bouldering is your passion, Holcomb has an abundance of problems scattered throughout the forest. Overall, the rock quality is exceptional, featuring large flakes and good edges.

The two developed campgrounds nearest Holcomb Valley Pinnacles are the first-come, first-served Holcomb Valley Campground ($23-25/night in 2020) and the by-reservation-only Tanglewood Group Campground, although many other options exist in the surrounding area. Both of these developed campgrounds offer toilets and limited amenities. Dispersed camping is also allowed throughout the national forest. For more information on rules and restrictions, please refer to the camping section in the introduction of this book or contact the Forest Service directly. Many climbers choose dispersed camping near Holcomb's southern parking lot, but using the developed campgrounds whenever possible will lessen our impact.

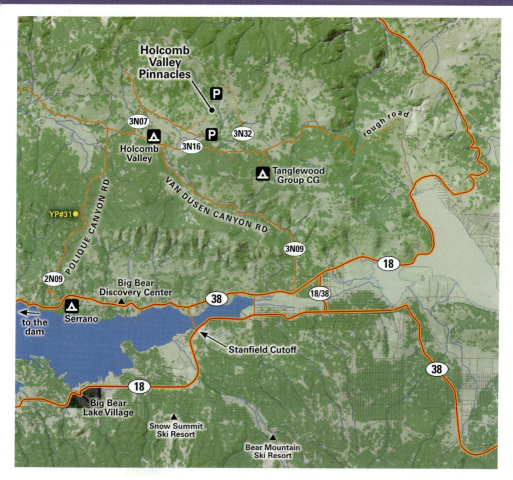

Approach: There are two primary driving approaches to Holcomb Valley Pinnacles' main southern parking lot, **Polique Canyon** Road and **Van Dusen Canyon** Road. Both are graded dirt roads that are passable with a 2WD vehicle in most conditions, although high-clearance vehicles are recommended. Be aware that after a rain, deep puddles on 3N07 can fill with several feet of water, making passage more difficult. Also, the parking area can get quite full on summer weekends. Please be courteous and park efficiently. Holcomb's northern parking area is accessed via an alternate route, where high clearance is a must and 4WD is recommended. Please note that larger vehicles may have trouble passing through the narrow squeezes between boulders on the final stretch to the northern parking area.

Polique Canyon Approach: This is the best approach if coming from the direction of the dam or in the off season, as this road is generally open year-round. From the stoplight at the dam, drive 5.1 miles on Highway 38 along Big Bear Lake's north shore. Turn left onto Polique Canyon Road (2N09). Continue for 3.8 miles to a righthand turn onto 3N16, marked by a brown Forest Service sign. Take 3N16 for 0.4 miles as it goes down and then up a large hill. Turn left at the top of the hill onto 3N07. 3N07 passes beside Wilbur's Grave and weaves through the trees (deep puddles possible here). In 0.4 miles, the road tees; turn right and continue to the road's terminus at Holcomb's southern parking area (1.1 miles past the tee).

Jacqueline Copp meets the *Gold Standard,* 5.6, Gold Wall, page 71. 📷 Brandon Copp

Van Dusen Canyon Approach: This approach is best if coming from the town of Big Bear, from Lucerne Valley, or up the backside of the San Bernardinos on Highway 38. Please note that Van Dusen Canyon Road may be closed and gated from November 1 to May 1 each year, depending on weather conditions. From the town of Big Bear, travel east to the Stanfield Cutoff. Cross the cutoff to the north shore of the lake and turn right on Highway 38. Drive 1.8 miles east on Highway 38 to Van Dusen Canyon Road, on the left. (From the dam, Van Dusen is located 9.0 miles east along Highway 38.)

HVP Southern Parking Area

Turn left onto Van Dusen Canyon Road (3N09), and drive for 3.8 miles to a tee with 3N16 at a Forest Service fire-danger sign. Turn left onto 3N16 and follow this past the Holcomb Valley Campground. Note: Be wary of the two big speed bumps on either side of the campground — taking these at anything but a crawl could seriously mess up your vehicle! Follow 3N16 for a total of 0.5 miles, then turn right onto 3N07. 3N07 passes beside Wilbur's grave and weaves through the trees (watch for deep puddles). In 0.4 miles, the road tees; turn right and continue to the road's terminus at Holcomb's southern parking area (1.1 miles past the tee).

Northern Parking Lot Approach: From Highway 38, turn left onto Van Dusen Canyon Road (3N09) 1.8 miles east of the Stanfield Cutoff, or 9.0 miles east of the stoplight at the dam. Drive north on Van Dusen Canyon Road (3N09) for 3.8 miles to a tee. Turn right onto 3N16 and follow this for 1.4 miles, passing the Belleville log cabin (a stop on the Gold Fever Trail). Turn left onto 3N32 and drive this road north for 1.1 miles to a fork with a cairn. Go left here, driving 0.5 miles on this bumpy road as it heads west and then eventually south to reach Holcomb's northern parking area. Note: The final stretch of road contains a narrow squeeze between boulders, where larger vehicles may not fit.

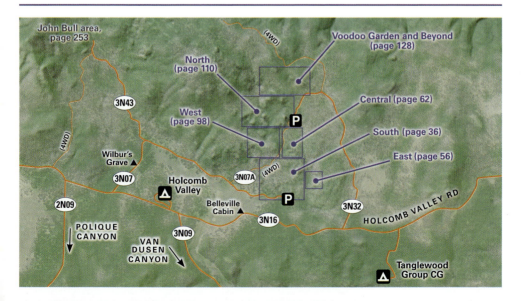

John Bull area, page 253

(4WD)

Voodoo Garden and Beyond (page 128)

North (page 110)

3N43

West (page 98)

Central (page 62)

P

South (page 36)

(4WD)

Wilbur's Grave

East (page 56)

3N07

3N07A

(4WD)

Holcomb Valley

2N09

P

Belleville Cabin

3N32

HOLCOMB VALLEY RD

3N16

POLIQUE CANYON

3N09

VAN DUSEN CANYON

Tanglewood Group CG

HOLCOMB VALLEY PINNACLES **SOUTH**

These are the first crags encountered from the southern parking area. Lost Orbit Rock is the standout wall in this area, with a high concentration of excellent climbs on good-quality rock. Many of the other smaller walls see little traffic, so this is a good place to escape the crowds and try something different. The routes are generally in the 40-50 foot range, fairly typical of Holcomb Valley, with Prowler Rocks having a few longer lines.

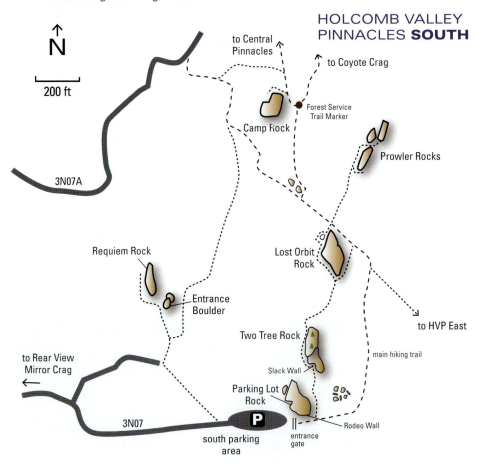

HOLCOMB VALLEY PINNACLES SOUTH

Approach: The drive into Holcomb Valley via Forest Road 3N07 will take you to the southern parking lot, where Parking Lot Rock will be obvious. Head east from the parking lot through a gap in the fence. The main trail leads to the majority of the crags, with the exceptions being Entrance Boulder, Requiem Rock, and Rear View Mirror Crag. Approach times vary from less than a minute to 10 min.

If you instead parked at the northern parking area, head south through the Central Pinnacles amphitheatre or along the 4WD road to reach Camp Rock. Approach times from this direction range from 10 to 20 minutes.

CLIMBING AREA	ELEVATION	HIKE	ROUTES	GRADE RANGE	CRAGS
REAR VIEW MIRROR *Mild trad routes* page 38	7400 ft.	1 min	2	≤.5 .6 .7 .8 .9 .10 .11 .12	
ENTRANCE AREA *Slab and crack climbs* page 38	7400 ft.	10 min	7	≤.5 .6 .7 .8 .9 .10 .11 .12	Entrance Boulder, Requiem Rock
PARKING LOT AREA *Range of difficulty and route quality, up to 5.13!* page 40	7400 ft.	1-2 min	18	≤.5 .6 .7 .8 .9 .10 .11 .12+	Parking Lot Rock, Rodeo Rock
TWO-TREE AREA *Must do:* Edu Zepic, *10c* page 44	7400 ft.	3-5 min	11	≤.5 .6 .7 .8 .9 .10 .11 .12	Slack Wall, Two Tree Rock
LOST ORBIT ROCK *Semi-popular, wide variety* page 47	7400 ft.	5 min	33	≤.5 .6 .7 .8 .9 .10 .11 .12	East Face, West Face, South End
PROWLER ROCKS *Variety of climbing styles* page 53	7500 ft.	10 min	5	≤.5 .6 .7 .8 .9 .10 .11 .12	
CAMP ROCK *Must do:* Oso Paws, *10a* page 54	7500 ft.	10 min	5	≤.5 .6 .7 .8 .9 .10 .11 .12	

REAR VIEW MIRROR CRAG

This little tower is located along 3N07 on the drive into Holcomb Valley Pinnacles. Often overlooked, this southeast-facing crag offers two mild trad routes with a minimal approach. A fine spot to run up a couple of routes with the rock to yourself.

AM **1 min**

Approach: From the Holcomb Valley Pinnacles southern parking lot, drive back down the entrance road (3N07) for 0.75 miles. The small tower will come into view on your right underneath a power line. Park on the south side of the road where the shoulder widens enough for a car. It's a super short 1-minute approach!
   Alternatively, if stopping here on the drive into HVP, the crag is located 0.4 miles from the fork in 3N07 where 3N43 splits off left. In this case, the rock will be on the left side of the road. **[GPS: 34.30692, -116.89161]**

❶ Rear View Mirror Crack 5.8 ★
This thin crack splits the middle of the tower and is located 5 feet right of a tree growing on the rock. A tough start on slick rock, with the crack getting more featured up higher. Skirt right underneath the block at the top.
25 ft. Gear to 2". Eric Odenthal, Kenn Kenaga, Brad Singer.

❷ Cracked Mirror 5.2
Easy climbing on blocks inside a dirty, lichen-covered crack. Finishes on large plated features on the arête. Miserably short. Shares anchors with *Rear View Mirror Crack*.
25 ft. Gear to 3". Kenn Kenaga (solo).

ENTRANCE BOULDER

This oversized boulder with a giant cap on the top lurks in the woods northwest of the parking area. The main climbs are located on the west face, with a single short crack climb on the east side. Most of the routes here are a mix of slab and dirty crack climbing.

PM **10 min**

Approach: Walk back along the road toward the exit of the southern parking area. At the edge of the parking lot, start up a wash on the right (recently a tree fell across the road here and has been sawn in half). You should quickly see a trail heading northwest. Hike uphill following this path for 200 yards to Entrance Boulder. **[GPS: 34.30445, -116.88075]**

❸ Green Slime 5.9
On the left side of Entrance Boulder is a grimy water channel. Take the flaring offwidth and finish in a hand crack on the right. Gear anchor.
40 ft. Gear to 6".
Eric Odenthal, Nathan Fitzhugh, Brad Singer, June 2005.

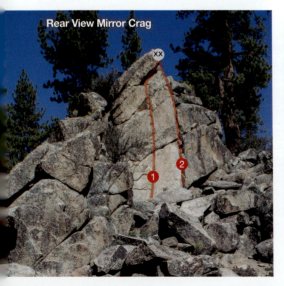

Rear View Mirror Crag

Entrance Boulder

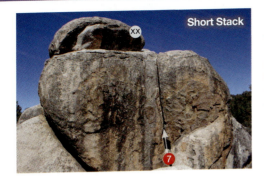

Short Stack

REQUIEM ROCK

Located 150 feet northwest of Entrance Boulder, this long west-facing formation currently has two quality lines.

Approach: From Entrance Boulder, head northwest through a grove of 10-15-foot-tall mountain mahogany shrubs. Requiem Rock is the next wall encountered.
[GPS: 34.30486, -116.88096]

4 Grimy Slimy 5.8 ★
5 feet left of the bolted route *Welcome to Pinnacles* is a left-slanting hand crack. Ascend the zigzagging line that widens underneath the giant boulder. Finish on the headwall sharing the final bolt and anchors with *Welcome to Pinnacles*.
50 ft. Gear to 4", 1 bolt. Brad Singer, June 2005.

5 Welcome to Pinnacles 5.9 ★★
Balancy slab moves with high feet provide a low crux on this thin face climb. Above the 3rd bolt, an optional piece of pro can be placed in a short crack. Crank up the lichen-covered, juggy headwall that guards the ledge with anchors.
50 ft. 4 bolts, optional gear to 1.5".
Chris Miller, Lisa Guindon, Sept. 2003.

6 Chimed 5.6
Not often climbed. Take the wide crack to the top of a small pillar. Work double cracks past a bush and finish on the same headwall as the previous two lines. Shares anchors with *Welcome to Pinnacles*.
50 ft. Gear to 3", optional 5" piece, 1 bolt.
Chris Miller, Lisa Guindon, Sept. 2003.

7 Short Stack 5.8 ★★
Located on the east face, in a corridor. Scramble up boulders to begin this striking wide-hands crack. Slightly overhanging, the lower section of the crack is bomber, growing ever so slightly wider until the top section begs to spit you out. Plentiful holds on the face throughout will help. Enjoyable yet unfortunately short, even for Holcomb standards. Note: There are no rap rings on the anchors, so you must scramble down the north end to descend.
25 ft. Gear to 4". Unknown

8 Requiem For a Dream 5.9 ★★
The best route in the immediate vicinity. Zip up a finger crack, then tread lightly through cruxy slab at the 2nd bolt. Place a 1-2" piece in the juggy crack system before a small ledge. Obliterate the short overhanging headwall by exploiting nice holds for a fun finish.
50 ft. 4 bolts, optional 1-2" piece.
Chris Miller, Craig Britton, Oct. 2011.

9 Requiem For a Lightweight 5.7 ★★
Climb a finger crack, then groove through plates above the ledge. Shares anchors with *Requiem For a Dream*.
50 ft. Gear to 3".
Alan Bartlett, Brandt Allen, Barbara Fredette, July 2009.

Requiem Rock

Parking Lot Left

PARKING LOT ROCK

This decent-sized formation hosts over a dozen lines that run the gamut of difficulty from 5.6 to 5.13b! The quality of the climbs here also span a wide range, with the standouts being the striking dihedral and roof crack on *Scapegoat* (5.10a), the splitter crack of *Two Cams Are Better Than None* (5.10a), and the timeless classic *Cling Plus* (5.11c).

The grove of trees surrounding the parking area provides late afternoon shade for much of this west-facing wall. Most of the routes here are only 40 feet tall, but there is a good mix of sport and trad lines on decent rock and the approach is nonexistent. Just pull into the parking lot, lace up your shoes, and start climbing! **Note:** The first four routes on the left end start from inside a corridor along the base of the wall. In addition, many of the climbs require gear anchors; however, it is usually possible to rappel off the bolted anchors of neighboring sport lines.

Approach: This wall is located at the east end of the southern parking area. The roof of *Scapegoat* on the corner of the formation should be obvious. **[GPS: 34.30330, -116.87887]**

❶ Two Cams Are Better Than None 5.10a ★ ★ ★
Very nice splitter hand crack! Reach this climb (and the next 3) by walking through a little chute into a 3-4-foot-wide corridor at the base of the wall. Stand atop a rock to gain the crack, then jam on up. It's too bad this quality route doesn't go on for another 80 feet or so! Note: It's best to set a directional piece at the top of the crack and use the anchors on *Smoke and Mirrors* instead of building a gear anchor and descending down the exposed 4th-Class gully directly behind the route.
35 ft. Gear to 2.5". Jim Hammerle, Chris Miller, 1990.

❷ Smoke and Mirrors 5.10a ★
Stem across the corridor to bypass the lower blank section, although a tough direct start is possible. Be careful not to fall bouldering up to the high first bolt, as it's a nasty landing in the corridor — a stick clip is recommended. Work through a series of horizontals and good edges above. Shares anchors with *Jedi Magic*.
40 ft. 3 bolts. Chris Miller, May 2003.

❸ Jedi Magic 5.11a ★
This IS the climb you're looking for. Like its neighbor, it has a high first bolt. Stand on a scoop and reach up into a thin undercling. Steep friction moves lead past the first bolt, leaving the good handholds out right as the line angles left.
40 ft. 3 bolts. Anthony Scalise, Brad Singer, Nov. 1999.

Cling Plus

4 Sleight of Hand 5.6 ★

Lieback the large flake marking the start of this route. Ride the rounded arête, placing gear in the crack to the right. Shares anchors with *Jedi Magic*.

40 ft. Gear to 2". Chris Miller, Oct. 2000.

5 Nice Cleavage 5.6 ★★

Unlike the previous 4 routes, this fun climb starts down below the corridor, 20 feet left of the big roof on *Scapegoat*. Wiggle up the partially hidden chimney, then negotiate the difficult transition into the hand crack that branches off right. Shares anchors with *Cling Plus*.

40 ft. Gear to 2". Jim Hammerle, 1991.

6 Cling Plus 5.11c ★★★

Utilize underclings and execute precision footwork throughout the lower portion of the route. Climb past a left-slanting crack to a horizontal (optional 1" cam). The upper portion of the wall is an easier romp to the top. This was the first route to be bolted in Holcomb Valley.

40 ft. 3 bolts, optional 1" piece. Rick Shull, 1989.

7 Five O'Clock Shadow 5.11b ★★

Stand on a boulder and stem across to reach the good underclings. Pull yourself onto the wall and use your sticky rubber to smear past a horizontal. Encounter thought-provoking moves on the enjoyable yet technical face. Shares anchors with *Cling Plus*.

40 ft. 5 bolts. Chris Miller, Oct. 2000.

8 Leech Master 5.7 ★

A bit contrived, this route links the lower corner of *Scapegoat* with the offwidth crack left of the roof. While making the cruxy traverse out from under the roof and around the arête, take care not to slip and smash yourself into the side of the dihedral. Gear anchor — you can rappel off the bolted anchors of *Cling Plus*.

40 ft. Gear to 5". Rick Shull, Brad Henderson, 1989.

9 Scapegoat 5.10a ★★★

A striking dihedral and roof crack on the orange corner of the wall. Jam and stem this beautiful corner for 20 feet until the roof is in your face. Using the roof crack, slide out right on slick feet and power through the tough crux sequence to turn the corner. Build a gear anchor and rappel from bolted anchors of *Cling Plus* to descend.

40 ft. Gear to 3". Rick Shull, 1989.

10 Hellbilly 5.10a ★

The right-leaning crack on the south face. Start in a tight chimney and move up on small plate features, made difficult by the boulder at the base. Transition into the hand crack and share the finish of *Billy Goat*. Gear anchor — can rappel off bolted anchors of *Cling Plus*.

40 ft. Gear to 3". Rick Shull, 1989.

Rachel Sahl climbs *Scapegoat*, 5.10a, page 41.
📷 Brandon Copp

TOP BEGINNER LEADS IN HOLCOMB VALLEY PINNACLES

So much of the rock in the Big Bear Lake area is beginner friendly. Are you just getting started climbing outside? Ready to try some leads? Already feel good on sport routes and want an easy intro to leading trad? Check the list below for some great, easier leads.

① **Fever Pitch** 5.3
Gunsmoke Wall,   page 84

② **Blasting Cap** 5.4
Motherlode Rock,   page 89

③ **Firewater** 5.5
Skyy Slab,   page 76

④ **Gold Standard** 5.6
Gold Wall,   page 71

⑤ **El Chico** 5.6
Slide Dome,   page 119

⑥ **Hook and Ladder** 5.6
Peyronie's Wall,   page 137

⑦ **Lap Dance** 5.6
Horny Boulder,   page 116

⑧ **Psychedelic Sluice** 5.6
Motherlode Rock,   page 90

⑨ **Bye Crackie** 5.7
Coyote Crag,   page 73

⑩ **Wild Turkey** 5.7
The Saloon,   page 107

⑪ **Lucky 7** 5.7
Pasqually Dome,   page 145

⑫ **Bear Pause** 5.7
Lost Orbit Rock,   page 51

⑪ **Billy Goat** 5.7 ★
Walk around the large boulder at the base to reach a corridor where this route starts. Slot jams in the enjoyable vertical hand crack and pop on top of the boulder. Launch into the upper portion, with so many face holds that it's difficult to stick with your crack technique. Build a gear anchor and rappel from bolted anchors atop *Cling Plus*.
35 ft. Gear to 3". Pat Brennan, Brad Singer, Eric Odenthal, May 2005.

⑫ **Big Man, Little Man** 5.8 ★
This route and the 2 to the right of it are really just boulder problems that start from a ledge (belay either from the ground or the ledge). Located on a west-facing portion of the wall, this super-short climb begins behind a small bush and follows the fist crack to a perched block. The squeeze chimney can be the crux depending on how wide you are. Gear anchor.
20 ft. Gear to 3.5", optional 5" piece for the upper section.
Pat Brennan, Charles Debruyn, Apr. 2005.

⑬ **Vicki Gill** 5.6 ★
Starts from the same ledge as *Big Man*. Follow the right-slanting hand crack. Gear belay. One of the earliest routes done at Holcomb.
20 ft. Gear to 3". Brad Singer, Steve Untch, 1986.

⑭ **Iron Horse** 5.9
A very thin crack that doesn't reach the ledge. Forge through the cruxy unprotected start to gain the flake and better crack above. Gear anchor.
20 ft. Gear to 3". Rick Shull, Jim Hammerle, 1989.

⑮ **4-Star 5.9** 5.13b ★★★
This little gem is the area's hardest climb, located on the far right side of the wall. Start on a rock behind the limbs of a dying pine tree and head into steep, fingery climbing with big moves on thin orange edges. Save enough gas for the interesting final sequence. Bolted anchor without rap rings.
30 ft. 5 bolts. Joe De Luca, 2011.

4-Star 5.9

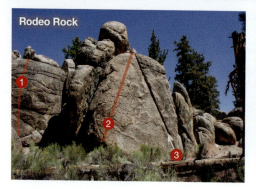

Rodeo Rock

Slack Wall

RODEO ROCK

A south-facing boulder near Parking Lot Rock. The two short lines on the main face were some of the original routes in the area.

☀ 🚶 2 min

Approach: From the south parking area, hike east along the main climber's trail. This formation is the first wall encountered on the left, roughly 100 feet from the fence. **[GPS: 34.30308, -116.87854]**

❶ John Gill 5.6 R/X ★ ▢
AKA *The Thimble*. Left of *New Pygmy* is a wall with several horizontal cracks. Climb the left side of the face with minimal pro. Gear anchor.
30 ft. Gear to 1.5". Alan Bartlett, Mary Ann Kelly, May 2005.

❷ New Pygmy 5.9 R ★ ▢
Climb the plates on the left side to a finish on slab. Not much pro on this one — small wires and gear between the plates. A gear anchor can be built in the *Watusi Rodeo* crack or you can sling the large boulder at the top.
30 ft. Gear to 1.5" with emphasis on small wires.
Rick Shull, Brad Henderson, 1989.

❸ Watusi Rodeo 5.9 ★★ ▢
Ascend the prominent diagonal seam cutting across the face. A hard, bouldery start on thin features guards the first bolt (added long after the FA), with very little gear down low. For an easier start, take the larger blocky crack out right, then traverse left into the seam once your hands are 10 feet off the ground. Gear anchor.
30 ft. Gear to 1", 1 bolt. Rick Shull, Brad Henderson, 1989.

SLACK WALL

A small south-facing wall with two ski-track cracks diagonalling across its face. There are no bolted anchors at the top of this formation. Scramble off the backside near a small pine tree.

☀ 🚶 3 min

Approach: Hike along the main climber's trail until Rodeo Rock comes into view. Just past Rodeo Rock is a downed dead tree that marks a faint climber's trail. Turn left and follow the trail north, wrapping around the backside of Rodeo and Parking Lot Rock to arrive at Slack Wall. **[GPS: 34.30373, -116.87833]**

❹ Wings of Slack 5.10b ★ ▢
Climb the giant flake on the wall's left side, exiting with a balancy crux sequence. Reach a horizontal dike and ledge, finishing on *Bulldada*. Could be led on gear.
40 ft. Chris Miller, May 2003.

❺ Bulldada 5.10d ★★ ▢
Climb the left "ski track." Tenuous moves with marginal fingers in the thin seam lead past 2 bolts to a horizontal dike with a giant ledge above. Once you can feel your fingertips again, fire up past the last bolt to the top. Gear anchor.
45 ft. 3 bolts, gear to 3" for anchor. Chris Miller, May 2003.

❻ The Stark Fist of Removal 5.10a ★ ▢
Start before the corridor in the obvious left-slanting crack (upper ski track). Sink good fist jams and pull over a slight bulge. Continue up a gritty crack that thins toward the top. Gear anchor.
40 ft. Gear to 4". Chris Miller, Nathan Fitzhugh, May 2003.

Two-Tree Rock Left

TWO-TREE ROCK

This long and squatty formation is home to a handful of lines, with the technical face climb *Edu Zepic* (5.10c) being the best. The namesake trees are located on top of the formation — a tiny one and a bigger one that can be used as an anchor. Climbs are on the west face, with an easy walk-off descent climber's right.

PM **5 min**

Approach: Hike along the main trail to Rodeo Rock. Turn left to follow the faint climber's trail north, wrapping around the backside of Rodeo and Parking Lot Rock. From Slack Wall, continue in the same direction, scrambling through boulders. On the left is a deep gully filled with massive boulders — stay out of there and hug the base of Two-Tree Rock on the right. **[GPS: 34.30416, -116.87845]**

7 Poker Face 5.10c ★

Tread lightly to a horizontal and figure out a way to get past the first bolt. Run the seam to where the angle lessens substantially, and finish on fairly easy slab. Note: Traversing left at the first bolt lowers the grade to 5.8. Shared anchor with *Edu Zepic*.

30 ft. 3 bolts. Chris Miller, Cheryl Basye, May 2000.

8 Edu Zepic 5.10c ★★★

A really good technical face climb! Look for the large broken flake, a white section amidst the black. Reach high to slot hands underneath this flake. Follow a ramp, trending left until it's possible to pop onto the slab. Finesse through the techy face, utilizing micro bumps and edges. A thin right-hand rail provides some relief between the 2nd and 3rd bolts. The anchor is on a ledge below the top.

35 ft. 3 bolts. FA: (TR) Rick Shull, John Marinovich, Tony Hunter, 1990; FL: Mike Rigney, Brad Singer, Oct. 1999.

Two-Tree Rock Right

9 Woodchuck 5.0

Climb an easy wide crack for 15 feet and finish up a dirty section to the large tree at the top.

45 ft. Gear to 5". Chris Miller (solo), May 2003.

10 Epic Zedu 5.6 ★

Boulder to a small ledge where the thin finger crack starts. Climb the crack with good gear and finish up the path of least resistance. Belay from the large tree.

45 ft. Gear to 1". Brad Singer, Mike Rigney, Oct. 1999.

11 Bark Beetle Blues 5.10c ★

Begin 2 feet right of *Epic Zedu*, taking the left side of the bulge to a small ledge. Crimp past a bolt to the thin crack and belay from the tree. Originally climbed as a toprope that followed the start of *Epic Zedu* and traversed right at the ledge, it was later led via the direct start.

40 ft. Gear to 1", 1 bolt. FA: (TR) Mike Rigney, Brad Singer, Oct. 1999; FL: Chris Miller, May 2003.

12 Wood Splitter 5.9+

25 feet right of the last climb is this hand crack, behind an annoying, difficult-to-avoid boulder. Either jam into the offwidth behind the boulder or stick to the crack as it flares toward the top. The rock is a bit crispy on this route — watch your pieces! There is a lone bolt on top of a boulder (15 feet back from the edge) that one can use when building an anchor.

45 ft. Gear to 4". Howard Yang, Sept. 2014.

13 Flared Wood 5.9- ★

Alternate start to *Wood Splitter*. Begin on the right margin of the same boulder and work left across a crack. The left lean to the flare prevents solid hand jams, which makes this route harder than it looks. Finish up the lichen-covered face the same way as *Wood Splitter*. Gear anchor.

45 ft. Gear to 4". Howard Yang, Sept. 2014.

14 Two Trees 5.8

A detached pillar another 25 feet right of the *Wood Splitter* crack. This wide climb becomes an insecure flaring squeeze chimney as the crack narrows toward the top. Gear anchor.

35 ft. Gear to 4". Eric Tipton, Bob Cable, June 2003.

LOST ORBIT ROCK

The close proximity to the main trail, coupled with the plethora of excellent routes, makes this the most popular crag in HVP South. Trad and sport, 5.5 to 5.12a, you'll find plenty of great options while escaping the crowds at the Central Pinnacles. It's possible to climb all day here chasing sun or shade. This is definitely a wall you don't want to miss!

The sunny south face hosts a handful of great bolted lines, with the powerful *Inch* (5.10d), *Yard* (5.10a), and *Millimeter* (5.10b) being the best of the bunch. The slabby west face has easy crack climbs plus a few bolted moderates. A stick clip is recommended for the sport routes, as the first bolts are high, with large boulders at the base. Check out *Bear Pause* (5.7), *Bear's Choice* (5.6), and *Ursa Major* (5.10c). The east face is steeper, with challenging lines on varied and unique features. Stand-out classics include *Lost Orbit* (5.10c), and *Lunar Eclipse* (5.11a) and *Road Crew* (5.12a).

Approach: Follow the main trail from the south parking area for 5 minutes until this large wall comes into view. The trail passes close to the east face, making these routes hard to miss. For the routes on the south and west faces, a faint climber's trail circles the base of the entire formation.

To reach Lost Orbit from the Central Pinnacles amphitheatre, a 5-minute hike south along the main trail will bring you to the north end of this formation near the climb *Hubble* (route #19).

Lost Orbit South
[GPS: 34.30486, -116.87782]

☀ 🚶 5 min

Lost Orbit South

❶ Grin and Bear It 5.10a ★
Ascend the thin seam in the right-facing corner. Tread lightly on the slab that steepens to vertical. Gear belay and rappel from any of the several bolted anchors atop the formation.
40 ft. Gear to 2". Chris Miller, Dave Masuo, 1990.

❷ Sloping Beauty 5.10b ★★
This bolted line tackles the center of the ramp. Begin in a scoop and make a difficult mantel to gain the low-angle slab. Cruise to a short blank section that guards the anchors.
40 ft. 4 bolts. Chris Miller, Oct. 2001.

❸ The Angry Inch 5.10d ★★★
An inch can make all the difference. An inch-thick edge on a slab climb is a godsend, and an extra inch of purchase on a hold can determine whether you slip off or stick the move. This route's reachy crux will have you wishing for an extra inch! Begin with bouldery moves on a left-slanting rail. The crux comes on thin crimps between the 2nd and 3rd bolts. Milk a jug, then contemplate how you'd like to finish — either heading left on *Sloping Beauty* (original finish) or right on *The Longest Yard* (more direct).
40 ft. 4 bolts. Chris Miller, Pete Paredes, Aug. 2001.

rock bridge

8

9 **10**

Road Crew

❹ The Longest Yard 5.10a ★★★

Hand-traverse the juggy rail, with feet on tiny jibs. Continue past 3 bolts as the features increase in size. At the final bolt, finagle your way through a tricky and insecure finish. It's all about the last 3 feet!

40 ft. 4 bolts. Nathan Fitzhugh, Chris Miller, July 2003.

❺ The Silly Millimeter 5.10b ★★★

This interesting slabby climb starts in the same place as *The Longest Yard*. Mantel onto the rail and head straight up the dark streak on the vertical face. Crimpy maneuvers gain a shallow seam that can be liebacked to slightly easier terrain. Spicy slab finish.

40 ft. 4 bolts. Chris Miller, Nathan Fitzhugh, July 2003.

❻ Call Me Ishmael 5.9 ★

Start as for *Stand Up Comedy*. Go up the fin to the first bolt, then branch off into the left-leaning hand crack. Get established under the roof and keep your cool as you crank through the awkward and tricky fist jams to surmount the bulge. Fire up the wide crack above and finish at the shared anchors on *Stand Up Comedy*.

45 ft. Gear to 5". Rob Stauder, Ishmael Chivite, Nov. 1999.

❼ Stand Up Comedy 5.10c ★★

This route starts behind a fallen tree. Ascend a fin of rock, then tech up the vertical orange wall on thin edges and underclings. Make the stand-up crux move on interesting holds, transitioning onto the easier black slab above.

45 ft. 5 bolts. Pete Paredes, Chris Miller, Loren Scott, Chuck Scott, Aug. 2003.

Lost Orbit East
[GPS: 34.30531, -116.87800]

AM

5 min

❽ You Know What I'm
Going to Do to You? 5.10a ★★

Scooch into the corner left of *Road Crew* to reach this climb, a striking wide-fist crack. Attack the overhanging crack exploiting the abundance of face holds. Gain a ledge and build a gear anchor. Rappel from the anchors atop *Road Crew*.

45 ft. Gear to 4". John Cardmon, David LePere, Nov. 1999.

❾ Road Crew 5.12a ★★★★

A coveted challenge, up plates on the beautiful orange face. Powerful and physical down low, technical and balancy up high, this aesthetic line has it all! Burly crimp-and-crank moves give way to positive plate-pulling on steep and sustained terrain. The incut plates run out at the 5th bolt, providing a second crux. Cruise the next overhanging section, as you'll need to keep your cool through the fierce finish! Fantastic and unrelenting, this climb is one of Holcomb's finest. Photo opposite.

50 ft. 6 bolts. Steve Shobe, Chris Miller, July 1992; Extended: Chris Miller, July 2001.

❿ Lost Highway 5.11a ★★★

Share the first 2 bolts of *Road Crew*, but instead of doing the initial bouldery crux, lieback and jam the steep crack to the right. Now head straight up, leaving your comfort zone and firing through the crimpfest. Transition onto the final slab with a challenging rock-over. Great line!

45 ft. 4 bolts. Chris Miller, July 2002.

Ian Umstead, *Road Crew*, 5.12a, opposite.
📷 Brandon Copp

Lost Orbit East

11 Lost Orbit 5.10c ★★★★
Just around the corner from *Road Crew* is this stellar climb.
Pluck and plunder the plentiful plates that pepper this path!
Power through pumpy edges and pull over a bulge onto the
vertical face. Pretty proud climbing on patina plates that
peter out toward the top. Great protection and excellent
movement positively make this a must-do route.
50 ft. 6 bolts. FA: (TR) Rick Shull, Jim Hammerle, 1990;
FL: Chris Miller, Dan Roth, 1991.

12 Lunar Eclipse 5.11a ★★★★
Walk up a ramp and stem across onto the vertical face. Cruise
positive patina plates to a lip, then crank over the bulge onto
the imposing upper face. Peruse your bag of tricks to perform
a reachy, delicate slab crux that guards the anchors.
50 ft. 6 bolts. Chris Miller, Dan Roth, 1991.

13 Love at First Bight 5.8 ★
The wide crack right of *Lunar Eclipse*. Head up the ramp
toward the first bolt of *Slacker*. Climb a bulge into the
widening crack behind it. Gear belay; rap a nearby route.
50 ft. Gear to 4", 1 bolt. Chris Miller, Aug. 2001.

14 Slacker 5.10c ★★
Ascend the slabby face above the ramp, with tenuous moves
past the 3rd bolt. Incut edges head left into a slight dish,
then right for a gritty finish.
50 ft. 6 bolts. Chris Miller, Adam Williams, Sean Godwin, Aug. 2001.

15 Real Men of Genius 5.10b ★★
Start in a scrappy left-facing corner. Tech up the clean
face above, shake out where a small roof becomes a great
undercling, then finish on slopers.
50 ft. 6 bolts. Chuck Scott, Chris Miller, Loren Scott,
Pete Paredes, Aug. 2003.

16 Exit Planet Dust 5.10a ★
A seldom-done toprope problem. Use *Hubble's* anchors.
Climb large features on dark rock that give way to blank
rock above. Fix a directional piece to prevent a major swing.
45 ft. Chris Miller, Aug. 2001.

17 Hannibal Lefter 5.7 ★
A left-leaning hand crack that starts between the bolted
routes *Nowhere to Go* and *Hubble*. When the crack splits,
go straight up. The crack soon fades — make a run to the
ramp above, then up and right to the anchors on *Hubble*.
Don't forget a directional piece at the ramp for your second!
45 ft. Gear to 2". David LePere, Brad Singer, Nov. 1999.

18 Nowhere to Go but Down 5.11d ★★★
If you love hard slab, this is a must-do! Fun, unobvious,
improbable, and unique for the wall. Warm up with an easy
section, then tiptoe out right to clip the 3rd bolt where the
action begins. The challenging friction moves may feel
desperate as you struggle to maintain your mental zen on
this unrelenting face. Shared anchors with *Hubble*.
45 ft. 6 bolts. Chris Miller, Aug. 2001.

Lost Orbit West

🔵19 Hubble 5.10b ★★

Begin at an undercut section and launch over the overhang. Smear up a steep slab using the thin crack out right, with the angle steepening at the top. Figure out the slightly contrived crux at the top and claim victory at the chains.

45 ft. 5 bolts. Brad Singer, Anthony Scalise, Nov. 1999.

Lost Orbit West
[GPS: 34.30524, -116.87817]

  5 min

🟢20 Henry's M.F. 5.12a ★★

This rarely-climbed TR problem is located on the SE corner of a large boulder separated from Lost Orbit's west face, in the vicinity of *Ursa Major*. Scramble up the backside of the block marked by a gnarled pine tree to set up on the anchor. Bring longer slings for the bolts (no rap rings). Sharp crimps on orange rock with a wicked crux up high.

30 ft. Jim Hammerle, 1990.

🔵21 Gravity Kills 5.10a ★

This climbs a skinny column on the far left end of the west face. Ascend the lichen-covered slab beside a prominent wide crack. Anchors are located on the rock behind the column's summit.

45 ft. 3 bolts. Chris Miller, Adam Williams, Aug. 2001.

🔴22 Chiller 5.8 ★

The obvious undulating offwidth crack in a left-facing corner. Shares anchors with *Gravity Kills*.

45 ft. Wide gear. Chris Miller, Adam Williams, Aug. 2001.

🟢23 Pablo Cruise 5.10a ★

Toprope the narrow buttress right of *Chiller*. Smear and edge up the corner on horizontal wave features. Set up this climb from the anchors of *Cruise Control*.

45 ft. Chris Miller, Pete Paredes, Aug. 2003.

🔵24 Cruise Control 5.10a ★★

Sweet slab! To reach the base, squeeze between a giant boulder and the wall. An unprotected start leads to a high first bolt. Slightly easier climbing leads to the 2nd bolt, then another noticeable runout. Heads up — this was the first climb put up on the wall and is "old school" in nature!

50 ft. 3 bolts. Bob Cable, Julia Cronk, 1989.

🔵25 Bear Essence 5.10a ★★

Start by stemming off a boulder (a direct start ups the grade a bit), with an optional 0.4" cam placement. Cross the crack system of *Bear Pause* and continue on lovely dish features that give way to heady moves on the clean upper slab. Shares anchors with *Cruise Control*.

50 ft. 5 bolts, optional gear to 0.4".
Chuck Scott, Loren Scott, Pete Paredes, Chris Miller, Aug. 2003.

🔴26 Bear Pause 5.7 ★★

Begin as for *Bear Essence*, stemming to a prominent ramp, but head right up the diagonal hand crack. A short flaring section leads to steeper terrain with good jams — an excellent lead with decent protection for the aspiring trad climber! Shares anchors with *Ursa Major*.

50 ft. Gear to 3". Chris Miller, Dave Masuo, 1990.

Bear's Choice

27 Bear Stroll 5.5 ★★

Starts as for *Bear Essence*. Stem up to a wide crack and traverse it right, crossing *Ursa Major*. Finish in the vertical slot of *La Paws*. Another great easy trad lead! Be sure to protect your second from decking or swinging into a boulder at the base. Gear belay; rappel from *Ursa Major*.
60 ft. Gear to 3". Alex Fletcher, July 2016.

28 Benevolent Bruin 5.9 ★★

A slabby mixed route left of *Ursa Major* requiring full commitment on the opening crux sequence. Make delicate and unprotected moves to a high first bolt, then reach for the large horizontal and place a piece. Blast up steep slab, trending right to finish in a V-shaped channel. Gear belay, then rappel from *Ursa Major*.
50 ft. Gear to 3.5", 2 bolts. Bruce Hawkins, Alan Bartlett, Nov. 1999.

29 Ursa Major 5.10c ★★

Identified by having a lower first bolt than any other climbs nearby. Work magic on a tough friction sequence to start. Breathe easy when you reach the "Thank God" chickenhead at the 2nd bolt. Step up onto the right-trending ramp to tackle the bulgy slab above. Spicy and enjoyable.
50 ft. 4 bolts. Chris Miller, Pete Paredes, Aug. 2003.

30 La Paws 5.10a ★★

Climb the dual crack system with bushes. Fingerlock and lieback the thin cracks, plugging small cams and nuts as you go. At the ledge, move right and zoom up the vertical hand crack. Gear belay and rappel from *Ursa Major*. The route is named for a tasty Mexican restaurant in town.
50 ft. Thin gear to 1". Chris Miller, Dave Masuo, 1990.
Variation 5.10a: Link the slightly easier start of *La Paws* with the last 2 bolts of *Ursa Major*.

31 Bear Elegance 5.8 ★

Start on a large block directly underneath the rightmost of the small bushes on the wall. Ascend the broken thin crack system that trends left to a corner. Gain the upper right-angling crack by negotiating the upper bush. Doesn't see a lot of traffic. Gear anchor and rappel from *Ursa Major*.
50 ft. Gear to 2". Chris Miller, Dave Masuo, 1990.

32 Bear's Choice 5.6 ★★

Enjoyable climbing on a monster flake. Head up the initial ramp, then pull a couple of face moves to transition into the flake. Lieback the flake that protects well and savor the ride to the top. Build a gear anchor and rappel from *Ursa Major*.
45 ft. Gear to 3.5". Chris Miller, Dave Masuo, 1990.

33 Lost My Nut 5.6 ★

Begin on a small ledge beneath another giant flake. Set a nut you can trust below the large left-facing flake, then climb to more solid gear in the crack above. Gear anchor, then rappel off *Ursa Major*.
45 ft. Gear to 3". Bob McDonald, P. Smeltz, July 2009.

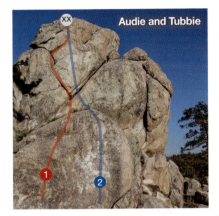

PROWLER ROCKS

These two formations are situated northeast of Lost Orbit Rock. The larger southern wall can be seen from the main trail, while the northern rock that houses *The Prowler* (5.12b) is hidden. The style of each climb here is a bit different, making the crag unique.

Approach: From Lost Orbit Rock, look northeast to see the prominent formation. Pick up the trail just past the north end of Lost Orbit that cuts right through a small wash. The southern wall is in view the entire way. Scramble over boulders to the left side of the wall, arriving at the base of *Audie*.

To get to the northern formation, hike around the west side of the formation until you see a large gully. Cut through the gully to reach this overhanging pinnacle.
GPS: 34.30622, -116.87760]

❶ Audie 5.8 ★
This is the first route encountered where the approach trail meets the wall. Edge through opening slab to a gigantic ledge. Follow the zigzagging crack as it weaves up the upper face. Fingers, hands, fists — this crack has it all. Cut right to finish with the last bolt and shared anchors of *Tubbie*. Watch for rope drag!
70 ft. Gear to 3", 3 bolts. Chris Miller, Pete Paredes, Apr. 2002.

❷ Tubbie 5.10a ★★
Use whatever small edges you can find to unlock the bouldery opening sequence. From the ledge, fire up the light-colored rock past 3 more bolts. An overall solid climb.
70 ft. 6 bolts. Chris Miller, Pete Paredes, Apr. 2002.
Variation 5.8+: A link-up that eliminates the smooth slab crux of *Tubbie*. Instead, climb the first 2 bolts of *Audie* to the ledge, then follow *Tubbie's* last 3 bolts.

❸ Trail of Tiers 5.11b ★★★
Further right on the south face is a burly route characterized by multiple bulges. Master each subsequent tier, culminating with a crux at the 3rd bolt. Battle through the roof bulge, then monkey up on jugs and big features near the top.
60 ft. 6 bolts. Chris Miller, Sept. 2001.

❹ George's Big Adventure 5.7 ★★★
A unique climb with lots of transitions. Climb the well-featured block to an alcove. Pop out onto the slick face on the left, then ascend the slightly dirty pinnacle until you can stand atop it. The anchors are located over on the rock on the left side and may be difficult to reach if you are short. It's easier to have a second clean this route, as it's a bit awkward to do on rappel.
40 ft. 5 bolts. Chris Miller, Reed Ames, Brandt Allen, June 2018.

❺ The Prowler 5.12b ★★
A lone climb weaves up the imposing, overhanging pinnacle of the northern formation. A short vertical section leads to a stance underneath the roof. Ignore your doubts and slowly creep out of your safe zone. Commit to holds on the prow, and don't pump out through the super-steep section — if you can hold on until the 3rd bolt, transition onto a more vertical face. Follow seams to a good horn and mantel onto a ledge. A final run on the fairly featured headwall takes you to the top. Don't blow the 2nd clip!
40 ft. 4 bolts. Grahm Doe, 1994.

Camp Rock

CAMP ROCK

A squatty formation marked by a giant dead tree that has fallen the length of the wall. *Oso Paws Left* (5.10a) is the main attraction here. Due to its proximity to the Central Pinnacles amphitheatre, some people drive the 4WD road (3N07A) and camp here. If you do so, please pack out trash and set up camp away from the base of the climbs.

PM 10 min

Approach: Walk the main trail from the south parking area for 5 minutes to Lost Orbit Rock. Just beyond, head up a hill where a large boulder on the right marks a split in the trail. Go right and continue hiking until you see a brown trail marker. Here, go left and approach Camp Rock from its east side, where it looks like a jumbled pile of boulders. Walk around to the northwest face and the routes.

Alternatively, this small crag is within view of the Central Pinnacles amphitheatre, and is a 2-3 minute jaunt south from there.
[GPS: 34.30706, -116.87893]

❶ **Moonlight Madness** 5.8 ★
Located on the north side of the formation, this wide crack splits the dark, lichen-covered face. The initial broken nature of the rock provides holds, but the middle section forces you to fully commit to the crack. Gear anchor, then rappel from *Target Practice*.
30 ft. Gear to 4". Jim Hammerle (solo), 1990.

❷ **Target Practice** 5.10b ★★
Balance up the blunt northwest arête. Milk the juggy horizontal, as the holds are sparse above, with desperate moves up a featureless corner. Not for the faint of heart.
30 ft. 3 bolts. FA: (TR) Jim Hammerle, Dave Masuo, Rick Shull, 1990; FL: Brad Singer, Ryan Scherler, Nov. 1999.

❸ **Dave's Crack** 5.6 ★
A decent easy trad route up the crack in the center of the west face. Easy climbing on a ramp leads to a ledge. Climb slowly up the nice hand crack to make the thrill last longer. A direct start (5.7) is possible by climbing the face straight to the ledge. Gear anchor, then rappel from *Target Practice*.
30 ft. Gear to 4". Dave Masuo, 1990.

❹ **Grain Scoop** 5.9 ★
A short toprope. Ride the ramp to the ledge. Climb red juggy plates to a neat round pocket, the only redeeming qualities of this route. Gear anchor.
30 ft. Chris Miller, 1991.

❺ **Oso Paws Left** 5.10a ★★★
Further right is this pillar, the best line on the wall. Motor through fairly easy terrain to a right-facing flake. Work up seams on the green and orange face to bolted anchors.
40 ft. 4 bolts. FA: (TR) Bob Cable, Julia Cronk, 1989; FL: Mike Rigney, Ryan Scherler, Nov. 1999.

Derek Volcan climbs *Trail of Tiers*, 5.11b,
Prowler Rocks, page 53. 📷 Landon Holman

HOLCOMB VALLEY PINNACLES **EAST**

This is a collection of small rocks just off the beaten path. Even though the formations are near the popular Lost Orbit Rock, you are almost always guaranteed to have the place to yourself. Expect a bit of lichen, but the climbs should clean up nicely with a bit more traffic. This is a worthwhile spot to escape the crowds on a busy holiday weekend, especially if you are looking for technical face climbs in the 5.10 range.

Approach: From the southern parking lot, follow the main trail for 5 minutes. Look for a thin trail (easy to miss) that cuts back right from the east face of Lost Orbit. You should be able to see the Bowery and Delancey formations at this turnoff. Follow the trail for about 100 yards as it crosses a seasonal creekbed to meet up with a well-defined dirtbike path. Turn left onto this path for all the formations in this area.

HOLCOMB VALLEY PINNACLES **EAST**

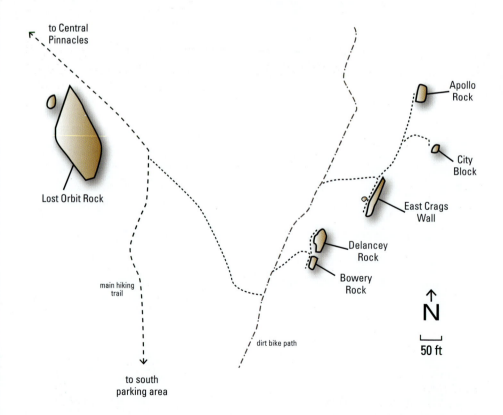

to Central Pinnacles

Lost Orbit Rock

Apollo Rock

City Block

East Crags Wall

Delancey Rock

Bowery Rock

main hiking trail

dirt bike path

N

50 ft

to south parking area

Leina Okamoto climbs *Bullish*, 5.9, Delancey Rock, page 59. 📷 Brandon Copp

CLIMBING AREA	ELEVATION	HIKE	ROUTES	GRADE RANGE	CRAGS
BOWERY ROCK *Thought-provoking slab* **page 58**	7450 ft.	🚶 10 min	3	≤.5 .6 .7 .8 .9 .10 .11 .12	
DELANCEY ROCK *Must do: Bearish, 10c* **page 58**	7450 ft.	🚶 10 min	6	≤.5 .6 .7 .8 .9 .10 .11 .12	
EAST CRAGS WALL *Short, technical 5.10s* **page 60**	7450 ft.	🚶 10 min	7	≤.5 .6 .7 .8 .9 .10 .11 .12	
CITY BLOCK *Crimps through bulges* **page 61**	7450 ft.	🚶 12 min	1	≤.5 .6 .7 .8 .9 .10 .11 .12	
APOLLO ROCK *Shaded lines with less-than-ideal anchors* **page 61**	7450 ft.	🚶 12 min	2	≤.5 .6 .7 .8 .9 .10 .11 .12	

BOWERY ROCK

Bowery and Delancey are sister formations separated by a broken section of rock. Brad Singer and the Rim of the World Climbing Club developed both areas in 2006. Bowery Rock is the smaller formation on the right, home to a few gritty lines on its west face.

Approach: Bowery Rock is the first formation encountered on the dirtbike path. **[GPS: 34.30435, -116.87615]**

Bowery Rock

1 Bowery Boys 5.9+ ★★
Start on a detached flake on the wall's left side — be careful as this large piece of rock can shift! Continue up well-protected slab where a thought-provoking crux leads to positive holds at the 3rd bolt. Anchors on a big ledge.
30 ft. 3 bolts. Brad Singer, Pete Paredes, Sept. 2006.

2 Central Park 5.10a ★★
This enjoyable route goes over a series of ledges in the middle of the wall. Using the edge of the corner lowers the difficulty of the bottom section to 5.8, whereas tackling the slab head-on is 5.10a. The upper section has no easy option, requiring precise footwork and balance on small holds.
40 ft. 5 bolts. Brad Singer, Pete Paredes, Sept. 2006.

Bowery Rock

Delancey Rock

3 Katz's Deli 5.10a ★★
Easily identified by a prominent dike. Climb a difficult slab, utilizing small knobs and divots. Gain the dike near the 2nd bolt and ride good features to the headwall. The finish is difficult and exciting on thin, grainy holds. Shares anchors with *Central Park*. Named for the restaurant in the movie *When Harry Met Sally* where the famous line, "I'll have what she's having" was spoken.
40 ft. 5 bolts. Pete Paredes, Brad Singer, Sept. 2006.

DELANCEY ROCK

Delancey Rock is larger and taller than its next-door neighbor. The best line in the HVP East area, *Bearish* (5.10c), is found on its west-facing wall. As with many of the nearby crags, the rock quality here is good but the lines may need a bit of cleaning.

Approach: Delancey Rock sits just north (left) of Bowery Rock. **[GPS: 34.30458, -116.87621]**

4 Bearish 5.10c ★★★
This fun and balancy route on delicate features tackles the far left side of the wall. A tough start on slopey holds gains a right-trending ramp. Mantel onto the ramp and ascend the face above, utilizing nice scoops and a large chickenhead.
50 ft. 6 bolts. Mike Williams, John Cardmon, Oct. 2006.

5 Skyscraper 5.10c ★
Unlock a thin crux to reach a large flake, then fire up the seam out right. Grab the ledge at the 3rd bolt and the rest is straightforward. Shares anchors with *Bearish*.
50 ft. 4 bolts. John Cardmon, Mike Williams, Brad Singer, Oct. 2006.

Delancey Rock

❻ Delancey Crack 5.7 ★

The obvious central crack. Place small gear in the thin section to start, then traverse left through the scoop (crux). Easier terrain leads to the anchors on *Bearish*.

50 ft. Gear to 1". John Cardmon, Mike Williams, Oct. 2006.

❼ Wall Street 5.10b ★★

This strenuous climb begins left of a large block, staying right of the bolt line. Work blocky features to a nice flake at the 2nd bolt. Follow this feature as it turns into an undercling, then make a difficult transition onto the headwall. Shares anchors with *Bullish*.

50 ft. 5 bolts. Brad Singer, Pete Paredes, Oct. 2006.

❽ Bullish 5.9 ★★

Look for a distinctive roof 15 feet up. Start under the big lieback flake, then pull the roof using decent holds on the lip. Fly through fun features above.

50 ft. 6 bolts. Pete Paredes, Brad Singer, Oct. 2006.

❾ Bullish Variation 5.8+ ★★

Start as for *Bullish* but instead of trending right to the roof, climb the thin crack out left. When the crack disappears, finish on the same plates above as *Bullish*.

50 ft. Thin gear to 2". Unknown.

Bullish

EAST CRAGS WALL

The East Crags Wall houses a handful of short technical 5.10s. The broken formation is divided into sections by dirty wide cracks, with a set of anchors atop each section. Although short even by Holcomb Valley standards, the concentration of climbs here makes this an attractive area to tick off many routes without moving your pack.

PM · 10 min

Approach: Approach as for Bowery and Delancey Rocks. The East Crags Wall is the next formation encountered on the trail, a 2-minute walk north of Delancey Rock.
[GPS: 34.30484, -116.87569]

1 Tongue Buckler 5.10c ★★
Start 5 feet left of the dike system. Funky moves on thin edges lead up to a right-facing corner under a small roof. Brace yourself for a few spicy moves as you bust past the roof.
40 ft. 4 bolts.
Chris Miller, Chuck Scott, Pete Paredes, Loren Scott, Aug. 2003.

2 Follow Your Dike 5.10b R ★
The dike system. It is possible to place a small piece in the horizontal or a 4" piece in the crack to the right to protect the opening moves. Boulder up to a high first bolt, then transition onto the dike. The climb gets more runout as you get higher. Shares anchors with *Tongue Buckler.*
40 ft. 2 bolts, optional gear. Bob Cable, Julia Cronk, 1989.

3 Hairy Eyeball 5.9
Grunt up the wide crack system and finish by transitioning right to the anchors of *Ritten on the Wall.*
40 ft. Pete Paredes, Loren Scott, Chuck Scott, Chris Miller, Aug. 2003.

4 Ritten on the Wall 5.10b ★★
Start with sidepulls and thin edges on a smooth face. Maneuver through an overlap using the flake out right and continue up the steep slab. There is a possible gear placement in the horizontal between the 2nd and 3rd bolts.
40 ft. 3 bolts, optional 0.75" piece. Bob Cable, Julia Cronk, 1989.

5 A Wrinkle in Time 5.10d ★★
Mantel onto the horizontal, pull over the lip, and tackle the crux slab above. Find the key hold that is the route's namesake! Share anchors with *Ritten on the Wall.*
40 ft. 4 bolts. Loren Scott, Pete Paredes, Chris Miller, Sept. 2003.

6 Prescription Pils 5.6 ★
Wedge up the initial squeeze chimney; about halfway up is a little ledge, above which good placements in the smaller range (up to 2") are plentiful. Bolts at the top of the crack have been chopped, so head up the low-angle face on the left to the anchors of *Ritten on the Wall.*
40 ft. Wide gear. Pete Paredes, Chris Miller, Aug. 2003.

7 Welcome to Sky Valley 5.10d ★★
An aesthetic line on the far right side of the wall. Work up to the bolt, using left-hand sidepulls and inconspicuous edges. Once through this crux, slip into the enjoyable finger crack that eats thin gear. Note: The 2-bolt anchor does not have rap rings, so descend off the backside behind *Prescription Pils.*
45 ft. Gear to 3", 1 bolt. Chris Miller, Sept. 2003.

East Crags Wall

City Block

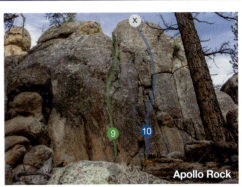

Apollo Rock

CITY BLOCK

A short satellite crag with a single line. From the East Crags Wall, find this block perched on a hillside to the north, with smaller boulders scattered below it.

PM · 12 min

Approach: Approach as for the East Crags Wall. Once at the base of that wall, hike north (left of the wall); City Block is easily visible on the hillside 100 yards away. Scramble up the boulders to the left of the block to reach a series of ledges. Traverse right along these to the start of the climb.
[GPS: 34.30511, -116.87515]

8 City Block 5.10c ★

This seldom-climbed route goes up the block's west face. Power up crimps through bulges coated in green lichen.
30 ft. 3 bolts. Pete Paredes, Brad Singer, Oct. 2007.

APOLLO ROCK

Apollo Rock is at the northern end of HVP East. While this crag has a couple of lines on its shady west face, the anchor situation is grim. **PM** · 12 min
At press time, the anchor for *Turn and Face the Music* has been chopped and *Harlem Shuffle's* anchor has only one hanger.

Approach: This wall does not have a well-defined trail leading from the main path; approach via a 2-minute flat hike north from the East Crags Wall.
[GPS: 34.30544, -116.87541]

9 Turn and Face the Music 5.11a ★

Since the anchor is chopped, hike around the backside and build a gear anchor behind a boulder in the gully. Tough liebacking in a thin, blocky crack. Could be led on gear.
35 ft. Gear to 2" for anchor. Brad Singer, Pete Paredes, Oct. 2007.

10 Harlem Shuffle 5.10b ★

Single-hanger anchor! As with its neighbor, the crux is low with slick feet and marginal hands in the crack system. Ascend the blocky corner, then ride parallel cracks right to finish on thin plates. Would be decent with a proper anchor.
40 ft. 4 bolts. Brad Singer, Pete Paredes, Oct. 2007.

HOLCOMB VALLEY PINNACLES **CENTRAL**

This is the most sought-out climbing region in the Big Bear Lake area, where tall walls and high-quality routes abound on excellent granite. Most of the routes are peppered with enjoyable plates and incut edges. No matter your skill level, you are sure to find a route here that fits the style and difficulty you're looking for. The climbs in the Central Pinnacles are predominately bolted sport routes, with the occasional crack line. Coyote Crag and Claim Jumper Wall are the most popular walls, and deservedly so. Arrive early or be prepared to wait in line!

Approach: Hike the main trail from the southern parking lot. After passing Lost Orbit Rock (page 47), the path heads uphill. Turn right at the split near the top of the hill, marked by a large boulder on the right. Follow this path, posted with brown Forest Service trail markers, as it heads past Camp Rock to the Central Pinnacles Amphitheatre. Approach time is 10-15 minutes.

Alternatively, if approaching from the northern parking area, hike south past the east face of Wilbur's Tombstone to Motherlode Rock's north end (Lizard Head). Wrap around the east face of the Motherlode to arrive at the top of the amphitheatre near the left end of Claim Jumper Wall. This approach takes approximately 10 minutes.

Note: As the Central Pinnacles become increasingly popular, it becomes more imperative for us as a climbing community to be conscious of our impact. Future access could be at stake. Please stick to established trails, don't trample vegetation, always pack out your trash, and properly dispose of human waste. Another way to lessen impact at these popular walls is to seek out other lesser-known crags nearby — there are many! Let's all do our part.

Skyy Slab   Tombstone Pit   The Tombstone   Claim Jumper Wall

Central Pinnacles Overview

HOLCOMB VALLEY
PINNACLES **CENTRAL**

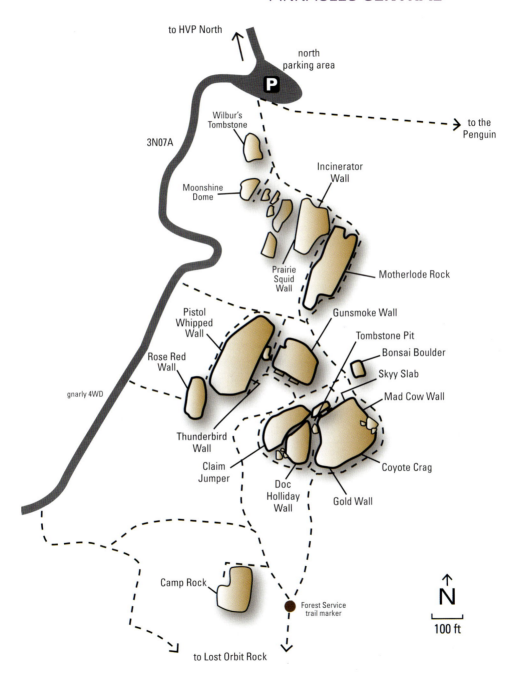

to HVP North

north parking area

P

to the Penguin

Wilbur's Tombstone

3N07A

Incinerator Wall

Moonshine Dome

Prairie Squid Wall

Motherlode Rock

Pistol Whipped Wall

Gunsmoke Wall

Tombstone Pit

Bonsai Boulder

Rose Red Wall

Skyy Slab

Mad Cow Wall

gnarly 4WD

Thunderbird Wall

Claim Jumper

Doc Holliday Wall

Gold Wall

Coyote Crag

Camp Rock

Forest Service trail marker

N

100 ft

to Lost Orbit Rock

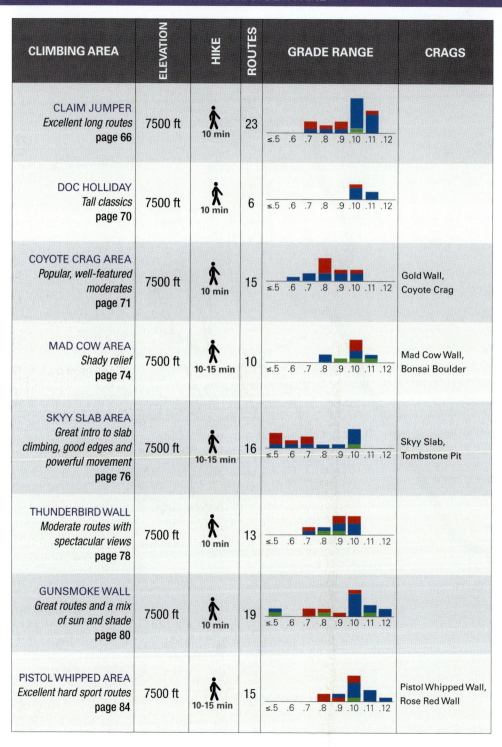

CLIMBING AREA	ELEVATION	HIKE	ROUTES	GRADE RANGE	CRAGS
CLAIM JUMPER *Excellent long routes* **page 66**	7500 ft	10 min	23	≤.5 .6 .7 .8 .9 .10 .11 .12	
DOC HOLLIDAY *Tall classics* **page 70**	7500 ft	10 min	6	≤.5 .6 .7 .8 .9 .10 .11 .12	
COYOTE CRAG AREA *Popular, well-featured moderates* **page 71**	7500 ft	10 min	15	≤.5 .6 .7 .8 .9 .10 .11 .12	Gold Wall, Coyote Crag
MAD COW AREA *Shady relief* **page 74**	7500 ft	10-15 min	10	≤.5 .6 .7 .8 .9 .10 .11 .12	Mad Cow Wall, Bonsai Boulder
SKYY SLAB AREA *Great intro to slab climbing, good edges and powerful movement* **page 76**	7500 ft	10-15 min	16	≤.5 .6 .7 .8 .9 .10 .11 .12	Skyy Slab, Tombstone Pit
THUNDERBIRD WALL *Moderate routes with spectacular views* **page 78**	7500 ft	10 min	13	≤.5 .6 .7 .8 .9 .10 .11 .12	
GUNSMOKE WALL *Great routes and a mix of sun and shade* **page 80**	7500 ft	10 min	19	≤.5 .6 .7 .8 .9 .10 .11 .12	
PISTOL WHIPPED AREA *Excellent hard sport routes* **page 84**	7500 ft	10-15 min	15	≤.5 .6 .7 .8 .9 .10 .11 .12	Pistol Whipped Wall, Rose Red Wall

Matthew Janse on *Tombstone Shadow*, 5.10b, page 77. 📷 Brandon Copp

CLIMBING AREA	ELEVATION	HIKE	ROUTES	GRADE RANGE	CRAGS
MOTHERLODE ROCK *Massive formation with many routes* page 88	7500 ft	🚶 15 min	37	≤.5 .6 .7 .8 .9 .10 .11 .12	East Face, West Face, Lizard Head
INCINERATOR WALL *Shady, overhanging testpieces* page 93	7500 ft	🚶 15 min	5	≤.5 .6 .7 .8 .9 .10 .11 .12	
WILBUR'S AREA *Stout, old-school mixed routes and easy trad* page 94	7500 ft	🚶 15 min	18	≤.5 .6 .7 .8 .9 .10 .11 .12	Prairie Squid Wall, Moonshine Dome, Wilbur's Tombstone
THE PENGUIN *Small and sunny* page 97	7500 ft	🚶 20 min	3	≤.5 .6 .7 .8 .9 .10 .11 .12	

CLAIM JUMPER WALL

One of the most popular walls in Holcomb Valley, with more than 20 nice, long routes. It is predominately northwest facing, with a handful of climbs on its narrow south face. The rock is quite good and sees a fair amount of traffic. Don't miss the challenging line *Coyotes in the Henhouse* (5.10d), or *Claim Jumper* (5.10a), the wall's namesake! As part of the Central Pinnacles Amphitheatre, this tall wall can get crowded on the weekends.

PM · 🚶 **10 min**

Approach: Hike the main trail from the southern parking lot. After passing Lost Orbit Rock, the path heads uphill. Turn right at the split near the top of the hill, marked by a large boulder on the right. Follow this path, posted with Forest Service trail markers, as it heads past Camp Rock to the Central Pinnacles Amphitheatre. Claim Jumper is the first wall encountered on the right side of the amphitheatre.
[GPS: 34.30793, -116.87861]

❶ **Better Luck Next Time** 5.10d ★★
Start up the green lichen-covered ramp at the very left end of the wall. Pass an optional 1" cam placement on the slightly runout slab heading to the 2nd bolt. Fire through a pumpy and slightly awkward sequence to slab above. Climbs better than it looks.
55 ft. 5 bolts, optional 1" piece. Chris Miller, Pete Paredes, May 2002.

❷ **Lady Luck** 5.9 ★★
Jam and lieback large flakes in the physical lower section. (Wait, jams on a sport route?!?) Huck yourself over a bulge in the grovelly crux section.
40 ft. 4 bolts. Chris Miller, Rick Shull, June 2000.

❸ **Lucky Cuss** 5.11a ★★
Climb through the steep overlaps, similar to many other climbs on this section of wall. Punch through underclings to a thrilling finish. Is luck on your side?
50 ft. 5 bolts. FA: (TR) Brad Singer, Travis McElvany, Aug. 1992; FL: Chris Miller, July 1997.

❹ **The Papper** 5.10c ★★★
This challenging route starts with powerful bouldery moves. Keep pushing through the steep section to a mantel at the 3rd bolt. Here the climb changes, requiring balancy friction moves as the holds thin out on green-colored rock.
50 ft. 5 bolts. Grahm Doe, Brent Webster, 1994.

❺ **The Hangin' Judge** 5.11c ★★★
Wicked first moves will have you screaming. Reach a slanting rail, which offers some relief until a 2nd crux hits hard at the 4th bolt. Claw your way through thin crimps that have dashed many redpoint attempts. Don't be caught a hangin' on this route!
70 ft. 6 bolts. Chris Miller, Sept. 2001.

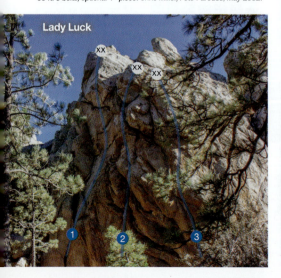

Lady Luck

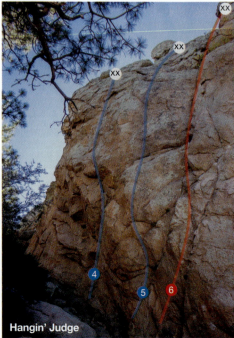

Hangin' Judge

Claim Jumper Wall

6 Colonial Ear Wax 5.8 ★

A rarely done crack with a tough start on dual seams. The main crack widens up higher for better gear placements. Finish right to anchors atop *Bum Steer*.

60 ft. Gear to 4". Tim Fearn, Chris Miller, 1990.

7 Bum Steer 5.10a ★★

This long route starts on thin but positive crimps. A definite crux at the 5th bolt steers you left to the rounded arête.

80 ft. 7 bolts. Chris Miller, Roger Stephens, July 1997.

8 Bobbing For Ear Snax 5.9 ★★

Another neglected trad climb, though actually quite enjoyable. Pick your way through the spiderweb of seams until they converge into a short section of crack. Alternate between cracks and positive face holds as the route squiggles up the center of the face. Use *Claim Jumper* anchors.

80 ft. Gear to 2.5". Tim Fearn, Chris Miller, 1990.

9 Claim Jumper 5.10a ★★★

This extremely popular route is one of the longest in the area, sporting a bit of everything. Master crimps and edges to arrive at a slanted rail. A short-lived crux at the 5th-bolt bulge offers multiple options. For the finale, a small roof/bulge will test your remaining strength. Expect a few funky clipping stances.

80 ft. 9 bolts. Chris Miller, Lisa Guindon, May 1997.

10 Get a Rope! 5.10a ★★

Recent addition that squeezes in another line on this densely packed cliff. TR from *Claim Jumper* anchors.

80 ft. Chris Miller, Reed Ames, Sept. 2019.

11 Green Goblin 5.7 ★★★

The obvious dihedral in the center of the wall. Wriggle up a flared squeeze chimney until the crack narrows down (need a 5-6" piece if you want to protect this lower section). Ascend the slick, steep, flaring corner by jamming, stemming, liebacking, or all three. Exit left to a crack that leads to the anchors. Stout, fun, and funky, with tricky pro.

70 ft. Wide gear. Bob Cable et al., 1988.

12 One-Armed Bandit 5.10a ★★★

This tackles the narrow pillar in the middle of the wall. Climb to a roof, pull over, and mantel onto a ledge. Get your friction on and burn rubber up the steep face. A sequential finish on hidden slots makes for an exhilarating ride. Sustained and stout for the grade. Shares anchors with *Green Goblin*.

75 ft. 8 bolts. Chris Miller, Chuck Scott, May 2001.

13 Bye Chimney 5.7 ★★

Stem and jam this wide crack that gets bigger, passing chockstones on the way. Build a gear anchor in the notch, or bump onto the face and finish on the last 2 bolts and anchors of *Chaps My Hide*. This finish ups the grade to 5.9.

70 ft. Gear to 5". Steve Untch, 1980s.

14 Chaps My Hide 5.11a ★★
Start on good sidepulls and positive holds to reach painful and sequential crimping at the bulge above the 3rd bolt. Muscle through and enjoy the cool finishing features!
60 ft. 6 bolts. Chris Miller, Chuck Scott, May 2002.

15 Brewed Awakening 5.11c ★★★
This route packs quite the kick! A challenging thin face gains a finger crack. Finish up steep rock on big jugs to anchors shared with *Coyotes in the Henhouse*. Named for a bygone coffee shop in Big Bear.
70 ft. Gear to 3", 4 bolts. Chris Miller, Chuck Scott, May 2001.

16 Coyotes in the Henhouse 5.10d ★★★★
One of HVP's best routes. Technical opening moves provide a crux right off the ground, with long reaches on thin crimps. Punch up the vertical face on stellar incut edges, admiring the well-placed bolts as you milk the rests where you can. Challenging sequences and enjoyable movement hold your attention throughout this full-value climb.
70 ft. 8 bolts. Sam Owings, Tony Egnozzi, Kevin Duck, 1995.

17 Public Hanging 5.11d ★★★
Ascend the face until the holds thin and it gets technical under a smooth roof. Muster up the courage to blindly clip the 4th bolt, making sure not to blow this one. Make a wild move over the lip, then fire up small crimps to a finish on larger plates. A bold lead that's sure to keep you on your toes. Many feel that this otherwise fun route is tarnished by the dicey 4th clip.
70 ft. 7 bolts. Chris Miller, July 2002.

Skyline Pillar

18 Blue Sky Mine 5.10c ★★★
Powerful climbing follows a seam to the 3rd bolt. Cut right, angling across the southwest face, with some runouts on big plates. Be cautious reaching the high first bolt.
70 ft. 5 bolts. Brad Singer, Mike Rigney, Aug. 1992.

19 Mad Season 5.11b ★★
Located in the center of the sunny southwest face, with a smooth and difficult opening sequence. Use the undercling to your advantage, reaching high for the decent features above. Shares the last bolt and anchors with *Blue Sky Mine*.
60 ft. 5 bolts. Grahm Doe, Brent Webster, 1994.

20 Necktie Party 5.10d ★★
Tackle a strenuous rounded arête, leaning hard into the left-hand seam, then deal with a bulge in your face that's sure to bring the frustration level up a few notches. This fun climb was originally done by traversing in from the left (5.10a).
50 ft. 5 bolts. FA: Chris Miller, Dana Adler, Linda Lynch, July 1997; Direct Start: Chris Miller, 2002.

21 Dos Dose 5.9 ★★
An off-hands/wide-fist crack. Fight through the uncomfortable start, jam up the middle, and do-si-do on good face holds at the finish. Gear belay, or cut left to the *Necktie Party* anchors.
50 ft. Wide gear to 4". Jim Hammerle, Mike Lee, 1990.

22 Whiskey Dave 5.8 ★★
Easily identified by its dark hangers and mussy-hook anchors. Clip the first bolt, then cut feet and swing up onto the wall for some good plate pulling. Named after a local saloon in Big Bear Lake. Legend has it that Whiskey Dave was a 1920s bootlegger who was sent to prison by Sheriff "Lefty" Dalton. After his release, Whiskey Dave fatally stabbed Lefty in the bar over a spat about who should marry a local gal, but not before Lefty shot Whiskey Dave through the heart! Whiskey Dave was buried in a whiskey casket under the bar, but his hell-raising spirit lives on still.
40 ft. 4 bolts. Reed Ames, Taylor Douglas, Dave Sharp, Aug. 2018.

23 Skyline Pillar 5.7 ★★
Approach this secluded route by scrambling up the boulder-filled gully beside *Whiskey Dave*. This neat little bolted line is the only route on this independent pillar. Jet up blocky features and big holds, then mantel onto a ledge and keep heading toward the sky.
40 ft. 4 bolts. Chris Miller, Eric Odenthal, July 2001.

DOC HOLLIDAY WALL

A tall wall located in a narrow corridor, offering belayers a bit of shade on hot summer days while climbers sample the extra long lines that are some of the most enjoyable around.

AM · 10 min

Approach: Doc Holliday Wall is located in the corridor west of Gold Wall.
[GPS: 34.30780, -116.87841]

1 Quick on the Draw 5.10d ★★

Leftmost of the 2 routes that start on the slab. Edge on thin holds past 2 bolts (crux) to a big ledge, then fire up the short face on blocky features.

60 ft. 5 bolts. Chris Miller, Brad Singer, July 2001.

2 Pistol Pete 5.10a ★★★★

This rootin' tootin' gunslinger's the best you've ever seen! A quintessential route that's one of Holcomb's longest — hopefully you can hang on till the anchors! Finesse through thin edges past 2 bolts on the lower slab. Reach an undercling flake, pop your feet out right, and commit to the strenuous lieback needed to snag decent holds above. Traverse left to the arête for a delicate and balancy finish. A superb climb packed with technical moves requiring a variety of techniques to succeed.

90 ft. 8 bolts. Chris Miller, Pete Paredes, Chuck Scott, July 2001.

3 Doc's Holiday 5.10d ★★★★

Another mega-classic, this super-sequential line is an unrelenting crimpfest. At the 4th bolt, mentally prepare yourself for a race-the-clock scenario on sparsely spaced holds. Leave your comfort zone, edging up the technical face on miniscule yet positive crimps. Originally started via a loose hand crack on the right; the direct start is much appreciated.

80 ft. 8 bolts. FA: (TR) Brad Singer, Mike Rigney, 1989; FL: Rich Scholes, Mike Rigney, 1990; Direct Start: Pete Paredes, Chuck Scott, Chris Miller, Nathan Mitts, July 2001.

4 Unforgiven 5.11b ★★

Lieback a left-facing flake to a blocky corner. An insecure crux hits abruptly above the 3rd bolt. Power through this committing sequence past a bush to easier climbing.

65 ft. 6 bolts. Chris Miller, Pete Paredes, Chuck Scott, July 2001.

5 Far Beyond Driven 5.11a R ★

Two shallow pockets above the first bolt mark this mediocre line on the green and orange face. Travel up on slopey/blocky holds that thin near the top.

70 ft. 7 bolts. Chris Miller, Sept. 2001.

6 Loose Women, Loose Rock 5.10a ★

A scrappy line starting in a right-facing wide-hands crack. Move right along the diagonal crack, then shoot straight up to share the last bolt and anchors with *Shoot at Will* — see the Tombstone Pit section (page 77) for more info.

65 ft. Gear to 3", 4 bolts. Craig Britton, Matt Hoch, 1997.

Doc Holliday Wall

Gold Wall

GOLD WALL

A nice place to warm up before tackling the harder routes on nearby Doc Holliday or Claim Jumper, and a great place for beginners since the face is well-featured. The base has only enough space to accommodate one or two parties, so unlike Coyote Crag, you won't be inundated with people while trying to learn. *Gold Standard* (5.6) is the classic climb here, with massive features, a standout for the grade.

10 min

Approach: Walk 50 feet left of Coyote Crag to Gold Wall, which is actually the south face of that same formation.
[GPS: 34.30772, -116.87827]

---

❶ Gold Bug 5.8 ★★

Pleasurable plate-pulling. The slab ramp leads to a steep transition onto the main face. Climb to a ledge with anchors.
45 ft. 5 bolts. Darren Jeffery, Chuck Scott, Chris Miller, June 2001.

❷ Flash For Hash 5.8 ★

Start in a thin crack between *Gold Bug* and *Hidden Gold*. Resist the good face features and practice your crack moves! On the upper face, climb between the two bolted lines, clipping the last 3 bolts and anchors of *Gold Bug* on the left. Usually toproped because of its indistinct finish.
40 ft. Gear to 2", 3 bolts. Jim Hammerle, Mike Lee, 1990.

❸ Hidden Gold 5.7 ★★★

Strike it rich with this fantastic moderate. Negotiate a low crux, then follow plentiful holds up the less-than-vertical face. A well-protected line for budding leaders.
40 ft. 4 bolts. Chris Miller, Lisa Guindon, June 2001.

❹ Gold Standard 5.6 ★★★★

This gem truly is the gold standard for the grade in Holcomb Valley. The movement is smooth and enjoyable, the holds are big and plentiful, the exposure is ever-present, and the top yields a beautiful, expansive view of Holcomb Valley, the climbing area, and the surrounding mountains. Monster plate features grace the entire climb, with challenging steep sections moving through the overlaps.
80 ft. 7 bolts. Chris Miller, Lisa Guindon, Mar. 2002.

COYOTE CRAG

This is probably the most popular wall in the San Bernardinos. It was one of the first walls in Holcomb to be developed, and for good reason. The routes are long and well-featured, the rock quality is excellent, and the frequent traffic has cleaned any loose flakes. Pick almost any route here and you'll be happy.

The southeast-facing wall soaks up the sun and can get a bit warm in summer, but that doesn't stop the crowds from setting up camp at the base. Come on a weekday during the fringe season and you might be lucky enough to have the place to yourself.

As a side note, Holcomb Valley Pinnacles used to be called Coyote Crags, since this cliff was the main climbing area, with the only developed routes aside from a few near the southern parking area.

Approach: Hike the main trail from the southern parking lot. After passing Lost Orbit Rock, the path heads uphill. Turn right at the split near the top of the hill, marked by a large boulder on the right. Follow this path until you reach a brown Forest Service trail marker, indicating another fork in the trail. Take the right fork to reach the formations on the east side (Gold Wall, Coyote Crag, Doc Holliday, etc.). The trail deposits you at the left end of Coyote Crag.

If you are already in the amphitheatre, there are trails leading to either side of this wall. **[GPS: 34.30767, -116.87811]**

① **Black Magic Poodle** 5.9 ★★★
Start atop an old log wedged in a slot, where an awkward maneuver lands you on the wall. Launch over a roof and proceed on good incuts through steepening terrain. A good mix of balance and power.
70 ft. 8 bolts. Chris Miller, Loren Scott, June 1997.

② **Golden Spike** 5.10c ★★
Hammer through a tricky start on an angling, fingertip crack. Milk a good stance below the 4th bolt and prepare for the intense redpoint crux on slick feet and gaston crimps. The awkward finish doesn't let up much, either.
70 ft. 7 bolts. FA: (TR) Chris Miller, Tim Fearn, 1990; FL: Chris Miller, Dave Evans, June 1997.

③ **High Noon** 5.10b ★★
Similar in character to *Golden Spike*, this route climbs good edges underneath a small roof. Surmount the bulge and work magic to get through the steep crux near the 4th bolt. Keep it together past runs between well-spaced bolts at the top.
70 ft. 7 bolts. Chris Miller, Chuck Scott, May 2001.

④ **Hootenanny** 5.10a ★★
Climb past the first 2 bolts on *High Noon*, then traverse right to the left-angling seam. Alternately, climb direct up the unprotected face directly below the crack. Clip the lone bolt at the crux (added long after the FA), or ignore it and protect this section with RPs like it was originally done. Share anchors with *Golden Spike*.
70 ft. Gear to 2", optional RPs, 1 bolt.
Steve Untch, Aaron Barnes, 1980s.

⑤ **Golden Poodle** 5.9+ ★★★★
Precision footwork and smooth, calculated movements are the key to sending this well-protected moderate. Romp through easy, blocky ledges (optional 2-3" cam) to the high first bolt. The crux comes fairly quickly after the 2nd bolt — find the thin edges near the seam. As you climb higher, the holds become better, while the bolt spacing grows wider, yielding an exciting finish.
75 ft. 6 bolts, optional gear to 3". FA: (TR) Bob Cable, Julia Cronk, 1988; FL: Dave Evans, Chris Miller, June 1997.

⑥ **Pass the Bucket** 5.8 R ★★
A thrilling line for practicing natural protection, put up shortly after *Bye Crackie*. Ascend a thin seam protectable by small wires and tie-offs on chickenheads. End in a left-slanting crack and share anchors with *Golden Poodle*.
75 ft. Natural pro, thin gear. Rick Shull, Jim Hammerle, 1989.

⑦ **Coyotes at Sunset** 5.8 ★★★★
Look for the gaggle of climbers waiting in line to do this route! This prominent line on the attractive face is the epitome of fun climbing at Holcomb Valley Pinnacles. Scale easy, broken terrain to reach the first bolt about 20 feet off the deck (optional 2-3" cam placement). Tackle the dead-vertical wall, making liberal use of the bomber plates and incut edges. An extremely popular route and a must-do if the waiting line's not too long!
75 ft. 6 bolts, optional gear to 3". FA: (TR) Bob Cable, Julia Cronk, 1988; FL: Kevin Duck, 1994.

Coyote Crag

8 Bye Crackie 5.7 ★★★★

One of the first bolted routes put up in HVP, this excellent line became an instant classic and remains one of the most sought-after moderate climbs in the Central Pinnacles. Burn rubber on the opening slabby section to reach a huge flake. The abundance of large face holds above is sure to make you smile. Savor the airy exposure of the arête as you climb extremely secure plates. The FA party originally did this route with 2 bolts and gear, but it was later fully bolted.

65 ft. 6 bolts. Jim Hammerle, Rick Shull, 1989.

9 Es Muy Bueno 5.8 ★★

Right of *Bye Crackie*, take the flake up a right-facing corner. Move right and finish with a short crack. Build a gear anchor and scramble down the gully to the right.

40 ft. Gear to 3". Jim Hammerle, 1989.

10 Western Farm Service 5.8 ★★

Another 1980s line, this flaring thin-hands crack protects easily with large nuts and 1-2" cams. Plentiful face holds pepper the sides of this crack. Gear anchor.

35 ft. Gear to 3". Rick Shull, Jim Hammerle, 1989.

11 Red Brewster 5.9 R ★★

Great exercise using thin gear and protection in opposition. If your protection skills are up to par, this is a neat climb, but if not .... Named for a cheap red ale from back in the day. Gear anchor.

35 ft. RPs and thin gear. Rick Shull, John Marinovich, 1989.

April Davidson on *Bye Crackie*,
5.7, Coyote Crag, page 73.
■ Eric Fallecker

MAD COW WALL

Since its base is elevated from the hiking path, most folks walk past this crag without noticing it. It's not suitable for children or dogs due to the scrambly approach, but it is home to a handful of neat climbs. Northeast-facing and shady, the wall offers relief from the sun on hot summer days.

AM 10-15 min

Approach: Continue past the right end of Coyote Crag to locate the first two climbs, on a separate pillar. This pillar sits on the lefthand side of the main wall's approach gully and has a small pine tree growing from it. Head up the boulder-filled gully, or alternately scramble up the slabs at the right end of Mad Cow Wall. **[GPS: 34.30792, -116.87811]**

❶ Eight-Second Ride 5.8 ★★

A short but enjoyable ride, yet few saddle up for it with many other longer routes nearby. Proceed up on easy terrain past the high first bolt to the crux sequence on the arête. Rounded holds threaten to buck you off this route — can you hold on long enough?
35 ft. 3 bolts. Ted Peace, Chris Miller, Aug. 2001.

❷ Saddle Tramp 5.9 ★

Another short-attention-span type route. Grab the reins, cowboy, and ascend the vertical face immediately right of *Eight-Second Ride*. Shares anchors.
35 ft. Chris Miller, Bryan Dennison, Sept. 2001.

❸ Black Angus 5.10a ★★

Head up the gully from the previous 2 routes to locate this cool traverse line. Take the arching crack across the main wall. Finish in a notch right of *Wild Kingdom* and share anchors with that route.
50 ft. Gear to 3". Grahm Doe, Brent Webster, 1994.

❹ Branding Iron 5.10a ★

Lieback the left side of a flake that looks like South America, or jam into the hand crack behind it. Transition onto the face and climb straight up on delicate holds past 3 closely spaced bolts.
40 ft. Gear to 3", 3 bolts. Chris Miller, Lisa Guindon, Loren Scott, Chuck Scott, Pete Paredes, Tyler Logan, June 2001.

❺ March of Dimes 5.11a ★★

Up the middle of the large flake, with balancy moves on dime-sized edges that may feel desperate. Once past the flake, enjoy better holds on the colorful rock above.
50 ft. 4 bolts. Chris Miller, June 2001.

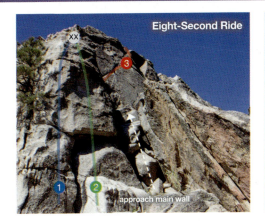

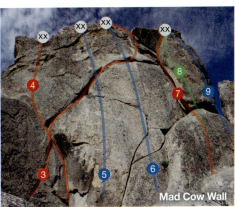

Mad Cow Wall

6 Wild Kingdom 5.10a ★★

Traverse the 4th-Class slab to reach the base of this climb. The first bolt will keep you from tumbling down the slab. Climb a flake that ends too quickly. Brave sharp microcrimps to reach a horizontal, where easier terrain leads to the top.

50 ft. 4 bolts. Chris Miller, Lisa Guindon, Loren Scott, Chuck Scott, Pete Paredes, Tyler Logan, June 2001.

Cross the heady, 4th-Class slab to reach a ledge where the next 3 climbs begin.

7 Cowdura 5.10b ★

Tackle the cruxy thin slab to reach a large block. Slither, squeeze, grunt, and slide up the short squeeze chimney. Cut right to finish at the anchors of *Down With the Herd*.

30 ft. Gear to 4", 1 bolt. Chris Miller, Sept. 2001.

8 Bovine Eyes 5.11a ★

Start as for *Cowdura* but ride the arête that angles right to shared anchors with *Down With the Herd*. Technical and balancy.

30 ft. Chris Miller, Sept. 2001.

9 Down With the Herd 5.10d ★★★

Cast off the ledge with opening 5.10a moves. The holds thin out, culminating in a fingery crux. Crank down on a savage right-hand crimp and reach high to the hold above. Anchors are located left of the giant mushroom cap.

30 ft. 4 bolts. Chris Miller, Pete Paredes, 2001.

10 Gorilla Tape 5.8 R ★

Situated on the far right side of the wall. Negotiate the low crux and progress up the dark wall to the gorilla. Stand atop the gorilla's head and reach across to the last bolt. A fall clipping this bolt could cause decking on the low-angle slab.

60 ft. 6 bolts. Mikey Griffitts, Dwain Porter, July 2019.

BONSAI BOULDER

A large boulder lurking down on the hillside behind Mad Cow Wall and Skyy Slab with one fun line on its north face. Scrambling up (and down) the slab on the backside to set up a TR takes gumption.

10-15 min

Approach: From Claim Jumper Wall, continue uphill past Skyy Slab to the back of the amphitheatre. Cross the trail and continue briefly downhill to Bonsai Boulder. Solo the slab beside a pine tree on the boulder's south face to set up the TR.
[GPS: 34.30825, -116.87812]

11 Coolie Crank 5.10c ★★

Often overlooked, this fun, albeit short line follows the rightmost orange streak on the overhanging face. Monkey up large plates until they peter out at darker rock. Execute the final moves on thin knobs to pull over the lip.

25 ft. Jim Hammerle, 1989.

Variation 5.10b: Take the orange streak on the left through shallower features. Engaging plate-pulling the whole way.

Bonsai Boulder

Skyy Slab

SKYY SLAB

A great introduction to slab climbing. A handful of well-protected lines in close proximity let you easily work through the grades.

PM 10-15 min

Approach: From the left end of Claim Jumper Wall, continue uphill to the north. Skyy Slab is the next section of rock. **[GPS: 34.30794, -116.87826]**

1 Naughty Pine 5.6 ★★

Start near a fallen dead pine and ascend a right-facing flake covered in green lichen. A bit dirty but enjoyable, starting with big features and culminating on a smooth upper slab. Shares anchors with *Skyy Pilot*.
45 ft. 4 bolts. Chris Miller, Rocky Smith, Lisa Guindon, June 2001.

2 Skyy Pilot 5.9 ★★

Left of the break in the wall is this fun bolted line. The short-lived crux is a beginning mantel move onto a ledge. Expect to fake it with your hands as you smear up the slab.
45 ft. 4 bolts. Chris Miller, Rocky Smith, Lisa Guindon, June 2001.

3 Liquid Courage 5.5

Just right of the large gully. Awkward liebacking in a grungy corner system. Traverse right to anchors on *Midsummer's*.
35 ft. Gear to 3". Chris Miller, Sept. 2001.

4 A Midsummer's Night Seam 5.7 ★★

Start atop a slanted boulder, using it to your advantage to reach nice holds to pull onto the slab. Follow a seam until it promptly runs out at the 2nd bolt, then make a few tenuous moves. Enjoyable throughout.
35 ft. 3 bolts. Chris Miller, Sept. 2001.

5 Firewater 5.5 ★★

This mild, well-protected, low-angle climb is a great intro route for the slab shy. A powerful start gains the slab, then breeze past 3 bolts. Shares anchors with *Midsummer's*.
35 ft. 3 bolts. Chris Miller, Sept. 2001.

6 Rotgut 5.4 ★

At the end of the slanted boulder is a set of twin cracks. Climb the left crack until they merge, then continue up the left-facing corner. Step left underneath a large block and finish at shared anchors with *Midsummer's*.
35 ft. Gear to 3". Chris Miller, 1992.
Variation 5.8+: Start in a pit and climb the right twin crack.

7 Here's Mud in Your Eye 5.10a ★

Toprope the middle of a large finger of rock via pumpy moves on a big flake, then face a challenging transition onto the thin slab. Use the *Master of Cylinders* anchors.
40 ft. Chris Miller, Sept. 2001.

8 Master of Cylinders 5.5 ★

Up the right side of the buttress via a hidden lieback crack.
40 ft. Gear to 3". Chris Miller, Sept. 2001.

TOMBSTONE PIT

The Tombstone Pit is a semi-secluded area formed by the intersection of many other Central Pinnacles formations. 10-15 min
The routes on the Tombstone itself tend to be longer and of better quality, although the short and powerful lines on the Firepower block are fierce, fun, and good for a quick burn.

Approach: Hike uphill from the left end of Claim Jumper Wall to Skyy Slab. The Tombstone Pit is sandwiched between these two formations. Scramble to the right end of Skyy Slab and drop down into the Tombstone Pit, where all of the lines except *Shoot at Will* start.
[GPS: 34.30796, -116.87835]

9 Shoot at Will 5.8 ★★★
Technically part of Doc Holliday Wall, this fun and popular route is approached from the Tombstone Pit. Atop the pit, walk toward Doc Holliday Wall, dropping down into a slot to the start of this line. Scale broken fins past 2 bolts. Transition to thin but good edges. Note: The last 3 bolts have recently been replaced with glue-ins.
45 ft. 5 bolts. FA: (TR) Jim Hammerle, Rick Shull, Dave Masuo, 1989; FL: Chris Miller, 1990.

10 Dead Man Chalking 5.10b ★★★
Start with bouldery moves on backwards holds. Grab a rail, turn it into an undercling, and gain the arête. Traipse up the arête to the top. Challenging and heady. Shares anchors with *Tombstone Shadow*.
45 ft. 5 bolts. FA: (TR) Bob Cable, Julia Cronk, 1989; FL: Chris Miller, Cheryl Basye, May 2000.

11 Tombstone Shadow 5.10b ★★★
A fun route up the center of the Tombstone's north face, characterized by slick feet, good left-hand holds, and underclings. Stick clip the high first bolt or slot a 0.5" cam to protect the lower moves above a rough landing zone.
45 ft. 4 bolts, optional 0.5" cam. FA: (TR) Bob Cable, Julia Cronk, 1989; FL: Dave Bridges, Mike Rigney, 1991.

12 Who's Will? 5.7
The easiest way to the top of the formation, via dirty and pebble-filled parallel cracks. Rappel from anchors atop *Tombstone Shadow* or *Shoot at Will*.
25 ft. Gear to 3". Bob Cable, 1989.

13 Fatboy Slim 5.6
The awkward and dirty chimney system.
30 ft. Wide gear to 5". Chris Miller, May 2000.

Tombstone Pit

Firepower

Ivan LaBianca climbs *Firepower,* **5.10d.**
📷 **Alex Vercio**

⑭ Suspended Sentence 5.7 ★★ ▢▢
Clamber up the face that is riddled with big holds, using sidepulls and underclings to reach a finger crack. Place thin gear in the crack and flaring pockets. Shares anchors with *Firepower.*
30 ft. Thin gear to 2". Chris Miller, May 2000.

⑮ Firepower 5.10d ★★★ ▢▢
A stellar route that packs a punch! Lieback, crimp, undercling, and just plain fight through the fierce initial sequence. Regain your composure at a nice shallow hueco, then use this to make a powerful transition out left. Fire up good holds to finish. The FA party took a grounder when a hook popped while bolting this one on lead — props to them for establishing this sweet line anyway!
30 ft. 3 bolts. Chris Miller, Mark Bowling, Aug. 1993.

⑯ Sentenced to Hang 5.10c ★★★ ▢▢
Powerful, gymnastic moves on big holds open this steep, exciting route. Like its neighbor, this line requires good footwork. Bust through to the arête, then make a tenuous traverse left from the 3rd bolt to the anchors. Go on, give this one a whirl, even if you hang!
30 ft. 3 bolts. Chris Miller, Cheryl Basye, May 2000.

THUNDERBIRD WALL

A popular Central Amphitheatre wall with spectacular views of the surrounding area from its top. The east-facing wall basks in the morning sun, and features moderate, well-protected sport routes in the 5.7 to 5.10 range. While not as tall as nearby walls, the featured rock is just as good and the routes are fun, especially *Medicine Man* (5.7+), *Bird of Prey* (5.8), and *Nervous Twitch Direct* (5.9).

🔆 AM   🚶 10 min

Approach: Hike the main trail from the southern parking lot. After passing Lost Orbit Rock, the path heads uphill. Turn right at the split near the top of the hill, marked by a large boulder on the right. Follow this path, posted with brown Forest Service markers, as it heads past Camp Rock to the Central Pinnacles Amphitheatre. Thunderbird is the first wall encountered on the amphitheatre's left side, with a bit of boulder-hopping required along its base.
[GPS: 34.30830, -116.87872]

Thunderbird Wall

Thunderbird Left

❶ Hot Wing 5.10b ★★

Behind a gnarled mountain mahogany bush lies this well-protected line. Tackle plated features with fantastic edges down low. Reach high and pull down hard to nail the crux mantel. The thin face above adds to the varied nature of this climb.

70 ft. 6 bolts. Chris Miller, Loren Scott, Pete Paredes, Apr. 2002.

❷ Deer Lick 5.10a ★★

Mixed. Place pro in a diagonal crack, then make a break for bolts along a thin seam. The crux involves difficult stemming in a flared corner. Shares anchors with *Fawnskin*.

60 ft. Gear to 2.5", 4 bolts.
Chris Miller, Loren Scott, Pete Paredes, Apr. 2002.

❸ Fawnskin 5.10b ★★★

Challenging start. Surmount the roof and follow good features that'll peter out and leave you hanging. Like its small-town neighbor, this climb has a spicy slab finish that's sure to keep you on your toes.

60 ft. 6 bolts. Chris Miller, Pete Paredes, Loren Scott, Apr. 2002.

❹ Sugarloaf 5.9 ★

So-so climbing on the corner, plugging gear in small seams and horizontals. Clamber over the crux bulge and finish past a bolt on the slab to shared anchors on *Fawnskin*.

60 ft. Small gear to 2", 1 bolt. Pat Brennan, Alan Bartlett, Aug. 1997.

❺ High Plains Drifter 5.10a ★★

Run up a dark streak on the smooth slab past 2 bolts to a large diagonal crack. Shares anchors with *Bird of Prey*.

50 ft. Gear to 1.5", 2 bolts. Chris Miller, Lisa Guindon, July 1999.

6 Bird of Prey 5.8 ★★★

Distinguished by 2 pointed flakes on either side of a finger crack. Paste your feet and blast up the lower slab. Battle the bulge using giant jugs out right. Traipse past 3 closely spaced bolts on nice flakes that are just where you need them. A nice easy climb, highly recommended.

45 ft. 5 bolts. Chris Miller, Lisa Guindon, July 1999.

7 A Thunder of Drums 5.8 ★

Set up this line from the anchors of *Bird of Prey*. The start is slabby with decent edges above.

40 ft. Chris Miller, Lisa Guindon, July 1999.

8 Last Call For Alcohol 5.7 ★★

The obvious left-slanting crack that splits the wall. Comfortable jams and plentiful face holds throughout. Share anchors with *Bird of Prey*.

40 ft. Gear to 3". Jim Hammerle, Rick Shull, 1989.

9 Thunderbird 5.9 ★★

Another enjoyable route on good features. A difficult thin sequence gives way to larger holds. Shared anchors with *Medicine Man*.

45 ft. 5 bolts. Loren Scott, Chris Miller, July 1997.

10 Ripple 5.9

Nondescript line on the smooth face past an oddly shaped pocket to the anchors of *Medicine Man*.

40 ft. Loren Scott, Chris Miller, July 1997.

11 Medicine Man 5.7+ ★★★

Look for the queue at the base of this popular line. Begin on the leftmost of the V-shaped finger cracks and progress on incut edges through steepening terrain. Anchors are on the left side of the prominent block sitting atop the formation.

40 ft. 4 bolts. Chris Miller, Dave Masuo, Loren Scott, July 1997.

12 Nervous Twitch 5.9 ★★

Try out this throwback to the original line. While the bolted direct start is more popular, the route initially went up the rightmost of the thin V-shaped finger cracks on gear. Finish on the bolted headwall.

50 ft. Gear to 3", 2 bolts. Bob Cockell, 1992.

13 Nervous Twitch Direct 5.9 ★★★

This bolted line goes directly up the middle of the obvious block atop the formation on holds that are better than they look from the ground. Relish the intriguing sequence on the impressive headwall.

50 ft. 5 bolts. Rick Shull, Chris Miller, June 2000.

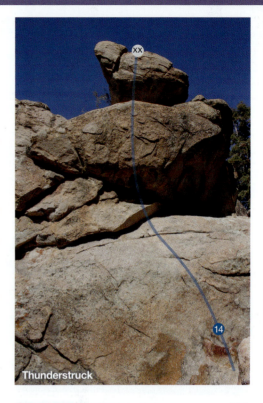

Thunderstruck

14 Thunderstruck 5.10c ★★

Located by itself in the corridor between Thunderbird and Gunsmoke walls. Once you start this baby, there's no turning back. You'll be shaking at the knees and there'll be no help, no help for you. Smear up the initial slab to seek respite beneath a huge roof. Cling to the obvious hueco and pray you can make the reach. Top out and you'll be thunderstruck.

40 ft. 4 bolts. Chris Miller, May 2002.

GUNSMOKE WALL

Gunsmoke is the large formation that stands sentinel at the top of the amphitheatre, distinguished by two prominent triangular blocks protruding from its south face. While the majority of the wall faces south and is sunny, there is a corridor on the west side that catches shade. This wall doesn't seem to attract the same traffic as other nearby walls, but there are some great routes here.

10 min

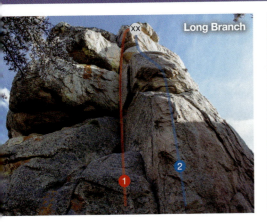

Long Branch

Powderhorn

Approach: The wall is perched atop a hill, forming the back end of the Central Pinnacles Amphitheatre. Continue uphill past Thunderbird Wall to its far right. Thunderbird forms a corridor with Gunsmoke, where its first lines are located. **[GPS: 34.30821, -116.87850]**

1 Triple Decker 5.7 ★

The obvious dihedral in the corridor, on lichen-covered rock. Discontinuous climbing past ledges with an awkward crux. Shares anchors with *Long Branch*.

50 ft. Gear to 3". Tim Fearn, Chris Miller, 1990.

2 Long Branch 5.10a ★

Up the sharp arête, then through bulges and a headwall.

50 ft. 4 bolts. FA: (TR) Chris Miller, 2001; FL: Unknown, 2011.

3 Powderhorn 5.10a ★★★

Boulder up to a series of huge undercling flakes to start this pumpy line. Transition onto a green slab that spits you out onto a sloped ledge. Pull the roof and fight the pump as you hang onto patina edges for the steep climax.

55 ft. 6 bolts. Chris Miller, Dave Masuo, June 1997.

4 Black Powder 5.7 ★★

Crank up the short crack with good protection throughout. End at the ledge and share anchors with *Gunsmoke*.

40 ft. Gear to 3.5". Rick Shull, 1989.

5 Smokin' the Rock 5.10b ★★

Start atop a flat boulder at the corridor's right end. Tread lightly on marginal edges up the orange and green face. Past the monster ledge, confront a blank section and a sporty mantel to shared anchors on *Finger Crimping Good*.

60 ft. 5 bolts. Chris Miller, Pete Paredes, May 2002.

6 Narcotic Prayer 5.11a ★

A neglected toprope problem that climbs the rounded arête on thin edges. Shares the upper section and anchors with *Smokin' the Rock*.

60 ft. Craig Pearson, Dean Goolsby, 1994.

7 Finger Crimping Good 5.11c ★★★

Round the corner and admire this thin, technical face climb. Warm up those fingers, then leave the ground on solid incuts and tiny sharp crimps. Higher up, the slightly negative nature of the wall becomes more apparent as you strain to hang on. Duck onto the large ledge for a well-deserved breather, then emerge to face the extension head-on. Throttle over the bulge on nasty crimps — this one ain't over til it's over.

65 ft. 7 bolts. FA: Chris Miller, Loren Scott, June 1997; Extension: Chris Miller, July 2001.

8 Drug of Choice 5.12a ★★★

Dive into the insanity on this superb crimpfest. Gently overhanging, that's about all that's gentle on this route! Lieback a crack that peters out around the first bolt. Fire up the face on sharp crimps that are sure to test your finger strength. Repeat until you redpoint or until your fingertips are raw and bleeding, whichever comes first. Shares anchors with *Gunsmoke*.

45 ft. 4 bolts. FA: (TR) Jim Hammerle, 1991; FL: Craig Pearson, Dean Goolsby, 1994.

9 Gunsmoke 5.9 ★★

Decent, pint-sized line. Lieback the crack, or palm and smear as you stem the left-facing corner to reach the top of the pillar. Run up the slab past a bolt to the anchor ledge.

45 ft. Gear to 4", 1 bolt. Jim Hammerle, Stuart Lochner, 1990.

Gunsmoke Wall

⑩ Rawhide 5.10b ★★

Try to get as many fingertip pads as you can on the thin holds that are a sharper and shallower than you'd like. Strenuous moves gain the arête, then pass a shared bolt on the way to *Gunsmoke's* anchors.

45 ft. 4 bolts. Pete Paredes, Chris Miller, Apr. 2004.

⑪ Smoking Gun 5.10b ★★

Tackles the prow of the small pillar. A tricky sequence pops out onto the arête. Take on the final slab past a bolt and anchors shared with *Gunsmoke*.

45 ft. 4 bolts. Chris Miller, Pete Paredes, May 2002.

⑫ Filet of Sole 5.8 ★★

Located on the rightmost pillar, this right-facing corner has more face holds than its neighbors. Surmount the final slab to a ledge. Build a gear anchor among the boulders and scramble 20 feet left to the anchor atop *Gunsmoke* to rappel.

45 ft. Gear to 2", 1 bolt. Chris Miller, Ernesto Ramirez, May 1991.

⑬ Dirty Captain Freeman 5.10c ★★

Slither up the slick dihedral and pop out right near the top of the feature. Flow through easier terrain in the middle and end on thin holds. Gear belay and walk off, or use anchors atop *Gunsmoke* to rappel.

45 ft. Gear to 2", 3 bolts. Alan Bartlett, Pat Brennan, Aug. 1997.

⑭ Testosterone Crack 5.11b ★★

Without stemming, slot your fists into this contrived corner crack and grunt and groove to the top. Gear anchor.

40 ft. Gear to 4". Chuck Scott, 1995.

Variation 5.10a: Much easier when a bit of stemming off the corner is added into the mix. A more natural and popular variation.

⑮ Joe's Dilemma 5.12c ★★★

Lieback a thin finger crack and smear on slick footholds. Fantastic fingerlocks and gastons on this one! Cut right at the 3rd bolt to an exhilarating huck at the finish.

40 ft. 4 bolts. Joe De Luca, 2007.

⑯ Bacon Taco 5.10a ★★

A spicy roof problem on the southeast corner. Climb up underneath the roof (optional 2" cam here), and lean back on big holds to clip the 2nd bolt above the lip. Overcome the roof and Tarzan through massive plates to the anchors. This climb was originally led on gear.

40 ft. 3 bolts, optional 2" piece.

FA: Chris Miller, Ernesto Ramirez, 1991; Equipped: Bob Cockell, 1991.

Adria Hendler, *Powderhorn,* **5.10a, Gunsmoke Wall, page 81.** 📷 Stephen Lê

Bacon Taco

xx

xx

variation

12 13 14 15 16 17

Fever Pitch

xx

18 19

17 After the Gold Rush 5.8 ★★

Either fire through the sequential direct start (5.7), or start on *Fever Pitch* and traverse left across the ramp. Tiptoe on small nubs to gain bigger features above, where a powerful crux guards the finish. Use anchors on *Bacon Taco*.
35 ft. Chris Miller, Sept. 2001.

18 Cali Gold 5.5 ★★

Once you've climbed *Fever Pitch*, toprope this slightly harder line. Climb *Fever Pitch* to the ramp, then step left and gravitate upward on large features, culminating in a bulge between two dark streaks. Great intro to steeper climbing.
30 ft. Chris Miller, Sept. 2001.

19 Fever Pitch 5.3 ★★

One of the easiest routes in all of Holcomb, and quite enjoyable. Short, with an abundance of large holds, this one is great for beginners, budding leaders, or those with a fear of heights. The nice ledge up top provides a perfect place to teach someone how to properly clean an anchor.
30 ft. 3 bolts. Chris Miller, Bryan Dennison, Sept. 2001.

PISTOL WHIPPED WALL

PM 10-15 min

This west-facing wall is actually the backside of Thunderbird. Though it is near the Central Amphitheatre, it rarely sees the crowds. It's a great spot to attempt excellent, hard sport routes on vertical to slightly overhanging terrain. *Ricochet* (5.10a), *Pistol Whipped* (5.11a), and *The Showdown* (5.12a) are all outstanding routes for breaking into their respective grades.

Approach: From Thunderbird Wall, hike north through the corridor between it and Gunsmoke. Pick up the faint trail heading downhill to the west. This trail snakes around, hugging the rock, to arrive at the left side of Pistol Whipped Wall near *Dangling Derelict*.
[GPS: 34.30825, -116.87896]

1 Dangling Derelict 5.10a ★★

100 feet left of the main wall is this easily recognizable roof problem. Tiptoe up a dirty slab to reach the monster roof. Slot bomber gear under the roof and get worked jamming up this short yet splendid crack. Belay from a dead pine or bring some wide gear. Walk off climber's left.
30 ft. Gear to 2.5". Chris Miller, Tim Fearn, 1989.

❷ Hang 'Em High 5.10d ★

Left of *Ricochet*, start underneath the prominent nose. Pick your way up the face past flakes, flakes, and more flakes. Use *Ricochet* anchors.

60 ft. Chris Miller, June 2001.

❸ Ricochet 5.10a ★★★★

A diamond in the rough. A short ramp leads to continuous climbing on the light-colored wall. Zip past a diagonal to reach the steep, imposing headwall. Savor the exposure as you bound up solid features with athletic movement. Reach the dike near the top and it's over. Spectacular, well-protected climbing— a high-caliber route.

60 ft. 7 bolts. Chris Miller, Chuck Scott, Rick Shull, Helen Shull, Lisa Guindon, Dave Masuo, June 2001.

❹ The Peacemaker 5.11b ★★

Grab your six-shooter and saddle up for this steep adventure. Trot up the wall to the right of the ramp, passing the alcove hideout. Gallop through thin crimps to a steep bulge. Don't let the crimpy headwall crux bamboozle you!

65 ft. 6 bolts. Chris Miller, Chuck Scott, July 2001.

❺ Shootin' Blanks 5.10b ★

Holster your doubts as you stare down the barrel of this twin crack line. A tough slab leads to the steep and somewhat chossy crack system that wants to spit you out. A painful left-hand jam at the crux might draw blood.

60 ft. 6 bolts. Loren Scott, Chris Miller, Mark Downey, Chuck Scott, Bryan Dennison, Aug. 2001.

❻ The Showdown 5.12a ★★★

Are you the fastest rope gun in the West? Square off with the thin lower face and shoot up single-pad edges to a stance below the headwall. Come out with guns blazin' to face the overhanging crux. When the smoke clears, you'll either emerge victorious or go down in a blaze of glory.

65 ft. 7 bolts. Chris Miller, June 2001.

❼ Pistol Whipped 5.11a ★★★

The initial blank slab quickly transitions to nice patina edges before the angle steepens. Gun for the big holds on the juggy headwall above. A fun challenge for the whole gang of outlaws.

70 ft. 8 bolts. Chris Miller, June 2000.

❽ A Good Day to Die 5.8 ★

Lots of rambling and scrambling for only 10 feet of good climbing in a left-facing corner. Finish in the unprotected chimney behind the pinnacle. Rappel from *Silver Bullet* anchors.

50 ft. Gear to 3". Jim Hammerle (solo), 1990.

Pistol Whipped Wall

9 Silver Bullet 5.10a ★★

Lieback a flake on the grainy green face. When the holds thin out, wrangle the prow. A tad awkward and dirty.

50 ft. 6 bolts. Chris Miller, Pete Paredes, May 2003.

10 Hair Trigger 5.10c ★★★

Situated on the outer face of the turret. Be quick on the draws while making tenuous moves on the blank face. The slightly negative lower section is harder than it looks. Increasing difficulty culminates with a tough sequence over a bulge — hang on to reach the chains!

50 ft. 5 bolts. Chris Miller, Pete Paredes, Oct. 2002.

11 Firing Line 5.11c ★★

Head down a boulder-filled gully to reach the base of this quality route, situated on the far right end of the wall. Although short, it packs a punch, with an intense and tricky sequence at the last 2 bolts.

50 ft. 4 bolts. Chris Miller, Oct. 2002.

ROSE RED WALL

A small, neglected wall with a few short burns. The anchors atop the formation are easily accessible from the vicinity of Pistol Whipped Wall.

PM   🚶 10-15 min

Approach: Set out on the main trail from the southern parking lot. Hike to the intersection with a 4WD road (3N07A) in the vicinity of Camp Rock. Turn north and walk the road, with the Central Pinnacles formations off to the right. Rose Red is a small formation that sits below the obvious Pistol Whipped Wall. Hike up a small incline through the trees to reach it. **[GPS: 34.30812, -116.87924]**

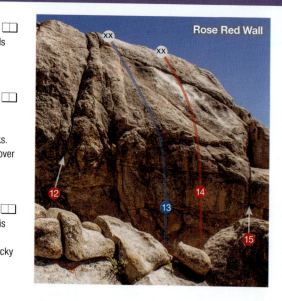

Rose Red Wall

12 Tangerine Dream 5.10a

Dirty, flared, right-slanting finger crack 10 feet left of *Pink Flamingo*; shares its anchors.

25 ft. Gear to 2". Eric Odenthal, Oct. 2005.

13 Pink Flamingo 5.9 ★

The only fully bolted line on the wall. Powerful, steep climbing on positive edges, then a technical slab.

35 ft. 4 bolts. Brad Singer, John Cardmon, Eric Odenthal, Oct. 2005.

14 Rose Red 5.9 ★

Boulder past the first bolt to better features. Use horizontals for gear and finish past a final bolt on the slab above. The 2-bolt anchor does not have rap rings.

35 ft. Gear to 2", 2 bolts. FA: (TR) Pete Paredes, Chris Miller, Mar. 2003; FL: Nathan Fitzhugh, Chris Miller, May 2003.

15 Apricot Brandy 5.8

Hard moves in a thin crack lead to a ledge. Meander up broken terrain to the top. Gear anchor.

35 ft. Gear to 2". Eric Odenthal (solo), Oct. 2002.

A busy day at Motherlode West.
📷 Brandon Copp

MOTHERLODE ROCK

This massive formation contains the most routes in Holcomb, satisfying trad and sport climbers alike. One can chase shade or sun throughout the day here. The Motherlode is typically less busy and a great place to check out when you've forgotten to phone in your reservation for Coyote Crag! The crag contains three main sectors. Motherlode East boasts a fair amount of everything — easy slab lines, a variety of bolted moderates, and even some excellent cracks. Motherlode North — AKA Lizard's Head — is distinguished by the bright green lichen-covered rock shaped like a giant lizard's head, which two unique and airy lines ascend. A massive roof on the left side has some spectacular climbs, often with a line of eager climbers waiting to give them a spin. Motherlode West is known for its powerful 5.10 sport routes.

Approach: Hike the main trail from the southern parking area to the Central Pinnacles Amphitheatre. Once at the amphitheatre, continue uphill between Gunsmoke Wall and Skyy Slab. Follow the trail northward along the back of Gunsmoke. The trail deposits you near *Blasting Cap* on Motherlode East, where the path splits and encircles the formation. To reach the north face, it is easiest to hike along the east face and follow the trail as it wraps around.

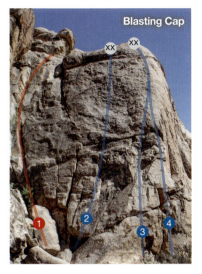

Blasting Cap

Motherlode

Motherlode East
[GPS: 34.30869, -116.87815]

AM 🚶 15 min

❶ Cap Gun 5.1
This low-angle gully/dihedral is the easiest way to the top of the formation. Gear anchor.
35 ft. Gear to 3". Unknown.

❷ Blasting Cap 5.4 ★★
A good introduction to slab. Big handholds and ledges lead past 2 bolts. Good friction and slab technique is gold on the upper section. Reach a ridge of good holds at the dike and smile — you've made it!
35 ft. 4 bolts. Chris Miller, 1989.

❸ Wildrose 5.7 ★★
Another low-angle slab route, but not a total gimme. Begin on the blunt arête and continue through a blocky corner. Tackle smooth features on the full-value slab above.
40 ft. 4 bolts. Chris Miller, Lisa Guindon, May 1997.

❹ The Prospector 5.7 ★★
Navigate the broken corner to a bulge. Go direct through the bulge to a slabby finale and the anchors of *Wildrose*.
40 ft. 5 bolts. FA: (TR) Unknown; FL: Bryn Owen, Chuck Scott, Chris Owen, Scott Nomi, Chris Miller, Oct. 2019.

❺ Fire in the Hole 5.10a ★★★
Down around the corner, this line features good movement on excellent incuts. Blast up the initial vertical section and then explode upward on great flakes and edges that thin toward the top.
40 ft. 4 bolts. Rick Shull, Chris Miller, 1989.

❻ Fool's Gold 5.6 ★★
Start this juggy crack system under the signature nugget. Be cautious when climbing past this block! Quite enjoyable, with plenty of pro and easy stances for placing it. Shares anchors with *Motherlode*.
45 ft. Thin gear to 2". Rick Shull, Chris Miller, 1989.

❼ Golden Nugget 5.10a ★★★
Fingerlock in the initial seam, transitioning to a bouldery crux on thin edges, then snag the "Thank God" hold on the dike. Pass a slab section and end with giant holds at the shared anchor of *Motherlode*.
45 ft. 5 bolts. Chris Miller, Rick Shull, 1989.

❽ Motherlode 5.11b ★★
Look for a black streak where the diagonal dike reaches the ground. Flail through (contrived) opening moves on blank rock. Stem a right-facing corner and climb the arête to the top.
45 ft. 5 bolts. Chris Miller, Jake Colella, May 2000.

❾ Golden Gloves 5.11b ★
A link-up of unappealing cruxes. Start with the first 3 bolts of *Motherlode* and finish past the last 3 bolts of *Black Bart*.
50 ft. 6 bolts. Chris Miller, May 2000.

❿ Lodestone 5.10b ★★★
The much more enjoyable inverse link-up that starts on *Black Bart* and finishes on *Motherlode*. A sweet line of least resistance that merges the best parts of each route.
50 ft. 6 bolts. Chris Miller, May 2000.

Out of Our Mines

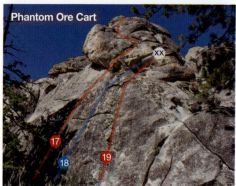

Phantom Ore Cart

⑪ Black Bart 5.11a ★★

Dance left on thin edges to a ledge. Trend back right to reach a miserable piece of slab on the upper section.

50 ft. 6 bolts. Chris Miller, Rick Shull, 1989.

⑫ Psychedelic Sluice 5.6 ★★★

Don't drink the juice! A superb, well-protected crack line. Tough start with slick feet, then plug gear and chug your way up the nice slanting crack. When you reach the tree, cut right to the anchors. Do it!

50 ft. Gear to 2.5". Chris Miller, Rick Shull, 1989.

⑬ Belleville 5.9+ ★★

Belleville was the original mining town in Holcomb Valley, established in 1860 and named after Belle Van Dusen, the blacksmith's daughter and the first child born in the area. Like raising a baby girl, this route is rough in the beginning, but it does get better! Shares anchors with *Psychedelic Sluice*.

50 ft. Chris Miller.

⑭ Shantytown Swing 5.8 ★★

A large block at the start of this climb recently fell off, bumping up the grade. Monkey past abundant plates to the final enjoyable slab. Shares anchors with *Psychedelic Sluice*.

50 ft. 6 bolts. Chris Miller, Ernie Ramirez, May 1991.

⑮ Dust in the Wind 5.7 ★★

As with the climb above, a new low crux now guards this attractive crack. Straightforward crack climbing leads up the right-facing corner toward a large roof. Before reaching the roof, branch off left and follow another crack that heads to the shared anchors atop *Psychedelic Sluice*.

50 ft. Gear to 3", 1 bolt. Chris Miller, 1989.

⑯ Out of Our Mines 5.11a ★★★

A tall and thought-provoking line with a little bit of everything. A low crux sports just enough holds, but a key hold on the direct start has broken since the first ascent. Tech through to reach an easy, runout slab, then power through the exciting roof on solid jugs to finish.

70 ft. 7 bolts. Chris Miller, Pete Paredes, June 2002.

⑰ Miner Forty-Niner 5.9+ ★★

Thin, technical crack. The insecure and sparse gear placements are the crux! Meander up the low-angle face to an easy gully on the massive upper block. Gear anchor.

80 ft. Gear to 3", mostly smaller pieces. Chris Miller, 1991.

⑱ Phantom Ore Cart 5.10b ★★

Start left of a small tree. Thin moves and scarce feet make for a tough start. Holds continue to improve as the angle slabs out, culminating in 20 feet of runout terrain to anchors.

50 ft. 4 bolts. Chris Miller, Reed Ames, June 2018.

⑲ Miner's Milk 5.9 ★★

Still cleaning up, but a smooth line nonetheless. Lieback the seam to a good flake. Launch up the face past a bolt to shared anchors with *Phantom Ore Cart*. If you like this route, try one of its delicious namesake brews next time you're out at the Joshua Tree Saloon!

50 ft. Gear to 3", 1 bolt. Reed Ames, Chris Miller, June 2018.

Lizard Head
[GPS: 34.30897, -116.87807]

15 min

⑳ Powder Keg 5.10a ★★★

A super-enjoyable and über-popular roof problem. Tiptoe up the cruxy slab, sink your mitts into monster pockets underneath the roof, lean back, and snag the big horn that looks further away than it really is. Cut feet, heel hook the arête, rock over, and romp to the top.

40 ft. 4 bolts. Chris Miller, Rick Shull, 1989.

Lizard Head

21 **Power Keg** 5.11a ★★

A burly link-up. Climb *Powder Keg* to the horn, then traverse the lip of the roof to join *Nitroglycerine* and finish on that route. Note: There is no connecting bolt for this traverse, so you risk a nasty swing if you blow it!
40 ft. 5 bolts. Ricky Steele, Aug. 2017.

22 **Nitroglycerine** 5.10b ★★

Don't hesitate at the strongman crux — blindly grab a sharp crack and muscle through the burly roof with a bulge in your stomach! Share the last bolt and anchors with *Powder Keg*.
40 ft. 4 bolts. Steve Gooden, Chris Miller, Aug. 1997.

23 **Boom Sauce** 5.8 ★★

A funky little right-facing dihedral around the corner from *Nitroglycerine*. Lieback or stem, clipping bolts on the left.
40 ft. 4 bolts. Reed Ames, Chris Miller, June 2018.

24 **Short Fuse** 5.10b ★★

Another short line packed in closely to its neighbors. A tough slab leads to an overhanging headwall that packs a punch.
40 ft. 4 bolts. Chris Miller, May 2002.

25 **Fun Police** 5.6 ★★

This fun, generously bolted line is a great beginning lead.

Advance past the initial slab and mount a bulge. Smear up more slab and travel through broken sections on splendid plates and horns. Pull your rope away from the water crack on the right to avoid getting the end stuck!
70 ft. 10 bolts. Aaron Lawrence, Brent Webster, 2012.

26 **Smackdown** 5.8 ★★

Scamper over bulges and slab to arrive at the impressive head of the lizard, where an easy traverse right out its mouth reaches the anchors shared with *Whiptail*. The crux spit off one of the first ascensionists, resulting in a fractured ankle and a fitting name for this route!
50 ft. 6 bolts. Pete Paredes, Nathan Mitts, Ted Peace, Diane Peace, Chris Miller, July 2001.

27 **Whiptail** 5.9 ★★★

This unique local gem climbs the rock that looks like the head of a giant whiptail lizard. Climb the belly of the beast past the first bolt in a right-facing corner. Thin, heady moves on the arête gain the lizard's neck. The airy exposure reaches its peak at the crux as you move through overhanging terrain below the 4th bolt. A slightly reachy sequence nabs the mouth of the lizard and the anchors above. Sure to get your heart pumping!
50 ft. 4 bolts. Chris Miller, Nathan Mitts, Pete Paredes, July 2001.

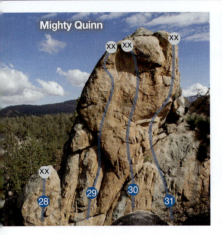

Mighty Quinn

Reach For the Sky

Motherlode West
[GPS: 34.30879, -116.87827]

PM   15 min

28 Highgrader 5.11a ★★
A short but stout route in the boulder-filled gully. Zip up the blocky seam to a bulge on the green-lichen-splattered wall. Throttle through the crimpy crux to the apex of a small pillar.
35 ft. 4 bolts. Chris Miller, July 2001.

29 Stake Your Claim 5.10d ★★★
Slick feet and mediocre hands make the initial moves difficult. Shake out above the 5th bolt and prepare for the final steep and sustained section. Wicked moves along a right-slanting rail end with a crimpy crux.
65 ft. 7 bolts. Chris Miller, July 2001.

30 Mighty Quinn 5.10c ★★★
A must-do route with gymnastic movement on steep rock. Climb patina flakes to a small rest stance. Excellent movement as you creep out and try not to pump out on the steep upper section. Launch into the heartbreaker crux protecting the chains — it's repelled many an onsight!
60 ft. 5 bolts. Grahm Doe, Brent Webster, 1994.

31 Long Arm of the Law 5.11a ★★★
If you like roof problems, give this one a go! Technical face climbing up a green streak leads to the monster roof. Explode upward, sticking the reachy crux move. Finish with a fabulous jug haul.
60 ft. 6 bolts. Chris Miller, June 2000.

32 Good Day For a Hangin' 5.10c ★★★
An exceptionally fun line that'll have you grinning from ear to ear. Climb the dihedral situated right of the break in the formation. Shake out at the ledge, calm the voices in your head, and apply Arno Ilgner's *Rock Warrior's Way*. Then

shock and awe your friends with a sick dyno to the big hold on the lip. Rock over the lip and revel in your badassery.
50 ft. 5 bolts. Chris Miller, Steve Gooden, Aug. 1997.

33 Funkadelia 5.9 ★
Take the nice hand crack until it pinches off. Traverse right on good flakes and end in a manky crack. Gear belay or use the bolted anchors atop *Reach For the Sky*.
50 ft. Gear to 3". Jim Hammerle, 1990.

34 Reach For the Sky 5.10b ★★★
Look for the stack of cheater stones at the start of this climb. Reach up sky-high into an undercling and make another reachy move to an edge. Blaze incut edges to a thin, fingery sequence up a short headwall block. Best to have a positive ape index for this line!
40 ft. 5 bolts. Chris Miller, Rick Shull, 1989.

35 Whiskeroo 5.10c ★★
A bouldery crux on a blocky dike guards the high first bolt. From the sloping ledge, stem up onto the incut-peppered headwall. Named for the Whiskeroo Beard Contest at the Mountain Top Days festival held annually in Running Springs.
40 ft. 5 bolts. Chris Miller, Adam Williams, Mark Downey, Aug. 2001.

36 Panning For Gold 5.10b ★★
Find the good holds among the slanting corners and slick edges and power through the roof section. Ride jugs on the dike to the chains. Fun, with a memorable ending.
40 ft. 4 bolts. FA: (TR) Chris Miller, Tim Fearn, 1990;
FL: Chris Miller, Sean Godwin, Nathan Fitzhugh, May 2002.

37 Golden Showers 5.9 ★★
A traverse route that follows the yellow lichen from a broken corner into an alcove. End at *RFTS* anchors.
50 ft. Gear to 3". Tim Fearn, 1990.

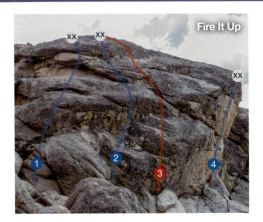

Fire It Up

The Incinerator

INCINERATOR WALL

A massively overhanging wall with two spectacular testpieces. There aren't many walls in the San Bernardinos like this! Shady and north-facing, perfect sending conditions can be found at this steep wall year-round.

15 min

Approach: Located across the narrow boulder-filled gully from the Lizard Head on Motherlode Rock. This wall can also be reached by hiking south from the northern parking lot past the east face of Wilbur's Tombstone.
[GPS: 34.30909, -116.87823]

1 Burning Man 5.9 ★

Locate a large roof ¾ of the way up the east face. Broken rock leads to a bulge with featured slab above. A little grungy down low but an enjoyable roof sequence.
45 ft. 3 bolts. Pete Paredes, Chris Miller, July 2001.

2 Fire It Up 5.10a ★★

Warm up on this fun line that's still cleaning up. Climb wavy features past bulges, with the crux up high. Bring an extendable draw for the 4th bolt.
50 ft. 5 bolts. Chris Miller, Reed Ames, June 2018.

3 Fire Walker 5.10a ★

A manky mixed line that starts atop a hunk of light-colored rock at the corner. Move past slanted ledges and a bulge, then take a thin finger crack to the top. Finish left at the anchors of *Fire It Up*, or build an anchor (gear to 3") as desired.
50 ft. Gear to 1", 3 bolts. Chris Miller, Sept. 2003.

4 Crematorium 5.12d ★★★

Get your feet wet on one of the easier routes nearby so you don't flame out on your attempt of this overhanging monster. Burn through blocky holds down low and fire straight up past a horizontal. Watch your forearms melt as you tech your way slightly right on increasingly smaller holds.
35 ft. 3 bolts. Matt Hulet, July 2010.

5 The Incinerator 5.12a ★★★★

An excellent steep sport route that's likely to extinguish any remaining strength you might have. Put your game face on as you throttle through the bouldery opening sequence. Explode out of the small alcove with forearms flaming and make the 3rd clip. Feeling pumped? Summon your inner beast and launch into the crux dyno. Powerful and well-protected, this is an area classic and deservedly so.
40 ft. 4 bolts. Chuck Scott, 1992.

Prairie Squid Wall

PRAIRIE SQUID WALL

This cephalopod-themed wall is home to half a dozen easy trad lines, many combining face and thin-crack climbing. A fun spot if you're looking to place gear in an out-of-the-way setting.

Approach: From the Lizard Head on Motherlode Rock, hike north past the Incinerator Wall. Just past this wall, turn left into a tight corridor. Prairie Squid is on the west side of the formation containing Incinerator Wall.

Alternately, reach this tight corridor by hiking south from the northern parking area and passing the east face of Wilbur's Tombstone. **[GPS: 34.30897, -116.87846]**

1 Squids in Blue 5.6 ★★
10 feet left of a boulder in the corridor is this right-leaning crack. Swim up to a small ledge, then trend left along a finger/hand crack through the middle portion of the wall. A 2-bolt anchor (no rap rings) is located on a wide ledge. Scramble off (unprotected) to the right or climb the upper headwall to a gear belay.
35 ft. Gear to 3". Unknown.

2 Squid Vicious 5.6 ★★
Begin right of the boulder and propel yourself up the face between two diagonal cracks, with horizontal seams providing protection. Same anchor situation as *Squids in Blue.*
35 ft. Gear to 2". Unknown.

3 Prairie Squid 5.6 ★
The obvious crack that splits the upper, middle, and lower sections of the wall but doesn't reach the ground. Sprout a couple extra appendages for the initial section that guards the high first placement. Follow the left-angling finger crack to the top. Gear anchor.
35 ft. Gear to 2". Unknown.

4 Smoked Squid 5.6 ★★
A left-angling thin seam left of a small pine. Cram your fingertips into the seam or sample the plentiful face holds nearby. Shimmy over a bulge to finish and gear belay from cracks at the top.
35 ft. Gear to 2". Unknown.

5 Calamari 5.7 ★
A dirty double crack system with a choose-your-own-adventure start. Go directly up the face under the left crack that doesn't reach the ground (5.7) or take the right crack and traverse left (5.6). Chug up the double crack system and bust through a final roof problem to a gear belay.
35 ft. Gear to 2". Unknown.

6 Squid Inked 5.7 ★★

Start 10 feet right of *Calamari* at a dirty, left-slanting hand crack. Climb past a boulder to a ledge. As the crack thins, ink out through a notch. Gear anchor.
30 ft. Gear to 2". Unknown.

MOONSHINE DOME

A 50-foot-tall dome situated on the northern fringe of the Central Pinnacles. It has a prominent dike running down its southwest face.

  15 min

Approach: From the Lizard Head on Motherlode Rock, hike north past the Incinerator Wall. Pass the tight corridor heading to Prairie Squid Wall. Turn left into the next channel that leads downhill to Moonshine Dome.

Hiking south from the northern parking area, the channel lies just past the east face of Wilbur's Tombstone.
[GPS: 34.30912, -116.87878]

7 Mule Kick 5.8 ★★

Head up an easy, broken section of the dike to a high first bolt (optional gear placement reaching the bolt). Amble up smooth rock to a small roof with huge jugs. Run it out on easy slab, passing an optional small cam placement.
50 ft. 3 bolts, optional gear to 2.5".
Chris Miller, Lisa Guindon, Mar. 2003.

8 Prohibited 5.7 ★★

Mediocre climbing leads to a small alcove. Jet out left, then shoot right up the nice hand crack that's sure to stimulate your senses. Shared anchor with *Mule Kick*.
50 ft. Gear to 4". Unknown.

9 Skull Cracker 5.8 ★

Start as for *Prohibited*. From the alcove, take the splitter hand-sized crack through a short but imposing overhanging section. Shared anchor with *Mule Kick*.
40 ft. Gear to 3". Chris Miller, Nathan Fitzhugh, May 2003.

10 Cool Water 5.7 ★

Same start to the alcove, but then move right on slab to a larger cave. Good hands provide security on the airy traverse underneath the roof. Squeeze through the slot and share anchors with *Mule Kick*.
40 ft. Gear to 4". Chris Miller, Nathan Fitzhugh, May 2003.

WILBUR'S TOMBSTONE

A tall fin with routes named in tribute to Charles Wilbur, a placer miner from the late 1800s whose gravesite you pass on the drive in to Holcomb. The challenging routes here are "old-school" in nature, and many of them require a piece or two of gear.

15 min

Approach: From the Lizard Head on Motherlode Rock, hike north past the Incinerator Wall. Wilbur's Tombstone is the next tall formation that you come to on the left. It sits at the edge of the northern parking lot.
[GPS: 34.30947, -116.87871]

❶ Wilbur Never Wore Lycra 5.7

This old, rarely done gear line takes a ramp on the left margin of the east face to a thin, sparsely protected crack. Shares anchors with *What a Woman*.
40 ft. Gear to 1.5". Jim Hammerle, Stuart Lochner, 1991.

❷ What a Woman 5.9+ ★★

Decent steep friction climbing. Starting direct involves some desperate slab moves; traversing in from the right is a slightly easier option. Slightly runout to the 2nd bolt, but an optional cam fits nicely in the horizontal.
50 ft. 4 bolts, optional 2" piece. Bob Cockell, 1992.

❸ Pumped-Up Woman 5.8 ★★

A mixed route in the center of the face. Climb knobs whilst stuffing gear in the seam or horizontal above. Mantel, then creep up the steep wall on thin edges. Fierce and challenging, with the jug rail at the dike offering some relief before the final thought-provoking blank section. Shared anchor with *What a Woman*.
50 ft. Gear to 2", 2 bolts. Bob Cockell, 1992.

❹ Rap Bolters Will Be Prosecuted 5.8 ★★

The unforgiving landing makes getting to the first bolt an exciting proposition. Navigate a plethora of seams past a chopped bolt (place gear here) to a big horn. Pure friction and balance takes you to the horizontal dike, with a final tricky sequence guarding the chains. Originally led entirely on gear, this was later retro-bolted; subsequently, 2 of those 5 bolts were chopped.
50 ft. Gear to 2", 3 bolts. Jim Hammerle, Chris Miller, 1988.

❺ Wilbur's Turning in His Grave 5.10b ★

Scale the narrow north arête to arrive beneath a bulge. The crux is a long reach straight over the bulge — moving left here feels more natural, but lowers the grade.
50 ft. 4 bolts. Kevin Duck et al, 1995.

❻ Killed by Death 5.10b ★★

Drop the needle on this Motörhead song as you follow the thin vertical seam. Have your groupies shout encouragement as you commit to reachy moves up the overhanging wall onto the finishing slab. It's 4 minutes and 40 seconds of hard rock. Share anchors with *Wilbur's Turning in His Grave*.
50 ft. 5 bolts. Eric Odenthal, Chris Miller, May 2003.

Wilbur East

Wilbur West

XX
The Penguin
11
9
10

7 Takes a Thief 5.11a R ★★

In the center of the west face. Fly up the unprotected low-angle slab to the main event, a powerful sequence on amazingly positive edges. Don't fall clipping the 2nd bolt! This short burner would be much improved with a dedicated anchor and another bolt. As it stands, most opt to TR; bring long cord to extend the anchors of *What a Woman*.
50 ft. 2 bolts. Chuck Scott, 1992.

8 Unknown

Easy scrambling gains access to a terribly short vertical headwall. Bearhug the blunt arête as you make your way up on decent incuts.
40 ft. 3 bolts. Unknown.

Steller's Jay

THE PENGUIN

Recently developed, this small, south-facing formation has good rock. There is one set of shared anchors on top (no rap rings) and easy access from the back. The penguin-shaped namesake rock is perched behind the actual wall.

☀ 🚶 20 min

Approach: Located 300 yards directly east of the northern parking area, beside the bike trail. Hike cross-country to the base.
[GPS: 34.30949, -116.87569]

9 Hodor 5.10a ★

The crack line 5 feet left of the bolts. The undercut base delivers an overhanging start, yet plentiful plates offer relief above. Shares anchors with *Three-Eyed Raven*.
25 ft. Gear to 2". Dave Evans, Todd Battey, Aug. 2019.

10 The Three-Eyed Raven 5.10d ★★

Another short burner on plates. The steep start is the crux.
25 ft. 3 bolts. Dave Evans, Todd Battey, Aug. 2019.

11 The Stupidest Lannister 5.9 ★

Toprope the good features left of the crack as they trend left to the shared anchors.
25 ft. Dave Evans, Todd Battey, Aug. 2019.

HOLCOMB VALLEY PINNACLES **WEST**

A land forgotten by most, Holcomb Valley Pinnacles West holds less-traveled routes that will delight sport and trad climbers alike. Composed mostly of smaller, blocky formations, this area is located west of Central Pinnacles and the 4WD road (3N07A). Most walls do not have well-defined approach trails.

Lost and Found (5.9), *Kodiak Arrest* (5.10d), *Golden Opportunity* (5.10d), and *Point Blank* (5.11d) are among some of the more notable routes found here. If you've brought a rack, seek out Lost and Found Crag, with the largest collection of crack climbs in Holcomb. As an added bonus while hiking, HVP West houses a collection of abandoned mine shafts that serve as a reminder of the area's gold rush days. For your own safety, observe posted signs and do not enter the mines.

HOLCOMB VALLEY PINNACLES **WEST**

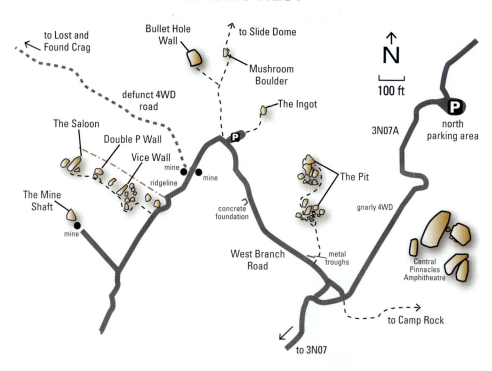

Approach: Set out on the main trail from the southern parking lot. Hike to the intersection with a 4WD road (3N07A) in the vicinity of Camp Rock (10-15 minutes). Locate the offshoot road heading west, leaving the Central Pinnacles behind. All of the HVP West crags are found along this west branch road.

It is possible to drive up 3N07A from 3N07 with a high-clearance 4WD vehicle. Take 3N07A for 1.3 miles and turn left onto the narrow west branch road. There are parking areas scattered along this road near most of the crags. With the exception of Lost and Found Crag, driving would cut the approach times to each of these walls to 5 minutes or less.

CLIMBING AREA	ELEVATION	HIKE	ROUTES	GRADE RANGE	CRAGS
THE PIT *Hidden and neat* page 100	7600 ft.	15 min	7	≤.5 .6 .7 .8 .9 .10 .11 .12	
THE INGOT *Handful of short climbs* page 101	7600 ft.	20 min	4	≤.5 .6 .7 .8 .9 .10 .11 .12	
MUSHROOM AREA *Testpiece: Harsh, 12c* page 103	7600 ft.	20-25 min	4	≤.5 .6 .7 .8 .9 .10 .11 .12	Bullet Hole Wall, Mushroom Boulder
LOST AND FOUND CRAG *Plethora of good cracks* page 104	7750 ft.	45 min	15	≤.5 .6 .7 .8 .9 .10 .11 .12	
VICE WALL AREA *Easy, fun trad lines* page 106	7600 ft.	25-30 min	11	≤.5 .6 .7 .8 .9 .10 .11 .12	Vice Wall, Double P, The Saloon
THE MINE SHAFT *Isolated, sunny wall* page 108	7500 ft.	30 min	4	≤.5 .6 .7 .8 .9 .10 .11 .12	

The Pit Approach

to Pit

Pit Approach 2

to Pit

THE PIT

The climbs on the main wall begin from down in an actual pit, whereas *Simple Lesson*, *Everclear*, and *Saddle Up* (#5-#7) are located on nearby boulders. The Pit's main wall faces south, but goes into shade in late afternoon. Though this crag is situated near the popular Central Pinnacles, its hidden nature has kept these enjoyable routes from seeing much action.

Approach: Where the west branch road heads out from 3N07A, walk uphill behind two rusty metal troughs, aiming for the prominent pinnacle seen from the road. Find a small cave beneath stacked boulders and scramble up to the left of the cave entrance. Stay on the main wall's left side and it will be possible to drop down into "the Pit." The challenging approach is not good for children or dogs.

To reach *Simple Lesson* and *Everclear*, instead of scrambling up beside the cave, stay low and continue west to these boulders. *Saddle Up* is found 100 yards to the north on the east face of a different pile of rocks. **[GPS: 34.30846, -116.88067]**

main Pit (routes #1-#4)
to *Everclear,*
Simple Lesson
to Pit

1 Whistleblower 5.10d ★★
Follow the black streak on the boulder left of *Sunkissed*. Slip into the great undercling and crimp your way to the top!
30 ft. 3 bolts. Stephen Lê, Nov. 2019.

2 Sunkissed 5.5 ★★
Easiest line of the bunch — if you can do the approach you should be able to do this climb! A fun slab route with lots of ledges and big holds. Similar in style to *Blasting Cap* and *Firewater* on Motherlode Rock.
50 ft. 4 bolts. Chris Miller, Pete Paredes, May 2002.

3 Down in a Hole 5.7 ★
Drop down into the Pit and grind out the difficult sidepull start on a thin finger crack, resisting the urge to use the block behind you. An awkward secondary crux hits as the crack widens. Easier terrain (but minimal gear) awaits at the finish. Shares anchors with *Sunkissed*.
50 ft. Gear to 3". Chris Miller, Pete Paredes, May 2002.

4 Heatseeker 5.10a ★★
Another tough start easily mitigated using the surrounding walls. Muscle through a mean lieback on the right-trending rail. Thin edges give way to jugs, culminating in a slabby finish. Shares anchors with *Sunkissed*.
50 ft. 5 bolts. Chris Miller, Pete Paredes, May 2002.

5 Simple Lesson 5.10d R
No anchors nor easy descent. From the main wall of the Pit, scramble over boulders around to the left and locate this 2-bolt line on the west face of the same huge boulder as *Whistleblower*. Good incut edges lead to a high first bolt above a bad landing (can place gear down low). Dig deep as the edges disappear and the blank vertical slab looms overhead.
35 ft. Gear to 2", 2 bolts. Dean Goolsby, Craig Pearson, 1993.

The Pit

Simple Lesson

5

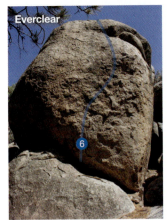

Everclear

6

Saddle Up

7

⑥ Everclear 5.12b ★

Situated on the south face of a stand-alone boulder near *Simple Lesson*. Begin on a ramp, with a reachy first clip. Angle right on small bumps and features. As of this writing, the hangers had been removed from the anchors — there's an easy scramble off the back, but you might have to get creative on how to get your gear back.

40 ft. 3 bolts. Dean Goolsby, Craig Pearson, 1993.

⑦ Saddle Up 5.10d ★★

100 yards north is a separate formation with this fun toprope on its east side. Scramble through boulders to the top of a hill and locate the bulging prow. Climb excellent flakes on the corner that thin to a blank section before big holds near the top. Gear anchor.

45 ft. Gear to 3" for the anchor. Jim Hammerle, 1990.

THE INGOT

A fin of rock hiding among the trees, with *Golden Opportunity* (5.10d) being the gem in the handful of short lines here.

PM

🚶 20 min

Approach: Take the road heading west past the Pit for 5 minutes to a small clearing/parking circle. This formation is partially hidden in the trees at the apex (east end) of the parking area. **[GPS: 34.30969, -116.88136]**

⑧ Goldfinch 5.7 ★

A one-move-wonder problem with an opening crux. Mantel onto a horizontal seam and run up the low-angle slab.

35 ft. 3 bolts. Brad Singer, Pat Brennan, May 2008.

⑨ The Melon Factor 5.11b ★

Gnarly moves through parallel finger cracks at the 2nd bolt present a short, painful crux. Reach the jugs and the climb is over. Shares the last 2 bolts and anchors with *Goldfinch*.

35 ft. 4 bolts. Pete Paredes, May 2008.

⑩ All That Glitters 5.10b ★★

Straightforward climbing leads to a dike with giant features. Mantel atop this and friction up the slab above.

35 ft. 3 bolts. Chris Miller, Oct. 2001.

⑪ Golden Opportunity 5.10d ★★

Around the corner is this short but quality line up a rounded arête. Throttle up to the dike on large holds, where an undercling can be useful getting above the horizontal, then smear up the textured face!

35 ft. 3 bolts. Chris Miller, Oct. 2001.

The Ingot

XX   XX   XX

11

8   9   10

Eoghan Kyne on *Everclear*, 5.12b, the Pit, page 101. ■ Stephen Lê

MUSHROOM BOULDER

This stone mushroom features three routes creeping up the east face of its distinctive cap. *Harsh* (5.12c) is a grueling spectacle that braves the blank face and wrestles with the largest part of the roof.

AM 20-25 min

Approach: Follow the approach to Bullet Hole Wall. Mushroom Boulder is the distinctly shaped rock sitting lower on the same hillside. **[GPS: 34.31026, -116.88184]**

BULLET HOLE WALL

A good-sized formation whose upper face is pockmarked with intriguing divots. One line has been done, but more potential exists.

20-25 min

Approach: Walk the west branch road for 5 minutes to a small clearing/parking circle. Look northwest from the parking area to locate this prominent wall. Walk toward the wall, staying low through a grove of mountain mahogany, crossing a seasonal streambed, and weaving uphill through boulders. **[GPS: 34.31016, -116.88232]**

12 Pocket Full of Shells 5.11c ★★
Comfortable crack climbing empties onto a ledge. Fire through the wicked sequence on the steep face littered with "bullet holes." A wild ride to the finish!
60 ft. Eric Odenthal.

13 Gold Fever 5.10a ★
Start from the left end of the boulder at the base. Use micro crimps to conquer the start until larger edges appear near the horizontal. Shared anchor with *Goldstrike*.
40 ft. Chris Miller, Oct. 2001.

14 Goldstrike 5.9 ★★
Begin atop a boulder and use a right-hand sidepull crack behind a small pine tree. Thin and balancy moves lead up to a horizontal, where the holds get larger. Fun finish on plates.
40 ft. 4 bolts. Chris Miller, Lisa Guindon, Aug. 1997.

15 Harsh 5.12c ★★
One of the hardest routes in Holcomb, with a low, bouldery crux sporting just enough holds to not be impossibly difficult. Tackle the white face where pure friction and balance transport the worthy over a sea of thin edges to the massive roof. Good holds grace the roof pull.
40 ft. 5 bolts. Eric Odenthal, May 2003.

Bullet Hole Wall

Mushroom Boulder

LOST AND FOUND CRAG

An outstanding crag hidden in a secluded corner of the woods. If you're willing to pack your trad rack all the way out here, you'll be rewarded with a full day's worth of gear-eating cracks. Offwidth climbing is an art that few perfect, but this crag is a good training ground for wide cracks. This large, square rock can easily host a few parties at once. Either sun or shade can be found throughout the day.

45 min

Approach: A long hike for HVP, but mainly on dirt roads. Take the west branch road past the parking circle by the Ingot, and continue as the road curves southwest toward Vice Wall. Turn right onto a defunct 4WD road just before a mine shaft on the right. (If you reach Vice Wall, you've gone too far.) Hike this old road for 0.5 miles, then head through a small clearing of manzanita and down a hill to reach the crag. The approach drops you near the climb *Rusted Root*, with the striking dihedral of *Lost and Found* easily visible as well. **[GPS: 34.31256, -116.88644]**

Lost and Found

❶ Throwing Logs 5.9 ★

Friction up a short ramp to reach the nice right-facing dihedral. Take the hand crack up this short but stout corner and finish on the separate pinnacle.
45 ft. Gear to 3", 1 bolt.
Brad Singer, Eric Odenthal, Kenn Kenaga, May 2005.

❷ Not For Sportclimbers 5.10a ★★★

No techy or dynamic moves here, just good ol' offwidth! 5 feet left of *Throwing Logs* is an outstanding splitter finger crack that grows as it goes. Excellent offwidth climbing that never feels thrutchy or weird. Cut slightly right to shared anchors on *Lichen the Eye*.
65 ft. Gear to 6". Kenn Kenaga, Eric Odenthal, Brad Singer, May 2005.

❸ Lost and Found 5.9 ★★★

The striking dihedral. Start down in a hole and lieback the obvious wide crack. Gets a bit wide at the top, but a little bit of hip scumming will get you through the final section.
50 ft. Gear to 4". Chris Miller, Nathan Fitzhugh, May 2003.

❹ Paradise Lost 5.9 ★★

Ascend a thin finger crack on the featured ramp just left of *Lost and Found*. An enjoyable venture.
40 ft. Gear to 2", 1 bolt. Chris Miller, Nathan Fitzhugh, May 2003.

❺ Paradise Found 5.11a ★

A difficult start on thin edges leads to a rounded arête. Slap up this, then deal with the overlap and slab above. Rappel from a nearby anchor since this one doesn't have rap rings.
55 ft. Gear to 2.5", 4 bolts. Chris Miller, Nathan Fitzhugh, May 2003.

❻ Rusted Root 5.11b ★★★

If you nailed the approach hike you should arrive near this excellent bolted line. Start with tough, crimpy goodness. Find the useful features on the fiercely technical face and end with a burly sequence on the clean orange slice of wall. Bring your A-game for this one!
55 ft. 6 bolts. Eric Odenthal, Brad Singer, May 2005.

❼ Peanut Business 5.7

The double crack system between two fins and left of a mountain mahogany. Climb up the arching crack. Gear belay.
50 ft. Gear to 4". Eric Odenthal, John Cardmon, June 2005.

❽ Just Breathe 5.9 ★★

This one's sure to get your heart pumping! A hand crack in the corner widens into a squeeze chimney. Wedge in and immediately regret your decision to do this climb. Take a deep breath — it'll be OK. Shimmy, wiggle, and squirm until the perched block is within reach. Finish past a single bolt on the face of the block. Gear anchor.
55 ft. Wide gear to 6", 1 bolt.
Kenn Kenaga, Eric Odenthal, Brad Singer, May 2005.

9 Lost and Found Roof (Open Project)

Gnarly and massively overhanging. Clip 2 bolts, then turn the corner as your feet beg to cut loose. Finish up a dirty, lichen-covered hand crack.

60 ft. Gear to 3", 2 bolts.

10 Point Blank 5.11d ★★★

An excellent hard sport route. Reach a good ledge below the first bolt. Claw through the roof, keeping it together as your fingers scream in agony on the small crimps. Milk every rest, as the redpoint crux awaits!

60 ft. 6 bolts. Eric Odenthal, May 2005.

11 Squeeze Me, Please Me 5.7 ★

Slither up the wash as the fist crack widens to a chimney and exit out right. Gear anchor.

60 ft. Wide gear to 6". Eric Odenthal, Nathan Fitzhugh, May 2005.

12 Unroped 5.7

Start in the same spot as *Squeeze Me* but take the water gully on the left. Climb up the right side of a block and tunnel through the chimney to reach the top. Gear anchor.

65 ft. Wide gear to 6". Nathan Fitzhugh (solo), May 2005.

13 Lichen the Eye 5.7 ★

Straightforward climbing on the right side of a triangular fin leads to a ledge. Dive into the chimney above and finish up the short, low-angle face.

65 ft. Wide gear to 6".

Eric Odenthal, Nathan Fitzhugh, Brad Singer, May 2005.

14 Where Have All the Good Holds Gone? 5.12a ★

This dark face climbs just as hard as it looks. When the miniscule bumps and knobs disappear, cut right. Savage and painful. Set up the TR from the anchor of *Lichen the Eye*, using the single bolt atop the face as a directional.

65 ft. Eric Odenthal, May 2005.

15 Eat Chimney 5.7 ★★

A steep hand crack quickly becomes wide. Fight through the offwidth — it doesn't have to look graceful! Delicate face climbing on the pillar past a single bolt provides the final mental crux. Shared anchor with *Throwing Logs*.

60 ft. Gear to 5", 1 bolt.

Eric Odenthal, Kenn Kenaga, Brad Singer, May 2005.

Just Breathe

Point Blank

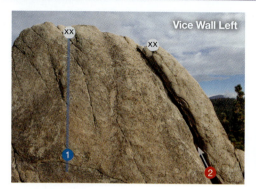

VICE WALL

An out-of-the-way wall with a mix of crack and face routes. *Kodiak* (5.10d) is the standout sport route here, contrasted by the two wide *Bandana Cracks* (5.8, 5.10a) that require a totally different set of skills.

Approach: Head down the road to the parking circle used for the Ingot. Continue on the road as it curves southwest, passing two old mines, to arrive at a flat clearing with a large dead tree stump near the east end of the crag. Tunnel through rocks or hike slightly downhill and around the large boulders to reach the base. **[GPS: 34.30869, -116.88343]**

1 Short Circuit 5.10d
Really thin slab climb up the middle of the northwest face.
30 ft. 3 bolts. Eric Odenthal, John Cardmon, Brad Singer, July 2004.

2 Left Bandana Crack 5.8 ★★
Obvious crack on the west corner, with a wide section down low. Motor up through the squeeze section, then stick your feet to the face for a few friction moves as the crack narrows. Use the bolted anchors atop *Kodiak*.
50 ft. Gear to 4".
Eric Odenthal, Brad Singer, John Cardmon, July 2004.

3 Redman 5.11a ★★
If you just climbed *Kodiak*, give this route a go. Work up the nice lieback feature on the left side of the narrow southwest face. Steep friction moves require your utmost attention.
50 ft. Chris Miller, May 2003.

4 Kodiak Arrest 5.10d ★★★
Enjoyable but rather balancy. Rock up and onto a ledge using high feet in good dishes and secret handholds. Sustained delicate moves on bumps and edges characterize the lower section. Right-angling seams attempt to push you toward the arête as you get higher.
50 ft. 5 bolts. Chris Miller, Loren Scott, Pete Paredes, July 2002.

5 Right Bandana Crack 5.10a ★★
A sweet wide crack with good pro throughout. Chimney/ squeeze into a cave 10 feet off the ground. Jam/lieback the fist-sized crack above, with feet on the ramp. Easiest to build a gear anchor, then rappel from *Kodiak*.
50 ft. Gear to 4".
John Cardmon, Brad Singer, Eric Odenthal, July 2004.

Double P Wall

DOUBLE P WALL

A slanted formation partially hidden behind another large rock, with the climbs starting from a narrow corridor. The top of the wall is often sunny but the bottom of the routes stay shady in the afternoon. A perfect supplement to a day at the nearby Vice Wall or Saloon.

25 min

Approach: Located 100 feet northwest from Vice Wall along the same ridge.
[GPS: 34.30888, -116.88372]

The Saloon

6 Peter's Out 5.7 ★
Scramble onto a fin leaning against the wall to reach a thin finger crack. Follow this crack up the middle of the formation until it peters out. Transition onto the slabby face and pass a bolt heading to the shared anchors with *Peter Built.*
35 ft. Gear to 2", 1 bolt. Chris Miller, Nathan Fitzhugh, Mar. 2003.

7 Peter Built 5.9 ★★
Fly past the first bolt on solid blocky holds and gain the rounded arête, making a burly move just below the 2nd bolt. Continue up the notion of the arête, placing gear in seams.
40 ft. Gear to 0.5", 3 bolts.
Nathan Fitzhugh, Pete Paredes, Chris Miller, Mar. 2003.

THE SALOON

Wild Turkey (5.7) and *Maker's Mark* (5.9) are definitely worth the hike out if you're looking for easy and fun trad lines. Their low-angle nature and large, secure features make both enjoyable, and they even sport a couple of bolts to protect the crux sections.

PM 30 min

Approach: Located 100 feet northwest of Double P Wall along the same ridge of inclined formations. **[GPS: 34.30895, -116.88416]**

8 Wild Turkey 5.7 ★★
Slither up the gully/chimney on the left margin to a ledge. Pleasant climbing on plates with gear placements in seams culminates in a final section of gritty slab protected by a bolt. Shares anchors with *Maker's Mark.*
70 ft. Gear to 1", 2 bolts. Chris Miller, Pete Paredes, Mar. 2003.

9 Maker's Mark 5.9 ★★
A fun line on the arête. Cruxy opening moves, then the angle eases as you continue up the well-featured face, passing good natural pro. Finish in a hand crack.
70 ft. Gear to 2", 2 bolts. Chris Miller, Pete Paredes, Mar. 2003.

10 Sourmash 5.8 ★
A slightly contrived line starting in the gully. Lieback the crack as you walk your feet up the slab on the right. At the top of the slab, move left over a small roof and into a thin crack, finishing at the *Maker's Mark* anchor.
60 ft. Gear to 3". Pat Brennan, Brad Singer, Eric Tipton, June 2005.

11 C.C. and Seven 5.6 R
Over to the right is a nice-looking slab, which at the time of this writing had a tree fallen across it. Solo the low-angle slab and walk off the back.
30 ft. No pro. Eric Tipton (solo), June 2005.

The Mine Shaft

THE MINE SHAFT

An isolated south-facing wall uniquely situated atop a mine on the western outskirts of the Pinnacles. At the time of this writing, both sets of anchors appear suspect. And — does it go without saying? — do not enter the mine shaft!

☀ 🚶 30 min

Approach: Follow the road past the parking circle used for the Ingot and the clearing near Vice Wall (10 minutes). Continue down a steep hill to a side road and turn right. There is a forked tree on the left side of the road that marks this turnoff. After 200 feet, the side road ends at a mine shaft, with the crag located above it.
[GPS: 34.30836, -116.88419]

❶ Fixed Carbon 5.4 ★

Dance up the super-low-angle wall. Slip a 1" piece in the horizontal, then zip up plates past 3 bolts. Large cams are needed for the gear anchor. The scrambling descent may be heady for someone climbing near the grade.
40 ft. Gear to 5", 3 bolts. Chris Miller, Pete Paredes, Mar. 2003.

❷ One Track Mine 5.6 ★

Crimp through the lower slab past a bolt. Continue up on larger features, passing horizontals that take gear.
45 ft. Gear to 2", 3 bolts. Chris Miller, Pete Paredes, Mar. 2003.

❸ Ground Control 5.8 ★

The obvious crack line. Bring big gear for the middle section and as the route curves left at the top, plug a few thin pieces. Shares anchors with *One Track Mine*.
50 ft. Gear to 4". Chris Miller, Pete Paredes, Mar. 2003.

❹ Angle of Repose 5.10a ★★

Step from a block to a sloping ramp. Bearhug the rib and tech up delicate features. Gear in horizontals can supplement the sparse bolt placements.
50 ft. 4 bolts, optional gear to 2".
Chris Miller, Pete Paredes, Mar. 2003.

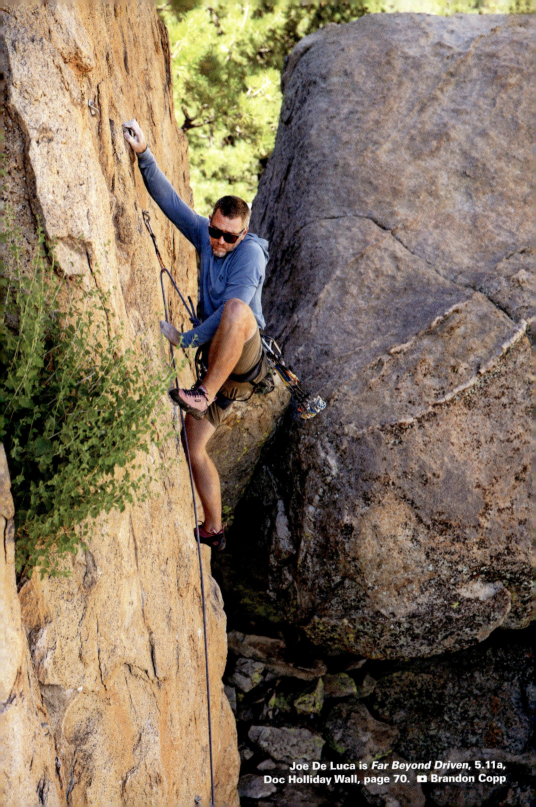

Joe De Luca is *Far Beyond Driven*, 5.11a, Doc Holliday Wall, page 70. 📷 Brandon Copp

HOLCOMB VALLEY PINNACLES **NORTH**

This part of the Pinnacles stretches from Wilbur's Tombstone north to the Voodoo Garden. It is bordered on its eastern edge by the entrance road to the northern parking area, which is also the primary access road for hiking to these crags. The majority of the walls are clustered along two ridgelines, with the rock ranging from amazing to flaky and gritty. Stone Wall features tall, top-notch lines and is a hidden gem close to the northern parking area. Slide Dome has one of the larger assortments of routes — don't miss *El Chico* (5.6) for a spectacular view of Holcomb Valley. Overall, traffic here is minimal, the climbing is good, and the approaches are fairly easy.

Approach: All of the walls are easily approached from the northern parking area. While it is possible to drive here with a high-clearance vehicle, many folks park at the main southern parking area and hoof it. It takes 15 minutes to hike between the two parking lots.

From the southern parking area, set out on the main trail. Hike along this path to the intersection with a 4WD road (3N07A) in the vicinity of Camp Rock. Turn north and walk the road, passing the Central Pinnacles formations and eventually arriving at the northern parking area. Directions to individual crags are given from here.

Holcomb Valley Pinnacles North Overview

HOLCOMB VALLEY PINNACLES **NORTH**

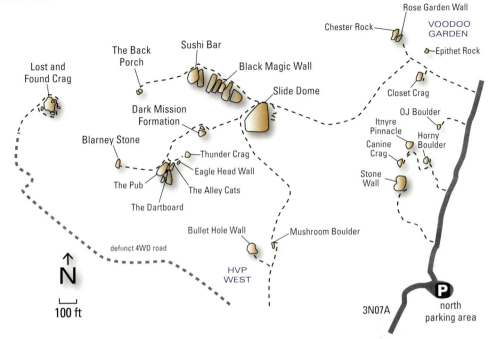

TOP 10 CRAGS FOR MIXED TEAMS

One of you digs 5.12, the other is happy on 5.7. You want to clip bolts, they want to plug gear. Where do you go? Try these mixed-bag crags.

1. **Motherlode Rock**
   page 88

2. **Lost Orbit Rock**
   page 47

3. **Castle Rock**
   page 166

4. **Fisherman's Buttress**
   page 161

5. **Black Bluff**
   page 190

6. **Physics Rock & Environs**
   page 310

7. **Voodoo Wall at the Coven**
   page 232

8. **Onyx Summit Crag**
   page 283

9. **Coyote Crag**
   page 72

10. **Lost and Found Crag**
    page 104

CLIMBING AREA	ELEVATION	HIKE	ROUTES	GRADE RANGE		CRAGS
STONE WALL *Tall, high-quality routes* **page 114**	7650 ft	20 min	5		≤.5 .6 .7 .8 .9 .10 .11 .12	
HORNY BOULDER AREA *Various small crags with decent climbs* **page 116**	7600 ft. 7700 ft	20-25 min	13		≤.5 .6 .7 .8 .9 .10 .11 .12	Horny Boulder, Canine Crag, Itnyre Pinnacle
OJ BOULDER *Rarely visited crag* **page 118**	7600 ft	20 min	3		≤.5 .6 .7 .8 .9 .10 .11 .12	
CLOSET CRAG *Quick warm-ups* **page 118**	7600 ft	25 min	3		≤.5 .6 .7 .8 .9 .10 .11 .12	
SLIDE DOME *Massive, lesser-known dome* **page 119**	7750 ft	30 min	9		≤.5 .6 .7 .8 .9 .10 .11 .12	
BLACK MAGIC AREA *Fun, powerful burns* **page 121**	7700 ft	35-40 min	13		≤.5 .6 .7 .8 .9 .10 .11 .12	Black Magic Wall, Sushi Bar, The Back Porch
DARK MISSION FORMATION *Cool, dark corridor* **page 124**	7700 ft	35 min	1		≤.5 .6 .7 .8 .9 .10 .11 .12	
DRY CREEK AREA *Conglomeration of quality formations* **page 124**	7700 ft	40 min	17		≤.5 .6 .7 .8 .9 .10 .11 .12	The Pub, Alley Cats, Eagle Head Wall, Thunder Crag, The Dartboard, Blarney Stone

STONE WALL

Named for the iconic SoCal brewery, this tall wall has high-quality routes for those who enjoy vertical to slightly overhanging terrain. It boasts magnificent views and receives all-day sun, great for the fringe seasons. Despite its close proximity to Central Pinnacles, it doesn't draw much of a crowd.

☀ 🚶 20 min

Approach: The rock is visible from the north parking area. Walk north along the road to a small clearing with a dead tree. Turn left onto the approach trail, following cairns leading to the wall's left end. 5 minutes from the north parking. **[GPS: 34.31116, -116.87936]**

❶ Supercalibelgolistic 5.9 ★★★
Start this long climb from the small, shaded alcove at the wall's left end. Climb over stacked boulders to a ledge. A high step and long reach are the keys to unlocking the first crux. Face a harder secondary crux at the next bulge, then enjoy decent flakes on the final section. Taller people have an advantage on this one.
90 ft. 10 bolts. Chris Owen, Chris Miller, Adam Stackhouse, Sept. 2014.

❷ Ruination 5.9 ★★★
A bold climb that's sure to redefine your perception of what constitutes a good route. Savor the initial large features that give way to a bitter crux at the 3rd bolt. Crimp and smear

this vertical section, then hop up and over pumpy bulges for an intense finish. A full-bodied climb that lasts!
85 ft. 10 bolts. Chris Miller, Chris Owen, Lisa Guindon, Sept. 2014.

❸ Old Guardian 5.10c ★★
This hefty brew starts on a thin face with no perceptible sweetness. The assertive bitterness necessitates precision edging on shallow crimps. Reach a ledge, and the end of the difficulties, as the route yields a touch of warmth. Sample a variety of features in the wandering upper portion.
70 ft. 6 bolts. Chris Miller, Pete Paredes, Sept. 2003.

❹ Vertical Epic 5.10a ★★★★
As with any good epic, herein lies the promise of a unique experience that defies expectations. This classic line has been aged to perfection and is arguably the best route of its grade in Holcomb. Rock up the thought-provoking vertical face sprinkled with positive incuts. An onslaught of roofs will challenge your abilities and endurance. Rip through a taste of slab to a corner and claim victory at the chains.
70 ft. 7 bolts. Pete Paredes, Chris Miller, Sept. 2003.

❺ Arrogant Bastard 5.11a ★★★★
Are you worthy? Aggressive and demanding, this steep, imposing line ain't for the faint of heart. A straightforward face leads to a fat flake on the overhanging wall. But where did all the holds go? Launch into the crux, powering through a heinous sequence on miniscule nubs. Fight the pump to the finish — this one's not letting up. Intense and uncompromising; if you make it to the top, you're one badass mofo.
70 ft. 7 bolts. Chris Miller, Pete Paredes, May 2003.

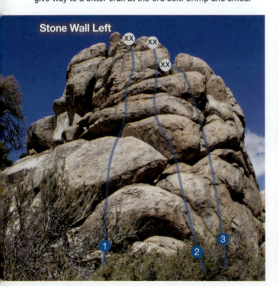
Stone Wall Left

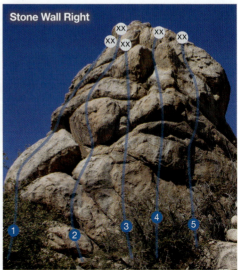
Stone Wall Right

Loralei Atchley shows the *Arrogant Bastard* (5.11a, opposite) who is boss. 📷 Brandon Copp

HORNY BOULDER

This large, flat-topped boulder hides among the trees on the east side of a ridge and downhill from Canine Crag and Itnyre Pinnacle. There is easy access to its top from the uphill side.

AM   20 min

Approach: From the northern parking area, hike along the road past the turnoff for Stone Wall. Locate Canine Crag high on the ridge and walk until you are directly east of the notch between it and Stone Wall. Find the path that heads through a small clearing and uphill into the trees. Follow this faint climber's trail as it leads directly to the base of Horny Boulder. Move right along the boulder's base to reach the main climbs.
[GPS: 34.31175, -116.87886]

❶ Al's Trumpet Fanfare 5.4
Located around on the south side of the boulder is this extremely short squeeze chimney.
20 ft. Wide gear. Brandon Copp (solo), Oct. 2018.

❷ Lap Dance 5.6 ★★
Great for beginners wanting large features or those scared of heights! Ride big plates past a dike on this short-lived but enjoyable climb. There's also an anchor bolt on the sloped ledge for your belayer.
25 ft. 3 bolts. Lori Brennan, Pat Brennan, Nov. 2016.

❸ Blue Balls 5.8 ★
This dirty little climb starts from the same sloped ledge as its neighbor and shares its first bolt. Crank on plates that turn into thin edges higher up. Will clean up with more traffic.
25 ft. 3 bolts. Marina Amador, Nick Reynaga, Angela Hwangpo, Kenn Kenaga, Aug. 2019.

❹ Early Morning Warm-Up 5.7 ★★
Head directly up the middle of the east face, climbing the tallest portion of Horny Boulder. Maneuver past a horizontal dike using nice incut edges.
25 ft. 3 bolts. FA: (TR) Jim Hammerle, 1990; FL: Pete Paredes, Brad Singer, Sept. 2007.

❺ Black Sabbath 5.10d ★
Ascend the light-colored rock on the far right margin of the face. Finesse up the thin crack until it peters out and decent holds present themselves. Note: The anchor is a single bolt with no rap ring.
20 ft. Jim Hammerle, 1990.

A small independent boulder lies 50 feet northeast of the main wall:

❻ Foreplay V0
Bury your fists in the splitter crack and jam up the low-angle face. An easy one to run laps on.

Foreplay

Horny Boulder

Canine Crag

Itnyre Pinnacle

CANINE CRAG

An east-facing wall that sits atop a ridge. This crag has a few neat slab-to-roof problems.

AM 🚶 25 min

Approach: From Horny Boulder, continue weaving uphill around small boulders to the top of the ridge.
[GPS: 34.31165, -116.87939]

7 Party Poodle 5.7 ★★
This route greets its climbers with a reachy, height-dependent start. Snag the big horn near the first bolt, then enjoy easier knobs and plates. Finish on the slopey, exposed arête. This fun climb packs in a variety of moves, with an airy crux at the top.
60 ft. 5 bolts. Chris Miller, Pete Paredes, July 2003.

8 Igor Unleashed 5.10c ★★
Begin in the middle of the slab below a seam in the roof. Place gear at the roof, then head up on decent incut edges until you can surf the wave. Conquer thin and balancy moves through the crux to finish. One bolt at the lip of the roof would make this a good, well-protected sport climb.
60 ft. Gear to 2", 5 bolts. Chris Miller, Pete Paredes, July 2003.

9 Fear of the Black Poodle 5.10b ★
Start on the slab and clip the good bolt (the other is bad). Follow the 2"-thick corner that arches right, fighting through the crux until you reach the roof. Finish up the obvious crack system to shared anchors with *Igor Unleashed*.
60 ft. Gear to 4", 1 bolt. Chris Miller, Pete Paredes, July 2003.

10 Powered by Hops 5.10a ★★
Start on the left side of a large block, making your way up the wide crack or using the arête. Pull the roof to encounter the crux off the ledge. Tackle the headwall on thin plates to gain the prominent dike, then cut right to the anchors. A fun climb with a rewarding view from the top.
60 ft. 5 bolts. Chris Miller, Pete Paredes, Jeff Brown, July 2003.

11 K-9 5.2
The west-face chimney. Ends at the *Igor Unleashed* anchors.
35 ft. Wide gear. Bob Cable, Pat Brennan, May 2005.

ITNYRE PINNACLE

A tall pinnacle with excellent 360° views of the Pinnacles. Both routes here are enjoyable.

☀️ 🚶 25 min

Approach: Situated beside Canine Crag and uphill from Horny Boulder.
[GPS: 34.31184, -116.87926]

12 AARP 5.7 ★★
Waltz up a corner to the perfect, slightly overhanging hand crack. Pop up onto a low-angle dirty section and pass the big ledge with anchors for *Por La Virgen*. Fly up on jugs to the top of the pinnacle. Note: As of this writing, the bolted anchor at the top lacks rap rings.
80 ft. Gear to 3". Mike Itnyre, Art Bertolina, Sept. 2001.

13 Por La Virgen 5.10c ★★
Head up the blunt arête to the steep, slightly negative face. Show off with powerful yet delicate moves on small features, ending at the anchors on a big ledge.
50 ft. 6 bolts. Brad Singer, Pete Paredes, Sept. 2007.

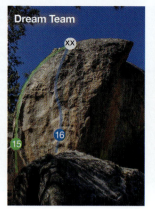

OJ BOULDER

This seldom-visited area has a few obscure routes on its east and south faces. The boulder is splashed in bright orange, but parties still pass it without knowing it's lurking in the trees. Access to the top is via a short vertical section on the west side.

  20 min

Approach: Hike the road from the north parking toward the turnoff for Voodoo Garden. 100 feet before the turnoff, a trail branches left, heading through small bushes and trees. The boulder is low on the hillside, 2-3 minutes off the road. **[GPS: 34.31225, -116.87862]**

14 The Bloody Glove 5.6 ★
Chimney or lieback to get established on the face. Follow the skinny crack to a dike and end on jugs. Shared anchor.
35 ft. Thin gear to 2". Alan Bartlett, Lenni Reeves, Chris Miller, 1994.

15 The Color of Fear 5.11a ★★
Ascend the striking arête, executing tough moves from the get-go as you reach high, cut feet, and struggle up the undercut section onto the face. Enjoyable plate pulling leads to the top. Shares anchors with *Dream Team*.
40 ft. Chris Miller, 1994.

16 Dream Team 5.10d ★★
Located on the aesthetic orange, green, and black face. Stem off the nearby boulder and creep onto the face. Progress upward on small bumps and edges that are better than they appear. Bolted anchor without rap rings.
40 ft. 3 bolts. Craig Pearson, Dean Goolsby, 1993.

CLOSET CRAG

A quick-tick wall to hit on the way to Voodoo Garden. A dead tree lies in the shallow gully at the foot of the east face where the first 2 climbs are found.

25 min

Approach: From the north parking area, walk north along the road for 5 minutes. Just before a dry streambed, turn left at a small clearing, the same as you would to approach the Voodoo Garden. Hike the climber's trail for 2-3 minutes, following the dry creek until you come to this small wall beside the trail on the left. **[GPS: 34.31297, -116.87902]**

17 Rope a Dope 5.7
Follow a wide crack up the slab. Angle right to shared anchors with *Crystal Closet Queen*.
30 ft. Wide gear to 4". Unknown.

18 Crystal Closet Queen 5.8 ★
Gravitate along a small flake to a right-facing corner. Tiptoe up the center of a diamond-shaped block, utilizing the good left-facing flake.
30 ft. 3 bolts. Pete Paredes, Brad Singer, Aug. 2007.

19 Voodoo Garden Men's Society 5.7 ★
To reach this route, hike around to the north face to find a slab climb on a skinny ramp. A slip on the crux mantel move risks an ankle-breaking fall!
50 ft. 4 bolts. Brad Singer, Pete Paredes, Kevin Graves, Aug. 2007.

SLIDE DOME

One of the taller formations in Holcomb outside of the Central Pinnacles. The routes on the east block provide stunning views of the surrounding area. *Slip-Sliding Away* (5.10c) is an awesome 80-foot slab line that's a must-do for the region. The rock is quite good here and the bit of lichen will clean away with more traffic. Overall, the northerly aspect of the wall provides shady relief on hot summer days for the majority of the routes.

☀ ⏀ 🚶 30 min

Approach: The easiest approach is via the Voodoo Garden turnoff. Hike 5 minutes north along the road from the north parking lot. Turn left (west) and follow a dry/seasonal creekbed as for Voodoo Garden. Where the trail to Voodoo Garden splits and crosses this creekbed, stay on its left embankment. Slide Dome will shortly come into view in the distance (10 minutes from the turnoff reaches its NE corner). Continue around the base of the wall to the desired climbs. A good landmark is the toadstool-shaped boulder located behind the routes on the northwest face.

Alternatively, it is possible to approach Slide Dome from Mushroom Boulder in HVP West (see map on page 98). From this vicinity, follow the cairned trail in a boulder-strewn wash heading north. This approach leads to the southern corner of Slide Dome, where you can continue around the base of the formation to reach the climbs. It is approximately a 10-minute hike from Mushroom Boulder. **[GPS: 34.31259, -116.88222]**

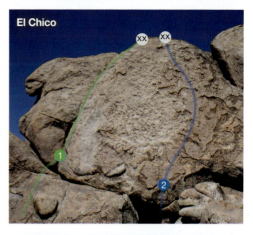

El Chico

Slip and Slide

❶ **El Gordo** 5.6 ★
Cruise the ramp/rounded arête on the left margin of the triangular summit block past a few flared sections of crack.
35 ft. Loren Scott, Pete Paredes, Sept. 2017.

❷ **El Chico** 5.6 ★★★
AKA *Bobbi's Bhavana*. High on the east face is this tantalizing route on excellent patina plates. This enjoyable route has some of the best views of the Pinnacles, Holcomb Valley, and the San Bernardinos. Feels quite exposed for such a short climb!
30 ft. 4 bolts. FA: (TR) Tyler Logan, Bobbi Kelleher, Chrystal Logan, Isaac Tait, Sept. 2007; FL: Pete Paredes, Loren Scott.

❸ **Slip and Slide** 5.9 ★★
Located on the northeast corner. Excellent hand-over-hand jamming in an arching crack attains a small ledge. Physical finish through the steep notch. Can share anchors with *Sub 2*.
60 ft. Gear to 3". Kenn Kenaga, Tyler Logan, Aug. 2007.

❹ **Slip-Sliding Away** 5.10c ★★★
A tall line that commences with desperate moves on a featureless slab. Optional gear under a flake between the 2nd and 3rd bolts. Pure friction and balance on tiny knobs is the key to reaching the large ledge. Pull the roof above, with the left side being tougher than the right.
80 ft. 8 bolts, optional gear to 0.75",
Brad Singer, Pete Paredes, Aug. 2007.

Slide Dome

5 **Slipping Into Darkness** 5.6 ★★

Climb easily up the elephant trunk. From the top of this feature, choose your own adventure.

Variation Sub 1: Finish up the left side of the gully on the arête.
Variation Sub 2: Climb the slab a few feet to the right of the arête. Bring a long draw for the 6th bolt.

80 ft. 7 bolts. Pete Paredes, Kiana Nakamura, Loren Scott, Aug. 2015.

6 **Zig Zag** 5.9 ★★

Sidestep right of the gully to a bolted slab. A varied climb with a dose of funkiness as you move through an undercling and onto vertical face. Share anchors with *Benchmark*.

75 ft. 5 bolts. Pete Paredes, Loren Scott, Chris Miller, Nov. 2015.

7 **Benchmark** 5.11c ★★

Run up an easy ramp past a bush. Stand tall to clip the 2nd bolt, step right, and then it's on like Donkey Kong. Undercling the seams and perform compression moves past 2 closely spaced bolts to reach lower-angle rock.

75 ft. 6 bolts. Ryan Crochiere, Aug. 2007.

8 **Thin Mint** 5.12 ★

Blast off straight through an undercling onto the face. Palm and smear the shallow waterchute where all the holds seem to have washed away. Set up this improbable line from *Benchmark's* anchors.

75 ft. Ryan Crochiere, Sept. 2007.

9 **Slip of the Tongue** 5.9

Lieback a dirty, right-facing flake near an alcove. End in a wide crack and gear belay.

75 ft. Gear to 4". Mike Williams, Ryan Crochiere, Pete Paredes, Brad Singer, Sept. 2007.

Variation 5.9: At the top of the flake, traverse left across the ledge and fire up the last bolt and anchors of *Benchmark*.

BLACK MAGIC WALL

The dark, northeast-facing wall is made up of four sections of rock, each with a couple of lines apiece.   35 min

The morning sun and afternoon shade make for pleasant climbing on both chilly and warm days. The routes here are a great supplement to a day of climbing at the nearby Slide Dome or Sushi Bar.

Approach: Hike as for Slide Dome, then continue 2 minutes northwest, hiking along the right side of the rock ridge seen from Slide Dome. **[GPS: 34.31282, -116.88275]**

Black Magic Wall

1 Wizard's Reach 5.9 ★

The light-colored undercut arête looks harder than it is. Powerful, fingery moves lead past a crux near the 2nd bolt. Shares anchors with *Black Magic*.

35 ft. 3 bolts. Tyler Logan, Pete Paredes, 2007.

2 Black Magic Fellatrix 5.7 ★

Move past 4 closely spaced bolts on the narrow face.

35 ft. 4 bolts. Pete Paredes, Loren Scott, 2008.

3 Black Magic Project (Closed)

4 Sleight of Hand 5.11c ★★

Set the feet, stand tall, and nab the roof. Improvise footwork while dealing with the massive hunk of rock jutting into your belly. Navigate a steep section of textured rock above.

35 ft. 4 bolts. Tyler Logan, 2007.

5 Wizard 5.11d ★★

Mixed. Work magic on the perplexing slick face, with a tricky pro placement between the first 2 bolts. Slip through the right side of the roof onto better features above and end in a finger crack. Shared anchor with *Sleight of Hand*.

35 ft. Gear to 3", 3 bolts. Tyler Logan, 2007.

6 Que Chichotas 5.10a ★★

Stimulating movement characterizes this route, with a crux near the last bolt as one crests the upper dome.

35 ft. 4 bolts. Pete Paredes, Loren Scott, 2008.

7 Chupacabra Hood 5.10b ★★

Begin from the lowest point possible for full value of the frictiony crux. Grapple with the yellow-speckled overhang and wrap around the north end of the formation to finish.

35 ft. 4 bolts. Pete Paredes, Loren Scott, 2008.

SUSHI BAR

Splashed with bright orange, yellow, and green, this colorful wall has more than a few good lines to sample. The routes are short and powerful burners on a dead-vertical face. The namesake of this wall is the rock bar along the lower left margin.

Approach: Approach as for Slide Dome. Hike northwest along the rock ridge past Black Magic Wall to this crag situated at the end of the ridge. 5 minutes from Slide Dome.

[GPS: 34.31319, -116.88363]

8 Wasabi Dude 5.10a ★★★

Gravitate toward the right on a myriad of orange plates flecked with gold lichen. An enjoyable, continuous, and attention-grabbing route. Be cautious of hollow flakes.

35 ft. 4 bolts. Pete Paredes, Tyler Logan, July 2008.

Sushi Bar

9 Sushi Project
A tough start leads to a good horizontal, with the wall becoming more featured above.
35 ft.

10 Miso Horny 5.11a ★
From the initial flake, gain fingery holds peppering the steep face with a painful crux at the 3rd bolt.
35 ft. 4 bolts. Loren Scott, Tyler Logan, Pete Paredes, Sept. 2008.

11 Uni Crack 5.10c ★★
Another route with a tough start on minute edges. Stem the right-facing corner using the crack and face features.
35 ft. 4 bolts. Loren Scott, Pete Paredes, Aug. 2009.

12 Biru 30 5.10a ★★★
This lesser-known gem is located under the large roof on the right margin. Fire up big holds to a shallow ledge, then advance with precision edging and a thin seam out right.
35 ft. 4 bolts. Pete Paredes, Loren Scott, July 2010.

THE BACK PORCH

A west-facing wall capped by an impressive roof. The clean, near perfect rock underneath is split by an exceptional finger crack.

PM   🚶 40 min

Approach: From Slide Dome, hike northwest past the Black Magic Wall to the Sushi Bar. The Back Porch can be found on the next hillside of boulders to the west, 100 yards from the Sushi Bar. **[GPS: 34.31301, -116.88456]**

13 Last Ray of Sunlight (Open Project)
This tantalizing finger crack will leave a marked impression on all hard crack climbers. Its flared nature adds spice to this brutal challenge, and finger size may make all the difference.
25 ft. Very thin gear. Equipped: Tyler Logan, 2007.

The Back Porch

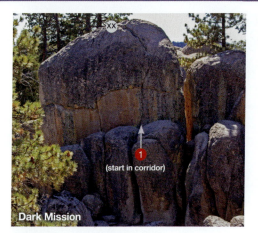

Dark Mission

(start in corridor)

DARK MISSION FORMATION

A dark, north-facing block with a narrow corridor situated in front. It is easiest to enter the corridor from climber's left.

35 min

Approach: Walk 100 yards west of Slide Dome. **[GPS: 34.31219, -116.88337]**

1 **Dark Mission** 5.10b ★★
Novel climbing as you chimney inside the dark and cool corridor to gain a splendid finger crack (rightmost of the wall's two cracks).
40 ft. Gear to 3". Tyler Logan, Kenn Kenaga, Oct. 2007.

THE PUB (AKA DRY CREEK WALL)

This rather large dome is the flagship wall of the small conglomeration of adjacent formations. It features half a dozen quality routes that scale its green northwest face.

40 min

Approach: From Slide Dome, walk 100 yards west to the Dark Mission Formation. Pass along the north end of this formation and locate a dry creek. Follow the dry creek southwest for an additional 100 yards to arrive at this large wall. **[GPS: 34.31166, -116.88420]**

2 **Free Dick** 5.9 ★★
This good climb sits separated from the main wall on its own piece of rock. Burly climbing on a slant snags a pocket and a horizontal with additional seams above. Thought-provoking and sustained movements.
35 ft. 4 bolts. Pete Paredes, Loren Scott, June 2013.

3 **Stout** 5.11a ★★
Lock in precision edging while struggling to find hands on the blank face. Creep upward as the thin seam turns vertical to face a crux at the 3rd bolt. Continue past a large overlap on decent holds.
50 ft. 5 bolts. Anthony Scalise, June 2010.

4 **You're Sitting in My Spot** 5.10d ★★
Be careful not to barn door on the stopper move at the first bolt! Clip the first 2 bolts that are shared with *China Doll* before sliding left along the giant undercling while finding good edges for feet. An enjoyable and varied line that ascends to the high point of the formation.
55 ft. Gear to 3", 4 bolts. Mike Rigney, June 2010.

5 **China Doll** 5.11b ★★★
Fantastic crimpy goodness. Pull the same challenging start as *You're Sitting in My Spot* before shaking out at the horizontal. An intricate sequence of small crimpers follows a water groove to the headwall, where a burly move protects the anchors.
50 ft. 5 bolts. Pete Paredes, Loren Scott, June 2014.

6 **Buda's Fingers** 5.10d ★★
Another great route that has a different style than its neighbor. Pass the first 2 bolts of *China Doll* before moving right across the horizontal. Confront the thin vertical fissure in the face above.
50 ft. 5 bolts. Pete Paredes, Loren Scott, June 2014.

7 **Boudica** 5.10d ★
Charge into battle with this grainy seam, where solid fingerlocks and thoughtful body positioning can make all the difference.
45 ft. Dan Rigney, June 2010.

The Pub

THE ALLEY CATS

Seek out this small buttress to put your skills to the test on *Alley Cat* (5.10b), a fantastic outing on the steep orange face! AM 40 min

Approach: Walk 100 feet east of the Pub. **[GPS: 34.31161, -116.88385]**

Alley Cats

8 Alley Cat 5.10b ★★★
Tie into the sharp end and get stoked for this sick line in the corridor! Pump past good flakes and positive edges on the overhanging orange face. An invigorating route packed with powerful and thoughtful movements on steep terrain.
30 ft. 4 bolts. Pete Paredes, Loren Scott, June 2009.

9 Gato Negro 5.9 ★
An awkward start leads to dirty slab up higher. Shares anchors with *Cat Ribs*.
35 ft. 4 bolts. Pete Paredes, Loren Scott, Sept. 2010.

10 Cat Ribs "Costillas Del Gato" 5.8 ★
Ascend the staircase on the right side of the dark buttress.
35 ft. 3 bolts. Pete Paredes, Loren Scott, July 2009.

Eagle Head Wall

Thunder Crag

THUNDER CRAG

A minor dome of clean rock with 2 routes that are more difficult than they appear.

PM 40 min

Approach: A brief 75-foot jaunt north of the Alley Cats.
[GPS: 34.31182, -116.88372]

⑫ Thunder Cat 5.10a ★★
Despite appearances, this route is actually quite a good challenge. Reach high for the undercling and pull onto the wall. Brave the heady slab moves that guard the 2nd bolt and breeze to the anchors.
35 ft. 3 bolts. Pete Paredes, Chuck Scott, Loren Scott, July 2010.

⑬ Cat Nip 5.11b ★
Set a line on the blank face to the right and chase it to the top.
35 ft. Loren Scott, Pete Paredes, Sept. 2010.

EAGLE HEAD WALL

The fractured northwest face of this pillar resembles an eagle's head.

PM 40 min

Approach: This conspicuous formation is situated a stone's throw away from the Alley Cats.
[GPS: 34.31166, -116.88377]

⑪ Lichen Eagle 5.9 ★
Soar up the multi-colored face, where fun yet slightly funky climbing awaits.
35 ft. 5 bolts. Pete Paredes, Loren Scott, Nov. 2008.

THE DARTBOARD

Take aim at these toprope problems — can you stick all three? This hidden wall is covered in a variety of different features, providing each line with its own unique flavor.

🕐 40 min

Approach: Hike 100 feet east of the Pub to the Alley Cats. Squeeze through a tunnel/corridor on the west side of the Alley Cats to reach the Dartboard.
[GPS: 34.31143, -116.88413]

14 Doubles 5.9 ★★
Good things come in small packages. Embrace this neat seam on the wall's left side.
20 ft. Dan Rigney, June 2010.

15 Bullseye 5.9 ★
Cautiously slip past a small tree that's taken root at the base of this crack. The climbing is a bit awkward in the pea pod.
35 ft. Dan Rigney, June 2010.

16 Triples 5.10a ★
Decipher the perplexing opening sequence before grabbing the cool alligator scales.
35 ft. Dan Rigney, June 2010.

BLARNEY STONE

A small, dark-streaked wall, partially in the shadow of a nearby tree.

🕐 40 min

Approach: This wall lies 200 feet west of the Pub.
[GPS: 34.31171, -116.88486]

17 Kiss Me 5.10a ★
Journey up the well-featured crack with a grainy pod in the middle. Make a shaky clip while confronting a high crux before grabbing the dike at the top.
30 ft. Gear to 2", 1 bolt. Mike Rigney, June 2010.

18 Lichen in My Teeth 5.9 ★★
Riddled with plates initially, this fun and fingery route draws you in before leaving you hanging as the holds disappear for a more technical finish!
30 ft. 4 bolts. Anthony Scalise, June 2010.

HOLCOMB VALLEY PINNACLES **VOODOO GARDEN AND BEYOND**

The Voodoo Garden is a moderate-climbing playground. The many small walls clustered together make it easy to spend the whole day hopping between spots. These formations house a large selection of predominately sport routes on good granite. Katrina Wall is the centerpiece, with standout lines that are some of the best for their grades in Holcomb. Stop at One-Eyed Cat wall for invigorating 5.10s, or hit up Reticent Rock if you're looking for a tougher challenge. Crags like Peyronie's Wall, Chester Rock, and Voodoo Pin are great for kids (and fine for dogs), while others such as Katrina, One-Eyed Cat, and Coral Sea are further up the hillside and require more scrambling to reach.

Beyond the Voodoo Garden lie additional crags with anywhere from a single to a half dozen routes. Many are situated along the western slope of the ridge that runs northwest from Voodoo Garden, with the exception being the Pasqually Outcropping. There are no real trails in this area — hardly anyone ever ventures up there! Most of the approaches follow paths of least resistance or seasonal streams, and may require minor bushwhacking or boulder scrambles. Seek out *Thor's Revenge* (5.12a) and *Coriander and the Special Blend* (5.11c), two of the best overhanging routes in this section.

Approach: To reach the Voodoo Garden, walk north along the road from the north parking area for 5 minutes (0.2 miles). Just before a dry streambed, turn left into a small clearing. Follow a climber's trail along the dry creek for 2-3 minutes, then cross the creekbed to reach the crags. The first formations encountered are Epithet Rock on the right and Rose Garden Wall in front. Approach time is 10 minutes from the north parking area, or 25 minutes from the south parking.

If parked at the south area, set out on the main trail. Hike along this path to the intersection with a 4WD road (3N07A) in the vicinity of Camp Rock. Turn north and walk the road to the north parking area (15-minute hike). Follow the above directions to reach the Voodoo Garden.

Ken Snyder, *Guys and Dolls*, 5.9, Voodoo Pin, page 136. 📷 Brandon Copp

HOLCOMB VALLEY PINNACLES
VOODOO GARDEN AND BEYOND

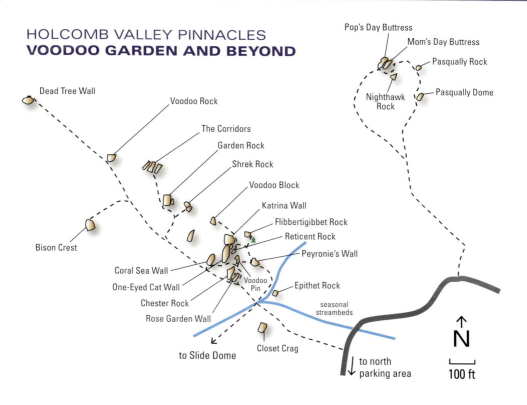

Dead Tree Wall

Voodoo Rock

Pop's Day Buttress

Mom's Day Buttress

Pasqually Rock

Nighthawk Rock

Pasqually Dome

The Corridors

Garden Rock

Shrek Rock

Voodoo Block

Katrina Wall

Flibbertigibbet Rock

Reticent Rock

Peyronie's Wall

Bison Crest

Coral Sea Wall

One-Eyed Cat Wall

Voodoo Pin

Epithet Rock

Chester Rock

Rose Garden Wall

seasonal streambeds

to Slide Dome

Closet Crag

to north parking area

N

100 ft

Voodoo Garden Overview

Coral Sea Wall

Rose Garden Wall

Chester Rock

One-Eyed Cat Wall

Voodoo Block

Katrina Wall

Reticent Rock

Voodoo Pin

Flibbertigibbet Rock

Peyronie's Wall

Epithet Rock

CLIMBING AREA	ELEVATION	HIKE	ROUTES	GRADE RANGE	CRAGS
VOODOO GARDEN *Moderate climber's playground* page 132	7650-7700 ft	25-30 min	37	≤.5 .6 .7 .8 .9 .10 .11 .12	Epithet, Rose Garden, Chester, Coral Sea, One-Eyed Cat, Voodoo Pin, Peyronie's Wall, Flibbertigibbet, Reticent, Katrina, Voodoo Block
GARDEN AREA *Don't miss: Coriander and the Special Blend, 11c and Thor's Revenge, 12a* page 140	7800 ft	40 min	7	≤.5 .6 .7 .8 .9 .10 .11 .12	Garden Rock, Shrek Rock, The Corridors
VOODOO ROCK *Barely visited routes* page 142	7800 ft	45 min	6	≤.5 .6 .7 .8 .9 .10 .11 .12	
BISON CREST CRAG *Secluded sport climbs* page 144	7800 ft	45 min	3	≤.5 .6 .7 .8 .9 .10 .11 .12	
DEAD TREE WALL *Obscure moderates* page 145	7800 ft	45 min	4	≤.5 .6 .7 .8 .9 .10 .11 .12	
PASQUALLY OUTCROPPING *Short crack lines; multi-tiered buttresses* page 145	7750 ft	40-45 min	8	≤.5 .6 .7 .8 .9 .10 .11 .12	Pasqually Dome, Pasqually Rock, Nighthawk Rock, Mom's Day Buttress, Pop's Day Buttress

HOLCOMB VALLEY 2019 REBOLTING PROJECT

In the summer of 2019, Joe and Carey De Luca took on the considerable task of rebolting popular routes in Holcomb Valley Pinnacles. Joe grew up climbing in the San Bernardino Mountains from the late 1980s to the 2000s and knew that the bolts in Holcomb needed help. He and Carey wanted to rebolt the area in the best way possible, using all ½-inch stainless-steel hardware. The American Safe Climbing Association provided bolts, hangers, and drill bits, while the Friends of Joshua Tree provided $1000 worth of other equipment. Members of the climbing community donated additional funds for necessary materials through a GoFundMe campaign.

The easiest way to rebolt is by chopping the old bolt, patch the hole, and move the new bolt 6-8 inches from the old hole to avoid weakening the rock. In addition to creating an eyesore if the patch isn't perfect or deteriorates, this process can alter the clips and movement on a route. Joe and Carey, however, made the exceptional effort to reuse (almost) all original holes, removing the old hardware using a custom bolt puller engineered by an old-school climber who specializes in replacing bolts in Joshua Tree. Once the old bolt was pulled and all of the associated metal removed, the hole was drilled out to ½-inch and a beefy new stainless-steel bolt and hanger was placed, torqued to the proper specs. This was a labor-intensive process — typically taking over an hour per bolt!

Joe and Carey's rebolting style is much more time consuming and physically demanding than the pull-and-patch method, but it protects the character and aesthetics of the routes and rock. Only when absolutely necessary (due to bad rock quality or for safety reasons), did they pull, patch, and move a bolt from its original location. Over the course of two months, many people came to Holcomb Valley to help, learn the process, or otherwise support the effort. It was a project that inspired many folks in the climbing community to volunteer time and learn the nuances of rebolting to make this area safer for all climbers.

While there are still many bolts needing replacement, 42 routes now have new ½-inch stainless steel bolts and anchors with at least a 50-year expected lifespan. Huge thanks to Joe and Carey for spending their entire summer working on the walls, and to everyone who participated in the Holcomb Valley rebolting effort.

Epithet Rock

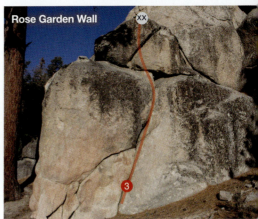

Rose Garden Wall

EPITHET ROCK

A northwest-facing block that guards the entrance to the Voodoo Garden. The attractive orange-and-black streaked rock is covered with wonderful plates.

Approach: When approaching the Voodoo Garden, cross the dry streambed and look right. This crag is situated beside the creek. **[GPS: 34.31343, -116.87901]**

1 Good Man 5.10c ★

Fingery edges provide passage up this dead-vertical wall. A tough challenge on thin features.

25 ft. 3 bolts. Mikey Griffitts, Joshua Horn, Sept. 2019.

2 Epithet 5.10c ★★

A 3-bolt gem on beautiful orange plates. Bouldery start off a low ledge leads into an enjoyable and cruisey middle. Dig deep as the plates run out before the rounded finish!

25 ft. 3 bolts. Tyler Logan, Loren Scott, Aug. 2007.

ROSE GARDEN WALL

This narrow wall sits in front of the southeast face of Chester Rock.

Approach: The approach to Voodoo Garden leads directly to this wall. **[GPS: 34.31355, -116.87955]**

3 Smells Like Roses 5.10a ★

Roses are red, violets are blue, this crack, though short, will challenge you! Slide up the diagonal crack that splits the mushroom-capped formation and climbs harder than it looks.

25 ft. Gear to 2". Jeff Brennan, Kenn Kenaga, Pat Brennan, July 2007.

CHESTER ROCK

This fin of rock rises like a pyramid behind the Rose Garden Wall. A crimpy moderate on its southeast face starts from a corridor, and a tougher slab is found on the west side.

Approach: Located directly behind the Rose Garden Wall. **[GPS: 34.31358, -116.87957]**

4 Duct Tape and Candy 5.11c ★★★

A thrilling crimpfest in a corridor. This route's crux involves desperate and painful crimping to get established on the wall. Difficult and sustained climbing on fragile flakes that groan when weighted is bound to keep your heart racing until you clip the chains!

45 ft. 4 bolts. John Cardmon, July 2007.

5 Forfeit the Bail 5.10b ★★

Reachy moves off the deck gain a narrow ramp, then crank through a difficult crossover move off the small shelf. Easier slab leads to the uniquely shaped top.

50 ft. 5 bolts. Brad Singer, Pete Paredes, July 2007.

Chester Rock Front

Coral Sea Front

Chester Rock Back

Coral Sea Back

CORAL SEA WALL

Another small wall that is covered with enjoyable plated features. The first two routes are on the southeast face while the second two ascend the northwest face. A single bolted anchor on top services all four climbs; it's advised to bring cord to extend the anchor and not shred your rope on the edge!

30 min

Approach: Hike into Voodoo Garden, staying low and keeping left of Chester Rock. Walk northwest until you can see this wall amidst boulders on the righthand hillside. Scramble through these large boulders to reach the base. **[GPS: 34.31373, -116.87983]**

6 Lurchin Urchin 5.7 ★★

Conquer the beginning roof crux to gain a nice horn. Cruise up jugs and chickenheads, angling right to the shared anchors atop *Neon Tetra*. Pure fun!

45 ft. 4 bolts. Pete Paredes, Brad Singer, May 2007.

7 Neon Tetra 5.8 ★

Mantel onto a rail and utilize the fantastic undercling. Pull the crux between the 2nd and 3rd bolts and claim your reward of plentiful jugs above.

35 ft. 4 bolts. Brad Singer, Pete Paredes, May 2007.

8 Angel Fish 5.7 ★

Grunt through the opening moves, then cruise super-positive flakes. Groundfall potential if you blow the 2nd clip! Shares the last bolt with *Hanging in Limbo*.

50 ft. 4 bolts. Tyler Logan, Kevin Graves, Loren Scott, Pete Paredes, Brad Singer, Aug. 2007.

9 Hanging in Limbo 5.9+ ★★

A good, challenging route with a demanding start over a bulge. Quickly shake out, then power through a crux sequence on sharp holds. Same anchor as *Neon Tetra*.

50 ft. 4 bolts. Tyler Logan, Kevin Graves, Loren Scott, Pete Paredes, Brad Singer, Aug. 2007.

Emily Wong on the *Lurchin Urchin*, 5.7, Coral Sea, page 133. ▶ Brandon Copp

One-Eyed Cat Wall

ONE-EYED CAT WALL

A long, narrow wall with a decent collection of lines. Make sure to try *One-Eyed Cat* (5.10a) and *Iceman Cometh* (5.10b). Beware a risky 2nd clip for many routes on this wall!

AM 🚶 **30 min**

Approach: Located 50 feet east of Coral Sea Wall. **[GPS: 34.31372, -116.87965]**

❶ One-Eyed Cat 5.10a ★★★
A burly move starts this climb off with a bang. Friction past a few plates on the blunt arête to the upper bulge. Trust the feet while moving through the high secondary crux.
70 ft. 6 bolts. Pete Paredes, Brad Singer, May 2007.

❷ Iceman Cometh 5.10b ★★★
Best on the wall? Blast up the interesting start, using small edges and underclings on the slightly overhanging face. The holds disappear before the headwall for a thought-provoking finish. Shared anchor with *One-Eyed Cat*.
50 ft. 5 bolts. Pete Paredes, Brad Singer, May 2007.

❸ Voodoo Glow Skulls 5.10b ★★
Cruxy down low under a small, squared roof. Pop over the roof and veer upward on edges that become more positive as you gain height. Shares anchors with *Had a Lean*.
40 ft. 3 bolts. Jonathan Bent, Chris Miller, Loren Scott, July 2009.

❹ Had a Lean in My Sole 5.8 ★★
A deceptively hard start from a slanted boulder gains the wall. Then enjoy holds that are even better than they look!
30 ft. 4 bolts. FA: (TR) Fred Maki, Chris Miller, 2005; FL: Brad Singer, Pete Paredes, May 2007.

❺ Mask of the Devil 5.10a ★★
Start from the slanted boulder and gain a V-shaped corner. Wander up, picking out the good holds until a slabby crux smacks you right in the face, mere feet from the anchors.
40 ft. 4 bolts. FA: (TR) Fred Maki, Chris Miller, 2005; FL: Mike Williams, May 2007.

❻ Flying High as the Sky 5.7 ★★
Start on the diagonal hand crack near *Mask of the Devil* and keep angling right. Best to follow the route to clean, then walk off the top, as the anchors don't have rap rings.
60 ft. Gear to 4". Eric Tipton, John Cardmon, June 2007.

❼ Beat the Devil 5.6 ★
Start at *Mask of the Devil* and take the hand crack that slants right (better) or begin on a flake to the right (easier). Follow the thin vertical seam to shared anchors on *Mask*.
40 ft. Gear to 2". Brad Singer, Pete Paredes, May 2007.

❽ Hole in the Ozone 5.10c ★★
Start low in a pit and move along thin features to a hole. Clip the 2nd bolt from here, then cruise decent nubs.
40 ft. 5 bolts. Pete Paredes, Brad Singer, May 2007.

❾ Classic Cowboy 5.7
Grovelly climbing in a dirty chimney to *Ozone* anchors.
40 ft. Gear to 4". Brad Singer, Pete Paredes, May 2007.

Sara Burchfiel goes for the clip, *When the Levee Breaks*, 5.9, Katrina Wall, page 139. 📷 Brandon Copp

VOODOO PIN

A prominent spire that is easily recognizable, rising from the lower slopes of the Voodoo Garden. Definitely plan a stop at this wall to sample the enticing moderates that ascend a large dike.

☀ 🚶 25 min

Approach: 50 feet northeast of Chester Rock/ Rose Garden Wall.
[GPS: 34.31369, -116.87947]

❶ Guys and Dolls 5.9 ★★
Take the dike to a horizontal, then spread those legs! Shimmy left across the ledge on marginal feet. Tackle the arête on grainy holds and burn rubber up the final slab.
45 ft. 6 bolts. Jeff Brown, Chris Miller, 2005.

❷ Girls in the Middle 5.9 ★★
Blast straight up out of the alcove into a right-facing flake. Lieback/undercling this excellent feature, then follow thin edges to the anchors on *Guys and Dolls*.
40 ft. Unknown.

❸ Lesbos in Love 5.8 ★★
Court the obvious dike that leads to the headwall. Squeeze knobs as you trend right on the slabby finish. Caution — be wary of hollow blocks on the dike!
40 ft. 6 bolts. Brad Singer, Pete Paredes, Loren Scott, July 2007.

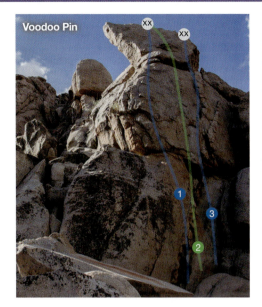

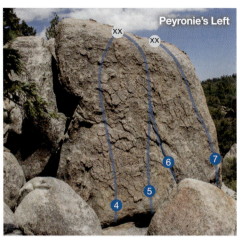

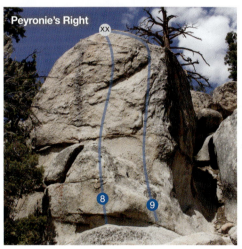

PEYRONIE'S WALL

A small block with great beginner climbs and a few more challenging lines. The first two routes start on a platform at the wall's left end, whereas the other four start down lower, past a notch. Peyronie's is probably the most easily accessible wall in the Voodoo Garden for setting up topropes.

Approach: From Voodoo Pin, continue 50 feet east to reach this block.
[GPS: 34.31375, -116.87929]

4 Hook and Ladder 5.6 ★★
A short line on plates that's especially enjoyable.
25 ft. 3 bolts. Pat Brennan, Pete Paredes, June 2007.

5 Snelled Hook 5.8 ★★
A logical step up from *Hook and Ladder,* with a difficult and reachy start. Well-featured, but the edges are smaller. Shares anchor with *Hook and Ladder.*
25 ft. 3 bolts. Brad Singer, Pete Paredes, Bill Olszewski, June 2007.

6 El Gancho 5.10b ★★
Start down below the notch for this engaging mix of slab, crack, and face climbing. Shares the last 2 bolts and anchor with *Snelled Hook.* Be careful not to blow the high 3rd clip!
35 ft. 4 bolts. Pete Paredes, Brad Singer, June 2007.

7 By Hook or Crook 5.11c ★★★
Start left of the pillar/arête in a scrappy offwidth. Thrash it out until you emerge from the crack, then hang on through the tenuous and sequential crux. Fun, yet tough is putting it mildly!
40 ft. 5 bolts. Jeff Brennan, July 2007.

8 Hook, Line, and Singer 5.10d ★★★
Leftmost route on the south face. Fly past the initial ramp to a blank white slab. Utilize edges and underclings on the tricky face that's sure to keep you on your toes.
45 ft. 5 bolts. Brad Singer, Pete Paredes, Sept. 2007.

9 Captain Hook 5.10d ★★★
Fun lieback moves on an awesome flake. Finish on the rounded top at anchors shared with *Hook, Line, and Singer.*
50 ft. 4 bolts. Pete Paredes, Loren Scott, Brad Singer, July 2007.

FLIBBERTIGIBBET ROCK

Secluded wall beside a large tree with a roof high on its east face.

AM 30 min

Approach: From Voodoo Pin, hike northeast past Peyronie's Wall and up a short gully as if you were heading toward Katrina Wall. Instead of scrambling uphill through boulders, stay low and look for the large pine. Duck underneath it to reach this semi-hidden wall.
[GPS: 34.31408, -116.87926]

❶ Flibbertigibbet 5.10d ★★
Climb the blocky arête past a series of ledges to a steep slab. If you don't know the password, use skill and balance to conquer the perplexing sequence.
45 ft. 6 bolts. Jeff Brown, Chris Miller, 2005.

❷ Tear the Roof Off the Sucker 5.11c ★★
Fire up the face from the low ramp to pull through the massive roof. Bouldery. Shares anchors with *Flibbertigibbet*.
45 ft. 5 bolts. Matthew Janse, Brandon Copp, June 2020.

RETICENT ROCK

A domed rock characterized by the vertical, color-streaked pane of glass that is its east face. If you climb 5.12, definitely give the single excellent route here a burn!

AM 30 min

Approach: Scramble slightly downhill from Katrina Wall.
[GPS: 34.31398, -116.87955]

❸ Reticent Arête 5.12b ★★★
Tinged with orange and black, this beautiful, smooth face sports one of the tougher lines in HVP. The remarkably sustained technical sequence is a puzzle worth solving. Devious arête holds are coupled with micro edges on the imposing slick face. Follow these as they lead upward through the crux. Shake out at a ledge and brace yourself for a finale on slightly bigger edges and flakes.
40 ft. 5 bolts. Ryan Crochiere, Sept. 2007.

Katrina Wall

KATRINA WALL

One of the most distinguishable walls in the Voodoo Garden, easily visible when approaching from the road. Its left side is home to some of the best 5.9-5.10 routes in the Voodoo Garden. The south-facing rock bakes on hot summer days.

30 min

Approach: From Voodoo Pin, hike northeast past Peyronie's Wall and up a short gully. With Katrina Wall in sight, scramble uphill through a boulder field.
[GPS: 34.31404, -116.87959]

④ When the Levee Breaks 5.9 ★★
Begin at the entrance to a chimney. Blast past a rounded flake on decent plates. Don't get washed off the wall by the thin edges and vertical slab at the finish!
60 ft. 6 bolts. Chris Miller, Lisa Guindon, 2005.

⑤ Bourbon Street 5.9 ★★★
A swig of liquid courage might help before attempting the whirlwind start on this one. Good technique will bring you over a ledge to face a heady secondary crux on the upper slab. Enjoyable and varied throughout its length.
60 ft. 6 bolts. Chris Miller, Lisa Guindon, 2005.

⑥ Mardi Gras 5.10b ★★★
Party on with this joy of a climb! A tricky, balancy sequence makes for an interesting start to reach key holds on the rail. Flash up to a ledge, then follow cool plates on the smooth patina face/arête.
60 ft. 6 bolts. Chris Miller, Lisa Guindon, 2005.

⑦ French Quartered 5.7 ★
Blast past 3 bolts, then tread carefully through easy runout terrain. The psychological crux is gathering the courage to pull onto the corner. A wandering line that is a bit contrived, and definitely not recommended for someone climbing at the grade. Shared anchor with *Blue Bayou.*
60 ft. 6 bolts. Sheila Romane, Brad Singer, Lee Clark, Noelle Ladd, June 2007.

⑧ Blue Bayou 5.7 ★★
Short and sweet, yet burlier than its neighbors. Swim out right to escape the blunt arête. Continue through pumpy terrain with a slight run to the anchors.
40 ft. 4 bolts. Brad Singer, Lee Clark, June 2007.

⑨ The Big Easy 5.8 ★
Set up from the anchor atop *Blue Bayou.* Lieback or jam a right-facing flake below a wedged boulder. Tech straight up an orange streak through a dish at the top.
30 ft. Craig Britton, Chris Miller, Oct. 2011.

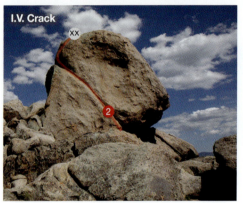

VOODOO BLOCK

A perched block that rests high on the ridge north of Katrina Wall, with two crack climbs.

Approach: From Katrina Wall, walk 100 feet uphill to the north.
[GPS: 34.31430, -116.87977]

SHREK ROCK

This massive perched boulder sits northwest of Voodoo Garden below the ridgeline. *Thor's Revenge* (5.12a) is the must-do route on its overhanging west face.

Approach: Begin by hiking to the Voodoo Garden. Head left around Chester Rock, but don't scramble up the boulders to the base of Coral Sea Wall. Instead, stay low and continue northwest, passing additional formations on your right until Shrek Rock appears high on the hillside. Scramble up the boulder-strewn hillside to reach the west face of this block.

While it is possible to approach this wall from Voodoo Block, it is more difficult. From that direction, drop down a steep gully and scramble around to the west face.
[GPS: 34.31454, -116.88022]

---

❶ The Misogynist 5.11a ★★

Located on the east face. Angle right on a steep, flared crack. Continue through the bulge to a roof, then make an airy hand-traverse out left along the horizontal. Ride big plates to bolted anchors.
40 ft. Gear to 4". Tyler Logan, Kenn Kenaga, Sept. 2007.

❷ I.V. Crack 5.10c ★

The diagonal seam splitting the west face. Shares anchors with *The Misogynist*.
40 ft. Gear to 1.5". Kenn Kenaga, Tyler Logan, Pete Paredes, Sept. 2007.

❸ Thor's Revenge 5.12a ★★★

Awesomely overhanging — but can you hang on? Easy moves to start, then lean wayyy back and clip the first bolt. Huck for a pinch near the 2nd bolt, then cling to plates and gain the upper face. Angle right across easy terrain to anchors. Steep and committing, with excellent movement.
65 ft. 5 bolts. Lee Clark, John Cardmon, Aug. 2007.

❹ Shrek 5.5 ★

Start with an easy chimney, then exit onto a plateau. Climb featured terrain on the south face of the giant egg past 2 well-spaced bolts to anchors shared with *Thor's Revenge*.
65 ft. Wide gear, 2 bolts. Pat Brennan, Aug. 2007.

The Corridors — *Just One More 5.8 Aréte*

Beyond the Voodoo Garden

Garden Rock

Shrek Rock

9

GARDEN ROCK

A large, south-facing formation high on the hillside. This wall rarely sees traffic due to the lengthy approach, but the climb *Coriander and the Special Blend* (5.11c) is not to be missed. Not very dog- or kid-friendly due to the boulder scrambling required.

40 min

Approach: Approach as for Shrek Rock. When that formation comes into view, Garden Rock can be seen further west. Scramble through the large boulder field toward the wall. **[GPS: 34.31452, -116.88052]**

Garden Rock Left

XX

5

6

⑤ Coriander and the Special Blend 5.11c ★★★★
An aesthetic line on beautiful, overhanging plates and incut edges. Slide up the crack in the left corner until you can creep out right to the high first bolt. From here, start crimping till you can't crimp no more! The rock is stellar — this would be a coveted classic if it was in the Central Pinnacles.
50 ft. 5 bolts. Jeff Brennan, June 2007.

⑥ Voodoo Soup 5.11a ★
Start the same as *Coriander*, but shove off right across a sloping ledge to the diagonal offwidth. Fight through, one inch at a time, until the crack becomes a horizontal on the south face. Extract your scraped and bloody limbs and finish up the easy south face to shared anchors with *Coriander*.
55 ft. Gear to 5". Kenn Kenaga, Jeff Brennan, June 2007.

⑦ Herb 5.7 ★
A zigzagging route that takes the easiest line to the tippy-top of the formation, passing a bolt on the upper face.
80 ft. Gear to 3", 1 bolt. Pat Brennan, Jeff Brennan, June 2007.

Garden Rock Right

XX

7

8

⑧ Ogre Veggies 5.7+ ★
Begin up the east side of a 35-foot fin, just east of Garden Rock. Step across to the main wall and follow a ramp angling right. Finish straight past a final bolt to anchors shared with *Herb*.
60 ft. Gear to 3", 3 bolts.
Jeff Brennan, Pat Brennan, Kenn Kenaga, July 2007.

THE CORRIDORS

Two big corridors can be seen at the top of the ridge, a short jaunt away from Garden Rock and Shrek Rock. The single climb here is located in the biggest and rightmost corridor, and ascends the middle rock of the formation. See photo on previous page.

🌞 🚶 40 min

Approach: From Garden Rock, continue hiking uphill to the northwest.
[GPS: 34.31483, -116.88071]

⑨ Just One More 5.8 Arête 5.8 ★★
An enjoyable romp on plates up the southeast arête. A bit of a hike for an OK climb. See photo on previous page, top.
50 ft. 4 bolts. Lee Clark, Sheila Romane, Aug. 2007.

VOODOO ROCK

A large, jumbly formation lurking in the woods north of the Corridors. Rarely visited, with climbs on its west and south faces, partially shaded by the large pines nearby.

🌞 🚶 45 min

Approach: Hike northwest up the dry creekbed from Garden Rock. This formation sits just past the Corridors at the far end of the ridge with Shrek Rock, Garden Rock, and the Corridors.
[GPS: 34.31498, -116.88139]

⑩ Gremlin's Best Friend 5.10d ★
Bearhug the arête and take the low-angle ramp to good undercling flakes. Crimp onto the steep, green wall above and tread lightly up the delicate face.
60 ft. 4 bolts. Jeff Brennan, Kenn Kenaga, June 2007.

⑪ Uncle Choss 5.11a ★
Ogle the bulging round corner, with an initial steep crux. Once through the difficulties, zoom up the sloping arête past 2 bolts and finish in the cool hand crack overhead. Shared anchor with *Gremlin's*.
50 ft. Gear to 3", 2 bolts. Jeff Brennan, June 2007.

⑫ Slammin' Doors 5.6 ★
Force your body into the offwidth crack and swim to the top. Shared anchor with *Gremlin's*.
50 ft. Gear to 5". Kenn Kenaga, Pat Brennan, Jeff Brennan, June 2007.

⑬ Who Do You Rock? 5.10a ★★
High feet and thin crimps on clean rock gain initial access onto the wall. Pass numerous ledges and gear belay at the top.
50 ft. Gear to 3.5", 2 bolts. Kenn Kenaga, Jeff Brennan, June 2007.

⑭ Free and Clear 5.8
Hop atop a fin and reach high to a finger crack. The heady start is thought-provoking, but the rest is discontinuous. Shared anchor with *Horizontal but Steep*.
45 ft. Gear to 3". Jeff Brennan, Pat Brennan, Kenn Kenaga, June 2007.

⑮ Horizontal but Steep 5.10c ★★
Enjoyable and powerful climbing. Leaning horizontals dictate the difficult opening sequence, then take plates and horns up the corner past a single bolt to anchors.
35 ft. Gear to 3", 1 bolt. Kenn Kenaga, Jeff Brennan, June 2007.

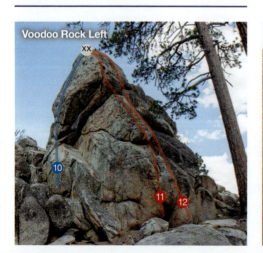
Voodoo Rock Left

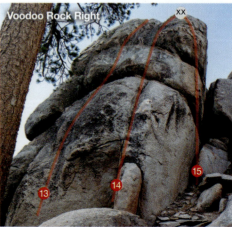
Voodoo Rock Right

Landon Holman on *Thor's Revenge,*
5.12a, Shrek Rock, page 140.
📷 Brandon Copp

UNTRODDEN CLASSICS

Too busy at your favorite crag? Seek out these routes for an adventure away from the crowds.

1 Chasm Spasm 5.9
Butt Rock Area,   page 327

2 Stellar Arête 5.10b
Pinnacle With a View,   page 214

3 Palm Pilot 5.10b
Onyx Summit Crag,   page 283

4 Out of Sight 5.10b
8000 Foot Crag,   page 288

5 Over the Hills and Far Away
5.10b, Zeppelin Dome,   page 337

6 Purgatory 5.10b
Underworld,   page 157

7 Kaleidoscope 5.10c
Arctic Temple,   page 187

8 Toaster Oven 5.10d
Toaster Oven,   page 245

9 Siberia Crack 5.10d
Siberia Creek Tower,   page 202

10 Waffle House 5.10d
Dragon Breath Wall,   page 235

11 Killer Crack 5.10d
The Far Side,   page 299

12 Canoe Slab 5.11a
Cap Rock Area,   page 303

13 Migs Over Moscow 5.11b
Big West Hanna,   page 226

14 Classic Crack 5.11b
Classic Crack,   page 332

15 Coriander and the Special Blend
5.11c, Garden Rock,   page 141

16 Exodus 5.11c
Black Bluff,   page 192

17 Thor's Revenge 5.12a
Shrek Rock,   page 140

18 Armageddon 5.12a
Seam Crag Area,   page 317

19 Swallow Your Pride 5.12a
Quartzite Bands,   page 268

20 Screaming Trees 5.12d
Dragonlance Wall,   page 229

BISON CREST CRAG

A secluded wall with a few bolted climbs on its uniquely shaped northwest face.

PM   🚶 45 min

Approach: Continue hiking northwest up the dry creekbed from Shrek Rock. This formation lies on the opposite side of the creekbed, 100 yards southwest of the Corridors.
[GPS: 34.31437, -116.88173]

Bison Crest Crag

1 Jojo the Dog Face Girl 5.10b ★
Begin by clipping the first bolt of *Cucaru*, then move left at the midway ledge and mosey up the green face.
50 ft. 4 bolts. Pete Paredes, Loren Scott, Aug. 2010.

2 Cucaru 5.10b ★★
Spar with the rock on the tough initial sequence. Perform a few mentally challenging moves above the midway ledge before clipping the 2nd bolt. Pass the overlap on small, sharp handholds.
50 ft. 4 bolts. Pete Paredes, Loren Scott, Aug. 2010.

3 The Low Down 5.8 ★
Follow the righthand arête past a triangular block and through the bulge.
40 ft. 5 bolts. Pete Paredes, Loren Scott, July 2010.

DEAD TREE WALL

A little-known wall tucked away in the northern reaches of HVP. Its small collection of routes are well-protected and on par with the quality of other moderate lines nearby. The wall's namesake tree lies at the base of the shady north face.

45 min

Approach: 125 yards northwest of Voodoo Rock. **[GPS: 34.31561, -116.88235]**

1 Canas y Ganas 5.9 ★★

Creep along the slabby, rounded arête past 2 bolts to where the bolt lines split. Go left up the slightly overhanging east face. Power past 3 more bolts to the chains.

40 ft. 5 bolts. Pete Paredes, Loren Scott, April 2012.

2 Chingon 5.8 ★★

Climb past 2 bolts shared with *Canas y Ganas*, but take the right fork, heading straight through a bulge. Angle right across the north face and motor past the last bolt to a separate set of anchors.

40 ft. 4 bolts. Pete Paredes, Loren Scott, June 2012.

3 The Slant 5.9 ★★

Lightly tread up the face to a lip. Make a long reach to pass the roof; another big move lies in wait at the top.

40 ft. 5 bolts. Pete Paredes, Loren Scott, Sept. 2011.

4 Passing the Stone 5.8 ★★

Follow the right margin of the face, with a high crux as the holds thin. Be wary of the flakes near the 2nd bolt.

35 ft. 4 bolts. Pete Paredes, Loren Scott, Aug. 2011.

Dead Tree Wall

PASQUALLY DOME

A long hike from the south parking area and even from the Central Pinnacles. There are two short crack lines on the south and southeast faces. No rap rings on the shared anchor, but it's an easy scramble off the back.

40 min

Approach: A long trek from the south parking and main climbing areas, but if you drive up the road from the north parking area and park by the road, the hike is only 5-10 minutes.

From the northern parking area, hike/drive up the road to the Voodoo Garden turnoff. Pass the turnoff and continue on the road for another 200 yards as the formation comes into view in front of you: look for the wide crack and the large pine tree beside the rock. Bushwhack to the base, taking washes/streambeds and natural paths of least resistance up the hillside (10 minutes).
[GPS: 34.31565, -116.87692]

5 The Leaning One 5.10b ★

Start via good fist jams in an overhanging crack. Turn the corner to an all-too-easy romp to *Lucky 7's* anchors.

25 ft. Gear to 5". Kenn Kenaga, July 2008.

6 Lucky 7 5.7 ★★

A splitter hand crack that would be a classic if it was 50 feet longer. Sink your mitts into this striking crack that angles right, with a unique 90-degree turn ¾ of the way to the anchor ledge. Great for someone who's getting into leading cracks; it eats gear, with good jams and features for feet.

25 ft. Gear to 3". Pat Brennan, Lori Brennan, Aug. 2007.

Pasqually Dome

Pasqually Outcropping

Pasqually Rock

Pop's Day Buttress

Mom's Day Buttress

Nighthawk Rock

Pasqually Dome

PASQUALLY ROCK

This rock sits uphill from Pasqually Dome, next to a big tree on the hillside. Good rock, but the lone route here is substandard, and setting up the anchor is a bit tricky.

  40 min

Approach: Approach as for Pasqually Dome. Upon reaching the dome, head left around the western side of that rock. Continue uphill to this formation, which sits left of a large pine tree. **[GPS: 34.31600, -116.87693]**

7 We Got Gold 5.7

You might try your hand at this climb … if you're already in the area. Start 10 feet left of the tree in a half-moon cutout and tread lightly on the fingery slab. Not much pro on this climb. Gear anchor.

25 ft. Thin gear to 1". Pat Brennan, Lori Brennan, Aug. 2007.

Pasqually Rock

NIGHTHAWK ROCK

A multi-tiered rock near Mom and Pop's Day buttresses, with a few short burners on its southwest face.

  45 min

Approach: Hike 5 minutes from Pasqually Rock, wrapping around the west slope of the hillside. **[GPS: 34.31589, -116.87735]**

8 Bonus 5.9 ★

Climb flakes and a shallow corner crack. Gear anchor.

30 ft. Gear to 2" for anchor Kenn Kenaga, July 2008.

9 Sawzall Crack 5.10c ★

A thin seam with tricky feet, then big plates. Finish on a monster pinch rail. Gear anchor.

30 ft. Gear to 2". Kenn Kenaga, July 2008.

10 Moving Down in Class 5.8 ★

Power past a bolt on the corner. Above a ledge the climbing eases, following big plates to thin cracks. Gear anchor.

30 ft. Gear to 2", 1 bolt.

Alan Bartlett, Kenn Kenaga, Pat Brennan, July 2008.

Nighthawk Rock

Mom's and Pop's Day Buttresses

MOM'S DAY BUTTRESS

A skinny pinnacle with one strange and discontinuous trad climb.   **45 min**

Approach: Approach as for Nighthawk Rock; this is only a stone's throw away. **[GPS: 34.31598, -116.87743]**

❶ Wednesday Night Romp 5.7 ★
A brief, plated section gains the main corner crack splitting the narrow fin. Climb past a ledge to a face with a single bolt. Reach the top, descend the back to a saddle, and finish at bolted anchors on a 2nd summit.
50 ft. Gear to 3.5", 1 bolt. Lori Brennan, Pat Brennan, June 2008.

POP'S DAY BUTTRESS

A south-facing buttress on the western slope of the hillside.   **45 min**

Approach: Next to Mom's Day Buttress. **[GPS: 34.31601, -116.87746]**

❷ Pal 5.9 ★★
A tiered climb. Pass the first bolt on the rounded arête, then tackle the slabby face of the 2nd block. Walk across the top and continue up the low-angle face to a decent roof. 2-bolt anchor without rap rings.
60 ft. 4 bolts. Pat Brennan, Adam Brennan, Lori Brennan, June 2008.

LAKESIDE CRAGS

Brandon Copp on *Rapala*, 5.10c, Fisherman's Buttress, page 164. 📷 Jacqueline Copp

LAKESIDE **CRAGS**

This collection of crags offers excellent climbing across all disciplines and grades, often with beautiful views of the lake. The rock quality overall is quite good, with enjoyable plates and more than enough crimps to go around. Temperatures at these south-shore crags tend to be a bit cooler than those located north of the lake, often helped by a late-afternoon breeze off the lake. Castle Rock is the tallest formation of the bunch, but it's hard to beat the minimal approach of the Fisherman's Buttress area.

Approach: All of the crags can be easily accessed by any type of vehicle, as the approaches consist of driving on Highway 18 and parking in roadside pullouts. The walls are located at the western end of Big Bear Lake, all within a couple miles of the dam. Crags are generally listed from west to east. There are two main clusters: those near Fisherman's Buttress, about half a mile east of the dam, and those near Castle Rock, another half-mile farther east. See individual crags for specific parking and approach directions.

Meg Kee aims her *Crossbow*, 5.8, Castle Rock, page 172.
▶ Stephen Lê

CLIMBING AREA	ELEVATION	HIKE	ROUTES	GRADE RANGE	CRAGS
TURNOUT BOULDERS *Peaceful roadside crag* page 152	6650 ft.	10 min	11	≤.5 .6 .7 .8 .9 .10 .11 .12	
ICEBOX CANYON *Easy cracks, hard face climbs* page 154	7000 ft. 7200 ft.	5-25 min	16	≤.5 .6 .7 .8 .9 .10 .11 .12	Toetally Broken Buttress, Underworld, Throne of the Mountain Gods
FISHERMAN'S AREA *Excellent technical routes* page 161	6900 ft.	5-10 min	31	≤.5 .6 .7 .8 .9 .10 .11 .12	Three Fishes Rock, Fisherman's Buttress
CASTLE ROCK AREA *Tall, varied lines* page 166	7300 ft.	20-30 min	49	≤.5 .6 .7 .8 .9 .10 .11 .12	Castle Rock, Camelot Crag, Castle Rock Slabs, Cracked Tower

TURNOUT BOULDERS

This small wall is located by itself just west of the Bear Valley Dam. It predominately faces south, with a few climbs on the southwest face, and receives partial sun and shade all day long. Located down in a canyon, this crag has a distinct feel, quite different from the majority of the Big Bear Lake hillside formations. It is peaceful, with the calm sound of Bear Creek babbling below and a unique view of the bridge spanning the dam. While not a premier climbing destination, it is nice change of venue. There are no bolted anchors here — all climbs require gear and long cord for slinging boulders to build anchors. Let the roadside adventures begin!

Approach: From the stoplight at the dam, go 0.1 miles west on Highway 18 to a big pullout on the left. If traveling from Running Springs to Big Bear, this is the last pullout on the right before the stoplight. The large pullout has a small stone wall lining it. Park here and hike through the break in the wall to a rocky outcropping. Scramble over the boulders until the terrain begins to drop down into the canyon. Tread carefully down the steep decline on the southeast corner of the point's apex toward the creek to reach the wall.
[GPS: 34.24088, -116.98114]

❶ Don't Make Me Turn This Car Around! (Project)
Desperate climbing on a thin dike with edges that dissolve before the jugs. Precision edging and good smearing will be needed for an ascent of this tough line.
25 ft.

❷ Street Sweeper 5.9 ★★
Bolted line on the southwest face. Mantel past a triangular pocket and reach high into the flaring crack that looks like a set of lips. Paste your feet to the wall and off you go!
35 ft. 3 bolts, gear to 3" for anchor.
Kenn Kenaga, Will Carlson, Mike McCarey, Sept. 2000.

❸ Litter Removal 5.10a ★
Start just left of the large pine tree and use the two ski-track seams to reach a block. Slide up the small gully to the finish.
40 ft. Kenn Kenaga, Will Carlson, Mike McCarey, Sept. 2000.

❹ Pull Over to Pass 5.10b ★★
Right of the big tree on the corner is a well-featured seam. Follow this to a nice ledge. Confront the roof problem and ride the arête above. Enjoyable.
45 ft. Mike McCarey, Kenn Kenaga, Sept. 2000.

❺ Park Off the Curb 5.10c ★
Step 3 feet right to good left-hand sidepulls. Bearhug the arête until you can pull onto the ledge. Bypass the roof by taking the finger crack on its right side.
45 ft. Mike McCarey, Kenn Kenaga, Aug. 2000.

❻ Scant Parking Zone 5.10a ★★
Bouldery slab moves on thin edges reach a widening seam that starts 10 feet above the ground. A tricky first placement; higher in the crack is better. Step right at the ledge to finish in a hand crack.
45 ft. Gear to 2". FA: (TR) Mike McCarey, Kenn Kenaga, Dan Thiele, Aug. 2000; FL: Brandon Copp, Matthew Janse, Sept. 2019.

❼ Overheated 5.8 ★★
Grunt up the chimney in the back of the alcove. Navigate around the wedged boulder to reach a ledge, then finish straight up a slick offwidth above. Fun with a dash of funky!
40 ft. Wide gear. Kenn Kenaga, Mike McCarey, Aug. 2000.

❽ Dead Battery 5.1
Weasel up the chimney past a few wedged blocks.
40 ft. Wide gear. Bob Cable, Julia Cronk, Pat Brennan, Aug. 2003.

❾ Boy's Gotta Pee 5.4
Wide hand crack surrounded by plentiful features located on the right side of the alcove's entrance. Not aesthetic, but fairly easy.
40 ft. Derek Wift, Tanner McCarey, Aug. 2000.

❿ Flat Spare Tire 5.7 ★
A quality sinker hand crack. Lieback and jam in the crack past a few ledges to a chimney section at the top.
30 ft. Gear to 3". Eric Tipton (solo), Feb. 2000.

⓫ Hitchhiker 5.7
A short, low-angle fist crack that climbs past a block.
25 ft. Gear to 4".
Kenn Kenaga, Will Carlson, Mike McCarey, Sept. 2000.

Turnout Boulders Left

Turnout Boulders Main

TOETALLY BROKEN BUTTRESS

A mostly sunny crag, close to the lake with a high concentration of traditionally protected cracks in the 5.8-and-under range. The buttress is completely broken and easily recognizable by the plethora of boulders surrounding it. The Lower Buttress lies partially hidden beneath the trees near Kidd Creek, while the Beer Tier is perched above 100 vertical feet of boulder-strewn hillside. This is not the best spot to bring children or dogs due to the precarious pebble-hopping involved in reaching the climbs.

PM   5-10 min

As of this writing, the anchor atop the climbs on the Lower Buttress is badly in need of replacement and should not be trusted as is. There is one set of good chain anchors with rap rings at the top of the Beer Tier to be shared among those climbs.

Approach: From the stoplight at the dam, drive 0.5 miles east along Highway 18 on the south shore of Big Bear Lake. Park in the pullout on the left side of the road that can fit half a dozen cars.

Getting to these climbs is half the fun! Just look at all the rocks you get to scramble on to reach these routes! Cross the highway and walk 50 feet up Icebox Lane. Just before the "neighborhood watch" sign, pick up the faint trail heading through the pine needles on the right side of Kidd Creek. Follow this boulder-filled gully until the formation comes into view on the hillside to your left. Hop across large boulders to reach the Lower Buttress. The climbs here are located on the right side of the wall next to a pine tree. Approach time to the Lower Buttress is a steep 5 minutes.

The upper Beer Tier should be visible after crossing the gully. Hike about 150 feet further upstream until you come to the chossy hillside covered with massive boulders. Climb straight up this obnoxious terrain. It's easiest to approach the Beer Tier from the right side by traversing in across a ledge to the starts of the lines. Approach time for the Beer Tier is a steeper 10 minutes. **[GPS: 34.23883, -116.97020]**

Beer Tier

Underworld

Lower Buttress

Toetally Broken Buttress Approaches

Jessi Reddick samples the spice on
Toetally Broken Again, 5.8, page 156.
📷 Brandon Copp

Lower Buttress

Lower Buttress

❶ Broken Toes 5.10b ★

This mixed route takes small gear and a large cam, plus three bolts. Hop up onto the toe of a long flake and climb lichen-covered slab to a seam. Follow the seam as it becomes a wide crack and ride easy slab above to the shared anchor on *Toetally Broken*.
60 ft. Small gear, 5" cam, 3 bolts.
Eric Odenthal, Brad Singer, June 2002.

❷ Toetally Broken 5.8 ★★

Lightning-bolt thin finger crack. Make cool mantel moves and then sink in good jams when it widens. Scramble up to the 2nd pitch above if desired. Note: The anchor on this route badly needs to be replaced as of this writing and should not be trusted as is.
55 ft. Gear to 4". Brad Singer, 1984.

Beer Tier

Beer Tier

❸ Toetally Broken Again 5.8 ★

Can be done as the 2nd pitch to *Toetally Broken* or as a stand-alone route starting from the Beer Tier. At the left end of the tier is a large, protruding tooth of rock. This route climbs left of the tooth in the finger-crack / monster-offwidth combo. Finish through the cruxy roof and gear belay above.

40 ft. Gear to 3" or 6" depending on which crack you choose.
Eric Odenthal, Brad Singer, June 2002.

❹ Pacifico 5.8 ★

Lieback the left side of a detached pillar at the base. Surf up the dihedral on the right side of the giant tooth to the shared anchor.

35 ft. Big gear. Unknown.

❺ Tecate 5.7 ★

Squeeze inside the gritty offwidth on the right side of the detached pillar or fly up the ramp outside the crack. Move up a left-facing dihedral with jugs above. Shared anchor on the ledge.

35 ft. Wide gear. Unknown.

❻ Negra Modelo 5.7 ★

This flared crack is a good challenge, both for climbing and placing pro. After the initial tough section, the route becomes better for jamming, with a final slab up high as the crack peters out. Shared anchor on the ledge.

35 ft. Gear to 3". Unknown.

❼ Corona 5.7 ★★

This crack starts as a hand crack and widens into an offwidth area wide enough to slip down in. When the crack branches about 25 feet up, go left.

35 ft. Gear to 4". Unknown.

❽ Modelo Especial 5.6 ★

Crack open a cold one and slosh your way up the undulating crack that weaves up the wall. Gear anchor.

30 ft. Gear to 4". Unknown.

❾ Tres Equis 5.6

This wide fist crack slants right and climbs through a series of horizontal ledges. Inconsistent climbing but mellow. Gear anchor.

30 ft. Gear to 3". Unknown.

UNDERWORLD

Located around to the north of Toetally Broken Buttress is this rarely trafficked little gem that is home to a few standout lines. *Purgatory* (5.10b) and *Downward Spiral* (5.11a) are both excellent face routes that would get another star if not for the lichen. This mostly shady, north-facing slab is quite tall.

  10 min

Approach: Park and approach as for the Toetally Broken's Lower Buttress. From the Lower Buttress, head left around the corner and follow the trail steeply uphill along the base of broken rock. Near the top, Underworld is the large, unbroken section of wall.
[GPS: 34.23907, -116.96983]

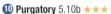

⑩ Purgatory 5.10b ★★★

Thought-provoking technical face climbing on a lichen-covered slab, staying relatively close to the arête. This superb route is quite long, finishing atop the short headwall block. Worth every minute of the short approach.
75 ft. 9 bolts. Eric Odenthal, John Cardmon, June 2002.

⑪ Downward Spiral 5.11a ★★★

Another fantastic line! A difficult yet short splitter finger crack in the middle of the wall leads to a ledge. Face climb on crystals, trending up and left following a break in the wall. Blast up the headwall, sharing the last bolt and anchors with *Purgatory*.
75 ft. 8 bolts, gear to 1.5". Eric Odenthal, June 2002.

⑫ Mr. Clean 5.9

This oxymoron of a climb takes the hand/fist-sized crack to a ledge with a tree. Belay from the tree or gear anchor.
30 ft. Gear to 4". John Cardmon, Eric Odenthal, June 2002.

⑬ Styx 5.8 ★★

A quality splitter hand crack, highly recommended. Start by scrambling up a gully or climbing *Mr. Clean*. Lieback the crack in the right-facing dihedral. Negotiate a small roof as the crack begins to widen. Gear anchor.
60 ft. Gear to 4". Unknown.

Underworld

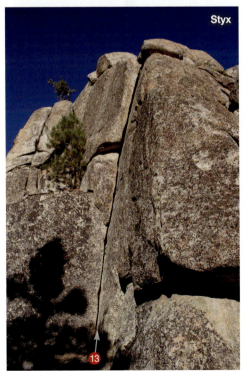

Styx

THRONE OF THE MOUNTAIN GODS

Like what you found at Underworld and itching for more? Take it up a notch and hike out to the Throne of the Mountain Gods, where the grades are a touch harder and the lichen's a bit thicker. This secluded block is perched atop the Kidd Creek gully, an almost forgotten sentinel. All three routes here are worth doing. Shady and north-facing, the entire face is covered in a layer of black and green lichen — best to brush before you crush!

25 min

Approach: Park as for Toetally Broken Buttress, cross the highway, and walk 50 feet up Icebox Lane to pick up the faint trail heading through the pine needles on the right side of Kidd Creek. Roughly 10 minutes in, the wash becomes more vegetated. It is best to cross the creek at this point and hike the left embankment, although not necessary. When the creek eventually curves to the right, Throne of the Mountain Gods will be straight up the hillside on the left embankment. Hike up the steep hill to the base of the formation. A strenuous 25-minute hike. **[GPS: 34.23614, -116.97026]**

Throne of the Mountain Gods

⑭ Aphrodite 5.10c ★★

Tech up seams on the left side of the block, heading past a couple bolts to a little ledge. Slant right, running along the arête, and finish straight up to the anchors.

40 ft. 5 bolts. Brad Singer, Eric Odenthal, May 2002.

⑮ Lord, Have Mercy 5.12a ★★★

Slab, slab, and more slab. Don't you need some hard, lichen-covered slab in your life? This super-thin line in the middle of the wall climbs the sea of green. Master perfect slab and smear technique, heading up shallow seams and bumps and making use of anything you can find. Arc left to share the final 2 bolts and anchors with *Aphrodite*. Brush it first!

40 ft. 5 bolts. Eric Odenthal, June 2002.

⑯ Apollo 5.11b ★★

Slink up the right side of the wall, using a nice groove on the left and the rounded corner on the right. Gain decent holds 2/3 of the way up to help you through the finish.

40 ft. 4 bolts. Eric Odenthal, Brad Singer, May 2002.

THREE FISHES ROCK

This small formation sits just east of Fisherman's Buttress. North-facing, this crag is home to only a few mediocre lines.

  5 min

Approach: From the parking for Fisherman's Buttress, hike up the hill heading west. Three Fishes Rock sits on the left as you follow the trail through the boulders toward Fisherman's. **[GPS: 34.24015, -116.96859]**

❶ Fisherman's Friend 5.10c ★

Set off under a small overlap with a bolt above it. Tech past horizontals to a gritty wide crack. After that fizzles out, pop back onto the wall to finish past the last bolt. Shares anchors with *Three Fishes*.

45 ft. Gear to 4", 2 bolts. Chris Miller, Pete Paredes, May 2001.

❷ Three Fishes 5.10a ★★

Lieback the striking hand crack that disappears just as you're getting excited. Smear up the cruxy slab above. It's too bad the crack is so short.

45 ft. Gear to 2.5", 3 bolts.

Brad Singer, Kenn Kenaga, Travis McElvany, July 1997.

Kenn Kenaga shows how it's done on *Zorro*, 5.10a, Castle Rock, page 173.
📷 Brandon Copp

Three Fishes

Splash Dancer

❸ Bass Assassin 5.12a ★★

Sneak around the corner to the right to an alcove marked by a crescent-shaped crack. Stab tiny crystals on the slick vertical slab under the arching crack. Kill the difficult upper section by smearing to the top. Try not to leave blood on the rock ...

40 ft. 4 bolts. Chris Miller, May 2001.

❹ Splash Dancer 5.11c ★★

From the ledge, creep out right to the first bolt. Slap and smear up the arête, bearhugging the blunt corner to squeeze past the crux.

40 ft. 4 bolts. Chris Miller, May 2001.

❺ 40 Lashes (Project)

Take a beating on unrelenting thin edges low on the west face. Thrash your way up to the final horizontal and breathe easier on the plates above. 2-bolt anchor without rap rings.

40 ft.

Derek Volcan on *Trouser Trout*, 5.12a, page 163.
📷 Marina Amador

FISHERMAN'S BUTTRESS

Fisherman's Buttress is an excellent roadside crag with numerous technical lines for the 5.10-5.12 climber. The popular crag sits on the south side of Big Bear Lake directly above Highway 18, unbeknownst to the carloads of visitors headed into the village. The crag receives some road noise, especially on busy weekends, but the views of the lake are unmatched, particularly at sunset.

10 min

The formation is relatively square, with climbs on the three tallest faces. The climbing tends toward thin and crimpy. The rock is fairly good, although there can be a bit of lichen on less traveled routes. Sun and shade can be found throughout the day, often with the occasional breeze off the lake. You can't go wrong choosing between *Trout Fishing in America* (5.11b), *Big-Mouth Fever* (5.11d), *Rumblefish* (5.12a), and *Trouser Trout* (5.12a) —all are spectacular lines with great exposure. *Roadside Crack* (5.10a) is a must-do for the crack enthusiast and *Crappie Corner* (5.10a) is a blast.

Approach: From the stoplight at the dam, drive 0.7 miles east along Highway 18 on the south shore of the lake. Limited parking is available just past the formation in a small pullout on the right (easy to miss), or across the highway near the wooden "Private Road" sign (do not block this road!). Alternatively, park in the larger pullout 0.2 miles to the west used for Toetally Broken Buttress.

From the small pullout, walk uphill, paralleling the road and heading toward the dam. The trail winds near the telephone pole cables, then traverses through boulders. Pass Three Fishes Rock on your left and continue hiking down across a pine-needle-filled crevice, where the east face of Fisherman's Buttress will appear across the gully. If heading to the west face, continue around the lower north face of the formation that sits just above the highway.

If parked at the Toetally Broken Buttress pullout near Icebox Lane, cross the highway and hike up Kidd Creek gully for roughly 100 feet. Traverse across the boulder-strewn creek so that you are high up on the hillside (being lower means more bushwhacking). Hike away from the dam, paralelling the road, skirting the large boulders on the hillside until the west face of Fisherman's Buttress comes into view. This is not a well-defined path, but it can be done. Expect to add 5 or 10 minutes to the approach time for Fisherman's Buttress and Three Fishes Rock, respectively. **[GPS: 34.24016, -116.96923]**

Note: In order to preserve climbing access, exercise extreme caution not to dislodge rocks or other debris onto the busy highway while at Fisherman's Buttress. In addition, **do not walk along the road** to reach this crag — it is a narrow stretch of highway with blind corners. It's better and safer to hike on the hillside.

❶ Fishbone 5.10b ★★
Lieback a dirty flake 5 feet left of the large chimney. Step right onto the face and scale the arête. The holds aren't quite as positive as you'd hoped.
40 ft. 5 bolts. Pete Paredes, Chris Miller, July 2000.

❷ Fishboner 5.9 ★★
Skip the flake and first bolt and instead plug up the short crack directly below the arête.
40 ft. Gear to 2", 4 bolts. Unknown.

❸ Catfish Crack 5.10b ★
A chimney quickly squeezes down to a hand crack. Awkward and dirty — perfect for a bottom feeder. Gear belay or set a directional and use the *Fish Out of Water* anchors.
40 ft. Gear to 4". Brad Singer, Eric Tipton, Eric Odenthal, Oct. 1999.

Fishbone

Fisherman's Buttress East Face

original start

4 Fish Out of Water 5.12a ★★★
Decipher the perplexing sequence, ascending edges to a challenging flaring crack. Like a fish out of water, you'll be struggling for oxygen, wondering what to do next to escape from this climb that looked much easier!
40 ft. 5 bolts. Chris Miller, Aug. 2000.

5 Catch of the Day 5.11c ★★★
Hand-traverse a ramp past the first bolt. A distinct strenuous sequence on thin, wavy features gives way to fun edges above. There is a low anchor bolt for the belayer since the belay stance is a bit precarious.
45 ft. 5 bolts. FA: (TR) Chris Miller, Rick Corbin, July 2000; FL: Chris Miller, July 2000.

6 Slack Line Leader 5.10b ★★
Smear past the ramp and first 2 bolts of *Catch of the Day*. Pop inside the righthand corner and follow the widening crack that angles right. Shares anchors with *Roadside Crack*.
45 ft. Gear to 4", 2 bolts. Chris Miller, July 2000.

7 Angler 5.9 ★
This is an easier and longer start to *Slack Line Leader*. Ride the mossy ramp, angling left to a corner, then zigzagging back right, following the wide crack to the top. Toprope from anchors on *Roadside Crack*.
50 ft. Chris Miller, Rick Corbin, July 2000.

8 Roadside Crack 5.10a ★★★
The recognizable crack on the east face. Quite good, albeit a little gritty. Perform the difficult stem in a right-facing dihedral to start (protected by a bolt). Mantel onto a ledge and step up to the splitter. A bit flaring at the bottom, it gets better as you go.
55 ft. Gear to 3", 1 bolt. Unknown.

The following two climbs have a low bolt to anchor the belayer and prevent a fall off the small ledge.

9 Shadowcaster 5.12c ★★★
Put your best rope gun on the end of the line and cast off! The original start takes the ramp out right, traversing back left across a horizontal with mediocre hands and marginal feet. The harder direct start takes miniscule edges to gain the horizontal and the 2nd bolt. Mash your fingertips into the thin seam above and dive into the insane crux sequence.
60 ft. 6 bolts. FA: (TR) Chris Miller, Apr. 2001; Direct Start (TR): David LePere, Aug. 2002; FL: Unknown, 2003.

10 Fishlips 5.10d ★★
From the mossy ledge, climb a thin ramp. Swim through the sea of decent edges into a dish and grab the good holds above the lip. Reachy finish. Shared anchor with *Trout Fishing*.
50 ft. 4 bolts. Chris Miller, Pete Paredes, June 2000.

⑪ Trout Fishing in America 5.11b ★★★★

Set sail on this classic line. Launch up a ramp toward a small pine, then steer directly into a wide horizontal with good jugs. Wade through thin edges and sidepulls, advancing with precision footwork and balance. The high crux is a puzzle worth solving. Fish around for the easiest line.

55 ft. 6 bolts. Brad Singer, Rob Stauder, July 1997.

Variation 5.11b: The original start was to ascend the *Big-Mouth Fever* arête past 2 bolts to the first horizontal, then traverse left to the 2nd bolt of *Trout Fishing*. 7 bolts.

⑫ Big-Mouth Fever 5.11d ★★★★

Exposure, excellent position, and an amazing view of the lake make for a spectacular arête climb. Work out the tough opening sequence, then hug the arête and don't let it slip away as you move past the big fang feature. Mentally prepare yourself for the abrupt crux that looms above the 3rd bolt. Stick the move and try to slow your breathing for the grainy, airy, and slightly runout finish.

55 ft. 5 bolts. Chris Miller, Aug. 2000.

⑬ Rumblefish 5.12a ★★★

Steep and sustained line located right of the arête on the north face. Flounder initially on sharp crimps until you can hook the giant undercling. Wicked edges are sure to test your finger strength as you finagle past the final challenge.

55 ft. 6 bolts. Chris Miller, Chuck Scott, Aug. 1999.

⑭ Trouser Trout 5.12a ★★★★

An enticing line just left of *Bass Crack*. Elegant opening moves on large plates quickly turn to insecure crimps and a tenuous mantel. A cool head will help for quickly deciphering the intricate sequence in this race-against-the-clock scenario. Exploit the weaknesses on the clean face as you enjoy this outstanding technical route.

55 ft. 6 bolts. Chris Miller, Chuck Scott, Sept. 1999.

⑮ Bass Crack 5.10b ★

Get your feet wet on this dirty crack system that shares anchors with *Trouser Trout*.

55 ft. Gear to 4". Rob Stauder, July 1997.

Variation 5.9: Avoid the hand crack start and traverse left across a ledge instead.

⑯ Catch and Release 5.11a ★★

Challenging climbing on a clean corner, liebacking to a wily roof problem. Bumble through the middle section and tackle the final slab guarding the anchors shared with *Crappie Corner*. If you want to eek out a bit of extra climbing, a grungy 5.10 start below takes gear to 3".

45 ft. 5 bolts. Brad Singer, Rob Stauder, July 1997.

Big-Mouth Fever

Fisherman's Buttress North Face

⑰ Crappie Corner 5.10a ★★★

Contort your body through an awkward and funky start. Quickly transition across the blunt corner to good holds and end with a healthy dose of slab.

45 ft. 5 bolts. Rob Stauder, Brad Singer, July 1997.

Fisherman's Buttress West Face

18 Power Bait 5.10d ★★

Strenuous liebacking ends all too quickly with a transition to a juggy crack and low-angle climbing. A strong bite in the beginning, but won't fight to the finish. Shares the last bolt and anchors with *Crappie Corner*.

45 ft. 5 bolts. FA: (TR) Brad Singer, Rob Stauder, July 1997; FL: Chris Miller, Aug. 2000.

19 Check Your Fly 5.12a ★★

Follow *Power Bait* for its first 3 bolts to a ledge. Place an extendable on the 3rd bolt, then fight and flail through increasingly difficult moves on small nuggets. Definitely full-on.

50 ft. 6 bolts. Chris Miller, May 2001.

20 Piece of Carp 5.7 ★

The obvious left-slanting crack system with a crux bulge in the middle. Shares anchors with *Crappie Corner*.

40 ft. Gear to 4". Unknown.

21 Rapala 5.10c ★★

Cast off on plates to an early crux at the overlap. Peel off the wall here and your partner will have to quickly reel in slack. Friction through insecure moves as the holds diminish, culminating with a heart-pumping mantel up high.

45 ft. 5 bolts. Brad Singer, July 1997.

There is gully between routes #21 and #22 allowing access to the top of the formation.

22 Bait and Switch 5.10d ★★

Located uphill on the short wall behind a large pine tree. TR from anchors on *Stanley-Slip Bobber*, climbing the flared hand crack 3 feet left of the bolt line.

35 ft. Chris Miller, June 2000.

23 Stanley-Slip Bobber 5.11a ★★

Great fun down low on plates diminishes as a savage crimpy crux is met at the top with tree branches encroaching.

35 ft. 4 bolts. Brad Singer, Travis McElvany, Aug. 1998.

24 Fish Face 5.11a ★★

Another fun climb a little too intimate with the nearby tree. Set up on *Trolling For Tuna's* anchors, utilizing the sidepulls and jugs whenever possible. Tougher than it looks!

30 ft. Chris Miller, July 2000.

25 Trolling For Tuna 5.8 ★

Short and sweet. Vertical face with huecos left of the *Professor Merten's* chimney.

30 ft. 3 bolts. Brad Singer, David LePere, John Cardmon, Oct. 1999.

26 Professor Merten's 5.5 ★

Wriggle up this short chimney until it pinches off, then cut left to shared anchors atop *Trolling For Tuna*.

30 ft. Gear to 4". Unknown.

Shehdad Khundmiri on *Big-Mouth Fever*, 5.11d, page 163. ◘ Brandon Copp

CASTLE ROCK

Castle Rock is a massive landmark formation with sheer walls over 100 feet tall. In addition to being an excellent climbing destination, this Big Bear gem is one of the most popular hiking locations in this part of the mountains, so don't expect solitude. The forest surrounding the walls provides pleasant shade, while the unobscured summit affords spectacular views of the lake and surrounding area. There is evidence of climbing at the Castle Rock area from the 1970s, '80s, and before, but much of that activity was never recorded. The information presented here includes the first known ascents (FKA). If you have a correction, please contact the author.

20 min

Castle Rock features a plethora of tall lines stacked in close proximity. There are routes here for every discipline over a wide range of grades, making this a great place not only to test your strengths, but also to practice and become competent at styles of climbing that may be out of your comfort zone. Face climbs, thin cracks, slab, offwidth, monster plates, tiny crimps — you name it, Castle Rock's got it! The east-facing slab is home to half a dozen easier sport lines, while the tall south face houses the harder sport climbs. Beginner-to-intermediate trad climbs are concentrated in between, with a few tougher traditional climbs scattered about. Recommended routes include the always-enjoyable mixed route *Knightline* (5.10a), the classic *Castle Crack* (5.10c), the sporty testpiece line of *The Roofs* (5.10d), and the demanding *King of the Castle* (5.12a).

It is best to **bring a 70m rope to this crag**. A few of the routes require a doubled 70m to descend and others are definitely 60m rope-stretchers. Be extremely cautious when lowering and tie knots in both ends of the rope when rappelling.

Approach: From the dam, drive 1.2 miles east on Highway 18 past the Castle Rock sign located on a hairpin turn. Park in the pullout on the left located a bit past the trailhead. The steep, 1-mile uphill trail is well traveled, marked sporadically with brown trail signs, and fairly well maintained. It does spiderweb with many additional spurs, especially toward the top, so keep your eyes peeled for trail markers. Just before the summit, the trail will pass directly under the main wall, arriving near route #20. **[GPS: 34.23123, -116.96145]**

---

1 Cryptology 5.10b ★★

Hike a bit farther up the trail and traverse out to a big ledge to start — don't begin in the slot by *Cheops*. Step across the chasm and pull onto the wall. Pleasant features and good friction characterize this quality line.

50 ft. 6 bolts. Craig Britton, Chris Miller, Sept. 2011.

2 The Great Steps of Cheops 5.8 ★★

Begin in the slot on the left side of the wall and locate a left-slanting crack. A low crux leads to a juggy vertical crack. Finish straight up when the crack ends.

90 ft. Gear to 3". Unknown.

Variation 5.6: Cut left along the crack at the end to independent anchors instead of climbing straight up.

3 The Sphynx 5.6 ★★

Just left of *Ball and Chain* is a thin finger/hand crack that leads to a large gully. Stem the wide crack that weaves up the heavily featured face past a small overhang. Shares anchors with *Ball and Chain*.

85 ft. Gear to 4". Unknown.

4 Ball and Chain 5.9+ ★★★

Stellar plate-pulling that plunders the giant features on the southwest corner. Above the 5th bolt, the jugs thin out, making for a spicy and heady finish.

85 ft. 6 bolts. Gary Henning, Brent Webster, 1997.

5 The Turret 5.8 ★★★

The steep and intimidating crack left of the detached block near the southwest corner of the formation. Technical jamming through the low crux leads past a small roof. Great pro and good rest stances abound throughout, making this a recommended route for the area. Shares the last bolt and anchors with *Holy Fingers*.

90 ft. Gear to 4", 1 bolt. Unknown.

6 Holy Fingers 5.11b ★★★

An engaging and sequential route on quality rock. Pass 2 bolts on the detached block, then transition onto a steep blank face that's anything but trivial.

95 ft. 9 bolts. Brent Webster, Gary Henning, 1997.

Castle Rock Left

approach #1

variation

---

7 Hammock Boys 5.11d ★★

Claw up the blunt arête left of the chimney. For the grade, avoid the chimney and opt for the tiny friable flakes.
70 ft. 8 bolts. Gary Henning, Brent Webster, 1997.

8 Hammock Boys Left 5.11d ★★

This challenging alternate finish makes for a less contrived route, eliminating the temptation of the chimney. Follow the previous route for the first 5 bolts, then cut left at the bush. Make use of the sparse edges while angling left to the chains. Shares the last bolt and anchors with *Holy Fingers*.
90 ft. 11 bolts. Gary Henning, Brent Webster, 1997.

*Routes 9-14 are 60m rope-stretchers. You **WILL NOT** make it all of the way down to the base, and will have to stop at the ledge and scramble down. Tie knots in both ends of your rope! Routes 15-16 **REQUIRE a 70m rope** to descend.*

9 Pigeon Wings 5.8+ ★★

The wide chimney that splits the south face of the formation. Squeeze in your body and jam, stem, and pigeon-wing to the top. Try not to get covered in guano. Gear belay or cut over to anchors atop *The Roofs* or *Hammock Boys*.
100 ft. Gear to 6". Unknown.

10 The Roofs 5.10d ★★★★

Testpiece. You can probably guess what to expect on this endurance route. Fire past 3 bolts, then launch into the series of roofs, watching your forearms swell as you take on these monsters. Slay the powerful sequences and cruise to the top. A formidable challenge for any noble rock warrior.
100 ft. 9 bolts. Brent Webster, Gary Henning, 1997.

11 Castle Crack 5.10c ★★★★

This outstanding crack line is a classic, with plenty of jams and excellent features throughout its long length. Wander up the finger crack to a small alcove. Head right and slot hands into this baby. Elegant climbing with splendid views of the lake below reward your efforts. Best to cut left and share anchors with *The Roofs*.
100 ft. Gear to 3". Unknown

12 Castle Crack Left 5.10d ★★★

Noteworthy variation that cuts out left down low. Charge up a seam and plates on the face to the top. Share anchors with *The Roofs*.
100 ft. Gear to 2". Unknown.

The Roofs

13 The Grappling Hooks 5.11a ★★★

Start up the striking, blank dihedral with 3 old, closely spaced bolts (originally used for aid). Stem up the dihedral and exit left to join *Castle Crack*. Do you have what it takes to lead it?

100 ft. 3 bolts, RPs, thin gear to 2".

FA: Unknown, FFA: Eoghan Kyne, Nov. 2019.

Variation 5.11c: Instead of exiting left to *Castle Crack*, traverse right and finish on *Kremlin Wall*.

95 ft. 8 bolts. *Aiden Maguire, 1990.*

14 Kremlin Wall 5.11d ★★

Ascend the tall, blank face on razor-sharp crimps that'll split your tips. Extremely thin features down low, better incuts in the middle, then good features toward the top. Shares anchors with *King of the Castle*.

95 ft. 10 bolts. Unknown.

15 King of the Castle 5.12a ★★★★

None shall pass! Decent features on the arête quickly dwindle, leading to desperate climbing on the blank middle portion of the route. Improvise by utilizing the seam out left to stick the grueling sequence. Long and demanding, this is one of the hardest lines on Castle Rock; redpoint it and you're definitely the king (or queen)!

95 ft. 11 bolts.

Sam Owings, Jack Marshall, Cecilia Hernandez, May 2014.

16 Knightline 5.10a ★★★★

Proud line showcasing exceptional climbing on splendid features. Don your best suit of armor and start off with good crack technique, placing pro on the way up to the first bolt. Gallop past bolts to arrive beneath the roof. A thrilling sequence here sets up a powerful gymnastic move to grab the ginormous flake that's just out of reach. Mount the gritty, rounded feature like a horse until you can get up and stand atop it. Ride off into the sunset.

105 ft. Gear to 2.5", 7 bolts. Brad Singer, Oct. 2001.

17 Waxed Candle 5.7 ★

Start as for *Knightline* and ooze up the left side of the fin. Melt into the chimney as you slide up underneath a wedged block. Shimmy up another chimney on the left wall above. Gear anchor, then rap from *Knightline*.

105 ft. Wide gear. Unknown.

Carolena Chang on *King of the Castle*, 5.12a, opposite. 📷 Stephen Lê

Knightline

The next routes — #18-24 — all end on a wide ledge with a single set of chain anchors. The upper face can be climbed at 5.7. To walk off from the ledge, climb through a notch on the right side and scramble up to the northwest corner of the formation. Descend via the hiking trail.

18 Taj 5.7 ★★

Stand atop the leaning boulder and saunter up a ramp. Engaging climbing on a pillar culminates in a slightly overhanging fist crack. Shared anchor on the ledge. *80 ft. Gear to 4". Unknown.*

Variation 5.7: Halfway up the climb, step right and follow the angling hand crack. Straight in jams on this slightly better and cleaner variant. *Gear to 2.5".*

19 Timeline 5.8 ★

Featured face climb between the cracks. Dance up to a shelf 3/4 of the way up. Take either the left-slanting or right-slanting crack to the shared anchor on the ledge. *80 ft. Unknown.*

20 The Murder Hole 5.7 ★

Find the wide chimney with a large, pointed chockstone sticking out of it. Climb over a pile of blocks and into a fist crack that wanders left of 2 pine trees. Squeeze through an offwidth section to the shared anchor on the ledge. *80 ft. Gear to 4". Unknown.*

Variation 5.9: Cut left from the first tree into a devious hand crack and finish on plates.

21 Round Table 5.6 ★★

Start as for *Murder Hole* but then sink solid jams into the clean hand crack to the right of the 2 pines. Shared anchor on the ledge. *80 ft. Gear to 3". Unknown.*

22 Crocs in the Moat 5.9 ★

An easy romp on big features leads to a thin, arching crack. Somewhat contrived upper plated section. Shared anchor on the ledge. *80 ft. Unknown.*

23 The Drawbridge 5.9 ★★

Follow a wavy wide crack to a shelf, then tackle the right arête of the well-featured upper headwall. Shared anchor on the ledge. *80 ft. Unknown.*

24 Chainmail 5.6 ★★

A little bit of everything on this enjoyable lead. Pop over lower tiers into a nook. Lean out onto fantastic face holds and head up the steep terrain. Chimney under the massive triangular block to end on the ledge with the shared anchor. *80 ft. Gear to 4". Unknown.*

Derek Volcan on *Knightline*, 5.10a, page 168.

📷 Brandon Copp

25 Crossbow 5.8 ★★★
The left-facing dihedral formed by the west face of Black Tower Buttress. Quality stemming in the corner whilst advancing up the hand/fist crack. A very enjoyable little climb that uses the shared anchor atop Black Tower Buttress.
60 ft. Gear to 5". *Unknown.*

26 Lower Black Tower 5.10a ★★
Really good climbing on thin holds. Lieback or fingerlock a seam, followed by a mantel to gain sidepulls near the first bolt. Traverse left on good hands and virtually no feet to the crack that snakes up the wall. After the ledge, finagle through reachy moves at the large lip and claim victory at the shared anchor atop Black Tower Buttress.
Note: The Leeper hangers on this route were recalled by the manufacturer decades ago, and the 1/4" bolts are just as unreliable! Hopefully, these will soon be replaced so that this climb can be enjoyed without peril!
60 ft. Thin gear to 2", 2 bolts. *Unknown.*

Black Tower Buttress

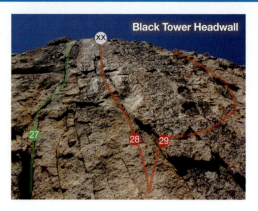

Black Tower Headwall

Routes #27-29 start from the top of Black Tower. Reach them via routes #25, #26, or #30-33.

27 Black Tower Headwall Left 5.10c ★★
Traverse left from the belay station to a short crack. Desperate climbing on delicate features leads to a shared anchor with *Headwall Center*. Loose anchor as of this writing.
30 ft. *Brad Singer.*

28 Black Tower Headwall Center 5.10b ★★★
Sick climbing on a thin splitter finger crack. Great positioning and a magnificent view of the lake below make this a memorable climb. Loose anchor as of this writing.
30 ft. Gear to 1.5", 1 bolt. *Brad Singer.*

29 Black Tower Headwall Right 5.10c ★★
An airy traverse right past 2 bolts provides passage to a seam. Dig through your bag of tricks to find a way up this difficult section, finishing on bigger holds near the shared anchor with *Headwall Center*. Loose anchor as of press time.
30 ft. Gear to 1.5", 2 bolts. *FFA: Steve Kravchuck.*

30 Damsel in Distress 5.9 ★
Interesting mixed line on the corner of the buttress in a shaded area. The steep initial face has a 2nd bolt that's out of reach for most climbers. Place a 1" cam behind the flake, then blast up onto the super-duper-easy ramp (a 20-foot run with more optional gear placements) that gives way to an exhilarating bulge sequence. Shares last 2 bolts and anchors with *EAYSBF*.
75 ft. 6 bolts, 1" piece, optional gear to 3". *Joan Bertini.*

31 Easy as Your Sister's Best Friend 5.5 ★★
Climb atop the detached rock at the base, then hike the low-angle slab. Head right to the 3rd bolt and smile as you squeeze the big features. Trust the rubber on the final slab. Shared anchor atop Black Tower Buttress. A fun romp.
70 ft. 7 bolts. *Brad Singer, David LePere, Oct. 2001.*

Castle Rock Right

32 **Trebuchet** 5.7 ★

Conquer the initial crack, moving onto the rounded arête. Like the rest of the climbs here, a slab guards the shared anchor atop Black Tower Buttress.

70 ft. Gear to 3". Brad Singer.

33 **Black Tower Crack** 5.7 ★★★

Excellent, secure crack climbing! Start up a vertical double crack system in the corner. Friction through enjoyable slab, plugging gear in the hand crack out right. A tricky section with slick feet but good hand jugs provides an exhilarating finish. Shared anchor atop Black Tower Buttress.

70 ft. Gear to 3". Unknown.

34 **Easy as Your Best Friend's Sister** 5.10b ★

Take the rightmost of the twin cracks all the way to a nice ledge. Get on top and keep going up the crack on the right side of the arête. Make a short traverse right to the anchor.

70 ft. Gear to 3". David LePere, Ryan Crochiere.

35 **Storm the Castle** 5.12b ★★

Begin on the narrow face between the arête and the offwidth. Grueling moves on a thin crack that arches left and ends in a pocket. Technical edging and a few awkward sidepulls lead up the stout face. Shares anchors with *EAYBFS*.

70 ft. Eric Odenthal, June 2005.

36 **Hard as Your Husband** 5.10c ★★

An offwidth on the shadier black face, identified by a small pine partway up the climb. Move right past the pine and continue up a finger crack that's slightly wider than desired. Traverse left to the shared anchors of *EAYBFS*.

70 ft. Gear to 5". David LePere, Brad Singer.

37 **Zorro** 5.10a ★

Challenging start, jamming and liebacking the crack with small edges providing tricky feet. Stand high to reach the horizontal, then skirt the roof to the right. Chossy and dirty above. Belay from a tree.

70 ft. Gear to 2". David LePere, Ryan Crochiere.

38 **Epee** 5.7

Start up a chimney and meander up indistinct thin cracks. Dirty and gritty. Belay from a tree.

50 ft. Gear to 2". David LePere, Ryan Crochiere.

39 **Pantshitter Splitter** V0

Not pictured. If you are at the summit of Castle Rock, you will undoubtably notice a short, beautiful crack on a boulder just down and west. This is an almost irresistable boulder problem, but disappointingly low-angle.

CAMELOT CRAG

A small, west-facing crag that's home to the great little splitter crack *Camelot*. The easiest way off the top is to the north (climber's left), scrambling over boulders. There are no anchors on top of the formation; you will need to belay in an awkward wide crack.

 25 min

Approach: From the climbs on Castle Rock, continue hiking around to the west side of the formation where the top of Castle Rock can be accessed. Look southwest for the wooden trail sign on a tree that says "Castle Rock" to locate this formation sitting alongside the hiking trail. **[GPS: 34.23116, -116.96204]**

1 Camelot 5.8 ★★
Great jams in this short hand crack that'll leave you wanting more! Continuous for 20 feet, then move through a few scoops. Gear belay.
30 ft. Gear to 4". Unknown.

2 Percival's Face 5.10c ★
While you're here, best set up a line on this smooth face route right of *Camelot*. Thin and balancy past a few horizontals, as you make use of the nubbins on the wall. End with a 5-foot crack section. Gear anchor.
30 ft. Gear to 4" for anchor. Unknown.

Camelot

CASTLE ROCK SLABS

Located about 100 yards northwest of the Castle Rock crag. The climbs listed are all on the more vertical west face, but the east face of these slabs is a great place to set up climbs in the 5.0-5.6 range for kids or beginners. Easy access to the top of the rock, with numerous locations for setting gear anchors. A few small trees have taken root atop this formation.

30 min

Approach: From the wooden sign near Camelot Crag, follow a faint trail downhill, heading northwest. Cross the seasonal stream as the slabs come into view. Hike around the formation to the left, traveling slightly uphill to reach the west face and the majority of the climbs. 5 minutes from the Castle Rock area. **[GPS: 34.23201, -116.96297]**

3 I Like It Dirty but You Like It Clean 5.9 ★
Scramble up a slot to reach the far north arête, or approach from the east face. Ascend a boulder to start, then transition into a lieback on the cruxy arête. Pop over onto the face and balance up the black, lichen-covered corner.
35 ft. Unknown.

4 Castle Doctrine 5.8 ★
A short stemming problem. Scramble onto the ledge or start from the crack below (5.10a) and pass the first bolt of *Big Bear Roots*. Stem up the flared corner above using the widening hand crack. Shared anchor with *Wing Span*.
35 ft. Gear to 4". Unknown.

5 Big Bear Roots 5.10a ★★
Slide up the thin slanting crack and make the difficult transition onto the white arête of this prominent detached block. Interesting movement but a bit scary and could have been better bolted. Shared anchor with *Wing Span*.
35 ft. 3 bolts. Bruce Rubio, Chris England, April 2008.

6 Wing Span 5.10d ★★
Smear through a dish onto slick slab, with a nice big flake above the 3rd bolt.
35 ft. 3 bolts. Chris England, Bruce Rubio, April 2008.

7 Easy Castle Crack 5.7
Short and uninspiring crack on the right side of the wall next to the gully. Shared anchor with *Wing Span*.
25 ft. Gear to 2". Andy Bussell, Eddie Page, Bruce Rubio, May 2008.

Castle Rock Slabs West Face

8 Conklin Face 5.12a ★★

Put your skills to the test on this short yet frustrating line. Scramble up the gully to reach the upper vertical wall. Tiptoe up this steep-slab face on lots of little crystals.

35 ft. 4 bolts. Bruce Rubio, Chris England, Eddie Page, May 2008.

CRACKED TOWER

As with Castle Rock Slabs, this wall is rarely visited due to its proximity to Castle Rock with its long, quality routes, yet both of these smaller crags boast aesthetic lines.

PM 30 min

Approach: Located 150 feet due north and slightly downhill from the west face of Castle Rock Slabs.
[GPS: 34.23239, -116.96303]

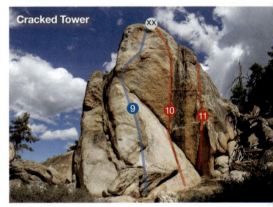

Cracked Tower

9 Unas, Slayer of the Gods 5.11a ★★

Despite appearances, this bouldery route is quite enjoyable. Step up to the white wall and punch up the edges and sparse plates. Slay the crux sequence on a slopey rail while trending right.

35 ft. 4 bolts. Andy Bussell, Eddie Page, May 2008.

10 What's Best in Life? 5.12a ★★

Rad overhanging finger crack on the attractive orange face left of a large black streak. Typically done as a TR due to the finicky placements, but a sweet project if you're looking for something tough. Shares anchors with *Unas*.

35 ft. Thin gear. Richard Cilley, 2010.

11 Kraken Takes Pawn 5.8 ★★

Not quite as aesthetic as the others but a fine line nonetheless. Lieback/fist jam the wide crack and gear belay in cracks at the top.

30 ft. Gear to 4". Eddie Page, Chris England, Bruce Rubio, May 2008.

BLUFF LAKE AREA

Angela Hwangpo, *Vodka and Tonic,*
5.9, Siberia Creek, page 202.
📷 Jacqueline Copp

BLUFF LAKE **AREA**

Home to unique wildlife, mature forests of lodgepole pines, and numerous species of wildflowers and native grasses, the Bluff Lake Reserve is a beautiful 20-acre alpine lake and meadow. Bluff Lake has a rich history as one of the turn-of-the-century stage stops on the road to Big Bear Lake. A hiker's loop trail passes through the meadows and serene forest, with a stop at a log cabin on its northeast shore, a reminder of the area's storied past.

While Bluff Lake is a popular hiking destination, the vast collection of rock in the vicinity has established it as an excellent climbing region as well. While most formations have at least a few routes, there is still plenty of potential for development. Abundant boulders and small roadside crags are a staple of this area. In contrast, the rim of the plateau is host to some of the tallest climbable walls in the San Bernardino Mountains, with Arctic Temple and Siberia Creek Tower clocking in at roughly 125 feet apiece.

The Bluff Lake area has many obscure crags, yet even the biggest and the best are rarely visited. Siberia Creek Tower is on a well-established trail and easy to find, but many of the other walls require bushwhack adventures to reach. Plan to spend additional time on the approach hikes if it's your first time visiting any of the crags on the plateau.

The majority of this region's climbs are traditional gear routes, the largest collection of which can be found at Black Bluff. The grading may seem a bit stiffer in the Bluff Lake area than at Holcomb or

CLIMBING AREA	ELEVATION	HIKE	ROUTES	GRADE RANGE	CRAGS
MILL CREEK TOWERS *Good warm-up stop* page 180	7550 ft.	5 min	8	≤.5 .6 .7 .8 .9 .10 .11 .12	Sleepy Bear Tower, Nightmare Tower
KIDD CREEK ROAD *Roadside routes* page 183	7600 ft.	1-10 min	22	≤.5 .6 .7 .8 .9 .10 .11 .12	Wall of Steel, Mercury, Care Bear, Terminator, Flatulence, OD, Forward Into Battle, Rapunzel's Tower
ARCTIC TEMPLE *Long trad routes* page 186	7400 ft.	40 min	6	≤.5 .6 .7 .8 .9 .10 .11 .12	
CASTLE GREY SKULL *Neglected and wild* page 188	7450 ft.	10 min	10	≤.5 .6 .7 .8 .9 .10 .11 .12	
BLACK BLUFF AREA *Stellar collection of cracks* page 190	7600 ft.	25-35 min	31	≤.5 .6 .7 .8 .9 .10 .11 .12	Big Juan, Black Bluff, Bing Bing, East Towers, Short Crag, Southside
SIBERIA CREEK AREA *Old-school cracks* page 200	7450 ft. 7650 ft.	35-45 min	23	≤.5 .6 .7 .8 .9 .10 .11 .12	Siberia Creek Tower, Upper Siberia, Triple Breasted Woman, Cape Thorn

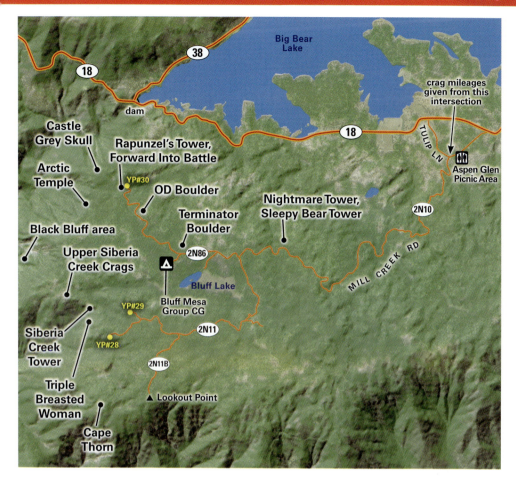

the north shore crags. The rock quality runs the gamut, from bomber quartz monzonite and fine-grained granite to crispy and lichen-covered. Seek out this area for its peaceful solitude and try your hand at a few of the striking, hard crack lines.

In terms of camping, there are 3 yellow-post campsites in the area, offering free places to pitch your tent or park your van close to the crags. If you want more amenities, the Bluff Mesa Group Campground can accommodate groups of up to 40 people and has a vault toilet. While the Aspen Glen Picnic Area is for day use only, there is also a toilet there for a pit stop.

Approach: From the stoplight at the dam, drive 2.9 miles on Highway 18 along the south shore of Big Bear Lake, then turn right onto Tulip Lane. Drive 0.4 miles and turn right onto Mill Creek Road (2N10). **All of the directions for the crags are given from this junction** of Tulip Lane and Mill Creek Road at Oak Knoll Lodge.

If coming from the town of Big Bear, drive west along Highway 18. Turn left onto Mill Creek Road just after the Alpine Slide. Drive 0.4 miles on Mill Creek Road, passing the Aspen Glen Picnic Area, and turn left at the Oak Knoll Lodge onto Mill Creek Road (2N10).

Please note that Mill Creek Road is typically closed and gated in winter, potentially from November 1 to May 1. The many Forest Service roads in this area are also subject to winter closure. Contact the Forest Service for seasonal road information.

Sleepy Bear and Nightmare Towers

Sleepy Bear

Nightmare

SLEEPY BEAR TOWER

This squatty tower sits in the shade of a tree, and has two routes on its east face. A Class-4 climb has been done as well, ascending the ledges on the northeast corner of the wall. Sleepy Bear Tower and its sister formation Nightmare Tower are not destination spots on their own, but a good stop on the way to somewhere else.

AM 5 min

Approach: Drive 3.0 miles on Mill Creek Road (2N10) to a bend in the road with a small parking pullout on the right. Walk briefly downhill from the wooded parking area and cross the Skyline multi-use trail (1E12) that parallels the road. Hike up a small rise, with the two towers in view. **[GPS: 34.22474, -116.95444]**

1 **Breakfast Burrito** 5.10d ★★

Protect the initial moves with gear as you wedge feet into a vertical seam. Thin edges give way to a decent rail and a horizontal. Follow the prow past a bolt, moving right to the top. *40 ft. Gear to 2", 2 bolts.* Pat Brennan, Mark Goldsmith, Aug. 1999.

2 **Eyes Wide Shut** 5.11b ★★

Begin your ascent of this head-scratcher in the middle of the east face. Solve the crux sequence at the 2nd bolt, then mount a series of ledges as you gallop through the upper section. Shared anchor with *Breakfast Burrito*. *40 ft. 4 bolts.* Chris Miller, June 2000.

NIGHTMARE TOWER

A thin formation with a handful of routes in a secluded setting. The drive from town is minimal and so is the approach, yet even so you're almost guaranteed to have the place to yourself. There is one set of chain anchors shared among all of the climbs on both the east and west faces.

5 min

Approach: Approach as for Sleepy Bear Tower. Nightmare Tower lies 100 feet to the east. **[GPS: 34.22475, -116.95396]**

XX

1   2

Sleepy Bear Tower

Nightmare Tower West Face

The first 4 routes are found on the west face, with the last 2 around on the east side.

③ Wrenched 5.9

Muscle through the steep face past sloped ledges. Once a fully equipped sport climb, but the lower bolts were chopped. Toprope it using an upper bolt as a directional.
30 ft. 4 bolts (currently 1).
Brad Singer, Eric Odenthal, John Cardmon, May 2005.

④ Tri-Tip and Corn 5.10a ★

This meal starts in the crack right of the bolt line, changes courses by moving left across a horizontal at mid-height, and finishes with a side of wide crack. Originally led on gear, this line has been retro-bolted.
35 ft. 4 bolts. Pat Brennan, Mark Goldsmith, Aug. 1999.

⑤ Cornbread 5.9 ★

An easier direct finish to the previous line that continues up the narrowing crack to a ledge. A technical mix of face and crack techniques, this too was originally led on gear.
35 ft. 4 bolts. Kenn Kenaga, Eric Tipton, Steve Gooden, Matt Reisling, Aug. 1999.

⑥ Dreamweaver 5.8+

The crack route underneath a tree. Slink up to the tree and weave left along a ramp.
35 ft. Gear to 3". Bob Cable, Art Bertolina, Julia Cronk, Jim Velie, Eric Odenthal, Kenn Kenaga, June 2000.

⑦ Stoneware 5.7 ★

Follow the southern prow, climbing large features past a bolt to a ledge with a tree. Transition to the steeper headwall where the edges become more sparse. Optional gear placements throughout.
35 ft. 2 bolts, optional gear to 2".
Mark Goldsmith, Pat Brennan, Aug. 1999.

⑧ Brownies and Beer 5.8 ★★

Leave the ground and ooze up the right-angling crack to a distinct gray knob. Catapult over the roof and blast up the face. Quite enjoyable.
35 ft. Gear to 2", 2 bolts. Pat Brennan, Kenn Kenaga, Sept. 1999.

Nightmare Tower East Face

WALL OF STEEL

A short, squatty formation located near the northeast corner of Bluff Lake, in the vicinity of an 1890s log cabin. A single set of bolted anchors (without rap rings) services all the topropes.

Approach: Drive 3.6 miles on Mill Creek Road (2N10) to the intersection with 2N86. Turn right and follow 2N86 for 0.3 miles. Turn left onto a small side road that ends in 0.1 miles at a gate. Park at the turnaround circle or on the side of the road. This boulder sits 100 feet to the west. **[GPS: 34.22231, -116.96729]**

1 Ground 5.9 ★
A quick warm-up that cruises the blunt southwest arête on horizontals and plated features.
20 ft. Craig Pearson, Julie Pearson, Dean Goolsby, 1990s.

2 Incisor 5.11d ★
Ignore the cheater stone and suss out the beta for the tough start. Explode through the burly sequence on slopers, bypass the mossy patch, and mantel above.
20 ft. Craig Pearson, Julie Pearson, Dean Goolsby, 1990s.

3 Brainstorm 5.10d ★
Use a positive, right-facing flake to get established on the wall, where it leaves you scratching your head with nothing but steep face above. Power through the finish.
20 ft. Craig Pearson, Julie Pearson, Dean Goolsby, 1990s.

Wall of Steel

Mercury Boulder

MERCURY BOULDER

A 10-foot tall boulder with five problems ranging from V0-V2, initially discovered and documented by Craig Pearson, Julie Pearson, and Dean Goolsby. A worthwhile stop in conjunction with a visit to Wall of Steel.

Approach: Follow the driving directions for Wall of Steel. Mercury Boulder is on the right (west) side of the road, 200 feet before reaching the gate.
[GPS: 34.22269, -116.96692]

CARE BEAR TOWER

A small roadside crag with a few mellow cracks on its southeast side. On the highest point of the wall, there is a bolt with a beefy quicklink that can be accessed for rappelling. No first-ascent information is known.

Approach: Drive 3.6 miles on Mill Creek Road (2N10) to the intersection with 2N86. Turn right and follow 2N86 for 0.3 miles. The tower will be visible through the trees on the right side of the road. Park and walk the 100 yards to its base.
[GPS: 34.22435, -116.96615]

4 The Care Bear Stare 5.9 ★★
This pumpy finger-to-hands crack is the most exhilarating line here. Make a committing move off a ledge on good jams and keep it together until you grasp the horns near the top. Bolted anchor without rap rings.
25 ft. Gear to 2.5". Unknown.

Care Bear Tower

Terminator Boulder

❺ I Don't Care, I'm Just a Bear 5.5 ★
Step over a small tree and slide into this nice, gear-eating crack with plentiful face holds to end in a notch between 2 large blocks. Bolted anchor without rap rings.
25 ft. Gear to 2". Unknown.

❻ The Land Without Feelings 5.6 ★
Scale the right-facing corner until you can move left across a ledge into a widening chimney. Flakes inside the chimney make for great footholds as you maneuver up past a horizontal gear placement.
25 ft. Gear to 1", optional wide piece. Unknown.

TERMINATOR BOULDER

Enjoy excellent tough problems on this stout boulder that has a sizable roof on its west face. Bring a rope to set up these overhanging lines as short topropes or swap the gear for a crash pad and boulder them instead.

PM

3 min

Approach: Drive 3.6 miles on Mill Creek Road (2N10) to the intersection with 2N86. Turn right and follow 2N86 for 0.5 miles. Park and hike 150 yards directly north, passing another sizable boulder sitting just 100 feet from the road on the way to Terminator Boulder.
[GPS: 34.22456, -116.96993]

❼ Terminator 5.11d ★★
Blast up the overhanging north face on thin horizontal seams. Intimidating. V3 if bouldered.
15 ft. Craig Pearson, Julie Pearson, Dean Goolsby, 1990s.

❽ Hasta La Vista 5.12a ★★
Power through the steep arête underneath the overhang. Tighten your core and stick the compression moves as you move along the sloped corner to the top. V4 if bouldered.
15 ft. Craig Pearson, Julie Pearson, Dean Goolsby, 1990s.

❾ I'll Be Back V3 ★★
Boulder the slick, light-colored face under the right side of the overhang. Keep it together as you reach high to a horizontal and pull through the roof.
Craig Pearson, Julie Pearson, Dean Goolsby, 1990s.

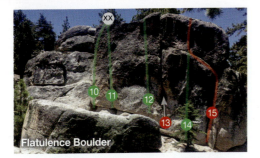

Flatulence Boulder

FLATULENCE BOULDER

This crag offers a few short routes in an out-of-the-way setting. To  reach the top, scramble up the gully behind the fin of rock with *Pull My Finger* and *King of the Blue Flame*. There are two bolts without rap rings on the fin that serve as anchors for these first two routes.

Approach: Drive 3.6 miles on Mill Creek Road (2N10) to the intersection with 2N86. Turn right and follow 2N86 for 1.0 mile to a locked gate on the left. Park and hike the closed road for 0.4 miles. The boulder is on the right side of the road. **[GPS: 34.22620, -116.98271]**

⑩ Pull My Finger 5.10b ★
Ascend the good arête on the left side of the wall.
30 ft. Craig Pearson, Julie Pearson, Dean Goolsby, 1990s.

⑪ King of the Blue Flame 5.11a ★
Start near a well-featured seam and brave the black slab.
30 ft. Craig Pearson, Julie Pearson, Dean Goolsby, 1990s.

⑫ Lofting Air Biscuit 5.10c
A technical climb on the lichen-covered face.
30 ft. Gear to 2" for anchor.
Craig Pearson, Julie Pearson, Dean Goolsby, 1990s.

⑬ Airy Bunger 5.9+ ★★
Surge past the uniquely shaped alcove, then cruise the upper portion of the crack to a gear belay.
30 ft. Gear to 2". Craig Pearson, Julie Pearson, Dean Goolsby, 1990s.

⑭ Stinky Boy 5.10b ★
Exploit a vertical rail and smear up the face behind a small pine tree. Finish in the same vertical seam as *Gas-X*.
30 ft. Gear to 2" for anchor.
Craig Pearson, Julie Pearson, Dean Goolsby, 1990s.

⑮ Gas-X 5.10a
A dirty crack on the right end of the face. Move left at the horizontal and end with a vertical seam. Tricky gear anchor.
30 ft. Gear to 3". Craig Pearson, Julie Pearson, Dean Goolsby, 1990s.

OD BOULDER

The routes on this large boulder were likely climbed years ago, but no first ascent records were kept. It is possible to bring crash pads and boulder these pint-sized routes.

Approach: Drive 3.6 miles on Mill Creek Road (2N10) to the intersection with 2N86. Turn right and follow 2N86 for 1.2 miles. Pull off the right side of the road; the boulder will be visible. **[GPS: 34.22846, -116.97688]**

⑯ Take What You Get 5.8- ★
Gritty offwidth on the north face with a cruxy undercut start. Gear anchor with wide pieces or belay from a tree.
20 ft. Gear to 5". Unknown.

⑰ Rain Delay 5.5 ★
The west-face dihedral. Lieback a nice rail and make your way up good features. Anchor from a tree.
25 ft. Gear to 3". Unknown.

OD Boulder

Forward into Battle

FORWARD INTO BATTLE BOULDERS

Two independent boulders make up this mostly shaded formation. These routes are best done as an addendum to a day at Castle Grey Skull or Arctic Temple, especially if camping at the nearby yellow post campsite.

🌑 🚶 1 min

Approach: Drive 3.6 miles on Mill Creek Road (2N10) to the intersection with 2N86. Turn right and follow 2N86 for 1.6 miles until it dead-ends at Yellow Post Campsite #30 and park nearby. These two boulders are on the left side of the road, 150 feet south of the campsite. **[GPS: 34.23158, -116.98000]**

18 Final Conquest 5.11c ★★
An opening mantel gains thin flakes near the high first bolt. Grapple with steep patina for the powerful crux before the slab transition. You may find yourself backing off to rethink the sequence on this stout, old-school line!
45 ft. 2 bolts. Craig Pearson, Julie Pearson, Dean Goolsby, 1990s.

19 Forward Into Battle 5.10b ★★
Hook the large flake on the west face and catapult onto a ledge above it, then take in the blank white face above. Charge past a single bolt to the shared anchors atop *Final Conquest*. Bring cord to extend the anchor to the lip.
40 ft. Gear to 4", 1 bolt.
Craig Pearson, Julie Pearson, Dean Goolsby, 1990s.

20 False Prophet 5.10b
Reach high for a flared fingertips seam, making tenuous moves until the seam widens. The gear is fiddly at the low crux. Sling a boulder or gear anchor.
25 ft. Thin gear to 1".
Craig Pearson, Julie Pearson, Dean Goolsby, 1990s.

Rapunzel's Tower

21 Dihedral 5.10b
Climb the slick, left-facing dihedral covered in lichen as it bypasses 2 square roofs. Sling a boulder or gear anchor.
25 ft. Craig Pearson, Julie Pearson, Dean Goolsby, 1990s.

RAPUNZEL'S TOWER

An easy line to hit on the way to or from Arctic Temple. Just off the trail is this 30-foot tower, distinguished by a flat rock that caps the formation and forms a roof over the single route.

 🚶 3 min

Approach: Follow the driving directions for Forward Into Battle Boulders. From Yellow Post Campsite #30, walk past the locked gate and turn left to follow an old road. Hike the road 150 yards and the formation will be on the left. **[GPS: 34.23103, -116.98073]**

22 Storming the Castle 5.7 ★
Stem and lieback the open book corner to a stance underneath the roof. Leave the crack and dihedral behind, transitioning to the right face as you maneuver past the roof. Gear belay and walk off. A bit dirty but enjoyable.
30 ft. Gear to 2". Brandon Copp, Angela Hwangpo, Nov. 2018.

ARCTIC TEMPLE

This striking 130-foot shield of fine-grained granite is home to many great lines, and some of the longest routes in the San Bernardino Mountains. The northwest-facing wall lies just below the rim of the plateau and can be seen from the Lakeview Point Scenic Overlook on Highway 18, gleaming in the afternoon sun. The exposure is phenomenal, as the ground drops steeply all the way down to Bear Creek 1500 feet below. The climbs are magnificent, but the rock can be somewhat grainy from lack of traffic. Build a gear anchor with long cords for all climbs, as there are no bolted anchors atop this formation. A full trad rack with doubles is recommended.

PM · 40 min

ARCTIC TEMPLE APPROACH

Approach: Drive 3.6 miles on Mill Creek Road (2N10) to the intersection with 2N86. Turn right and follow 2N86 for 1.6 miles until it dead-ends at Yellow Post Campsite #30. Park near the campsite, being respectful of campers.

Walk past the closed gate and turn left to hike southwest along an old logging road for 0.3 miles. As the road begins to fade, continue straight ahead through the bushes and into a ditch. Hike the ditch for 1-2 minutes to a large cairn on the right. Pop out of the ditch on its right side and follow a thin, cairned trail through boulders and up a small hill. This will lead to a second ditch. Follow this ditch uphill and right, continuing southwest. After 5 minutes, this ditch will open up and become a larger creekbed. Hike through this creekbed over boulders and fallen logs for about 350 feet.

At this point, the entire hike has taken you generally southwest. As the creekbed begins to dwindle, head out of this creekbed (tricky to find the best exit point). Go west about 250 feet, across the plateau, and locate the descent gully marked with cairns. Make your way down the gully to the top/rear of the formation. **Note:** It is easy to get lost on the plateau; it is almost a right of passage. There are few landmarks, and an abundance of misleading cairns. Allow extra time!

It is possible to descend down the steep gullies on either side of Arctic Temple to the base of the climbs, but the right (north) side is best. However, most parties build an anchor and rap in. To do this, hike around the back of the formation and hug the north side of the wall. At the last fin of rock that is flanked by a tree, carefully scramble up to the top of the wall and build your anchor. Please note that the descent is 35m rappel — **a 70m rope is needed for a double-line rappel.** Tie knots at the ends of your rope! **[GPS: 34.22756, -116.98829]**

Arctic Temple

❶ Arctic Arête 5.10d ★★★

A spectacular, varied route. An insecure off-fingers crack provides a desperate crux right off the deck; 20 feet of wicked crack climbing ends at a ledge, where a bolted arête begins. Outstanding and exposed moves along the aesthetic arête lead to a roof. Extend the last bolt under the roof to reduce rope drag and run it out on easier terrain.

110 ft. Gear to 2", 7 bolts.

Kenn Kenaga, Eric Tipton, Pat Brennan, July 2000.

❷ Kaleidoscope 5.10c ★★★

A stellar right-leaning crack that begins from the platform on the wall's left side. The crack becomes progressively harder as it widens to offwidth. Dive into the wide section and push through to a ledge. Meander right, following chickenheads, then lieback a thin crack. The gear is good throughout the climb, although care is required to protect the flares.

110 ft. Gear to 5". Eric Tipton, Bob Cable, Kenn Kenaga, Pat Brennan, June 2000.

❸ Hoodoo Temple 5.10c ★★★

A tantalizing hand crack with a sketchy start. Coax yourself along a cruxy, thin, slanted crack. Hoot and holler when you reach the awesome hand crack that extends to a small tree. Take in your surroundings as you breeze up the final corner.

130 ft. Gear to 3" with extra thin pieces for the start.

Kenn Kenaga, Eric Tipton, Bob Cable, Pat Brennan, June 2000.

❹ Drunks in Tow 5.10b ★★

An alternate start and finish to *Hoodoo Temple*. Begin with the vertical section of *Land of the Midnight Sun* and continue straight up into the hand crack of *Hoodoo Temple*. Follow this to a ledge midway up the route. Cut left from here, moving into an interesting flaring crack. Save enough in the tank for a thin crux high on the wall!

130 ft. Gear to 3", with thin gear for the crux.

Kenn Kenaga, Eric Tipton, Pat Brennan, July 2000.

❺ Land of the Midnight Sun 5.10b ★★★

Begin by conquering a leaning off-hands crack. Muster the courage to chickenwing and strongman your way across the low traverse, cautious of the groundfall potential, with one foot inside the crack and the other dangling. If that wasn't challenging enough, a finger-crack crux appears in your face when you're tired and sweating. Dig deep, progressing ever closer to relief at the small tree. Finish as for *Hoodoo Temple*. An adventure through and through.

130 ft. Gear to 5". Eric Tipton, Kenn Kenaga, Pat Brennan, June 2000.

❻ Wild Turkey Arête 5.9 ★★

Another exciting route with a fierce start. Look for its lone bolt on the far right side of the wall. Place a piece to protect a potential tumble down the gully, then commit to the opening crux near the bolt. Ascend the arête and follow discontinuous but delightful cracks to the top.

110 ft. Gear to 3", 1 bolt.

Eric Tipton, Kenn Kenaga, Pat Brennan, June 2000.

Battle Cat

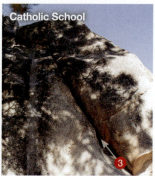

Catholic School

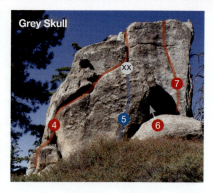

Grey Skull

CASTLE GREY SKULL

This neglected spot has the feel of a wild crag in a remote setting, yet requires only a minimal approach. Perched on the edge of the Bluff Mesa Plateau, it offers outstanding views of the lake, Highway 18, and the massive valley below. This square chunk of rock has routes on all four faces and, with the exception of *Grey Skull* (5.10c), a gear anchor is required for all climbs. A gully on the east face provides easy access to the top.

10 min

Approach: As for Arctic Temple, drive and park near Yellow Post Campsite #30. Hike straight past the locked gate on an old logging road, following it over a small hill and into a circular clearing (3-5 minutes). At this point, there are roads that branch in three directions. Continue straight, following the middle path up a small rise where it peters out. It's a bushwhack from here, so be prepared with long pants or suffer through the brambles. Cut across a small gully heading northwest to the crag.
[GPS: 34.23381, -116.98294]

❶ Battle Cat 5.9+ ★
The leftmost crack line. Its bread-and-butter is the upper finger-sized portion beside a roof. Sustained throughout.
40 ft. Gear to 3". Craig Pearson, Julie Pearson, Dean Goolsby, 1990s.

❷ Over the Band Gap 5.10a ★
Slip into a seam that becomes a corner as it approaches the small roof. Easier on the slab above. Could be led on gear.
40 ft. Jeff Botimer, June 2013.

❸ Catholic Grade School 5.10b ★
The obvious diagonal crack right of the water streak. Sew it up while working hands along the slant and smearing feet.
45 ft. Gear to 3". Craig Pearson, Julie Pearson, Dean Goolsby, 1990s.

❹ Retarded Arête 5.7
A silly route that starts on the southwest corner and climbs the left side of the flake with minimal pro before joining *Flairvoyant* for the final wide crack.
45 ft. Wide gear. Alan Bartlett, Brandt Allen, Laurel Colella, Aug. 2000.

❺ Grey Skull 5.10c ★
A short route on the detached slab that leads to bolted anchors without rap rings. It's best to bring a bit of wide gear and continue to the top of the formation via a 20-foot crack rather than downclimbing the chimney behind the flake.
25 ft. 2 bolts. Craig Pearson, Julie Pearson, Dean Goolsby, 1990s.

❻ Flairvoyant 5.6
A flared chimney behind the flake leads to a wide crack.
40 ft. Wide gear. Alan Bartlett (solo), Aug. 2000.

❼ He-Man Slab 5.10b ★★
A tough bout of slender edges is the first adversary encountered on this route. Fight past the lone bolt to gain a crack that provides minimal relief. Power past a horizontal and wrestle with the last bit of face to reach the top.
40 ft. Gear to 1.5", 1 bolt.
Craig Pearson, Julie Pearson, Dean Goolsby, 1990s.

❽ Skeletor 5.10d ★★
This invigorating line on the narrow east face is not to be missed. After an attention-grabbing start, comfortable flakes offer a moment's relief. Fight the pump as you punch up a seam and small edges. Plug a small cam underneath the overlap and thrash through the final face.
45 ft. Gear to 1.5", 2 bolts.
Craig Pearson, Julie Pearson, Dean Goolsby, 1990s.

Brad MacArthur on *Arctic Arête*, 5.10d,
Arctic Temple, page 187. ◘ Brandon Copp

Skeletor

to top of formation

8

Oxidation

9   10

9 Oxidation 5.10a

Build an anchor atop the main formation and throw your
rope over this thin fin of rock that's inundated with lichen.
Move from a ledge into an undercling before a set of long
reaches lead up the bright yellow wall.

25 ft. Jeff Botimer, June 2013.

10 Rust 5.7

Right of *Oxidation*, this follows red lichen to a notch.

20 ft. Sean Thomas, June 2013.

BLACK BLUFF

Perched on the rim of the plateau, this long, unbroken cliff line of fine-grained granite sits peacefully immersed in forested beauty. Its stellar collection of classic cracks makes this gorgeous wall the best traditional crag in the San Bernardinos. Home to continuous splitters, outstanding offwidths, thin seams, beautiful arêtes, and perfect corners, this wall has it all. Climbers of all abilities will find routes here to suit them. For the crack connoisseur of any level, *Aurora Borealis* (5.9) is a spectacular line that should not be missed!

Black Bluff's northern aspect ensures pleasant and cool summer climbing on all but the hottest days. In addition, the wall's right end wraps around to the west and these routes bask in the afternoon sun, making them attractive on chilly or breezy afternoons. A 60m rope is sufficient for all lines, and a standard rack with doubles in the mid-sizes is recommended.

BLACK BLUFF

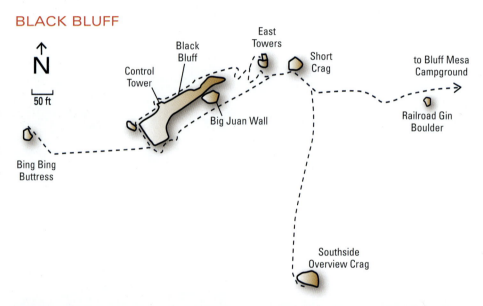

Approach: Drive 3.6 miles on Mill Creek Road (2N10) to the intersection with 2N86. Turn right and follow 2N86 for 0.6 miles to a fork in the road. Turn left on 2N86A at the sign for the Bluff Mesa Group Campground and drive 0.25 miles until the road dead-ends at the campground. Park nearby, being respectful of campers.

Hike west from the campground, picking up the trail that weaves through the woods. The beginning of the trail is obscure, but it quickly becomes well-marked with cairns and brown plastic signposts. Head west for 10-15 minutes to reach a logging road. Turn left and walk this road to a clearing. Pick up the trail again at the back of the clearing, and continue hiking up and over a rise. Snake through boulders on the plateau for another 10 minutes, following cairns as the trail heads toward the rim.

You will be approaching from the backside of the cliff, and the easiest way to the base is to find the cairned descent gully near Short Crag. This trail passes East Towers on its way to the left end of the main wall. Alternatively, it is possible to hike along the top of the wall for easy anchor access, then descend via a path to the wall's right side. Hiking distance from car to crag is 1.25 miles. Overall, the hike to the crag is moderate and pleasantly enjoyable, as you are immersed in the forested beauty of the San Bernardino Mountains. If you get lost, don't worry. It's customary to get lost on your first time hiking out to any crag on the plateau.

PAT BRENNAN

Prolific local climber Pat Brennan has developed over 1000 routes in the San Bernardino Mountains. The countless hours he and his friends have spent putting up new routes have had an immense impact on shaping the area into the remarkable rock-climbing destination it is today. In addition, Pat and his wife, Lori, are both founding members of the Rim of the World Climbing Club and have been active since the club was established in 1989.

Pat's life has always been intertwined with the mountains. Born in San Bernardino, Pat began roaming the foothills of the San Bernardinos in grade school, hiking, exploring caves, and soloing up dry waterfalls. When he was 14 years old, he started backpacking, completing the John Muir Trail and half of the Tahoe-Yosemite Trail. This soon evolved into winter backpacking and cross-country skiing, which in turn led him to climbing on frozen waterfalls. After two years of climbing ice, Pat transitioned to rock. His first rock climb was the Praying Monk on Camelback Mountain near Phoenix. Back home, Mt. Rubidoux became his gym, as there were no indoor climbing gyms at the time. Soon, Pat visited Tahquitz, and after doing the 700-foot-tall *Sahara Terror* (5.7), he thought he had done it all. Yet a mere three months later, he was headed off to climb the East Buttress of El Cap with his friend Bruce Bindner.

The Sierra became the big draw for Pat and his climbing partners, who spent years putting up new routes there and freeing aid lines. At that time, the crags in the San Bernardinos were their training ground, a place that they didn't take too seriously or record anything they did. When sport climbing took off in the late '80s and early '90s, Pat and his friends started exploring new areas, only to realize that the rock in their backyard was much better than these new crags. With that knowledge, they went on to develop over 1000 lines in the local mountains over the next 20+ years. Pat is responsible for numerous classics around Big Bear Lake, from the stellar crack routes at Black Bluff and Arctic Temple, to the excellent bolted face climbs on the lake's north shore, to wildly adventurous lines well off the beaten path.

After 45 years of climbing, Pat has amassed countless memories with a multitude of climbing partners; Bruce Bindner, Keith Tasker, Royce Landman, Dave Ohlsen, Rick Lynski, Todd Gordon, Kelly (The Troll) Vaught, Dan Kipper, Kevin (Bosco) Malone, Alan Bartlett, Dave Evans, Steve Untch, Kenn Kenaga, Bob Cable, Eric Tipton, Pete Mack, Bob Gaines, his wife Lori, his sons Jeff and Adam, and many more. His most eventful stories are from climbing on El Cap, putting up new routes in the Sierra, and about night hikes and bouldering with Todd Gordon and the Joshua Tree gang. All his stories are good; spend time sitting around a campfire with Pat and he's bound to share his wisdom from the mountains.

Pat and Lori have been married for 37 years and have two sons, Jeff and Adam. Together, they've run Patrick Brennan Construction since 1985. In 1987, they built their house in Deer Lodge Park, where they raised their family. When the Rim of the World Climbing Club began in 1989, it was an opportunity to meet the few other climbers in the Lake Arrowhead area. At the time, everyone had families with kids and the club brought the climbing community together for many camping trips and climbing adventures. As a result, the entire Brennan family all became climbers. Adam climbed until he received his ROWCC 10-Climb Award and then hung it up; he is now married with twin boys. Jeff still climbs hard and has moved to Moab, Utah. Lori and Pat spent many years as climbing partners, establishing first ascents together. Today, they remain integral members of the local climbing community and the ROWCC.

Big Juan Wall

Exodus

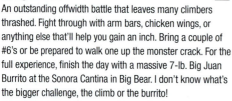

Big Juan Wall

The first two routes are situated on a short face above the left end of the main wall.
[GPS: 34.21989, -116.99221]

25 min

❶ Big Juan 5.9+ ★★★

An outstanding offwidth battle that leaves many climbers thrashed. Fight through with arm bars, chicken wings, or anything else that'll help you gain an inch. Bring a couple of #6's or be prepared to walk one up the monster crack. For the full experience, finish the day with a massive 7-lb. Big Juan Burrito at the Sonora Cantina in Big Bear. I don't know what's the bigger challenge, the climb or the burrito!

40 ft. Gear to 6". Eric Tipton, Kenn Kenaga, Pat Brennan, Aug. 1999.

❷ Green Planet 5.12a ★★★

Take your skills to the next level on this challenging testpiece. Heinous fingertip seams offer little purchase, with a distinct crux above the 3rd bolt. Don't pump out before the thrilling finish! Distinctly different and high-caliber; shares a bolted anchor (no rap rings) with *Big Juan*.

45 ft. 4 bolts. David LePere, Sept. 1999.

Black Bluff Main Cliff

[GPS: 34.21980, -116.99265]

30 min

❸ Mr. Fister 5.9 ★

Slink up this manky offwidth-to-roof that sits neglected on the far left margin of the main wall.

50 ft. Gear to 5".

Pat Brennan, Brad Singer, Eric Tipton, Kenn Kenaga, Aug. 1999.

❹ Sierra Route 5.8 ★

The obvious wide chimney beneath the end of the *Exodus* traverse. Work up the chimney and transition to a lieback as it pinches off. Share anchors with *Mr. Fister.*

50 ft. Gear to 4". Pat Brennan, Linda Hall, Sept. 1999.

❺ Exodus 5.11c ★★★★

Locate this massive traverse line in a recessed section of wall that's splattered with orange lichen. Start on *Die Hard's* initial flake and clip its first bolt. Quell your fears, paste feet to the slick face, and inch left, underclinging the monster flake. If the Elvis twitch takes hold halfway through, throw in a kneebar, regain your composure, and push through. Turn the corner, throw in a blind cam, and race the pump to the anchor atop *Mr. Fister.* Bring 2 #4's — this climb eats gear.

70 ft. Gear to 4", 1 bolt. Ryan Crochiere, David LePere, Aug. 2004.

❻ Die Hard 5.11c ★★★

A powerful mixed line on the lichen-covered face. Better than it looks! Fly up a flake to the first bolt and barrel up a thin finger crack. Exploit fingerlocks near the 2nd bolt as this steep face threatens to spit you off. Bolted anchor without rap rings. Get some!

50 ft. Gear to 1", 3 bolts.

FA: (TR) Chris Miller, Aug. 1999; FL: Brad Singer.

❼ Black Beard 5.10c ★★

Right of *Die Hard* is a green section of wall where this climb resides. Motor along a curved crack until it runs out, master a crux mantel, and blast past the final slab. Shares anchors with *Arctic Circle Jerk.*

70 ft. Gear to 2", 2 bolts.

Brad Singer, Kenn Kenaga, Pat Brennan, Aug. 1999.

Derek Volcan exits *Exodus*, 5.11c, opposite. 📷 Brandon Copp

Social D

Control Tower

NOTE: For Black Bart and Scratch and Sniff, be extremely careful climbing past the completely detached, refrigerator-sized block at the top: this massive rock could topple, causing serious injury or death.

🔟 Black Bart 5.8+ ★★★

Size matters for this wide fist crack. Strenuous jamming stays continuous through the grueling lower section until you arrive at a giant ledge. Finish in a right-facing dihedral. *70 ft. Gear to 3". Pat Brennan, Eric Tipton, June 1999.*

⓫ Scratch and Sniff 5.7 ★★★

Hand-over-hand jamming will have you grinning from ear to ear. This splitter hand crack leads to the ledge with the precarious refrigerator block. Slide up a final crack to shared anchors with *Black Bart*. *70 ft. Gear to 3". Pat Brennan, Brad Singer, John Cardmon, July 1999.*

⓬ Control Tower 5.10b ★

The bolted line up the tower. Fun moves past a roof and onto crimpers, cutting right across the west face. Optional gear placement under the rectangular block that caps the tower. *35 ft. 3 bolts , optional gear to 1.5". Brad Singer, Kenn Kenaga, David LePere, Eric Odenthal, June 2000.*

❽ Arctic Circle Jerk 5.9 ★★

A fist-eating wide crack ripe for deep jams and liebacks. Like any circle jerk, it's awkward, especially in the beginning. *70 ft. Gear to 4". Eric Tipton, Pat Brennan, June 1999.*

❾ Social D 5.10b ★★★★

Steep and sustained, this thrilling crack line is exceptional, flowing nicely throughout with good stances for gear placement. A demanding flared seam leads past 2 bolts, then move left into a slanting hand crack. Slot your hands into this beauty and smile. Shares anchors with *Arctic Circle Jerk*. *70 ft. Gear to 3", 2 bolts.*
Kenn Kenaga, Pat Brennan, Brad Singer, Aug. 1999.

Derek Volcan goes the distance on *Social D,*
5.10b, opposite. 📷 Brandon Copp

Landon Holman on *Aurora Borealis*, 5.9, opposite. 📷 Brandon Copp

Aurora Borealis

13 Best of Both Worlds 5.7 ★★
Though only 5.7, this climb can be a real workout! Dive into the chimney between the main wall and the tower and/or climb the hidden crack. Gravitate up cracks on the main wall. Belay at the tree or continue to the anchors of *Aurora Borealis*.
90 ft. Gear to 3". John Cardmon (solo), July 1999
Variation 5.7: At the top of the chimney, make a thin traverse left to pull the small roof and tag the anchors on *Control Tower* instead.

14 After the Fire 5.9 ★★
The flake/zigzagging crack system between *Best of Both Worlds* and *Aurora Borealis*. Belay at the tree or continue to the anchors of *Aurora Borealis*.
90 ft. Gear to 4". Brad Singer, Pat Brennan, July 1999.

15 Aurora Borealis 5.9 ★★★★
Brad Singer called this, "One of the best crack climbs in the San Bernardinos." An offwidth section up the right side of a flake will get the adrenaline pumping. Next, perform a brief yet tenuous traverse left and zip past bulges to the start of THE CRACK. Elegant and beautiful, this marvelous splitter snakes its way toward the top. Find yourself giddy as you rise above the treetops, then embrace the wide flare at the finish. Delight in your accomplishment, taking a moment to soak in the breathtaking landscape.
90 ft. Gear to 4". Eric Tipton, Pat Brennan, June 1999.

16 Powder Finger 5.11a ★★★
The direct start and finish to *Shooting Star*. Face climb to a high first bolt at the bottom of a thin seam, then join *Shooting Star*

for its undercling traverse. Part ways after the thin flake section, staying direct past 3 more bolts on a difficult slab. Micro edges and crystals take you to the *Shooting Star* anchor.
90 ft. Gear to 1", 9 bolts. Direct Start: John Cardmon, Brad Singer, Pat Brennan, Aug. 1999; Direct Finish: Brad Singer, Eric Odenthal, Chris Miller, David LePere, June 2000.

17 Shooting Star 5.10b ★★★
Another exceptional route that ascends a crack in the open-book corner. Move left along an undercling, where a shallow flake presents a fingery challenge above. At the top of the flake, cut right to a ledge and face climb past a final bolt.
90 ft. Gear to 3", 5 bolts.
Pat Brennan, Brad Singer, John Cardmon, Aug. 1999.

18 Beauty in Darkness 5.12a ★★
Did *Shooting Star* leave you hungry for more? Set this one up from the same anchors. Begin with the crack/corner, but instead of executing the traverse, climb directly up the arête. This line may leave you thrashed and confused until the deviant holds finally reveal themselves.
90 ft. Chris Miller, Sept. 2001.

19 Slap and Tickle 5.10d ★★★
Excellent position and exposure on this varied line! Slip into a pleasurable splitter crack (5.8) and ascend the right side of a triangular block. From a ledge, move left to the arête. Slap, crimp, and curse your way up the blunt arête.
60 ft. Gear to 3.5", 5 bolts.
Pat Brennan, John Cardmon, Brad Singer, July 1999.

Black Bluff Right

BING BING BUTTRESS

An often-overlooked buttress with a lone sport climb.

  35 min

Approach: From the right end of Black Bluff, hike 100 yards west. Scramble down a steep slope to the wall and wrap around to its northwest face. 5 minutes from Black Bluff. **[GPS: 34.21965, -116.99365]**

20 Blackout 5.11c ★★

Begin with the same hand crack as *Slap and Tickle*, but then commit to the perplexing seam angling right from the ledge. Tech-tastic slab climbing leads to the last 2 bolts and anchors of *Slap and Tickle*.
60 ft. Gear to 3.5", 6 bolts. Chris Miller, Aug. 1999.

21 Black and Tan 5.11c ★★★

Start from a cutout in the middle of the west face. Lieback the left-facing corner above the roof, followed by a long reach to slopers on the side of a block. A bouldery offwidth sequence around the block transitions to slab technique along a seam. Varied skills needed to succeed!
60 ft. 6 bolts. Chris Miller, Brad Singer, Aug. 1999.

22 Firewalker 5.12a ★★★

A thin seam 5 feet right of *Black and Tan*, with a grueling start. Outlast the low crux with heinous crimping and technical footwork, gunning past a bulge at the 3rd bolt. More enjoyable slab lies above. Share anchors with *Black and Tan*.
60 ft. 7 bolts. Eric Odenthal, June 2000.

23 Fire on the Mountain 5.12a ★★

Climb the same ridiculous start as *Firewalker*, but keep angling right past the 3rd bolt to another thin crack. Watch the swing as you blast straight up the vertical groove to the top. TR from anchors on *Black and Tan*.
60 ft. Chris Miller, June 2000.

24 Shout in the Dark 5.11a ★★

Mantel, then follow a shallow channel beside a flake. A delicate traverse left gains the arête. Breathe easy, sliding hands up the arête and smearing feet to the chains.
50 ft. 6 bolts. Eric Odenthal, John Cardmon, Aug. 2003.

EAST TOWERS

Two buttresses, with the one nearest the trail having a large, tilted boulder balanced on top.

  25 min

Approach: East of the main wall and found midway down the final descent to Black Bluff. **[GPS: 34.22013, -116.99182]**

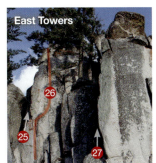

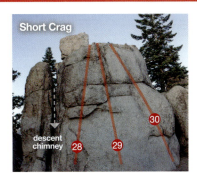

25 Waterloo 5.10c

On the left side of the left tower is this dirty, left-facing corner that starts finger-sized and ends with fists.

35 ft. Gear to 4". Kenn Kenaga, Pat Brennan, Sept. 1999.

26 The Sheriff 5.10b ★★

Start down in a pit and ascend flakes to a midway ledge. Climb the thin, flared seam past a bolt and into a widening hand crack. Belay from a tree.

45 ft. Gear to 3", 1 bolt. Kenn Kenaga, Pat Brennan, Sept. 1999.

27 Wildfire 5.8

A manky offwidth on the left side of the rightmost tower with the perched block on top. Gear anchor.

35 ft. Wide gear. Kenn Kenaga, Pat Brennan, Sept. 1999.

SHORT CRAG

Hardly worth the stop with such outstanding cracks nearby at Black Bluff, but the backside has potential for a few tough bolted lines.

 25 min

Approach: To the right of the trail before descending the final gully to Black Bluff, this crag is perched on the rim of the plateau, east of the main wall. **[GPS: 34.22011, -116.99157]**

28 Chicken Chat 5.5

Step up past underclings on the slab beside the chimney, slinging a chickenhead near the top. Gear anchor.

25 ft. Thin gear to 2" and slings for pro. Unknown.

29 Easy Feet 5.6

Execute balancy moves on tiny features up the initial unprotected slab. Whiz up the right-facing flake. Gear belay.

25 ft. Gear to 2". Pat Brennan, Jeff Brennan, Matt Rubio, Sept. 1999.

30 Paper Weight 5.7

5 feet right of *Easy Feet* is a set of parallel cracks. Start on the better right crack, place gear in the horizontal, and cross over to the left crack to finish. Gear anchor.

25 ft. Gear to 2". Pat Brennan, Jeff Brennan, Matt Rubio, Sept. 1999.

SOUTHSIDE OVERVIEW

An out-of-the-way formation on the plateau with a prominent hand crack on its south face. The setting at this crag is utterly beautiful.

25 min

Approach: Follow Black Bluff's approach to Short Crag. From here, turn and hike 200 yards south to reach a nondescript jumble of boulders that is the backside of this crag. **[GPS: 34.21866, -116.99158]**

31 Solo Paws 5.8 ★★

A striking, vertical hand crack up the middle of the south face. Finish on the zigzagging crack ending right of the boulder or up a flake to its left. Gear anchor.

40 ft. Gear to 3". Unknown.

Southside Overview Crag

SIBERIA CREEK TOWER

The main attraction of the Siberia Creek area is a massive, 120-foot-tall formation featuring fine-grain granite similar to Arctic Temple and Black Bluff. Most climbs here are old-school cracks of great quality, but the slick, near-featureless rock also sports an excellent 5.12d face route called *Silk* that ascends a shallow waterchute. The crag has great views of the area off the backside of the mountains — take a minute to enjoy the scenery from the top. It can get quite windy here, so consider that on wind-advisory days. Make sure to take the short detour to see the amazing 440-year-old Champion Lodgepole Pine on the way to the crag!

Note: With the exception of *Vodka and Tonic* (5.9) and *Californication* (5.7), the intermediate anchors on the tower do not have rap rings, only the anchors on the summit do. In addition, there is a 25-foot section of unprotected 5.3 slab at the top of all the climbs leading up the main tower, so be aware of this runout if climbing those routes.

35 min

Approach: Atypically for the San Bernardinos, the wall is next to a well-kept trail.

Drive 3.6 miles on Mill Creek Road (2N10) to the intersection with 2N86. Turn left to continue following 2N10 for an additional 0.7 miles. Next, turn right onto 2N11 at the Lodgepole Pine sign. Drive 1.0 mile on 2N11 to a large parking pullout at the Siberia Creek trailhead.

Hike 5 minutes down the Siberia Creek trail to a tee, passing 10 wooden markers. Turn left here. A sign indicating the Champion Lodgepole Pine will immediately become visible. It's a worthwhile 1-minute detour to see the gigantic, 110-foot-tall tree.

Follow the Siberia Creek trail west for about a mile as it parallels the seasonal stream, meandering alongside meadows and through peaceful stands of trees. The relatively flat path crosses a wooden bridge at approximately 20 minutes in, at which point large rocks will become visible on the right. 100 yards before the second wooden bridge (roughly 25 minutes of hiking total), cut up the hill on the right to the backside of Siberia Creek Tower. The triangular summit block with *Californication* can be seen and approached from here.

The easiest path to the main wall is to head right, going around the tower's northern end to descend beside the west face. Exercise caution when hiking down the steep slope, as the pine needles can make for a slick descent. This approach should deposit you at the base of *Siberia Crack*. If you miss the turnoff to the formation entirely and continue on the trail, both Siberia Creek Tower and the Upper Siberia Creek Crags will be easily visible across a steep gully on your right. **[GPS: 34.21680, -116.98421]**

Alternate Approach: It is also possible to approach this crag from the Bluff Mesa Group Campground. The drive is 5 minutes shorter but the hike is that much longer. From the camp, walk 100 yards back up the road (2N86A) to locate the Bluff Mesa Trail (1W16). Hike south on this trail until it passes the Champion Lodgepole Pine and meets up with the Siberia Creek trail. Turn right and follow the Siberia Creek trail to the crag as above.

Shehdad Khundmiri climbs *Siberia Crack,* 5.10d, next page. 📷 Brandon Copp

Siberia Creek Tower Left

❶ Siberia Crack 5.10d ★★★

Ready to put those crack skills to the test? Step right up to this sick, 2-pitch line. Start in the shadow of the large pine below the southwest face. From an undercling, battle up a thin seam past 3 bolts and plop onto a belay ledge with anchors. The move off the ledge may throw you for a loop. Power up the excruciating finger crack. Pass a 2nd set of anchors and end with a run of easy, unprotected slab.
100 ft. Gear to 2" with emphasis on small pieces, 3 bolts. Chris Miller, Sept. 2002.

❷ Northern Lights 5.12a ★★★

As my friend Don once said, "There are no hard moves on toprope!" Pull past a U-shaped flake and commit to the difficult face. Elusive holds consisting of tiny crystals and delicate edges add to the allure while you desperately attempt to reach the ledge before peeling off the wall.
40 ft. Chris Miller, Sept. 2002.

❸ Silk 5.12d ★★★★

This smooth and balancy route commands impeccable technique, smearing and edging on dimes in a slick waterchute. "Really hard" would be putting it mildly.
50 ft. 8 bolts. David LePere, Sept. 2003.

❹ Mysterious Ways 5.10d ★★★

An exciting upper pitch that starts from a ledge above the improbable route *Silk*. Traverse right past a bolt, executing a demanding sequence to gain the arête. Delightful climbing along the rounded arête quickly takes you above the treetops.
65 ft. 6 bolts. Eric Odenthal, Sept. 2002.

❺ Disorderly Conduct 5.12b ★★

The leftmost of 3 cracks, marked with a lone bolt low on the face. Master a burly, bouldery sequence in a right-facing corner that repels even the most seasoned climbers. This crack serves as a variation start to *Matrix* and merges with that climb as it moves left on a slanted finger crack.
120 ft. Gear to 4", 1 bolt. Eric Odenthal.

❻ Matrix 5.9+ ★★

The middle crack, solid for the grade. Wedge into a squeeze section and wiggle awkwardly through it. Transition left across a slanted finger crack, using small foot chips. Continue up a gully and keep moving left along a hand crack that evaporates near the lower set of anchors. Run up the final unprotected slab to the top.
120 ft. Gear to 4". John Cardmon, Pat Brennan, Aug. 2000.

❼ Matrix Direct Finish 5.10a ★★

Climb *Matrix* to the top of the gully. Where the regular route heads left into the hand crack, instead stay straight and smear past 4 bolts on the minimally featured face. To ease rope drag you can build an anchor and do this as a 2nd pitch.
110 ft. Gear to 4", 4 bolts. Brad Singer, John Cardmon, Sept. 2002.

❽ Vodka and Tonic 5.9 ★

The rightmost of the 3 crack lines. Surge up the dirty, flared crack, followed by a spooky slab.
80 ft. Gear to 3", 5 bolts. Brad Singer.

❾ Poke You With My Stick 5.9

Underwhelming roof-to-face route up a block in the gully.
40 ft. Chris Miller, Eric Odenthal, Sept. 2002.

The following 4 routes are located up and right of the main tower on a separate wall that faces southeast.

❿ Cold Hearted 5.5

Locate the flake of *Free Be Free*, then scramble over boulders to the squeeze chimney 20 feet left. Its low-angled nature makes it a good confidence-builder. Gear anchor.
80 ft. Gear to 5". Unknown.

Siberia Creek Tower Right

11 Warm Blooded 5.7

Get the blood pumping on this flaring fist crack. Gear anchor.
60 ft. Gear to 3". Brad Singer, Eric Odenthal, June 2002.

12 Free Be Free 5.10a

Climb the conspicuous right-facing flake and float directly
up it to the face above. Extremely poor rock on the upper
section. Gear anchor.
60 ft. Gear to 2" for anchor. Brad Singer, Eric Odenthal, June 2002.

13 Harold 5.9 ★

10 feet of decent climbing in a fist crack gives way to a
disappointing finish on the loose and gritty face. Gear anchor.
60 ft. Gear to 4". Eric Odenthal, Brad Singer, June 2002.

14 Californication 5.7 ★

On the triangular summit block of the main tower, climb
divots and knobs past 2 bolts.
25 ft. 2 bolts. Pat Brennan, John Cardmon, Aug. 2000.

Upper Siberia Creek Crags

UPPER SIBERIA CREEK CRAGS

Upper Siberia Creek Crags comprises two separate rock formations. Upper Siberia Creek Tower is home to the majority of the lines on various cracks and fins, while Wicked Pinnacle sits slightly uphill, with the single route *Swamp Gas* (5.7). These rarely traveled crags need some TLC, so be prepared to bushwhack heavily around the base. The route to climb here is the 5.8+ dihedral *Cold Crack*.

45 min

Approach: From the top/back of Siberia Creek Tower, strike off northwest along the ridgeline, heading fairly continuously uphill. Reach a flat-topped rock near the top of the hillside, at which point you can head downhill to arrive near *Cracked Ice*. For a better approach to routes 15-17, stay high on the ridgeline, passing behind the formation, and dropping down into a gully. The Upper Siberia Creek Crags lie 300 yards away from Siberia Creek Tower, a 10-15 minute bushwhack. **[GPS: 34.21758, -116.98724]**

15 Swamp Gas 5.7

Climb the crack in the middle of the wall past a pointed block to a flared squeeze chimney. Gear anchor. Descend with a slightly exposed scramble down climber's left.
50 ft. Gear to 4". John Cardmon, Pat Brennan, Aug. 2000.

16 Cloudburst 5.6 ★

Hone your chimney technique while using the wall behind. Wedge hands and feet into the crack and take this past a perched block. Gear anchor.
75 ft. Gear to 4". Eric Tipton, John Cardmon, Kenn Kenaga, June 2006.

17 Nighthawk 5.10a ★

An interesting line that begins from a ledge. Move past a roof and toil on the slick and challenging crack that arches left. Tired and desperate near the top, find a way past the crux bulge. Gear anchor.
70 ft. Gear to 3". Brad Singer, Eric Tipton, June 2006.

18 Cold Crack 5.8+ ★★

A nice open-book route situated 5 feet right of a tree on the wall. Stem the corner to the Y-shaped fork in the crack, then choose the right side. Gear anchor.
70 ft. Gear to 3". John Cardmon, Pat Brennan, Aug. 2000.

19 Cracked Ice 5.8 R

The gritty, low-angle face/arête beside a recess. Runout. Gear anchor.
55 ft. 3 bolts, gear to 3" for anchor. Unknown.

TRIPLE BREASTED WOMAN

For slab lovers, this crag is worth the quick hike out to explore these short but sweet climbs. Since these are less traveled lines, the rock may need a bit of cleaning up.

10 min

Approach: From the Siberia Creek trailhead's parking pullout, drive an additional 0.2 miles on 2N11 to a fork in the road. Take the left fork leading 0.2 miles further to Yellow Post Campsite #28. Park near this campsite.

Hike cross-country, heading west/northwest, across a clearing of dead manzanita. Continue past boulders to where the slope drops dramatically down to Siberia Creek. The approach leads to the backside of the crag, which sits on the rim overlooking the valley. **[GPS: 34.21479, -116.98409]**

20 Left Breast Left (Open Project)

Pat Brennan and company were working this project that ascends a 2"-thick flake on the green lichenous face.
40 ft.

Triple Breasted Woman

㉑ 3 Nipples 5.10d ★★

Throttle past a series of overlaps, squeezing the underclings and milking the upside-down holds on the path to the top.

30 ft. 4 bolts. Kenn Kenaga, Nov. 2007.

㉒ Witch's Tit 5.10a

Cling to the right margin of the low-angle face on this balancy route. Shared anchor with *3 Nipples*.

30 ft. 3 bolts. Kenn Kenaga, Pat Brennan, Nov. 2007.

Variation 5.7: If you use the crack it's a lot easier!

㉓ D-Cup 5.8 ★

Grip a large flake, mantel onto a ledge and clip the 4th bolt, then avoid the difficult-looking blank face by strolling up easy blocks to the left.

35 ft. 4 bolts. Pat Brennan, Alan Bartlett, Mary Ann Kelly, Lori Brennan, June 2008.

CAPE THORN

An isolated pinnacle with majestic views of the mountains and the basin below. It is doubtful that the solitary line has seen many ascents, but the rock is surprisingly good.

☀ 🚶 50 min

Approach: A difficult wall to locate. The approach can be heinous if you end up in a valley of thorns. Definitely pull out the GPS to locate this crag.

Drive 3.6 miles on Mill Creek Road (2N10) to the intersection with 2N86. Turn left to continue following 2N10 for an additional 0.7 miles. Turn right onto 2N11 at the Lodgepole Pine sign. Drive 0.7 miles on 2N11, then turn left on 2N11B. Take this for 0.7 miles until it dead-ends in a clearing at Lookout Point.

From the clearing, hike west cross-country, dropping down into a wash. After 5-10 minutes you'll see a large rock on the right — if only that were it. Make your way to the top of the ridge on your right, staying high where the thorn bushes are thinnest. Ride the ridge as long as you can (about 0.6 miles) and locate the backside of Cape Thorn off to the southwest. It looks like a pile of boulders out on a point. Follow a path of least resistance in the seasonal streambeds, cutting trail through small stands of thorns to reach the base of the wall. **[GPS: 34.20377, -116.98380]**

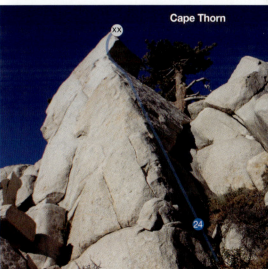

Cape Thorn

㉔ Cape Thorn South Face 5.10a ★★

Use caution in reaching the high first bolt, and embrace the southwest arête. At the roof, move to the arête's left side and master a final thin face. The anchor likely needs a couple of quicklinks for rappelling.

50 ft. 4 bolts. Kenn Kenaga, Pat Brennan, Sept. 1999.

FAWNSKIN CRAGS

Tim Trigg on *Migs Over Moscow*, 5.11b,
Big West Hanna, page 226. 📷 Brandon Copp

FAWNSKIN **CRAGS**

This section encompasses the crags north and west of the town of Fawnskin on the north side of Big Bear Lake. The area is a bit remote and less traveled than other spots near the lake. As a result, while the rock quality is generally good, expect some loose crystals from lack of traffic. The largest concentration of climbs is found at the Coven, an area initially developed by Craig Pearson and Dean Goolsby in the 1990s.

The crags are an even mix of sport and traditional lines on fine- to coarse-grained granite. Driving to many of these crags involves a fair amount of time on Forest Service backroads, and approach hikes range from 5 minutes to an hour for the more remote spots. Crag elevations are in the 7000-8000-foot range. Over the last few decades, fires have sadly devastated much of the vegetation on many of the hillsides, so it can get quite windy at hilltop crags, and buckthorn has often taken over in the large trees' absence. Much of the Holcomb Creek drainage is still in a period of regrowth, so please exercise additional care and adhere to Leave No Trace principles when traveling in this area.

Many camping options exist near the crags. The Hanna Flat Campground and the Big Pine Flat Campground are managed by the Forest Service, with some sites operating on a reservation system and others first-come, first-served. In addition, Gray's Peak and Ironwood are group campgrounds that can accommodate 25+ people each. If you're looking for free camping options, there are several yellow-post campsites in the area.

Brandon Copp on *Waffle House*, 5.10d, the Coven, page 235.
📷 Jacqueline Copp

Beyond the restrooms in the town of Fawnskin, Gray's Peak Group Camp has a pit toilet, which is located near the parking for Hanna Rocks, Legoland, and the Coven. The other Forest Service campgrounds maintain toilets as well, and there is a restroom near town at the Gray's Peak trailhead off North Shore Drive.

Approach: From the stoplight at the dam, drive Highway 38 for 3.3 miles along the north shore of Big Bear Lake to reach the tiny town of Fawnskin. In Fawnskin, turn left (north) onto Rim of the World Drive (Forest Road 3N14), near the fire station. All of the crags are reached from this road, which is paved for the first 0.4 miles before turning to dirt.

For navigating to these off-the-beaten-path crags, it's helpful to grab a (free) map of the Forest Service roads from the Big Bear Discovery Center, located along North Shore Drive about halfway between Fawnskin and Big Bear. The driving is all on dirt roads that are for the most part well-maintained. While 4WD is not mandatory, a high-clearance vehicle is recommended. Also be aware that after heavy rains or a particularly snowy winter, the roads can become deeply rutted or have washouts.

Jeremy Saqr on *Eddie the Eagle*, 5.10a,
World Cup Tower, page 247. 📷 Brandon Copp

CLIMBING AREA	ELEVATION	HIKE	ROUTES	GRADE RANGE		CRAGS
CLOSE TO TOWN CRAGS *Isolated adventures* page 212	6950 ft. 8000 ft.	15-40 min	12			Fawnskin Tower, Delamar Mountain
PINNACLE WITH A VIEW *Outstanding views* page 214	7500 ft.	20 min	14			
OLD SNOW SLIDE RD. *Secluded playtime* page 216	7300 ft.	20-50 min	9			Toot Sweet, Mugavero Peak
LEGOLAND *Sunny moderates* page 219	7600 ft.	5 min	19			Kid Power Towers, Tot Pinnacle, Miniland
HANNA ROCKS *Must do: Migs Over Moscow, 11b* page 223	7800 ft.	10-30 min	12			Trash on the Floorboard, Hanna Cappa Island, Heatwave, Summit Block, Rendezvous Rock, Big West Hanna
THE COVEN *Excellent and uncrowded* page 227	7600 ft.	5-15 min	67			Cauldron, Dragonlance, Voodoo, Dragon Breath, Mortal Sin, HP Wall, Gargoyle, Warlock Spires, Bear Paw, Lost Souls Slab
HOLCOMB CREEK CRAGS *Remote slabs and cracks* page 242	5300 ft. 7000 ft.	15-45 min	18			Red Bull, HC Tower, Slashed Tower, HC Dome, Toaster Oven, World Cup Tower, Monster Garage

FAWNSKIN TOWER

Fawnskin Tower is a square-shaped freestanding tower located on the outskirts of the town of Fawnskin, with climbs on 3 faces. A single 2-bolt anchor with chains services all of the climbs. Most of the routes are lichenous and many of the low-angle cracks are filled with pine needles from an overhanging tree.

15 min

Approach: Turn onto Rim of the World Drive (3N14) in Fawnskin and drive 0.6 miles, past where the pavement ends, to a large pullout on the left. Park here, before a gate and an old overgrown road. Walk down the old road, crossing a bridge, to a boarded-up cabin. Locate the faint trail that continues southeast, curling around a hillside. Roughly 5 minutes past the cabin, the tower will be visible on the hillside to the right. Hike up the steep hillside to the crag. **[GPS: 34.27170, -116.95213]**

Ironside

Pickle Deer

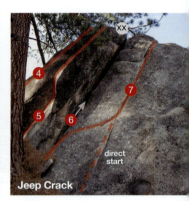
Jeep Crack
direct start

❶ Ironside Direct 5.10b ★★

Sprint up the easy hand crack on the right margin of the northeast face to a comfy stance. Continue up slightly negative terrain past 2 bolts to a horizontal. Traverse left using the undercling and end in a right-slanting finger crack. Much better than the wandering original route.

65 ft. Gear to 3", 3 bolts. Kenn Kenaga, Pat Brennan, Sept. 1999.

❷ Ironside 5.10a

Start as above, but branch right on a halfway ledge. Scoot along the ledge to a ramp and crack that slant back left.

70 ft. Gear to 3". John Cardmon, Pat Brennan, July 1999.

❸ Jeep Crack 5.7 ★

The short diagonal crack on the northwest face. Easy but dirty climbing in a wide crack leads to a big ledge. Head up the same nice ramp and crack used by *Ironside*.

50 ft. Gear to 4". Mike Itnyre, John Cardmon, Pat Brennan, July 1999.

❹ Bear Hug 5.4

A one-move-wonder up a pine needle-filled crack. Situated on the far left side of the uphill southwest face.

30 ft. Gear to 1". Mike Itnyre, John Cardmon, July 1999.

❺ Tree Fort 5.5

Hand crack with a committing opening move.

30 ft. Gear to 3". Alan Bartlett, Mary Ann Kelly, Kevin Graves, Pat Brennan, June 2006.

❻ Zargen 5.5

Shimmy up the sloping squeeze chimney right of the pine tree.

30 ft. Wide gear to 4". Pat Brennan, Kenn Kenaga, Steve Kravchuck, David LePere, Sept. 1999.

❼ Pickle Deer 5.8+ ★

From the start of *Zargen*, make a thin, tricky traverse right (protected by a bolt) to the crack system that doesn't quite reach the ground. Gain the seam and lieback the flake. Alternatively, a slabby 5.10a direct start can be done, but be careful not to tumble down the steep slope on the right.

35 ft. Gear to 2", 1 bolt. FA: Steve Kravchuck, David LePere, Sept. 1999; Direct Start: Chris Miller, Aug. 2001.

DELAMAR MOUNTAIN

Two small backcountry crags near the summit of Delamar Mountain, with a smattering of undeveloped rocks higher on the hillside. If you're up for the trek, they are bound to be all yours for the day! The squatty lower formation sits right at 8000 feet and the towers of the upper formation have expansive views of the lake. Both face southwest, with all-day sun. There are no bolted anchors, and all routes require gear.

35-40 min

Approach: From Fawnskin, take Rim of the World Drive (3N14) for 1.8 miles. Turn right onto 3N12 (gravel road) and go 0.4 miles. Turn right onto 2N71, a dirt road that can get very muddy after a rain. Take 2N71 for 0.8 miles to a parking turnout on the right that can fit half a dozen cars.

No trail, only bushwhacking! Plug in the GPS coordinates or hike about 30 degrees northeast. Start up a wash, cross an old overgrown road, then climb steeply uphill, navigating loose talus on the slope near the lower crag. From Lower Delamar Rock, hike uphill from the right end of the crag through loose rock for 5 minutes to reach Upper Delamar Rock.

Lower Delamar Rock
[GPS: 34.28821, -116.94816]

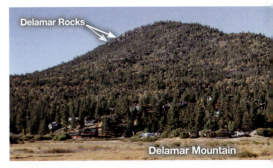
Delamar Rocks
Delamar Mountain

8 **8000 Feet and Still Climbing** 5.10d ★★
Carefully proceed up the V-shaped corner to the high first bolt. Precision footwork is your friend on the slick water-washed face. An easy slab runout gains the top. Gear anchor.
60 ft. Gear to 2", 3 bolts. Kenn Kenaga, Pat Brennan, July 2000.

9 **Premium Processing** 5.8+ ★
Start as for *8000 Feet* but branch right after the first bolt, heading to the blocky arête. Pop through a small notch to an easy slab finish. Gear anchor.
60 ft. Gear to 2", 1 bolt. Kenn Kenaga, Pat Brennan, July 2000.

Lower Delamar Rock

Upper Delamar Rock
[GPS: 34.28855, -116.94769]

10 **Tin Roof Sunday** 5.8 ★★
A fun, varied route. Make your way up the leftmost tower past 2 bolts and horizontals for gear. Decide how to tackle the roof and push through the bulge that guards the summit. Gear anchor.
40 ft. Gear to 2", 2 bolts. Kenn Kenaga, Pat Brennan, July 2000.

11 **Twin Lake View** 5.7
Wide hand/fist crack right of the corner. Gear anchor.
40 ft. Gear to 4". Kenn Kenaga, Pat Brennan, July 2000.

12 **Watch Your Hold** 5.8+ ★
Begin down low and stair-step up the blocky right side of the arête. Easy, low-angle terrain leads to a final section of crack. Gear anchor.
50 ft. Gear to 2", 3 bolts. Kenn Kenaga, Pat Brennan, July 2000.

Upper Delamar Rock

PINNACLE WITH A VIEW

As the name suggests, this pinnacle has amazing views of the lake and surrounding mountains. It can get a bit breezy at this wall since the fire that occurred years ago wiped out many of the area's trees. The routes here are split between the north and south faces, allowing for soaking-in-the-sun or shade-chasing days. The aptly-named *Stellar Arête* (5.10b) and the *Under the Influence* roof problem (5.12c) are the climbs to do here.

20 min

Approach: Take Rim of the World Drive (3N14) for 1.2 miles. Turn left onto 2N13. Drive 2.1 miles on 2N13 to a right turn to stay on 2N13. Continue for another 0.25 miles to a sharp right turn onto 2N68, where that road heads steeply uphill. (If you find yourself heading downhill on 2N13, you've missed the turn and gone too far.) Take 2N68 for 0.2 miles to the parking pullout for the Coven, located on the hairpin turn just before a downhill section.

It is recommended to park here and walk down 2N86 for 0.5 miles (10 minutes), as this road has been closed for many years and is not maintained. Walk northeast along 2N86 to Yellow Post Campsite #4. Looking across the road from the campsite, if you squint your eyes and turn your head sideways you will see the faint memory of an old 4x4 road heading uphill to the south. Hike this overgrown track beside a seasonal wash until it crests the top of the hill and ends in a clearing. Pinnacle With a View is visible from here. There is no trail to the base, so take the path of least resistance to the pinnacle.
[GPS: 34.27151, -116.98318]

Routes 1-7 are located on the north face of the formation while routes 8-13 are situated on the south face.

❶ Tyrone 5.9+ ★
Low crux on the initial undercut section of this wide-hands crack. Move right to shared anchors atop *Observatory*.
60 ft. Gear to 4". Brad Singer, May 2001.

❷ Beatrice 5.7 ★
Pull onto the slab, clip a bolt, and cruise along finger cracks to an easy V-shaped notch. Shares *Observatory* anchors.
60 ft. Gear to 3", 1 bolt. Brad Singer, Eric Odenthal, May 2001.

❸ Observatory 5.10b ★★
Delicate! Tiptoe on slab past the high first bolt to gain the arête. Mantel a shelf and advance up the textured face.
60 ft. 4 bolts. Brad Singer, Eric Odenthal, May 2001.

❹ Hy-Pro-Glo 5.11a ★★
Throttle through the tiny technicolor topography trying this thrilling, technical tower.
55 ft. 4 bolts. Eric Odenthal, Brad Singer, May 2001.

❺ Stellar Arête 5.10b ★★★
Spectacular arête climbing with airy exposure in a gorgeous setting. Reach high for the good opening handholds and master a bouldery start, then smile as you lieback the sharp arête. Transport this line to Holcomb and it'd be an instant classic!
60 ft. 6 bolts. Eric Odenthal, Brad Singer, May 2001.

❻ View to a Kill 5.9 ★★
5 feet right of the arête is this right-angling hand crack. Progress straight up the upper face in a thin crack that's tricky to protect. Shares anchors with *Stellar Arête*.
60 ft. Gear to 3". Chris Miller, June 2001.

❼ Agnes 5.5 ★★
Begin climbing in the same hand crack as above, but step right onto a block and ascend giant flakes. Surprisingly enjoyable. Shares anchors with *Stellar Arête*.
60 ft. Gear to 4". Brad Singer, Eric Odenthal, May 2001.

❽ Harlan Pepper 5.7 ★★
Mellow climbing on the leftmost slab of the south face. Place a 1" cam in the crack after the 3rd bolt if you like. Shares anchors with *As the Crow Flies*.
70 ft. 4 bolts, optional gear to 1".
Brad Singer, Eric Odenthal, May 2001.

❾ Winkie 5.6
A fat fist crack that shares anchors with *As the Crow Flies*.
70 ft. Gear to 5". Unknown.

❿ As the Crow Flies 5.10a ★★
Stand tall and creep up the south face past 3 bolts, then tread slightly right toward the horizontal. (Moving left to the good holds drops the grade a couple notches.) Clip the final bolt and run it out on big holds.
70 ft. 4 bolts, optional gear to 1". Brad Singer, Eric Odenthal, May 2001.

Pinnacle With a View North

Pinnacle With a View South

⑪ Hubert 5.6 ★

Slip and slide in a chimney until it becomes too wide to continue inside. Cut left to the *As the Crow Flies* anchors.

70 ft. Wide gear. Unknown.

⑫ Under the Influence 5.12c ★★★★

An impressive roof problem caps a deviously thin section of slab. Smear past the high first bolt, then unlock the wild sequence out the intimidating roof.

75 ft. 5 bolts. Eric Odenthal, Ryan Scherler, June 2001.

⑬ Around the Influence 5.11b ★★★

For this toprope variant, climb the initial thin slab, then surmount the roof on the easier left side.

75 ft. Eric Odenthal, June 2001.

⑭ Butch the Bitch 5.9 ★★

A discontinuous crack line that goes beside the roof to the right. Negotiating the wide fist crack at the top can be exciting. Shared anchor with *Under the Influence*.

70 ft. Gear to 4". Unknown.

TOOT SWEET

A decent southeast-facing formation with a couple of easy crack lines and potential for a few hard face routes. The cracks here are a little dirty with slightly poorer rock quality, but it's worth a trip to play around on this chunk of rock. Easy walk-off from the top.

20 min

Approach: The crag sits alongside the Hanna Flats singletrack bike trail and has a fairly easy and flat approach. Take Rim of the World Drive (3N14) north out of Fawnskin. After 2.0 miles (just past the YMCA Camp Whittle), turn left onto 2N01X/2N68 (the Old Snow Slide Road). In less than 0.1 mile there will be a large parking area on the right, just before a locked gate closing the road to vehicles. Park here and hike past the gate along the road.

Hike 0.1 miles to arrive at a fork in the road and a 2nd locked gate. Head right to follow 2N01X. An additional 0.4 miles of road hiking brings you to another fork. This time, stay left to stay on 2N01X. Immediately past the fork on the left is the signposted bike trail (about 10 minutes of hiking from the parking area). Turn left and follow the well-defined bike trail for 0.75 miles. As you crest a slight rise, the formation will be in view on the right side of the path, just off the trail. **[GPS: 34.28073, -116.97771]**

Toot Sweet

① Sun Blisters 5.7+ ★★

Lieback the rounded fin to get established in the crack. Slip in fist and foot jams while you can, then navigate thinner seams and finish in a slot. Sling a tree or boulder to anchor. *45 ft. Gear to 4". FA: (TR) Sheri Immel, Nov. 2012.*

② Toot Sweet 5.7+ ★★

Slide up the wide crack in the middle of the wall, getting funky at the finish with chicken wings in an offwidth. Same anchor situation as *Sun Blisters* — bring extra cord if you want to extend it. *40 ft. Gear to 5". FA: (TR) Sheri Immel, Nov. 2012.*

**Tim Mullis on *Stellar Arête*, 5.10b,
Pinnacle With a View, page 214.**
📷 Brandon Copp

MUGAVERO PEAK

A nice, secluded crag to spend the day climbing half a dozen short lines. Located north of Hanna Rocks and the Coven, the crag consists of 3 main summit blocks atop Mugavero Peak, plus a nearby formation with the route *Bite the Bullet* (5.9).

50 min

Approach: A bit of a hike! Park as for Toot Sweet (see previous page). Hike 0.1 miles past the first gate to arrive at a fork in the road and a 2nd gate. Turn right to follow 2N01X. Hike 0.4 miles to another fork; stay left on 2N01X. At 15 minutes in, you will pass an old yellow-post campsite. After about 30 minutes total (1.25 miles), stay left as the road forks again. Walk uphill for 5 minutes to a small rise. Instead of following the road as it curves downhill and left, leave the road and strike out northwest, going cross-country over the crest of the first summit. Continue downhill along the ridge/saddle, then make a final uphill push to reach the 2nd summit: Mugavero Peak. The approach should deposit you at the route *Here We Go*. Total distance: 1.75 miles.

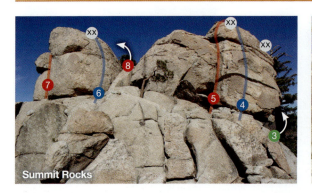

Summit Rocks

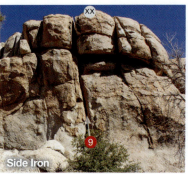

Side Iron

Summit Rocks
[GPS: 34.28153, -116.99278]

③ Mugavero Project
A TR project on the northeast face. Start from the sloping ledge and climb the slightly overhanging face on horizontals.
25 ft. Bolted anchor.

④ Here We Go 5.6 ★★
Mild face climb on good patina with one big move over a bulge. Quite enjoyable.
30 ft. 3 bolts. Pat Brennan, Lori Brennan, Jeff Brennan, July 2011.

⑤ Split Pea 5.6
From the ledge with a small tree, scoot into the wide crack between 2 blocks, then motor up the face on the right. Share anchors with *Here We Go*.
30 ft. Gear to 5". Pat Brennan, Lori Brennan, July 2011.

⑥ Strawberry Torte 5.8 ★★
A thought-provoking, technical line located in a corridor. Follow bumps and ridges on the face.
30 ft. 4 bolts. Pat Brennan, Lori Brennan, Adam Brennan, July 2011.

⑦ Candy Corner 5.6 ★
An interesting lower corner to a small roof. Step left and continue up the well-featured face above. Rappel from anchors atop *Strawberry Torte*.
25 ft. Thin gear to 2". Pat Brennan, Lori Brennan, July 2011.

⑧ Noisemaker 5.10a ★
Right-slanting crack on the northeast face. Short yet powerful, starting with fingers and ending with fists. Rappel from *Strawberry Torte* anchors.
25 ft. Gear to 3.5". Kevin Graves, Pat Brennan, Aug. 2012.

Side Iron
[GPS: 34.28079, -116.99267]

⑨ Bite the Bullet 5.9 ★★
Have a ball as you slip and slide up the gully/crack left of the bolted anchor.
35 ft. Wide gear to 5". Kenn Kenaga, Aug. 2011.

LEGOLAND

This collection of sunny, south-facing walls is a great learning spot, with nearly 20 routes in the 5.6-5.10 range. You will likely be the only party at the crag, the routes are short, and it's very easy to set up topropes. Many of the anchors are set back from the edge, however, so long runners are definitely helpful.

5 min

Approach: Take Rim of the World Drive (3N14) for 1.2 miles. Turn left onto 2N13. Drive 2.1 miles on 2N13 to a right turn to stay on 2N13. Continue for another 0.25 miles to a sharp right turn onto 2N68, where that road heads steeply uphill. (If you find yourself heading downhill on 2N13, you've missed the turn and gone too far.) At the top of the hill, approximately 100 yards along 2N68, is a small clearing in the pines. Park here for Legoland (same parking as for Hanna Rocks).

From the parking area, face south and hike up the small hill, taking the path of least resistance. Crest the top and continue downhill to the formations. You will be approaching from the back side of the walls, and the first one encountered on your right will be Upper Kid Power Tower.

Upper Kid Power Tower

Upper Kid Power Tower

The well-featured, 30-foot-tall rock that sits closest to the top of the hill. All of the climbs here ascend numerous horizontals. In addition to the listed routes, try out the *Lower Boulder Traverse* (V0), an easy back-and-forth across the bottom of the wall utilizing a good rail system. **[GPS: 34.26886, -116.98883]**

❶ Swabbies Deck 5.7 ★★

A pleasant romp on horizontals, using a short left-facing corner to start. Anchor from *Brickmaster* with an extension.
30 ft. 4 bolts. Brad Singer, Mike Williams, Aug. 2006.

❷ Block Party 5.8+ ★★

Enjoyable climbing with a neat finishing bulge that adds a little spice. Shared anchor with *Brickmaster*.
30 ft. 3 bolts. Brad Singer, Mike Williams, Aug. 2006.

❸ Brickmaster 5.8+ ★★

In the middle of the wall, this route lures climbers in with the easy moves down low, only to catch them off guard with a reachy challenge at the top.
30 ft. 5 bolts. Brad Singer, Mike Williams, Aug. 2006.

❹ Log Cabin 5.7 ★★

Identify this fun easy route by the orange diagonal dike running beside its first bolt. Shares anchors with *Brickmaster*.
30 ft. 4 bolts. Brad Singer, Mike Williams, Aug. 2006.

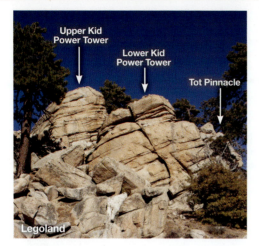

Upper Kid Power Tower

Lower Kid Power Tower

Tot Pinnacle

Legoland

5 Block on Block 5.6 ★★

Stack solid move upon solid move as you climb the huge jugs of this broken corner. Good route for someone learning to lead.

30 ft. 4 bolts. Brad Singer, Mike Williams, Aug. 2006.

6 Sky Ride 5.9 ★★

A novel traverse route beginning on the first 2 bolts of *Swabbies Deck*, moving right across the wall, and finishing on the last bolt of *Block on Block*. Stay above the obvious ledge to keep the thin traverse interesting.

40 ft. 6 bolts. Chris Owen, Scott Nomi, June 2018.

Lower Kid Power Tower

The lower of the 2 main formations, 50 feet downhill from UKPT, and home to the majority of the tougher routes at Legoland.

7 Sky Cruiser 5.10b ★★

Cruise the sequential face with holds right where you need them. Culminates with a steep finish. No rap rings at press time — walk off or use nearby anchors to rappel.

35 ft. 3 bolts. Brad Singer, Mike Williams, Aug. 2006.

8 Bionicle 5.10a ★★★

An exciting route that crosses the prominent arching crack and passes a conspicuous chickenhead. Fierce finish as you punch out the lip with a long reach to a distant crimp.

40 ft. 4 bolts. Brad Singer, John Cardmon, Aug. 2006.

9 Water Works 5.7 ★

Paddle up the obvious wide crack in the center of the formation. Swim through the offwidth at the top to shared anchors of *Sky Cruiser*.

40 ft. Gear to 6". Kenn Kenaga, John Cardmon, Aug. 2006.

10 Sky Patrol 5.9 ★★★

Short but sweet line on a giant flake that kicks back for the final steep overhang. The movement flows very well, powerful with a dash of finesse.

40 ft. 5 bolts. Brad Singer, Mike Williams, Aug. 2006.

11 Flight Squadron 5.10a ★

Blast past numerous horizontals on good face holds. Share anchors with *Sky Patrol*.

40 ft. 5 bolts. Brad Singer, Mike Williams, Aug. 2006.

12 The Big Test 5.10d ★

This short roof puzzle is the toughest line at Legoland. Stand high on blocks and pull the height-dependent crux. Run through a series of overlaps on the right margin of the wall. Set up from the anchors of *Sky Patrol*.

40 ft. Ryan Crochiere, John Cardmon, Aug. 2006.

Tot Pinnacle
Located 50 feet right of LKPT

13 Brickolini 5.9+ ★★

Rock up and over the neat roof problem, making the cruxy long reach to a distant edge. Caution: there's potential for groundfall as you climb easy terrain to the 2nd bolt. Smear to the top, where the fun is over too darn quickly.

30 ft. 3 bolts. Brad Singer, Mike Williams, Aug. 2006.

Miniland
A squatty little formation, home to a collection of short climbs. The rock is the poorest at Legoland, being gritty and crumbly. Exercise caution especially on the trad routes and expect to perform some exfoliation.

Approach: Located approximately 100 yards southeast of Lower Kid Power Tower. The easiest approach is to hike straight downhill from the Lower Tower and then walk east toward the wall. There is no defined trail, but the approach is only 3-5 minutes from the other crags.
[GPS: 34.26796, -116.98795]

14 Block of Fame 5.8 ★

Climb underneath the small overlap on the left side of the south face. Charge through incut edges that become sparse toward the top.

40 ft. 4 bolts. Brad Singer, Eric Odenthal, Mike Williams, Pat Brennan, Kevin Graves, Aug. 2006.

Lower Kid Power Tower

15 Art of Lego 5.7

Head directly up easy terrain to right-facing flakes. Shares anchors with *Block of Fame*. Loose rock.

40 ft. Gear to 2". Eric Odenthal, Aug. 2006.

16 Master Builders 5.10c ★

Climb plates on the arête. Tricky moves guard the upper section of the slopey corner near the 3rd bolt.

45 ft. 4 bolts. Eric Odenthal, Brad Singer, Aug. 2006.

17 Legotechnic 5.9 ★

A gritty groove/finger crack 5 feet right of the corner. Gear anchor. The tree branches behind you can be obnoxious.

40 ft. Gear to 2". Pat Brennan, Kevin Graves, Aug. 2006.

18 Model Shop 5.7

Climb into a cutout, then jam the crack. Worse rock than some of the others. Gear anchor.

40 ft. Gear to 3". Eric Odenthal (solo), Aug. 2006.

19 Coast Cruise 5.8

On the east face. Take a ramp past a bolt and climb the narrow chunk of rock that looks like the bow of a ship. Gear anchor.

30 ft. Gear to 2", 1 bolt. Pat Brennan, Kevin Graves, Aug. 2006.

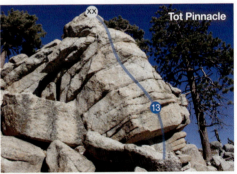

Tot Pinnacle

Miniland

HANNA ROCKS

This is a collection of south-facing formations scattered atop a hillside, with Big West Hanna being the largest and best of the bunch. The rock is generally good, with plates, horns, and chickenheads that make for enjoyable climbing. *Migs Over Moscow* (5.11b) is the only fully bolted sport line here, and a route that should definitely be on your tick list. There is no distinct trail system — one must follow landmarks or GPS coordinates to locate the walls. The area has recently burned, and as a result the buckthorn has flourished in the trees' absence. The buckthorn and downed trees make the tramping a bit tougher here, but not unbearable.

Approach: Hanna Rocks has the same parking as Legoland. From the town of Fawnskin, take Rim of the World Drive (3N14) for 1.2 miles. Turn left onto 2N13. Drive 2.1 miles on 2N13 to a right turn to stay on 2N13. Continue for another 0.25 miles to a sharp right turn onto 2N68, where that road heads steeply uphill. (If you find yourself heading downhill on 2N13, you've missed the turn and gone too far.) At the top of the hill, approximately 100 yards along 2N68, is a small clearing in the pines. Park here.

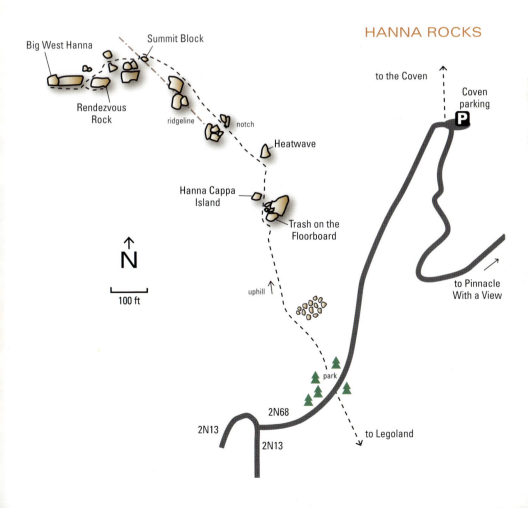

HANNA ROCKS

Big West Hanna
Summit Block
Rendezvous Rock
ridgeline
notch
Heatwave
Hanna Cappa Island
Trash on the Floorboard
uphill
to the Coven
Coven parking
P
to Pinnacle With a View
N
100 ft
park
2N68
2N13
2N13
to Legoland

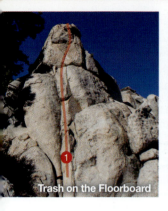
Trash on the Floorboard

variation
Hanna Cappa Island

Heatwave

Trash on the Floorboard

The first formation encountered at Hanna Rocks. The base of the wall is a gully filled with debris from dead trees.

  10 min

Approach: From the parking area, locate a pile of boulders to the north. Head around the left side of these boulders to a wash. Hike up the wash to the first formation encountered directly behind the boulders.
[GPS: 34.27149, -116.98951]

❶ Trash on the Floorboard 5.7 ★

Chug up the railroad-track cracks. Straddle the ridge of rock between, climbing to a thin diagonal seam. Skirt the bulge on the right and finish on big plates. Gear anchor.
40 ft. Gear to 3". Pat Brennan, Bob Cable, John Halushka, July 1998.

Hanna Cappa Island

This formation has a single thought-provoking route leading to its summit.

10 min

Approach: Continue uphill past Trash on the Floorboard. This is the next rock encountered, situated smack dab in the middle of a large gully filled with buckthorn.
[GPS: 34.27174, -116.98959]

❷ Hanna Cappa Island 5.7 ★

Set sail across a shallow ledge, traversing right to a slanting finger crack. Thinning plates provide a runout finish.
40 ft. Thin gear. Bob Cable, John Halushka, Pat Brennan, July 1998.
Variation 5.9+: The direct start underneath the roof is a short boulder problem with slick feet.

Heatwave

A south-facing formation capped by a roof, located high on the slope. Summit could use a bolted anchor!

  15 min

Approach: The next formation uphill from Hanna Cappa Island.
[GPS: 34.27217, -116.98959]

❸ Heatwave 5.10a ★★

An excellent little line up the center seam of the formation. Climb up underneath the roof, then blast out left to giant horns and plates that can be slung for natural pro. Gear anchor.
35 ft. 3 bolts, gear to 3" for the anchor.
Bob Cable, Pat Brennan, John Halushka, July 1998.

Summit Block

This 20-foot-tall formation houses the hiker's summit register on its north side, marked by cairns. Only hit these routes if you're in the neighborhood, bored, and looking for more cracks.

25 min

Approach: From the parking area, head around the left side of the initial boulders. Hike up a gully past the first 3 formations. From Heatwave, continue up the hill through a notch in the ridge, then travel northwest along the ridgeline to the summit block.
[GPS: 34.27297, -116.99084]

❹ Green Machine 5.6

A very short wide-hands crack on the north face that angles right. Lichen, lichen, and more lichen. Gear anchor.
20 ft. Gear to 2.5". Pat Brennan, David LePere, July 1999.

Summit Block North

Summit Block South

Rendezvous Rock

⑤ Pebble Pusher 5.8

The south-face crack line with a low crux. Climb direct or take the left slant to big horns. Gear anchor.

20 ft. Gear to 2.5". Pat Brennan, David LePere, July 1999.

Rendezvous Rock

Squatty south-facing formation home to 2 cracks and distinguished by a fin of rock on the left side, climbed by the route *Allison's Chance*.

  30 min

Approach: Downhill to the west of Summit Block. Easily visible from the vicinity of Big West Hanna.
[GPS: 34.27278, -116.99129]

⑥ Allison's Chance 5.10b ★★

Ride this granite fin, exploiting the crack on its right and the awesome plate features as they present themselves. Gear anchor.

45 ft. Gear to 2.5", 1 bolt. Pat Brennan, Kenn Kenaga, June 1999.

⑦ Hanna-Barbera 5.8 ★

Broken crack system on the right side of the wall. Gear anchor.

45 ft. Gear to 2". Pat Brennan, David LePere, July 1999.

Big West Hanna

The biggest and best wall at Hanna Rocks, easily visible from the road. Magnificent views, good rock, and the routes have great movement—what's not to like?

30 min

Approach: From Summit Block, hike downhill to the west.
[GPS: 34.27269, -116.99176]

Big West Hanna

8 Weber 5.9 ★★

A crack-to-traverse line that wraps around the formation. Jet up the leftmost hand crack past a bolt to a ledge 40 feet up. Quit here by building a gear anchor and walking off the ledge, or continue climbing up a flake. Cut left across the west face, pop onto the low-angle north face, and slab it to shared anchors atop *Migs*. Expect rope drag for the full version.
80 ft. Gear to 3", 1 bolt.
Pat Brennan, Kenn Kenaga, Eric Tipton, July 1998.

9 Hurricane Hanna 5.10a ★

An alternate, slightly tougher starting crack. Slick and flaring down low, becoming solid fist jamming. Ending options are the same as for *Weber* — bail left or top out.
80 ft. Gear to 3", 1 bolt.
Kenn Kenaga, Eric Tipton, Pat Brennan, July 1998.

10 Migs Over Moscow 5.11b ★★★★

Stellar climbing up the signature landmark at Hanna Rocks. Pristine rock, majestic views, excellent movement, airy exposure, and a remote setting all contribute to a memorable experience on this mega-classic line. Flow up a left-facing dihedral/ramp to a burly crux at the 3rd bolt. Balance and friction past 3 closely spaced bolts to a secondary crux near the 6th bolt. Punch out the roof and claim victory at the chains.
80 ft. 10 bolts. David LePere, Sept. 1998.

11 Kahanna 5.10a ★★★

Exploit the weaknesses of the wall with this line. Start down low in an offwidth behind a fat flake (wide gear needed to protect this section). Stand atop the flake to clip a bolt and traverse left across a blank face to reach a ramp. Move right of the roof, zipping up a finger crack to the summit. Shares anchors with *Migs*.
70 ft. Gear to 2", 1 bolt.
Eric Tipton, Kenn Kenaga, Pat Brennan, July 1998.

12 Barbara Ann 5.10a ★★

Exceptional dihedral climbing for 30 feet, but the roof section is unfortunately crusted in lichen. Save a couple of larger pieces for a gear anchor. Descend via a plated juggy downclimb on climber's right.
50 ft. Gear to 4". Pat Brennan, Kenn Kenaga, Eric Tipton, July 1998.

THE COVEN

Nestled atop a ridge, this excellent outcropping is home to 60+ routes. The ridge runs southeast to northwest, with many formations facing south or southwest and receiving all day sun. This granite amalgamation has routes scattered among a dozen different walls, with Voodoo Wall and Dragonlance Wall having the highest concentrations of lines. Many routes are sport bolted, but there are plenty of excellent traditionally protected cracks. The rock is generally good, although more traffic will help clean the slightly crumbly exterior on some routes. Grades range across the spectrum, from 5.3 to 5.12d, often featuring solid movement on good plates. This extensive area is an excellent alternative to the popular Holcomb Valley Pinnacles, without the crowds.

Approach: From Fawnskin, take Rim of the World Drive (3N14) for 1.2 miles. Turn left onto 2N13. Drive 2.1 miles on 2N13 to a right turn to stay on 2N13. Continue for another 0.25 miles to a sharp right turn onto 2N68, where that road heads steeply uphill. (If you find yourself heading downhill on 2N13, you've missed the turn and gone too far.) Drive along 2N68 for 0.2 miles to the parking pullout on a hairpin turn just before a downhill section.

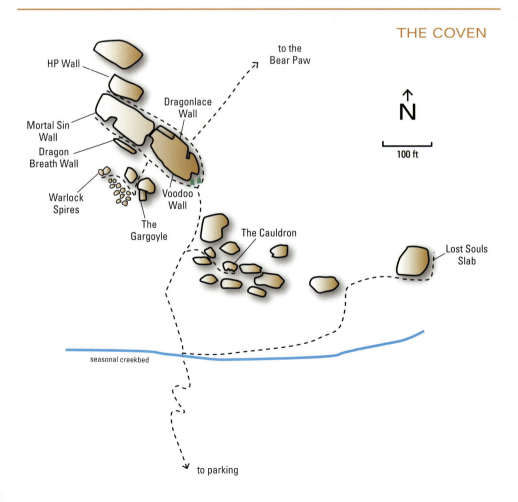

THE COVEN

HP Wall

to the
Bear Paw

Dragonlace
Wall

Mortal Sin
Wall

Dragon
Breath Wall

Warlock
Spires

Voodoo
Wall

The
Gargoyle

The Cauldron

Lost Souls
Slab

N

100 ft

seasonal creekbed

to parking

The Cauldron

A small, south-facing formation, often bypassed while heading to the main walls.

5 min

Approach: Approach as for Dragonlance Wall, but on the final push uphill through the boulders, locate cairns marking the righthand turnoff. Scramble east through broken terrain in the back corner of a corridor that leads to the base of the Cauldron.
[GPS: 34.27439, -116.98753]

Cauldron Approach

1 Boil, Boil 5.10b ★

Toil and trouble, arms burn and fingers bubble as you fire up this thin diagonal crack that shares anchors with *Eye of Newt*.
40 ft. Gear to 3". Brad Singer, Chris Miller, David LePere, Steve Kravchuck, Sept. 2000.

The Cauldron

2 Eye of Newt 5.10a

Difficult start with poor feet. Climb past the obvious flake between the two cracks.
40 ft. Chris Miller, Steve Kravchuck, Brad Singer, David LePere, Sept. 2000.

3 Toil and Trouble 5.11a ★★

Tricky little line that opens with a mantel onto a small ledge. Make use of both the right (flaring) crack and the left (fingertips) crack to reach a horizontal. Worm up the widening hand crack to shared anchors on *Eye of Newt*.
40 ft. Gear to 3". David LePere, Chris Miller, Brad Singer, Steve Kravchuck, Sept. 2000.

Dragonlance Wall

One of the longest walls at the Coven, this predominately east-facing wall gets morning sun and afternoon shade. It is home to the ultra-classic testpiece *Screaming Trees* (5.12d), plus a mix of sport and trad lines across the grades. This crag can satisfy climbers of all abilities, but is best if you're climbing in the 5.10 or 5.12 ranges.

10 min

Approach: From the parking area on the hairpin turn, hike north to pick up the faint climber's trail. Follow the trail underneath pine trees, heading around the corner while keeping the hill to your left. After 2-3 minutes the trail will reach its apex, with the collection of crags coming into view across a small gully. Head downhill, cross a seasonal creek, and continue up the next hill, weaving through boulders. Hike the well-cairned trail through a notch to arrive at twin pines that mark the left end of Dragonlance Wall.
[GPS: 34.27502, -116.98777]

4 Squeal Like a Pig 5.9

Finger crack located 2 feet left of *Wide Body*. Shares anchors with *Dragonlance*.
45 ft. Gear to 2". Pat Brennan, Brad Singer, Aug. 2001.

5 Wide Body 5.8

Wiggle up the flaring wide crack and scum around the right side of a block to shared anchors with *Dragonlance*.
45 ft. Gear to 6". Brad Singer, Rob Stauder, Sept. 2001.

6 Dragonlance 5.10a ★

A hazardous, so-so bolted line that starts in *Wide Body*, then tackles the face right of the wide crack. Decking potential getting to the high 2nd bolt! Has a 2-bolt anchor without rap rings; you can clip these and keep climbing higher to the chain anchors on *Gorilla Dance* to descend.

45 ft. 3-4 bolts. Dean Goolsby, Craig Pearson, 1990s.

7 Gorilla Dance 5.10a ★

Strenuously lieback a finger crack, then monkey through ledges on knobby holds. Caution: the too-low first bolt does not protect the crux!

45 ft. 4 bolts. Brad Singer, John Cardmon, Aug. 2001.

8 Dancing on a Broomstick 5.7 ★

Scuttle up this chimney with wedged chockstones. Shared anchors atop *Fierce*.

35 ft. Very wide gear, slung chockstones. Rob Stauder, Sept. 2001.

9 Fierce 5.12c ★★★

This bouldery route will steal your time and skin. Reachy moves on sharp crimps and single-pad edges lead to a dyno that's sure to peel you off the wall. A bit contrived where it stays left, avoiding a large plate near the top.

35 ft. 4 bolts. Eric Odenthal, Aug. 2001.

10 Screaming Trees 5.12d ★★★★

Named for the strange noises heard during the equipping of the route one cold, windy day. This is the "money route" at the Coven, bound to leave an impression on any 5.12 climber who lays eyes on it. Fight the pump as you move quickly through sequential and slightly overhanging moves to the arête above.

70 ft. 10 bolts. Eric Odenthal, Mar. 2002.

11 Walk Up 5.3

The ramp to the right of *Screaming Trees* is the access climb for the following 2 routes that start from the upper ledge.

30 ft. 2 bolts.

FA: John Cardmon (solo), Equipped: Chris Miller, Pete Paredes, 2003.

Dragonlance Left

Dragonlance Center

Dragonlance Right

Electricity

The next 2 climbs start from a ledge. Climb Walk Up *(5.3) or* Hammer and Anvil *(5.10d) to access.*

⑫ El Guapo 5.10d ★
Ascend a shallow water gully to plates above.
50 ft. 5 bolts. Chris Miller, Pete Paredes, 2003.

⑬ Lichen Nightmare 5.10d ★
Scale a dirty slab to reach a J-shaped crack. Shares anchors with *El Guapo*.
50 ft. Gear to 3", 2 bolts. Chris Miller, Pete Paredes, 2003.

⑭ Hammer and Anvil 5.10d ★★
A demanding climb with a distinct crux above the 2nd bolt. When the holds peter out, grab the horn, plaster your feet, and perform a mad dyno! Exciting to say the least!
35 ft. 3 bolts. Chris Miller, Pete Paredes, 2003.

⑮ Thermatology 5.10b ★★
50 feet right of *Hammer and Anvil* is this beautiful splitter crack above a flake. Slide your rope up under this route and sink killer jams and cams in all the way to the ledge. Repeat until satisfied. Gear anchor.
40 ft. Gear to 3". Dean Goolsby, Craig Pearson, 1990s.

The following 3 routes begin from the ledge atop Thermatology. *Gain the ledge via a short gully on the right.*

⑯ Alchemy 5.12a ★★
Hairy climbing on the multi-colored upper wall. Identified by a big gray cobble.
35 ft. 2 bolts. Dean Goolsby, Craig Pearson, 1990s.

⑰ Dragonlance Seam (Open Project)
The beautiful seam. Use any and all face holds that come your way, with tiny nuts and brassies as pro on this extremely thin line.
40 ft. Thin gear and RPs.

⑱ Sorcery 5.12c ★★★
Work magic on the pockmarks and thin crimps that pepper the difficult face. Originally a 4-bolt sport climb, this excellent route has sadly had its bolts chopped, but it can still be done as a toprope. Bolted anchor.
45 ft. Dean Goolsby, Craig Pearson, 1990s.

⑲ Electricity 5.10c
Right of the walk-up gully is a short, broken section of wall. Start left of a dead pine and climb a dirty, flared crack system. Belay from a tree.
25 ft. Gear to 2". Dean Goolsby, Craig Pearson, 1990s.

Tim Mullis on *Hammer and Anvil*, 5.10d, opposite. 📷 Brandon Copp

Voodoo Left

Voodoo Wall

The routes here alternate between crack and face climbing, most being of moderate difficulty. This is one of the most popular walls at the Coven, but that doesn't mean you'll see another party here on your visit! Bask in the sun as you climb to your heart's content on this southwest-facing wall.

 10 min

Approach: Approach as for Dragonlance Wall. When the twin pine trees are reached, head left up the boulders/gully to reach Voodoo Wall. **[GPS: 34.27500, -116.98807]**

20 Witch Hunt 5.10b

This slab route was located 50 feet around the corner from the main wall and started behind a tree. As of this writing, all of the bolts have been chopped. Included for historical purposes only.
40 ft. 4 bolts (currently zero).
Dean Goolsby, Craig Pearson, 1990s.

21 Lighten My Load 5.6 ★

A well-featured, left-leaning wide crack. Belay from the pine tree on the massive ledge.
35 ft. Gear to 5". Unknown.

22 Voodoo Highway 5.10c ★

Start in an alcove and climb the rounded arête on sidepulls and edges. Thin finish! 2-bolt anchor without rap rings.
40 ft. 3 bolts. Dean Goolsby, Craig Pearson, 1990s.

23 Chimney-a-Go-Go 5.6 ★

Obvious flaring chimney. Start stemming, then shove any body part that will fit into the offwidth as you squeeze up this widening crack. Shares anchors with *Voodoo Highway*.
40 ft. Wide gear. Unknown.

24 The Sceptre 5.10b ★★★

Bearhug the arête, strenuously scooching and smearing up this sustained spine. Memorable! No rap rings — add some, or walk across the top to a nearby anchor to descend.
50 ft. 4 bolts. Dean Goolsby, Craig Pearson, 1990s.

25 Bruja 5.8 ★

An easy flake leads to a chimney. Wriggle up the chimney for 10 feet until it narrows, then plug in fist jams and pop out onto the cruxy face. Shares anchors with *Bat Wings*.
45 ft. Gear to 6". Unknown.

26 Bat Wings and Blood 5.10a ★★

An enjoyable route with incut patina edges. Don't pop off clipping the 2nd bolt or the boulder at the bottom is likely to bite! Bolted anchor but no rap rings — descend from anchors atop *The Holler*.
45 ft. 4 bolts. Dean Goolsby, Craig Pearson, 1990s.

Rachel Sahl on *Thermatology*, 5.10b, Dragonlance, page 230. 📷 Brandon Copp

Voodoo Right

㉗ Witching Hour 5.11a ★

Launch upward from a small dish through pinkish plates.
Solve the technical sequence on the slick, vertical wall.
Shared anchor with *Bat Wings*.
45 ft. Eric Odenthal, Sept. 2000.

Scramble up onto a ledge to reach the following routes.

㉘ The Holler 5.7 ★★

Sweep that leaning chimney climb on the left end of the
ledge! Gear placements are pretty deep inside the crack.
45 ft. Gear to 4". Rob Stauder, Sept. 2000.

㉙ Witches' Brew 5.10a ★★

Nice, well-protected line on big holds. Work up a rail,
liebacking through a steep section at the 2nd bolt. Tarzan
through the huge holds up higher.
35 ft. 4 bolts. Steve Kravchuck, Brad Singer, David LePere, Sept. 2000.

㉚ Merlin 5.10b ★★

Toprope the blank face between *Witches' Brew* and *Snape*.
Take the large crack up higher to finish.
35 ft. Brad Singer, Kevin Graves, Sept. 2006.

㉛ Snape 5.8 ★★

A one-move-wonder start with high feet on a blank wall.
Positive features, but thinner than the nearby *Malfoy*.
35 ft. 4 bolts. Pete Paredes, Chris Miller, Aug. 2004.

㉜ Harry's Crack 5.7 ★

Start with nice jams and thrash up this gritty wide crack.
Hand stacks at the top! Shares anchors with *Malfoy*.
35 ft. Gear to 4". David LePere, Brad Singer, Sept. 2000.

㉝ Malfoy 5.7 ★★

Fun climb that's pretty cruisy throughout, with plenty of
patina flakes and features.
35 ft. 4 bolts. Chris Miller, Bryan Dennison, Soo Dennison, July 2003.

㉞ Goblin Roof 5.10a ★★

The large roof located right of a tree. Devious slab moves
lead to the roof. Yard past the roof on jugs and follow a
vertical dike past the final 2 bolts.
*35 ft. 4 bolts. Pete Paredes, Brad Singer, Steve Kravchuck,
David LePere, Chris Miller, Sept. 2000.*

㉟ Voodoo Jive 5.10d ★

Toprope the tough slab just right of *Goblin Roof*. Pull the
right side of the roof and dance up the arête to the *Goblin
Roof* anchors.
35 ft. Chris Miller, Pete Paredes, Sept. 2000.

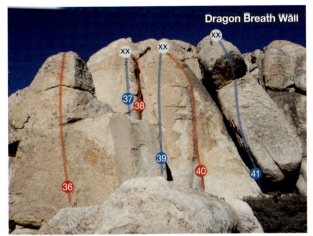

Dragon Breath Wall

Baby Hobbit Roof

Dragon Breath Wall

Located in a small corridor a stone's throw away from Voodoo Wall. The distinct roof on *Waffle House* (5.10d) makes this southwest-facing wall easy to identify.

10 min

Approach: Walk 100 feet left of Voodoo Wall past a broken section to reach the right end of the wall.
[GPS: 34.27513, -116.98822]

---

36 Dragon Balls 5.8
Found on the backside of the rock that forms a corridor with the main wall. Pull on bumps and knobs past horizontals. Get creative with the gear and anchor on this one!
30 ft. Thin gear to 1.5".
John Cardmon, Noelle Ladd, Ryan Scherler, Aug. 2001.

37 The Altar 5.6 ★★
Left of the wide crack is this enjoyable easy route on flakes with a low crux.
30 ft. 3 bolts. Dean Goolsby, Craig Pearson, 1990s.

38 Dracarys 5.7 ★★
Stand atop a boulder and scuttle into the pocket 15 feet up. Slay the upper section of this wide crack with awesome offwidth technique. Shares anchors with *The Altar*.
30 ft. Wide gear to 6". Unknown.

39 Dragon Breath 5.8 ★★
Another great, well-featured line on incuts right of the wide crack. Don't get burned by the crux above the 2nd bolt!
30 ft. 3 bolts. Dean Goolsby, Craig Pearson, 1990s.

40 Spellbound 5.10a ★
Lieback a crack to finish on patina features above. As the crack peters out, the angle subsides. Shares anchors with *Dragon Breath*.
30 ft. Gear to 4", 2 bolts. Dean Goolsby, Craig Pearson, 1990s.

41 Waffle House 5.10d ★★★
Powerful and excellent! From the left side of a block, rock up and over onto the slab. Motor up to the slanting roof. Make a long reach to good holds, throw a heel hook, and make the hero move.
35 ft. 4 bolts. Eric Odenthal, Ryan Scherler, Aug. 2001.

42 Hogwarts 5.5 R ★
Climb a dirty, featured crack to its end, step left and go up an unprotected slab. This route could use a bolt at the top. Gear anchor.
25 ft. Gear to 3". Alan Bartlett, Brandt Allen, Aubrey Adams, June 2015.

43 Baby Hobbit Roof 5.9+ ★
A short roof route around the corner between Dragon Breath and Voodoo Walls. Gracefully climb the lower slab, then sink good jams into the hand crack above the roof.
25 ft. Gear to 3". Brad Singer, Pat Brennan, Aug. 2001.

Mortal Sin Wall

A small southwest face with a few tough trad lines. Build a gear anchor and walk off climber's right.

Approach: Walk through the corridor at the base of Dragon Breath and continue heading downhill past the left end of that wall. Scramble past boulders; Mortal Sin is the next wall encountered. **[GPS: 34.27524, -116.98843]**

44 Whipped 5.11d ★★★
An imposing overhanging finger crack on the left side of the wall. Demanding, unrelenting, and sure to test your mental fortitude. Gear anchor.
40 ft. Gear to 2". John Cardmon, Rob Stauder.

45 Mortal Sin 5.10a ★★
Stem up the dihedral past an overlap to a nice hand-sized crack that widens to fists. Gear anchor.
40 ft. Gear to 4". Dean Goolsby, Craig Pearson, 1990s.

46 Weave the Magic 5.11b R ★
Start in the dihedral and climb to a large flake, then take the finger crack that arcs out right. Precision footwork makes all the difference on this tough route. Gear anchor.
45 ft. Gear to 2". Dean Goolsby, Craig Pearson, 1990s.

Mortal Sin Wall

HP Wall

Yer a wizard, Harry! This spot has beautiful views of the surrounding mountains and valleys, and its climbs either start from a ledge or are located in a corridor. The sport routes *Gryffindor* (5.11a) and *Slytherin* (5.11b) are well worth the hike down to this wall.

Approach: Head steadily uphill past the far right end of Dragonlance Wall until you reach the top of the ridge. Pick your way down the steep gully/corridor until it ends in a pile of boulders. *Evil Deed* and *Lesser of Two Evils* are located on the right side of this corridor. Carefully swing around the corner to your right onto a large ledge that forms the base of HP Wall. **[GPS: 34.27542, -116.98831]**

47 Gryffindor 5.11a ★★
Found on the northeast corner. Start up a yellow undercut section with reachy moves to a horizontal. Plates galore on the low-angle ramp lead to a headwall block. Cast your favorite spell to float past thin, crimpy challenges on slicker rock. Bolted anchor without rap rings.
60 ft. 5 bolts. Chris Miller, Pete Paredes, 2003.

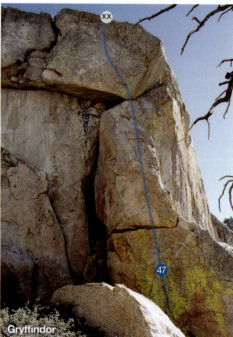

Gryffindor

DEAN GOOLSBY

Dean Goolsby grew up in Southern California and is best known for developing the Coven with Craig Pearson in the 1990s. His passion for adventure has resulted in over 50 first ascents in the Big Bear Lake area. His climbing career has spanned the greater part of his life and has truly defined and shaped who he is. Dean's introduction to climbing came on a backpacking trip in the Sierra Nevada, where he did a Class-4 scramble up Mt. Humphries. He was so elated that the very next week he went out and bought a pair of climbing shoes, and a lifelong love was born.

Dean met Craig Pearson while climbing locally in Orange County. At that time, climbers were establishing "glue-ups" — typically bouldering traverses and occasionally taller bolted routes created by gluing thin rocks or bricks to concrete walls and bridges (an interesting part of Southern California's climbing history that pre-dated gyms: look it up!). The two would boulder together after work on these local walls and take weekend trips to Deadman's Summit and the Bachar Boulders on the Sierra East Side. In the summer of 1992, Dean, Craig, and Craig's wife Julie started exploring the local San Bernardino Mountains in search of new bouldering spots, where they discovered the vast potential hidden among the trees on the south shore of Big Bear Lake.

One winter while cross-country skiing in Holcomb Valley, Dean spotted tall rock formations in the distance, vowing to return the next summer to climb at what would become the Coven. Dean and Craig spent the next couple of years on a frenzy, developing numerous memorable routes on the granite spires. Dean's first ascent of *Sorcery* (5.12c), a challenging face climb utilizing pristine holds on Dragonlance Wall, is in his opinion his most noteworthy. The pair also discovered nearby Jacoby Canyon, developing a handful of routes on the unique quartzite wall.

Dean drew inspiration from various prominent climbers of the day. He was fortunate enough to know John Bachar, who was inspirational because of the way he climbed at a high level with such conviction and confidence. Dean also spent time climbing with and photographing Peter Croft, another premier soloist who seemed to climb so effortlessly, yet was still humble and easy to talk to — good qualities that Dean wanted to emulate. When Dean was trying to push himself, Wolfgang Güllich's training regimen provided motivation and set an example for pushing the boundaries of climbing grades.

Over the past 30 years Dean has climbed throughout the world. His favorite places include the immaculate limestone cliffs of Céüse, France, and Hueco Tanks for bouldering. Today, Dean continues to develop boulder problems in the Santa Ana Mountains. While he hasn't roped up in years, he enjoys the solitude of the mountains and searching every hill and gully for quality boulders.

Dean has been married to his beautiful wife, Janel, for 15 years, with whom he has a daughter, a stepdaughter, and a stepson. Outside of climbing, Dean enjoys freshwater fishing, and is a die-hard fan of Manchester United, having played soccer competitively himself for many years.

His message to the climbing community: We must as a group work on the overcrowding issue to minimize our impact on our fragile climbing resources. Climbers today need to police themselves and take responsibility for their actions. Please take care of these beautiful places we all love so that those privileges are not taken away.

48 Goblet of Fire 5.9 ★★★

Excellent wide splitter crack forming the left side of the "V". Double-fisting at its finest as you work magic on this challenging offwidth. When you're tired of grunting, find a plate feature inside the crack or on the face to regain your composure. Complete the trial by finishing up the left side of the headwall to the shared anchor with *Slytherin*.

50 ft. Gear to 6". Kenn Kenaga, John Cardmon, June 2006.

49 Out of Print 5.10b ★

Climb the crack on the right side of the "V", working up a ramp to the big ledge. Continue into a crux sequence on a seam, passing 2 bolts. Shared anchor with *Slytherin*.

50 ft. Gear to 3", 2 bolts. Kenn Kenaga, Brad Singer, June 2006.

50 Slytherin 5.11b ★★★

It's all fun and games on the steep and cruisy features down low. From the big ledge, surmount the slick steep wall above, making powerful moves on thin crimps, and slither left through the final crux bulge.

50 ft. 5 bolts. John Cardmon, June 2006.

51 Evil Deed 5.10d ★

Around the righthand corner in the corridor. Plug up the leftmost crack, passing a rounded horn. Tricky pro. Bolted anchor without rap rings.

35 ft. Gear to 1". Dean Goolsby, Craig Pearson, 1990s.

52 Lesser of Two Evils 5.10a ★

Rightmost and easier of the cracks. Smear feet while liebacking the rounded corner/flake and slotting gear in the finger crack. No anchor — bring some long cord to build one.

30 ft. Gear to 2". Dean Goolsby, Craig Pearson, 1990s.

The Gargoyle

A small west-facing crag located just downhill from Voodoo Wall.

  10 min

Approach: From the left end of Voodoo Wall, locate the large pine behind the cliff. Facing the tree from the wall (looking southwest), you will see a gully framed by large rocks on either side. Hike 100-150 feet down the gully; the Gargoyle is the wall on the left.
[GPS: 34.27483, -116.98815]

53 The Gargoyle 5.11b ★★

Stout crimpfest with incuts that just keep getting better. 1-bolt anchor (no rap ring).

30 ft. 3 bolts. Dean Goolsby, Craig Pearson, 1990s.

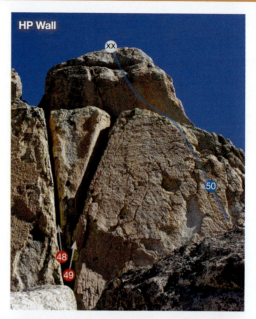

HP Wall

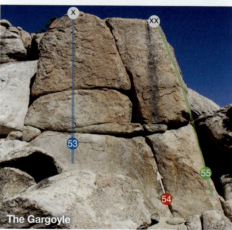

The Gargoyle

54 The Griffin 5.10c ★★

This is the main crack splitting the formation. A frustrating start leads to a good ledge. Power up the nice finger-to-hands crack above. Shared anchor with *The Gargoyle*.

35 ft. Gear to 2.5". Dean Goolsby, Craig Pearson, 1990s.

55 The Spectre 5.10a ★

A short burn up the fairly blank and rounded arête. Bring longer slings for the 2-bolt anchor (no rap rings).

35 ft. Dean Goolsby, Craig Pearson, 1990s.

Jeremy Saqr on *Which Crack*, 5.8,
Warlock Spires, page 240. 📷 Brandon Copp

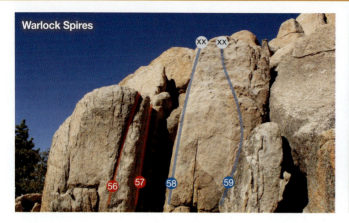

Warlock Spires

The Bear Paw

Warlock Spires

A set of two spires. Use the bolted anchors on the right spire for all routes.

☀ 🚶 15 min

Approach: Go down the same gully as for the Gargoyle, but continue heading downhill. The two spires should be visible from the Gargoyle. Scramble over and through boulders, moving to the right (west).
[GPS: 34.27493, -116.98846]

 Thunderclap Crack 5.10b ★★   ☐☐
A right-trending crack that doesn't quite touch the ground. Scratch your head and unlock the lower sequence to reach the crack. Gear anchor. For full value, do it in a thunderstorm like the first ascensionists!
35 ft. Gear to 2.5". Brad Singer, Kevin Graves, July 2006.

 Which Crack 5.8 ★★   ☐☐
Jam up this quality fist crack in a corner situated left of the wide chimney. A solid climb that's good fun! Gear anchor.
35 ft. Gear to 4".
Kenn Kenaga, Mike Williams, John Cardmon, July 2006.

58 **Warlock** 5.10d ★★   ☐☐
Friction and balance along the blunt arête on the right spire, using any small chips you can find. Just when it seems like the difficulties have passed, confront a desperate and surprising finish.
40 ft. 3 bolts. Dean Goolsby, Craig Pearson, 1990s.

59 **Williams Whine** 5.8+ ★   ☐☐
Reach high for the thin flakes and you're off! Enjoy the slabby finish!
30 ft. 2 bolts. Mike Williams.

The Bear Paw

An independent pillar located a short distance from Dragonlance Wall, beside a drainage channel. There are no rap rings on either bolted anchor—a 4th Class scramble off the back of the formation is required to descend.

☀ 🚶 15 min

Approach: Locate the gully that leads to the *Walk Up* route (page 229) on Dragonlance Wall. From here, strike out east to get a visual of the wall before approaching. Head north and east, down into a drainage gully. Follow this drainage and it will bring you right to the base of this pillar. While it is a fairly easy landmark to locate visually, the path isn't obvious. 5 minutes from Dragonlance Wall.
[GPS: 34.27639, -116.98625]

---

60 **Big Toe** 5.10c ★★★
Clamber up the lefthand arête of the foot-shaped face. Slabby down low with nice edges and good features up higher. At the 4th bolt, transition right to the crack that separates the big toe from the rest of the foot. A slight runout here on easier terrain (optional 1-2" cam) adds spice to the finish.
45 ft. 4 bolts, optional 1-2" piece.
Reed Ames, Pete Scollan, Kyle Campbell, Sept. 2015.

61 **Little Toe** 5.11c ★   ☐☐
Tackle a right-facing flake head-on to reach a thin crack. Tickle the toe as you follow the crack up the right corner of the face to much better features above.
50 ft. Reed Ames, Pete Scollan, Kyle Campbell, Sept. 2015.

Lost Souls Slab

Lost Souls Slab

An east-facing slab separate from the main Coven formations. The wall is speckled white and black, with 2 roofs capping the crag.

AM   15 min

Approach: Hike along the main trail to the Coven until you reach the seasonal creekbed. Turn right and walk east to the right end of a line of boulders. Pop over a small rise; from here you will see 2 domes, which mark the backside of the Lost Souls Slab. Cut downhill slightly and hike around the rightmost formation to its east face and the climbs. Only slightly harder to find and reach than the other walls at the Coven.
[GPS: 34.27439, -116.98603]

62 Soul Doubt 5.11b ★
Trust those feet to smear on a thin seam (past a bolt). Pray you make it through the sea of nothing and reach the overlap. Shares anchors with *Elizabeth Reed*.
45 ft. David LePere, Chris Miller, June 2002.

63 In Memory of Elizabeth Reed 5.10a ★★★
Like the Allman Brothers song, this remarkable line keeps changing, but is enjoyable throughout. A long reach to a dish provides relief from the steep opening slab. Throttle over an overlap and into the flared finger crack that leads to a roof.
50 ft. 6 bolts. Brad Singer, Eric Odenthal, Mar. 2002.

64 Night Shift 5.11c ★
Shares the first bolt and anchors with *Elizabeth Reed*. Cut right from the dish across blank slab and finish in a slot. The bolting leaves some bad fall potential.
50 ft. 5 bolts. David LePere, Mar. 2002.

65 Open Project
Utilize the gray knob as a foothold to pop onto the slab. Surf directly into the overhung wave feature. Slap up the blunt arête and skirt the roof on its right side to anchors atop *Hooters*.
50 ft.

66 Hooters 5.10d ★★
Easy climbing on a ramp using bumps and knobs. The crux hits hard on the perplexing face above the 2nd bolt. Higher up, grab the honkers sticking out of the wall and soar on up to the anchors on the right side of a block.
45 ft. 3 bolts. Eric Odenthal, Brad Singer, Mar. 2002.

67 Youth of a Nation 5.9 ★★
Delicate slab climb on the right margin of the wall that shares anchors with *Hooters*.
45 ft. 5 bolts. Brad Singer, Eric Odenthal, Mar. 2002.

HOLCOMB CREEK CRAGS

This smattering of small crags near the Holcomb Creek drainage is rarely visited. Most of the walls are in the 40- to 60-foot range. The rock quality is decent, although there can be a bit of loose grit, as is common for many of the crags around Big Bear Lake that don't see a lot of traffic. Holcomb Creek Tower and World Cup Tower have the largest collections of routes, with most of the other formations only sporting a route or two. There is near-endless potential here among the copious piles of boulders if you are interested in putting up new 40-foot routes.

Approach: From the stoplight at the dam, drive 3.3 miles along the north shore on Highway 38/North Shore Drive to the small town of Fawnskin. Turn left onto Rim of the World Drive (3N14) near the fire station. The driving directions for all crags start from the intersection of 38 and 3N14.

Red Bull Pinnacle

A narrow formation with two climbs on its shady northeast face.

AM · 15 min

Red Bull Pinnacle

Approach: Drive north from Fawnskin along Rim of the World Drive (3N14) for 2.9 miles in total. The road passes the Hanna Flat campground and heads downhill. Park beside a fence row on the left, 0.2 miles after the pavement ends.

Hike 100 yards southwest, cresting a small hill. Turn south and hike down into a ravine. Just before the bottom of the ravine is a mountain bike trail. From the bike trail, the pinnacle's northeast face is visible on the opposite embankment. The approach is a 15-minute, steep downhill and uphill trek (0.25 miles). **[GPS: 34.28837, -116.98337]**

1 **Red Legs** 5.9+ ★★

The obvious squeeze chimney formed by the main pinnacle and a squatty boulder. Writhe up the pebbled chimney that's sure to chew up your knees! Exit the chimney at the 3rd bolt and delicately climb the blunt arête. Shares anchors with *Red Bull*.

50 ft. 6 bolts. Brad Singer, Eric Odenthal, John Cardmon, June 2002.

2 **Red Bull** 5.11b ★★★

You'll need fingers of steel for this splendid overhanging finger crack! Chug an energy drink, then dive into ringlocks on this pumpy splitter as you gun for the wide flare 25 feet up. Step left and mantel atop the formation to an anchor without rap rings.

50 ft. Gear to 4". FA: (TR) Eric Tipton, June 2002; FL: Eric Odenthal, June 2002.

Holcomb Creek Tower

A secluded, south-facing tower that sits high on a hillside overlooking the Pacific Crest Trail and picturesque Holcomb Creek. The routes here are all steep slab climbs, with *The Rocker* (5.10b) being the best. Nearby formations offer a couple of additional climbs.

30 min

Approach: Drive north out of Fawnskin on 3N14 for 4.3 miles, then turn left onto 3N93. Follow this road, beside Holcomb Creek, for 0.7 miles to a circular parking area just before the road crosses the creek. The parking circle has a section of barbed wire fence beside the road.

Holcomb Creek Tower and Slashed Tower

The hiking approach is fairly easy and follows the well-maintained Pacific Crest Trail (PCT) for the majority of the time, with a final scramble up a hillside to reach the tower. From the right side of the fence, walk perpendicular to the road for 150 feet until you meet up with the PCT. Turn left and hike southwest along the fairly flat trail, paralleling the creek, for 0.75 miles until the trail begins to leave the creek, making a long curve away to the right. At this point, the tower should come into view on the hillside. Leave the trail as it makes a hairpin turn to the left and continue cross-country over boulders and brush to reach the base of the tower.
[GPS: 34.29117, -117.00172]

❸ **Long Tom** 5.9+ ★★
Start with a low crux on thin, fragile edges that give way to a well-featured arête and a final short slab as you ascend the left margin of the tower.
55 ft. 6 bolts. Pat Brennan, Kenn Kenaga, Aug. 1998.

❹ **South American Cruise** 5.10b ★
Locate the large flake shaped like South America. Start your adventure by traveling up the coast of Argentina, then navigate straight through the heart of Brazil. Reach the northernmost point of the continent and set sail on the open ocean, plundering small holds on the slab above.
55 ft. Brad Singer, June 1999.

❺ **Holcomb Lode** 5.10d R ★★
Mantel onto a rail and use the South America flake to make the scary traverse right along the Brazilian coast. Balancy and delicate slab climbing.
55 ft. 5 bolts. Kenn Kenaga, Pat Brennan, Sept. 1998.

❻ **The Rocker** 5.10b ★★★
A real calf burner. Thin features lead up to a ledge. Reach high on the blank section for better knobs and edges. Continuous slab climbing along the tower's corner.
65 ft. 6 bolts. Bob Cable, Pat Brennan, Eric Tipton, Aug. 1998.

❼ **Rainbow** 5.10c ★★
Stem a slot to reach a short section of crack and a good gear placement. Transition to face features, traversing left across the steep wall on small nubbins. Best to extend the shared anchor.
60 ft. Gear to 1", 5 bolts.
John Halushka, Bob Cable, Pat Brennan, Sept. 1998.

Slashed Tower
Located 50 feet west of Holcomb Creek Tower.

30 min

❽ **Wolverine** 5.9- ★
Claw up the right-angling crack, then make a slightly hairy traverse left across patina before following another wide hand crack and knobs to the top.
35 ft. Gear to 2". Matthew Janse, Brandon Copp, Sept. 2019.

Alex Hamo on *Long Tom*, 5.9+,
Holcomb Creek Tower, page 243.

📷 Brandon Copp

Holcomb Creek Dome

Located 150 yards northeast from Holcomb Creek Tower, a low-angle dome with a distinctive pine tree above it.   40 min
[GPS: 34.29208, -117.00092]

9 Three Amigos 5.8+ ★

Initially ascend easy terrain on a small buttress. Saunter up the slab above sombrero-style, making sure to cha-cha real slow. This slab-tastic line rewards good footwork with spectacular views of Holcomb Creek.
65 ft. 6 bolts. Tim Trigg, Matthew Janse, Tim Mullis, Sept. 2019.

Toaster Oven

It's a bit of a hike for just one route, but the single splitter crack line is worth the trek. A rectangular block with an overhanging crack climb on its northeast face, marked by a dead tree leaning against the wall. 45 min

Approach: Take Rim of the World Drive (3N14) north out of Fawnskin for 6.7 miles. Turn left onto 3N16 near the Big Pine Flats campground. Drive 5.3 miles on 3N16 to a pullout on the right. The last 0.25 miles of road is paved, with parking just after a hairpin turn and the intersection with the 3N93 4x4 trail.

Locate the Pacific Crest Trail beside the creek and hike along it for 30-40 minutes (1.3 miles) until Toaster Oven comes into view on the left embankment of Holcomb Creek. Head down the steep slope, cross the creek, and hike uphill to reach the wall.
[GPS: 34.27791, -117.06882]

Holcomb Creek Dome

Toaster Oven

10 Toaster Oven 5.10d ★★★

A sick slightly overhanging crack climb. A few slab moves lead to a horizontal, where a horn will allow you to lean back, pop in a cam, and slot fingers into the crack. The crack size goes from fingers to hands as it arches across the wall. Even though it's short, this line is an extremely fun challenge for the grade. Gear anchor.
40 ft. Gear to 3". John Cardmon, Eric Odenthal, June 2000.

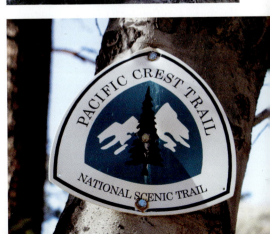

World Cup Tower West

World Cup Tower

If you like slab lines or wide cracks with no crowds, then World Cup Tower is for you! A distinct formation capped by a prominent dome, where sun or shade can be chased all day with east-, south-, and west-facing climbs.

15 min

Approach: Take Rim of the World Drive (3N14) for 6.7 miles and turn left onto 3N16. Follow 3N16 for 1.5 miles to a left turn onto 3N97. Continue on 3N97 for 0.3 miles to the end of the road and park here. Hike along the right side of a meadow for 0.25 miles following an overgrown road. Trek up the steep hillside on the right, heading west. At the top of the hill, World Cup Tower's dome will be visible. **[GPS: 34.29448, -117.02090]**

11 Rope Tow 5.7 ★
After a low crux with slick feet, cruise neat features that the rest of the wall lacks. Be careful with the bit of rotten rock on the blocky corner.
40 ft. 3 bolts. Brad Singer, Eric Odenthal, Sept. 2001.

12 Hermanator 5.8 ★★
A flaring wide crack splitting the west face. Build a gear anchor and rappel from anchors atop *Rope Tow*.
45 ft. Gear to 5". Eric Tipton, Kenn Kenaga, July 1999.

13 Sugar 5.12a ★★
Stiff climbing and long reaches on this friction scare-a-thon. Clamber atop a triangular fin and execute a tenuous mantel onto a small ridge. Dance right across the delicate face, passing a gray xenolith. Underneath the dome, regain your composure before punching out the final headwall. Shares the last two bolts and anchors with *Bird of Prey*.
60 ft. 7 bolts. Ryan Scherler, Eric Odenthal, Sept. 2001.

14 Bird of Prey 5.10b ★★★
A sustained slab route on the southwest corner. Quality technical climbing on bumps and knobs that's tough right from the get-go.
60 ft. 6 bolts. Brad Singer, John Cardmon, July 1999.

15 Hahnenkamm 5.11b ★★★
Straight up the south face. This extremely thin slab route has a crux at the 2nd bolt on crispy edges that don't help the situation. Place a 2" cam under the roof and share anchors with *Bird of Prey*.
60 ft. 5 bolts, gear to 2". Eric Tipton, July 1999.

World Cup Tower East

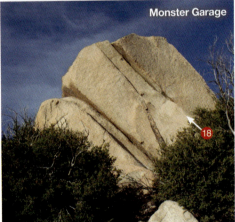

Monster Garage

16 Eddie the Eagle 5.10a ★★

Soar through slab on the southeast arête to a big ledge. Throw a heel hook and rock up onto the top of the dome. Share anchors with *Bird of Prey*.

55 ft. 5 bolts.

Benjamin Oberman, Eric Tipton, Kenn Kenaga, June 2005.

17 Downhill Skidmarks 5.9+ ★★

Fat fist crack/offwidth on the east face. Boogie up past a constriction before being spit out of the widening slot. Gear belay from the ledge and rappel from *Rope Tow* anchors.

35 ft. Gear to 3". John Cardmon, Brad Singer, July 1999.

Monster Garage

A large rock that overlooks Cienaga Larga Meadow. A single route takes the slanting crack on the south face.

20 min

Approach: Follow driving directions for World Cup Tower. Hike along the old road, then trudge through the meadow; Monster Garage is on the opposite side of the meadow from World Cup Tower. Weave through the large bushes on the hillside to reach the climb on the south face. **[GPS: 34.29304, -117.01644]**

18 Monsters Under My Bed 5.9 ★★★

The upper of the two left-slanting cracks. Gear anchor. Punch up the initial ramp to the midway point, where the widening fist-sized crack requires hand stacks. The first ascensionist used a clutch head jam on the send. Be afraid.

50 ft. Gear to 6". Kenn Kenaga, Pat Brennan, Bob Cable, June 2005.

VAN DUSEN CRAGS

Agustin Florido on *Freeze-Dried Lizard Direct*, 5.9+, Alpine Rock, page 263. 📷 Brandon Copp

VAN DUSEN **CRAGS**

These crags are scattered northeast of Big Bear Lake, east and west of Holcomb Valley Pinnacles (which have a dedicated chapter), with the majority accessible by Van Dusen Canyon Road. Overall, the area is void of any large walls, but tight collections of lesser formations are prevalent. North Shore Boulders, with its close proximity to town, is great for a workout when you have only a few hours to climb. Jacoby Canyon and the Quartzitte Bands are unique quartzite crags worth an exploratory visit, and Tanglewood has a low-angle slab that is an ideal spot for beginners. The John Bull area is an out-of-the-way spot with a high concentration of 40-foot moderates on good stone. The majority of the Van Dusen Crags tend to face south, making this area best suited for chilly days.

Approach: To reach the turnoff for Van Dusen Canyon Road, drive east for 9.0 miles from the stoplight at the dam, along the north shore of the lake.

Note that Van Dusen Canyon Road can be closed and gated from November 1 to May 1 each year, depending on conditions. It is possible to drive Polique Canyon Road instead to reach many of these crags.

CLIMBING AREA	ELEVATION	HIKE	ROUTES	GRADE RANGE	CRAGS
JOHN BULL CRAG *Decent crack climbs* page 254	7600 ft.	5-10 min	7	≤.5 .6 .7 .8 .9 .10 .11 .12	
J.B.'S BOX CANYON LEFT *30- to 40-foot-tall crags* page 255	7800 ft.	10-15 min	8	≤.5 .6 .7 .8 .9 .10 .11 .12	California's Gold Rock, JB's Pinnacle, Fat Daddy Rock, Crack Masters Rock, JB Weld Rock, PBR Tower
J.B.'S BOX CANYON RIGHT *Clustered crags, varied climbing* page 258	7800 ft.	10-30 min	9	≤.5 .6 .7 .8 .9 .10 .11 .12	For Brutus of Wyde, Gold Rock, Foggy Rock, Big Bull Rock, Fish Fin, Tumor Pinnacle
TANGLE WOOD *Perfect training ground* page 261	7650 ft.	5-10 min	19	≤.5 .6 .7 .8 .9 .10 .11 .12	Tanglewood Slab, Greenhouse Rock, Alpine Rock
JACOBY CANYON *Polished, beautiful quartzite by a creek* page 265	7350 ft.	5-10 min	15	≤.5 .6 .7 .8 .9 .10 .11 .12	Shooting Gallery, Gunslinger Rock
QUARTZITE BANDS *Thought-provoking sequences on unique rock* page 268	7000 ft. 7200 ft.	10-20 min	17	≤.5 .6 .7 .8 .9 .10 .11 .12	
NORTH SHORE BOULDERS *Sunny, knobby boulders close to town* page 270	7100 ft.	15-20 min	24	≤.5 .6 .7 .8 .9 .10 .11 .12	Big Bubba, Epicenter, Shark Fin, Secret Spot Rock, Table Top Rock, Bear's Behind, The Egg, Cockell's Dome, Lime-Aid, Taggers

Elliot Warden sizes up *Humbolt Hunnies*, 5.8, page 254. 📷 Brandon Copp

JOHN BULL AREA

This peaceful climbing area — from John Bull Crag, page 254, to Tumor Pinnacle, page 260 — is nestled in the woods northeast of Holcomb Valley, clustered around the John Bull 4WD Trail. The John Bull Crag has the largest concentration of routes, with the remainder of the walls containing only one or two lines. Most of these small formations are within John Bull's Box Canyon, an area developed from 2009-2010 by Pat Brennan, Kenn Kenaga, and friends, yet there is still much potential for many more quality routes. There are no trails in this area, so use the GPS coordinates and follow the path of least resistance to reach these crags.

You likely won't see any other climbers at this area. The climbing is actually quite good, with the face climb *Goldfinger* (5.10c) and the offwidth *For Brutus of Wyde* (5.11a) being standouts. The rock can be a bit gritty due to lack of traffic, but there is more than a full day's worth of moderately graded routes waiting for those who make the trek.

JOHN BULL AREA

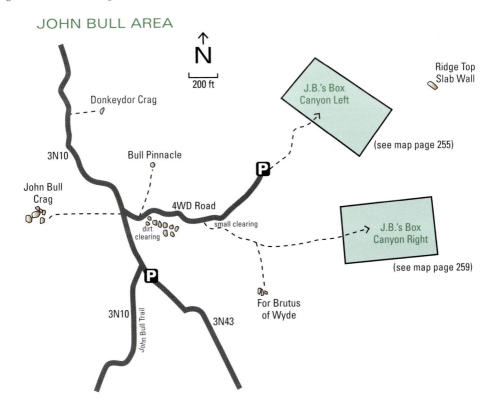

Approach: It is best to have a high-clearance vehicle with 4WD for the last stretch on 3N43.

Drive along Van Dusen Canyon Road (3N09) for 3.8 miles to a tee with 3N16 at a Forest Service fire-danger sign. Turn left onto 3N16 and follow this, past the Holcomb Valley Campground, for a total of 0.5 miles. Turn right onto 3N07 and drive for 0.4 miles. Turn left at the tee onto 3N43 and drive this for 0.75 miles to the junction with the John Bull 4WD Trail (3N10). Park before the junction at the large turn-around circle.

Alternate driving approach: If you have a 4WD rock crawler want to have a little fun, take the John Bull Trail (3N10) to the crags instead. The entrance to the trail is off of Polique Canyon Road.

JOHN BULL CRAG

This pile of large boulders is one of the biggest formations in the John Bull area, with a decent number of crack lines. Deep chasms between large boulders make this crag unsuitable for small children and dogs. In addition, the walk-off descents can be a bit convoluted, often with scrambling required to get back to the base. Sun or shade can be found throughout the day, as routes face a variety of directions.

5-10 min

Approach: From the parking area, turn right and hike north along the John Bull Trail (3N10) for 500 feet. The John Bull Crag will be visible through the trees on the left side of the road. Be careful scrambling over/through large boulders to reach the climbs on the left side of the wall. **[GPS: 34.31961, -116.90709]**

1 **Having Funnies With the Hunnies** 5.10c ★
The obvious overhanging offwidth around the corner from *Barefoot and Drunk*. Gear anchor.
40 ft. Wide gear. John Cardmon, Jeff Brennan, Nov. 2005.

2 **Barefoot and Drunk** 5.7 ★★
Sew up this splitter crack on the low-angle face. Fingerlocks offer excellent security throughout the initial section, as do the hand and fist jams as the crack widens. Gear anchor.
50 ft. Gear to 4". John Cardmon (solo), Aug. 2005.

3 **Humbolt Hunt** 5.2
Lackluster climbing on the slab beside *Barefoot and Drunk*.
50 ft. Gear to 4". Pat Brennan, Marissa Parish, Nov. 2005.

4 **Grab the Bull by the Horns** (Open Project)
Located 10 feet left of *Wrangling the Bull* is a thin seam snaking up the wall. Pro may be a bit sparse in the first 20 feet, but higher up the crack widens as the angle of the face kicks back. Maybe you could be the first to complete this one?
40 ft. Thin gear to 2".

5 **Wrangling the Bull** 5.10c ★★
Enjoyable crimping on the less-than-vertical face. Angle right on tiny nubs, dodging the kitty litter under the roof. (Decking potential going to the 2nd bolt.) A blind reach above the roof yields a nice jug. Bolted anchor without rings.
40 ft. 3 bolts. Unknown

6 **Bunnies and Hunnies** (Open Project)
This wide-crack line is on a separate chunk of rock located roughly 150 feet north of *Wrangling the Bull*. Start from a small cave, then traverse right underneath a block. Gear anchor. Similar in nature to *Humbolt Hunnies*.
45 ft. Wide gear.

7 **Humbolt Hunnies** 5.8 ★★
A challenging offwidth on the north face. Climb out from a cave, plugging large gear overhead. Engage beast mode to power through the corner and continue fighting the wide crack. Gear anchor. The spicy, Class-5 downclimb on crumbly rock is this climb's main demerit.
40 ft. Wide gear to 6". John Cardmon, Jeff Brennan, Nov. 2005.

Barefoot and Drunk

Wrangling the Bull

Humbolt Hunnies

J.B.'S BOX CANYON — LEFT SIDE

The following formations — from California's Gold Rock, page 256 to PBR Tower, page 257 — are located on the left side of a box canyon. The crags lie in and around a boulder field, and range in height from 30 to 40 feet.

Approach: From the intersection of 3N43 with 3N10, drive north on 3N10 for 500 feet. Turn right and head through a circular clearing, picking up an old 4WD road. Drive east along this spur road for 0.25 miles until it dead-ends at a loop. Park here. Cross-country hike 500 feet to the northeast, following a seasonal wash to the boulder field surrounding the crags.

J.B.'S BOX CANYON **LEFT SIDE**

J.B.'s Pinnacle

California's
Gold Rock

Fat Daddy Rock

PBR Tower

Crack Masters
Rock

JB Weld Rock

edge of boulder field

↑
N

50 ft

P

4WD road

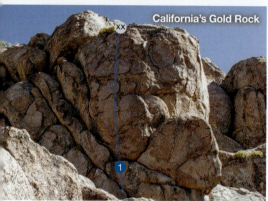

California's Gold Rock

J.B.'s Pinnacle

CALIFORNIA'S GOLD ROCK

A small rock with two highly enjoyable routes - a sport climb on splendid plates and a challenging finger crack.

PM 🚶 10 min

Approach: This crag is located high on the left side of the boulder field. **[GPS: 34.32185, -116.90081]**

1 **Wondrous Stories** 5.7 ★★
An easy romp on the plated west face. A great warm-up.
30 ft. 4 bolts. Pat Brennan, John Harrison, May 2009.

2 **First Impressions** 5.10b ★★
Stick the tough bouldery sequence as you grapple with this finger crack on the east face.
25 ft. Gear to 1". Matthew Janse, May 2020.

J.B.'S PINNACLE

A stacked tower with one nice route on its south face.

☀️ 🚶 15 min

Approach: Hike uphill from Fat Daddy Rock to reach this isolated pinnacle. **[GPS: 34.32216, -116.90020]**

3 **Ophuckme** 5.9 ★★
More technical than most other nearby lines. Coax the orange plates into allowing passage to the apex of the pinnacle. Reachy in spots and a bit blank at the top.
35 ft. 4 bolts. Pat Brennan, Dave O'Brian, Kenn Kenaga, July 2009.

FAT DADDY ROCK

This skinny formation stars a single warm-up route that blasts up a low-angle face.

PM 🚶 10 min

Approach: In the midst of the boulder field. **[GPS: 34.32151, -116.90038]**

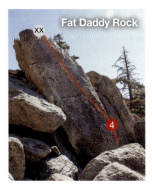

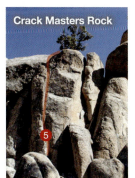

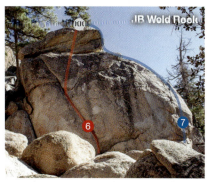

❹ Daddy 5.6 ★

Good incuts lead past a bolt to a well-featured crack section, followed by a final bolt on the upper slab.

35 ft. Gear to 2", 2 bolts. Pat Brennan, John Harrison, Craig Harrison, Charlie Dobbs, June 2009.

CRACK MASTERS ROCK

A jumbled pile of boulders forms this disjointed wall.

PM 🚶 10 min

Approach: Situated low on the right side of the boulder field, 100 feet south of Fat Daddy Rock. **[GPS: 34.32124, -116.90038]**

❺ Stranded in the SB's 5.9 ★

Scamper up a pillar/flake hiding a wide crack and navigate the short face above it. Gear anchor.

35 ft. Gear to 5".

Kenn Kenaga, John Harrison, Christian Trask, May 2009.

JB WELD ROCK

A squatty formation capped with a thin, flat rock.

PM 🚶 10 min

Approach: Walk 50 feet southeast of Crack Masters Rock. **[GPS: 34.32107, -116.90032]**

❻ Carburetor Crack 5.10a ★

The tight finger crack angling left across the face. Make the move on the upper block as fun as you want it to be — throw a heel hook and flop on top like a baby seal, or skirt the roof to the side. Shares anchors with *Piston Pumper*.

30 ft. Gear to 1", 2 bolts. Kenn Kenaga, Dave Daley, Oct. 2010.

❼ Piston Pumper 5.10a ★

Muscle through the start, then follow incuts as the route wraps around the south corner. Bolted anchor without rings.

35 ft. 4 bolts. Kenn Kenaga, Dave Daley, Oct. 2010.

PBR TOWER

An offwidth crack splits this colorful miniature tower.

☀ 🚶 10 min

Approach: Hike uphill (east) from JB Weld Rock to this formation marked by a large pine. Wrap around to its shady north face to find the climb. **[GPS: 34.32134, -116.89986]**

❽ Can Opener 5.9 ★★

Pop the top off this wide crack and get intimate with the rock. If you're sliding your face and hips against the rock, you're doing it right.

30 ft. Wide gear. Kenn Kenaga, Oct. 2010.

J.B.'S BOX CANYON — RIGHT SIDE

The right side of the box canyon lies 250 yards southeast of the left-side crags, separated by a ridge. With the exception of For Brutus of Wyde, all of the formations from Gold Rock to Tumor Pinnacle are clustered together on a hillside.

Approach: From the intersection of 3N43 with 3N10, drive north on 3N10 for 500 feet. Turn right and head through a circular clearing, pickup up an old 4WD road. Follow this spur road east for 0.1 miles to a small clearing. Park here. Cross-country hike 0.25 miles east for all walls except For Brutus of Wyde. There is no trail system in J.B's Box Canyon, so follow a seasonal creek bed or the path of least resistance to the ridge, then head uphill to the crags.

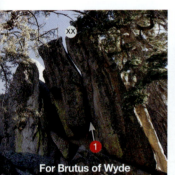
For Brutus of Wyde

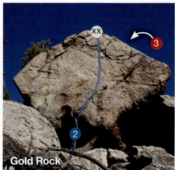
Gold Rock

Search For Goldfinger

FOR BRUTUS OF WYDE

An outlying formation with a short yet excellent offwidth challenge on its shady north face.

10 min

Approach: From the small clearing on the 4WD road, hike southeast for 200 yards, crossing a seasonal creek bed before arriving at the small hillside containing this wall.
[GPS: 34.31815, -116.90189]

❶ For Brutus of Wyde 5.11a ★★★

Get ready! Bury body parts inside the wide crack and inch along. Fight the urge to give up as the crack curves and widens ever so slightly near the finish. Named in honor of friend and fellow climber Bruce Bindner, who was tragically killed in a car accident.

20 ft. Gear to 5". Kenn Kenaga, July 2009.

GOLD ROCK

A diamond-shaped block with the fantastic sport route *Goldfinger* (5.10c) on the featured southwest face. Perched high on the hillside, this rock has wonderful views of Holcomb Valley and the surrounding mountains.

30 min

Approach: Hike cross-country from the small clearing, traveling 0.25 miles to the east. Follow the path of least resistance through the trees before the final uphill trek to the crag.
[GPS: 34.31942, -116.89920]

❷ Goldfinger 5.10c ★★★

Too short? Jump to reach the first holds and rock up onto the diamond-shaped face. Float good edges past an optional gear placement and mantel above the 2nd bolt. Pass a thinner section before the final plates. A nice, varied line.
35 ft. 4 bolts, optional gear to 1". Kenn Kenaga, July 2009.

❸ Search For Goldfinger 5.7

A leaning, crack-to-slab on the backside.
25 ft. Wide gear. Kenn Kenaga, July 2009.

J.B.'S BOX CANYON **RIGHT SIDE**

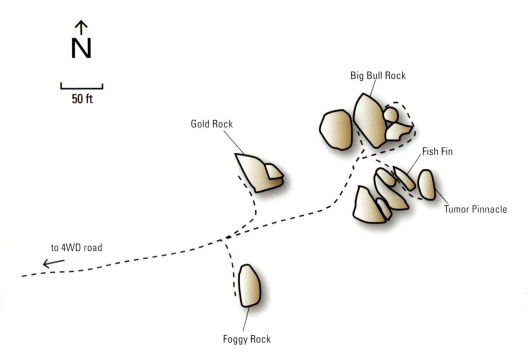

FOGGY ROCK

This squatty wide formation basks in the afternoon light. **PM** 🚶 30 min

Approach: 150 feet south of Gold Rock.
[GPS: 34.31904, -116.89925]

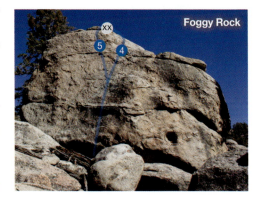

Foggy Rock

4 **Fog Head** 5.6 ★
A pleasant route up the line of least resistance on the wall.
30 ft. 3 bolts. Pat Brennan, Elain Tipton, July 2009.

5 **Fog Head Direct** 5.9 R ★
This variation fires straight up from the 2nd bolt to a horn and thin vertical seam. Runout.
30 ft. 2 bolts. Eric Tipton, Kenn Kenaga, July 2009.

Big Bull Rock

Fish Fin

Tumor Pinnacle

BIG BULL ROCK

A massive 70-foot-tall hunk of granite, home to the bold *El Matador* (5.11b).

30 min

Approach: Uphill 150 feet east from Gold Rock. **[GPS: 34.31950, -116.89869]**

6 El Matador 5.11b ★★★
A grueling line employing various techniques. Wrestle with a roof crack in the recess at the wall's left end to start, then take a breather on a ledge. Master the thin face above with fingers of steel and good footwork as the line wraps around the corner.
65 ft. Gear to 3", 3 bolts. John Cardmon, July 2009.
Variation 5.10c: Step left for a 5.9 start on a jumble of rocks that eliminates the opening difficulties. Join the previous line at the ledge for the technical 3-bolt corner.

7 Heifer 5.4
This mellow route begins down in a pit on the northeast face. It's the easiest way to the top of this large formation.
40 ft. 2 bolts. Pat Brennan, Lori Brennan, July 2009.

FISH FIN

A thin fin with the splendid face-to-arête climb *Freeky Deeky* (5.8).

PM   30 min

Approach: 50 feet southeast of Big Bull Rock. **[GPS: 34.31939, -116.89853]**

8 Freeky Deeky 5.8 ★★★
An invigorating line up a delightful arête. Tread lightly across the blank face, trending right over the void as the exposure mounts. Grasp the arête and veer left along it to the anchors.
35 ft. 4 bolts. Kenn Kenaga, Pat Brennan, July 2009.

TUMOR PINNACLE

A funky formation that's aptly named; you can't miss this distinct-looking rock!

PM   30 min

Approach: Head 50 feet downhill from Fish Fin, or 100 feet southeast of Big Bull Rock. **[GPS: 34.31934, -116.89840]**

9 Hematoma 5.10b ★★
Trickier than it looks. Climb along a dike on the west face until it is possible to move right underneath the gigantic tumor. Wiggle through a slot at the end. Note: There is a fallen tree currently encroaching on this route.
45 ft. 5 bolts. Kenn Kenaga, Craig Harrison, July 2009.

Tanglewood Slab

TANGLEWOOD AREA

A semi-secluded set of roadside crags that are fun if you like slab routes or want to learn to lead on trad gear. The vast majority of lines are low-angle climbs of modest grades, creating a perfect environment for beginner or intermediate climbers. The standout routes include the mixed line *Queenie's Dish* (5.8), the powerful *Canned Lizard* (5.10c), and the novel dihedral *Smith* (5.10b).

Approach: Drive Van Dusen Canyon Road (3N09) for 3.8 miles until it tees with 3N16. Turn right onto 3N16 and continue for 2.1 miles to a parking area on the left. You're close when you see the right turn for Tanglewood Group Campground — the parking is 0.3 miles further up the road.

TANGLEWOOD SLAB

A perfect training ground: a low-angle wall, excellent rock quality, well-protected cracks, and easy access to the anchors for setting topropes. The routes on this south-facing wall all share the same two-bolt anchor (no rap rings) and walk-off descent to climber's left.

Approach: The slab is visible from the parking pullout. Walk around the fence and take the climber's trail uphill toward the crag, which is in sight for the entire 5-minute hike. **[GPS: 34.30286, -116.85805]**

1 Email 5.5 ★
Motor up the left-facing dihedral to reach a roof with a slot above that eats gear. Comfortable climbing.
40 ft. Gear to 2". Pat Brennan, Lori Brennan, Mike Itnyre, June 2007.

2 Toner 5.3 ★
Hand-to-finger crack on the mellow slab.
40 ft. Gear to 2". Pat Brennan, Lori Brennan, Mike Itnyre, June 2007.

3 Fax 5.4 ★
A good introduction to slab climbing with an exhilarating run to the high first bolt. Cross over the *Tevo* crack and scamper past the last bolt on the upper face.
40 ft. 2 bolts. Pat Brennan, Lori Brennan, Mike Itnyre, June 2007.

4 Tevo 5.2 ★
An easy, left-slanting diagonal crack.
40 ft. Thin gear to 1".
Pat Brennan, Lori Brennan, Mike Itnyre, June 2007.

5 Hi Def 5.2 ★
Shimmy up the gully in the corner, then traipse along a finger crack on the low-angle slab to a thin finish.
40 ft. Gear to 2". Pat Brennan, Lori Brennan, Mike Itnyre, June 2007.

Greenhouse
Rock

Alpine
Rock

Tanglewood
Slab

10

Tanglewood Overview

6 Go Green 5.2

An alternate start on broken features/crack. Take the right side of the nook and merge with *Hi Def*.

40 ft. Gear to 2". Pat Brennan, Lori Brennan, Mike Itnyre, June 2007.

7 Enterprise 5.6 ★

Hop onto the slippery slab and tiptoe to the overlap. Clear the lip and run to the 2nd bolt on better holds.

40 ft. 2 bolts. Pat Brennan, Lori Brennan, Mike Itnyre, June 2007.

8 Canon 5.5

Chicken-wing up the gritty offwidth uphill from *Enterprise*.

20 ft. Gear to 5". Pat Brennan, Lori Brennan, Mike Itnyre, June 2007.

9 Fine Point 5.7

A very short and rarely traveled finger crack.

20 ft. Thin gear to 1".

Pat Brennan, Lori Brennan, Mike Itnyre, June 2007.

The following route is located on a small buttress atop Tanglewood Slab. See photo above.

10 Fast and Easy 5.3

Brief low-angle slab climb with a bulge/overlap mid-route.

20 ft. 2 bolts, gear to 3" for anchor.

Pat Brennan, Lori Brennan, Mike Itnyre, June 2007.

Greenhouse Rock

XX
XX

14

12   13

GREENHOUSE ROCK

Greenhouse and Alpine Rocks are sister formations on the western slope of the hillside. Greenhouse is the left one, with a couple stout routes on its southwest face.

PM   🚶 10 min

Approach: Skirt the base of Tanglewood Slab, heading past the left end and through the talus field. Continue around the hillside, staying at roughly the same elevation. Greenhouse Rock is approximately 150 yards northwest of Tanglewood Slab. **[GPS: 34.30359, -116.85896]**

11 Lud 5.9

An uninspiring line on the lichen-dotted face 50 feet left of *Canned Lizard*. Gear anchor. No photo.

30 ft. Gear to 3" for anchor, 2 bolts. Pat Brennan, Lori Brennan, Jeff Brennan, Adam Brennan, June 2007.

12 Canned Lizard 5.10c ★★

Burly start, with a high foot and a powerful lieback on thin crimps. After that, this decent line is fairly chill to the top.

40 ft. 4 bolts. Jeff Brennan, Kenn Kenaga, Mary Ann Kelly, June 2007.

13 Smith 5.10b ★★

Neat route with another high-foot start on the undercut wall. Stem the corner and pull the roof above on sharp crimps.

40 ft. 3 bolts. Jeff Brennan, Pat Brennan, June 2007.

14 Pop's Day 5.5 R ★

Lil' shorty route on the well-featured south face that ends at the anchors on *Smith*. Exhilarating, as it's a tad runout though the terrain is easy. You can clip the last bolt of *Smith* with a long draw to minimize decking potential.

30 ft. 1 bolt. Pat Brennan, Jeff Brennan, Lori Brennan, Adam Brennan, June 2007.

Alpine Rock

ALPINE ROCK

This is the uphill formation with loose talus along the base of its sunny south face. Many routes and variations are packed in closely on this small wall, so it's easy to get confused as to which features belong to which route.

10 min

Approach: Just right of Greenhouse Rock. **[GPS: 34.30368, -116.85882]**

15 Chicken Lizard 5.7 ★

Ascend a ramp to where the climb really begins. So-so climbing on decent features with a large bulge to overcome. Bolted anchor without rap rings.

25 ft. 2 bolts. Pat Brennan, Lori Brennan, Jeff Brennan, June 2007.

16 Freeze-Dried Lizard 5.7 ★

Start up the same ramp as *Chicken Lizard* but traverse out underneath the large tooth feature and scuttle up easy slab.

30 ft. 2 bolts. Pat Brennan, Jeff Brennan, Kenn Kenaga, June 2007.

Variation 5.9+: A tough one-move-wonder direct start on backward-slanting holds. There's one committing move, then it's a breeze to the top.

17 Queenie's Lizard 5.7+ ★

A linkup starting with the initial finger crack on *Queenie's Dish* but bypassing the roof and cutting out left to finish on *Freeze-Dried Lizard*.

30 ft. Gear to 1", 1 bolt. Unknown.

18 Queenie's Dish 5.8 ★★

Fingerlock up excellent, secure slots. Sink in a bomber cam and mosey up to an overlap/small roof. Pull the roof using the rail above and share anchors with *Freeze-Dried Lizard*.

30 ft. Gear to 1", 2 bolts.

Kenn Kenaga, Jeff Brennan, Pat Brennan, June 2007.

19 Sunflower 5.0

A jumbled crack system that meanders up the right side to shared anchors with *Freeze-Dried Lizard*.

25 ft. Gear to 6". Kenn Kenaga, Pat Brennan, June 2007.

Angela Hwangpo climbs *Smith*, 5.10b,
Greenhouse Rock, page 262.
Brandon Copp

JACOBY CANYON

A set of unique quartzite cliffbands, distinctly different from the rest of the climbable rock in the San Bernardinos. With the walls situated beside a creek, most of the beautiful quartzite is polished and slick. Even though the routes are on the shorter side, the style of climbing on the fractured rock's blocky features makes this area worth a visit. Be extra careful of loose rock at these crags!

Approach: Drive Van Dusen Canyon Road (3N09) for 3.8 miles until it tees with 3N16. Turn right onto 3N16 and continue for 2.9 miles to the intersection with 3N02. Turn left and drive 100 yards down the road. Park next to the fence.

SHOOTING GALLERY

When Dean and Craig discovered this wall in the early '90s, there were bullet casings scattered all over the place, hence the name. The wall wasn't bolted as thoroughly as it might have been because the extremely hard quartzite chewed through so many drill bits! The climbs here are predominately pumpy encounters on steep terrain — good for an explosive burn! None of the anchors here have rap rings, but it is an easy hike off the top.

5 min

Approach: Walk around the fence and hike down into the streambed heading east. The Shooting Gallery is the first cliffband reached, a 5-minute hike along this streambed. **[GPS: 34.30481, -116.84557]**

❶ Firearms 5.10a
A short-attention-span type of route around the corner from *Ricochet* that shares anchors with that route.
20 ft. 2 bolts. Craig Pearson, Dean Goolsby, 1990s.

❷ Magnum Force 5.9 ★
Pleasant climbing as you balance up the south face and lieback the arête. Shares anchors with *Ricochet*.
20 ft. Craig Pearson, Dean Goolsby, 1990s.

❸ Ricochet 5.11b ★★
Shoot straight up this sequential face starting 5 feet left of the wide split in the wall. Tread lightly on glassy feet and thin edges.
25 ft. 2 bolts. Craig Pearson, Dean Goolsby, 1990s.

❹ Sitting Duck 5.10c ★
Gun for the top as you squeeze blocky holds on the slick overhanging face. TR from *Ballistic Test* anchors.
30 ft. Craig Pearson, Dean Goolsby, 1990s.

❺ Muzzleloader 5.11c ★
Prepare the forearms for a short burn on this pumpy and powerful line on the overhanging arête. TR from the *Ballistic Test* anchors.
35 ft. Craig Pearson, Dean Goolsby, 1990s.

❻ Ballistic Test 5.9+ ★★
Hike up easy terrain to a ledge. Blast through the slightly negative main face on blocky corners. A splendid sampling of different quartzite features.
35 ft. 2 bolts. Craig Pearson, Dean Goolsby, 1990s.

Gunslinger Left

Gunslinger Right

❼ Target Practice 5.10b

A slick initial sequence of delicate face climbing on thin edges becomes a romp on big holds. The single-bolt anchor can be backed up with the tree.

35 ft. Craig Pearson, Dean Goolsby, 1990s.

❽ Shell Casings 5.7 ★

A cruxy start with recessed feet gains the crack. Blocky holds lead to the top. Anchor from the tree.

35 ft. Gear to 3". Angela Hwangpo, Brandon Copp, Elliot Warden, Gene Yonemoto, Jacqueline Copp, Sept. 2019.

❾ Buckshot 5.10b ★★

Start beside an orange incut corner. Traverse left using whatever holds exist. Reach a hand rail and mantel.

35 ft. 2 bolts. Craig Pearson, Dean Goolsby, 1990s.

GUNSLINGER ROCK

The second and larger of the two walls in Jacoby Canyon, with climbs on both its west and south faces. No bolted anchors exist atop the formation, so bring cord to sling a boulder or build a gear anchor for all climbs. *Quartz Crack* (5.6) and *Detour* (5.10a) are by far the best routes on this small wall.

10 min

Approach: Continue another 150 yards down the streambed from the Shooting Gallery. **[GPS: 34.30455, -116.84395]**

❿ Gem Climb 5.6 ★

Don't get too excited, as this blocky face climb is more akin to finding fool's gold than the real stuff.

40 ft. 2 bolts, gear for anchor. Kenn Kenaga, July 2007.

⓫ Quartz Crack 5.6 ★★

The hand crack on the green west face. Enjoyable climbing on the unique quartzite.

45 ft. Gear to 3". Kenn Kenaga, Pat Brennan, July 2007.

⓬ Globetrotter 5.5

A slick, left-facing dihedral leads to a brown flake and finishes up a slot. Dirty and loose.

45 ft. Gear to 2". Pat Brennan, John Cardmon, July 2007.

⓭ Attachment 5.6

Blocky ladder 5 feet right of *Globetrotter*.

45 ft. 2 bolts, gear for anchor. Pat Brennan, John Cardmon, July 2007.

⓮ Detour 5.10a ★★

Locate the large roof near a pine tree. Deliberate footwork on glassy holds is clutch, or risk peeling off the slick, brown slab! Incut edges and liebacks on the right side of the roof allow challenging moves to reach the blocky arête. Fun!

45 ft. 4 bolts, gear for anchor. Kenn Kenaga, July 2007.

⓯ Jacoby's Ladder 5.6 ★

Haul yourself up the chimney-to-fist crack right of *Detour*.

45 ft. Wide gear. Alan Bartlett, Mary Ann Kelly, May 2009.

Jacqueline Copp climbs *Buckshot*, 5.10b, opposite. 📷 Brandon Copp

QUARTZITE BANDS

Another good change of pace from the standard granite climbing in the area. The crag overlooks Baldwin Lake, gathering morning sun and afternoon shade. The slick, highly fractured rock encourages good footwork and presents thought-provoking sequences. Make sure to check out the remarkable lines on the TNT Wall — must-do routes for the 5.12 climber. Kudos to the first ascensionists who had the patience to expend the time and drill bits needed to put these routes up!

Approach: From the stoplight at the dam, drive Highway 38 along the lake's north shore for 9.6 miles to reach the Highway 38/18 intersection at Greenway Drive. Continue straight for an additional 2.6 miles on Highway 18 around Baldwin Lake to a pullout on the right side of the road. Park here, where both quartzite bands are visible on the hillside, along with a massive quartzite boulder near the road.

Trek up the boulder-laden slope, carefully navigating the loose talus. 10 minutes of steep hiking will reach the routes on the lower band. Cross a talus field and continue another 10 minutes uphill to arrive at the upper band, where climbs are concentrated on its left end.

Quartzite Bands

Lower Band
[GPS: 34.28370, -116.82043]   10 min

1 Lower QB #1 5.10a ★
Neat little burn that starts from a cave around the left corner of the wall.
25 ft. 3 bolts. Unknown.

2 Lower QB #2 5.7 R
Wandering line with only a single bolt down low. Climb easy terrain behind a flake to drop-in anchors.
40 ft. Unknown.

The following three routes are located on a section of rock named the TNT Wall.

3 Swallow Your Pride 5.12a ★★★
Sick route on the steep arête. Surge through the challenging start, watching your forearms swell. Power through one overlap after another, passing swallow nests along the way. Bolted anchor without rap rings.
50 ft. Jim Voss, Billy Holder, 2015.

4 Dynamite 5.12b ★★★
This bitching line beside the orange streak also starts from the ledge. Shoot up scant features on the vertical pane of glass. Bolted anchor without rap rings.
45 ft. Jim Voss, Billy Holder, 2015.

5 Fire in the Hole 5.11b ★★
Blast out of a hole on the right side of the wall. Fire up seams and square edges past a midway ledge, continuing through lighter rock above. Bolted anchor without rap rings.
55 ft. Jim Voss, Billy Holder, 2015.

6 Rosy Cheeks 5.7 ★
Ascends a small pillar to the right of the TNT Wall.
35 ft. Jim Voss, Laura Voss, 2015.

7 Rosy Boa 5.10d ★★
Cope with a large block and capitalize on decent holds as they appear. Alternate between steeps and slabs as you brave the overlaps. A tricky but enjoyable climb.
55 ft. 6 bolts. Jim Voss, Billy Holder, 2015.

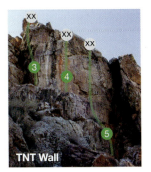

TNT Wall

Red Roof Inn

Quartzite Pillars

Quartzite Quandary

8 Red Roof Inn 5.10a ★★

Begin this unique crack line from the concave corner. Plug gear overhead and explode through the first roof. Take a breather on big features and suss out the next roof problem. Shares anchors with *Rosy Boa*.

55 ft. Gear to 4". Jim Voss, Billy Holder, 2015.

9 Redline 5.11a ★★

Grasp good edges on the fractured face, making your way up past a bush. The wall saves a cruxy overhanging section of slick face to thwart you at the finish!

40 ft. 4 bolts. Jim Voss, Billy Holder, 2015.

10 Lower QB #3 5.10b ★★

A bolted face climb situated 50 feet right of *Redline*, on a separate block. Bolted anchor without rap rings. No photo.

35 ft. 4 bolts. Unknown.

Upper Band
[GPS: 34.28443, -116.82210]

  20 min

11 Upper QB #1 5.10a ★★

Tucked away in a corner on a beautiful orange and red face. Hone your technique as you ascend slick blocks, edging on numerous horizontals. Slip into a finger crack that ends below a single bolt. Bolted anchor without rap rings.

35 ft. Gear to 1", 1 bolt. Unknown.

12 Upper QB #2 5.10b ★

Toprope the dihedral right of the previous route.

35 ft. Unknown.

13 Left Quartzite Pillar 5.9 ★

Climb slick face on the leftmost of the two bolted pillars.

25 ft. 3 bolts. Unknown.

14 Right Quartzite Pillar 5.10a ★★

Blast up the rightmost of the two bolted pillars.

25 ft. 3 bolts. Unknown.

15 Upper QB #3 5.8

Left of *Quartzite Quandary*, meander up from the undercut base to a midway ledge. Force your way through overlaps on the upper face. Bolted anchor without rap rings.

55 ft. Unknown.

16 Quartzite Quandary 5.10d ★★★

Exciting climbing on the undercut corner and the fractured face beside it. Tuck in under the overhang, find the key handhold, and pull off the gymnastic crux sequence. Monkey through big holds to a ledge, from which sustained climbing leads to the bolted anchor (no rap rings).

55 ft. Unknown.

Variation 5.9+: Ascend blockier terrain, slanting left. Pull a height-dependent move off the ledge and join *QQ*.

17 Upper QB #4 5.9 ★

A short route on an orange wall at the far right side of the band. Bolted anchor without rap rings.

30 ft. Unknown.

NORTH SHORE BOULDERS

North Shore Boulders is a conglomeration of small but closely spaced crags on a hillside south of Gold Mountain. The proximity to town and the south-facing nature of the knobby, granite boulders makes this one of the few spots near Big Bear Lake that climbing can be enjoyed year-round. With a short approach time, these walls are great if you want to get in a workout before or after work.

In addition to a variety of 25- to 40-foot roped routes, there is a wealth of bouldering, with one particularly concentrated area called the Gardens. Sadly, this area has a fair bit of trash and graffiti. Please do your part to help clean up these crags when you visit. Also, be aware that most anchors will not have rap rings, although the necessary downclimbs are typically straightforward.

Approach: From the stoplight at the dam, take Highway 38 along the north shore of Big Bear Lake. Drive 9.6 miles, passing the Van Dusen Canyon turnoff, to the Highway 38/18 intersection at Greenway Drive. Turn left onto Greenway Drive and continue briefly north until the road tees with Pioneer Lane. Park alongside Pioneer Lane and hike north to the crags on the hillside.

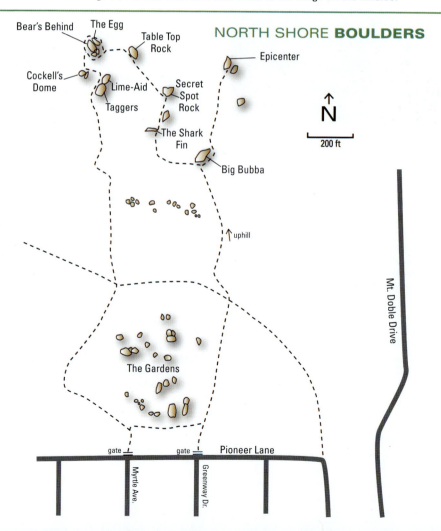

BIG BUBBA

One of the bigger and better boulders and the centerpiece of roped climbing in the area. Seek out the climbs on its southeast face for a technical challenge on thin features.

15 min

Approach: From the Greenway Drive entrance gate, hike north on a well-defined path that passes the right side of the Gardens bouldering area. Cross a hiking trail and take the path of least resistance uphill. Big Bubba is situated halfway up the hillside, 0.3 miles north of the entrance gate.
[GPS: 34.27554, -116.84679]

❶ Trembling Tips 5.10b ★
A fingery toprope on small plates and textured edges. Angle left on crimps from the first bolt of *Dancing Digits* to a rail near the top, then cut right to the shared anchor.
35 ft. Bob Cockell, 1991.

❷ Dancing Digits 5.10b ★★
From the good flake near the first bolt, slant right to a crux. Edge on thin features, being careful not to blow it on the long run to the 2nd bolt. Bolted anchor without rap rings.
35 ft. 3 bolts. FA: (TR) Bob Cockell, 1991; FL: Brad Singer, 1992.

❸ Hubba Bubba 5.10c ★★
A powerful route up bulges and scoops along the right margin of the wall. Bolted anchor without rap rings.
35 ft. 3 bolts. Bob Cockell, 1992.

EPICENTER

A 40-foot dome with the exciting slab route *Richter Scale* (5.11a) on its blank south face.

20 min

Approach: Located 125 yards northeast of Big Bubba near the top of the hill.
[GPS: 34.27653, -116.84647]

❹ Richter Scale 5.11a ★★
A clean slab line. Tiptoe up a tough start, hoping for the best! The climb eases up higher, culminating with a seam-to-flake (optional gear placement). Gear anchor.
40 ft. 3 bolts, gear to 3" for anchor. Bob Cockell, 1991.
Variation 5.10c: Eliminate the difficult direct start, climbing the blunt corner and traversing in. Still not a gimme.

❺ The Fracture 5.10b ★
Exploit the fracture line near the dark lichen streak. Embrace the small scoops and milk the good holds as they come.
35 ft. Gear to 3" for anchor. Bob Cockell, 1991.

Big Bubba

Epicenter

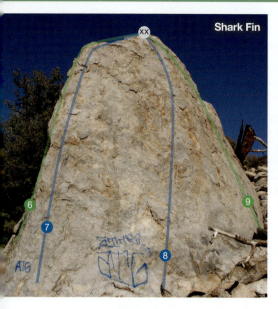

Shark Fin

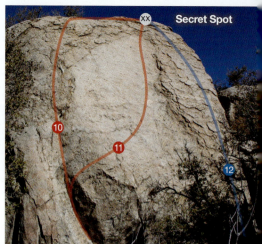

Secret Spot

SHARK FIN

A small fin with one bolted anchor that services all the climbs.

🌞 🚶 15 min

Approach: Hike 75 yards west and slightly north of Big Bubba.
[GPS: 34.27580, -116.84753]

6 Lakeview Arête 5.6 ★
TR (or solo) the left side of the well-featured southeast arête. A fun and easy jaunt on nice plates.
30 ft. Chris Miller (solo).

7 Arête You Can 5.8+ ★
Prepare for a dash of funkiness while ascending the clean face on the arête's right side.
30 ft. 2 bolts. Bob Cockell, 1992.

8 Barking Fish 5.8 ★★
A cool climb on edges in the center of the near-vertical face.
30 ft. 2 bolts. Bob Cockell, 1992.

9 Sharkface 5.7 ★
Clamber up a flake to a ledge. It's slightly airy cutting left onto the face before riding good plates to the top.
25 ft. Chris Miller (solo).

SECRET SPOT ROCK

A nondescript rock with a few short routes up its sunny southwest face.

🌞 🚶 20 min

Approach: Located 100 yards northwest of Big Bubba and directly uphill from the Shark Fin.
[GPS: 34.27621, -116.84738]

10 Dirty Little Secret 5.8 R ★
Saunter up a ramp, then wiggle finicky pro into the flare behind a flake. Punch straight up on decent holds. Shares anchors with *Hardstart*.
30 ft. Thin gear to 2". Chris Miller.

11 Mr. Friction 5.9 ★★
Take the same initial ramp and plug gear high in the crack. Creep right onto the face toward the first bolt. Cautiously balance through the slab above. Shares anchors with *Hardstart*. Spicy!
30 ft. Gear to 2", 2 bolts. Unknown.

12 Hardstart 5.10a ★★
Ascend nice plates and square edges along the bolt line to an anchor without rap rings.
30 ft. 2 bolts. Unknown.
Variation 5.7: Nix the hard start and chimney or climb the boulder leaning against the wall.

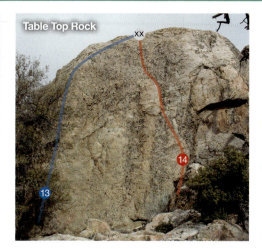

Table Top Rock

14

13

Avenue, hike north on a well-defined path that passes to the left side of the Gardens. Cross a hiking trail and take the path of least resistance uphill. Bear's Behind lies near the top of the hillside, 0.3 miles north of the entrance gate.

If approaching from Table Top Rock, Bear's Behind is located 75 yards due west. **[GPS: 34.27675, -116.84856]**

TABLE TOP ROCK

A flat-topped boulder with two routes on its sunny southwest face.

☀ 🚶 20 min

Approach: Situated 175 yards northwest of Big Bubba or 75 yards northwest from Secret Spot. **[GPS: 34.27676, -116.84786]**

13 **Pinch It or Leave It** 5.9 ★
Use any of the slopers or small edges to your advantage as you navigate the cruxy slab. Clip the first bolt from a pinch and find the good edges on your way to the top. Bolted anchor without rap rings.
25 ft. 2 bolts. Bob Cockell.

14 **Pinch It and Leave It** 5.7
Begin from a boulder and launch upward on tiny holds to a flake. Slightly runout terrain leads to the shared anchor.
25 ft. Gear to 2". Chris Miller.

BEAR'S BEHIND

One of the taller formations here. The clean southwest face is devoid of lichen, in contrast to many of the neighboring boulders.

☀ 🚶 20 min

Approach: This formation and the collection of rocks near it can be approached directly from the parking on Pioneer Lane, or from the walls listed above. From the entrance gate at Myrtle

15 **Hairy Bear** 5.8
Hand traverse the crack 15 feet off the deck, joining *Sunkiss* at its last bolt. Protect your second on the traverse!
40 ft. Gear to 1", 1 bolt. Unknown.

16 **Sunkiss** 5.10c ★★
One of the better and taller lines at North Shore Boulders. Pass the first bolt on small edges, then launch upward through a series of bulges on the rounded arête. Bolted anchor without rap rings.
40 ft. 4 bolts. Kenn Kenaga, Jeff Brennan, June 2007.

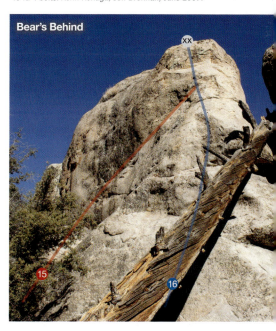

Bear's Behind

xx

15

16

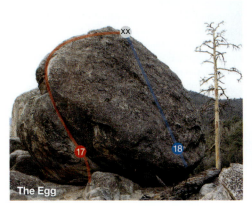

The Egg

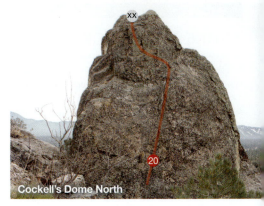

Cockell's Dome Southeast

Cockell's Dome North

THE EGG

An appropriately named rock with two routes on its dark-colored northeast face.

20 min

Approach: 50 feet northeast of Bear's Behind. **[GPS: 34.27687, -116.84843]**

17 Split Open and Melt 5.7 ★

This wide crack is no yolk. High feet are the ticket on the undercut start (or use the boulder to bring the grade down a notch). Continue up a slot to end on plates. Shares anchors with *Deviled Egg* (no rap rings).

25 ft. Gear to 3". Jeff Brennan, Pat Brennan, Kenn Kenaga, June 2007.

18 Deviled Egg 5.8 ★★

This egg-cellent climb tackles the center of the dark face with consistent climbing throughout. The bolted anchor has no rings — add some if you can.

25 ft. 2 bolts. Pat Brennan, Jeff Brennan, Kenn Kenaga, June 2007.

COCKELL'S DOME

Bob Cockell was a local fireman and climber who lived across the street from the crags; the North Shore Boulders were primarily developed by Bob and his friends in the early 1990s. Bob's home was destroyed twice, once from a house fire and the second time by the 1992 Big Bear earthquake, after which he moved to Oregon.

20 min

Approach: 100 feet due south of Bear's Behind. **[GPS: 34.27649, -116.84860]**

19 Duck and Cover 5.7 R

A rarely traveled miniature line that climbs past an overlap on the southeast face to shared anchors atop the dome.

25 ft. 1 bolt. Bob Cockell, early 1990s.

20 Stop, Drop, and Roll 5.8 ★

Make quick work of the pocketed seam on the north face.

25 ft. Small gear to 0.5". Bob Cockell, early 1990s.

LIME-AID

This green, lichen-spackled northwest face houses a few decent sport routes. Note: At the time of this writing, a large tree has fallen across the base of these routes; until it is removed, there is a potential for injury in the case of a climbing fall.

☀ PM   🚶 20 min

Approach: 125 feet southeast of Bear's Behind. **[GPS: 34.27645, -116.84834]**

㉑ Rinds of Good Times 5.10c ★
Edge up thin slab to the rounded arête. Shares anchors (no rings) with *The Fun Never Ends*. Scramble off climber's left.
25 ft. 2 bolts. Jeff Brennan, June 2007.

㉒ The Fun Never Ends 5.10b ★
A low crux on the blank face leads to a bolted anchor (no rap rings) on a ledge.
25 ft. 2 bolts. Jeff Brennan, Pat Brennan, June 2007.

㉓ Fresh Squeezed 5.11a ★
Creep along fingery seams to the first bolt, where the fun begins. Grip lichen-covered features while working the feet higher, finessing tenuous moves to reach the slanting ledge. Shares anchors (no rings) with *The Fun Never Ends*.
30 ft. 2 bolts. Jeff Brennan, June 2007.

Lime-Aid

Taggers

TAGGERS

A low-angle dome with a prominent band near the top of its west face.

☀ PM   🚶 20 min

Approach: Located 50 feet downhill and due south of Lime-Aid or 175 feet southeast of Bear's Behind. **[GPS: 34.27626, -116.84837]**

㉔ ASCA 5.2
Crawl up the initial slab, then meander along a crack system. At the prominent band, traverse 5 feet left to ascend a seam. Gear anchor.
30 ft. Gear to 2". Pat Brennan, Kenn Kenaga, July 2007.

Roland Castro on *El Rayo*, 5.10a,
8000-Foot Crag, page 290. 📷 Harrison Weinberg

FRINGE AREAS

FRINGE **AREAS**

The crags listed here — predominately roadside walls with short approaches — are on the eastern fringe of the Big Bear region, scattered northeast and southeast of the lake. These are good spots to seek out to get away from the crowds, or for shoulder-season climbing; if you want slightly cooler or warmer temps, these walls differ in elevation from the rest of the Big Bear area. Many of the walls have enough routes to keep a party busy for a day, and often you'll have the entire place to yourself.

Approach: The crags are located along highways 38 and 18, east of Big Bear Lake. Blackhawk Pinnacle and Whosville are reached by following Highway 18 past Baldwin Lake and north toward Lucerne Valley. The other 4 crags are along Highway 38 heading south toward Redlands.

Clark Reinholtz on *Opiate*, 5.11c,
Onyx Summit Crag, page 285.
📷 Harrison Weinberg

CLIMBING AREA	ELEVATION	HIKE	ROUTES	GRADE RANGE	CRAGS
BLACKHAWK PINNACLE *Fringe-season spot* page 280	5900 ft.	10 min	7	≤.5 .6 .7 .8 .9 .10 .11 .12	
WHOSVILLE *Remote and sunny* page 282	5900 ft.	50 min	2	≤.5 .6 .7 .8 .9 .10 .11 .12	
ONYX SUMMIT CRAG *Accessible, high-quality granite* page 283	8450 ft.	5 min	19	≤.5 .6 .7 .8 .9 .10 .11 .12	
ONYX OUTBACK *Serene alpine setting* page 287	8500 ft.	5 min	4	≤.5 .6 .7 .8 .9 .10 .11 .12	
8000-FOOT CRAG *Cool temps, great climbing* page 288	8000 ft.	5 min	15	≤.5 .6 .7 .8 .9 .10 .11 .12	
COON CREEK ROCK *Roadside crag near camping* page 291	7450 ft.	1 min	4	≤.5 .6 .7 .8 .9 .10 .11 .12	

BLACKHAWK PINNACLE

This small crag sits in the transition zone between mountains and desert along Highway 18 near Cactus Flats. It can be a bit warmer than spots up in the mountains, even though it's predominately north-facing with a bit of shade at the base. In the fringe season when the weather starts to turn cold, this is a great crag to visit. Pull out the trad rack and warm up on the moderate cracks, but be sure to get on *Blackhawk Arête* (5.10b), the only bolted line here. This wall has a super-easy walk-off from the top.

PM | **10 min**

Approach: From the intersection of highways 38 and 18 on the northeast end of Big Bear Lake, take Highway 18 east past Baldwin Lake for 4.3 miles to the crest of a small hill and the start of the Cushenbury Grade. Continue following Highway 18 downhill to Cactus Flats and check the odometer. Turn right onto 3N62 (a faint road that's easy to miss) at 0.6 miles past the Cactus Flats sign (7.2 miles in total). Follow 3N62 for 0.4 miles, staying right at all junctions to continue following the dirt road. At this point, you will come to an old road that's been fenced off to vehicles and marked with a restoration sign. Park just past the fence on the right in a parking area big enough for 3 cars.

  The crag should be visible in the distance on a hillside to the east. Walk past the fence along the old road for 5 minutes, eventually veering right off the road and heading uphill to the base of the crag. Bushwhack and boulder hop for another 5 minutes to reach the wall.
[GPS: 34.32427, -116.81006]

Blackhawk Pinnacle

1 Grapevine 5.8+ ★
Tricky climbing in a flared hand crack on the left end of the wall. Get sucked into the alcove underneath a large block and contemplate your options. Either fire up the fist crack on the left or take the thin finger crack out right. Gear anchor.
30 ft. Gear to 4". Pat Brennan, Brad Singer, Nov. 1998.

2 Cactus 5.8 ★★
Step 5 feet right of a tree at the base and start up the wide fist crack. At the triangular notch, pull through an awkward move to gain the wall. The longer your reach, the better you can sink your fingertips into the thin crack! Gear anchor.
35 ft. Gear to 3" with a wide piece for the anchor.
Brad Singer, Pat Brennan, Nov. 1998.

❸ Stabbing Westward 5.10b ★★

Tough line with slick feet. Slink up the right side of a block that has cleaved off the wall. Slot fingers into the undercling and creep onto the slick face above, making the cruxy stand-up move. Technical face climbing past a bolt finishes with a thin seam. Gear anchor.

40 ft. Thin gear to 2", 1 bolt.
Brad Singer, Dave Honeywell, David LePere, Nov. 2000.

❹ Silver 5.9 ★

Fist crack. Numerous seams on the undercut base lead to a sporty overhanging crux. Proceed up the interesting crack through a series of steps. Gear anchor or share with *Blackhawk Arête.*

40 ft. Gear to 4". *Pat Brennan, Brad Singer, Nov. 1998.*

❺ Blackhawk Arête 5.10b ★★★

The standout route for the crag and definitely worth a spin. Boulder up blocky terrain until it's possible to lean back and clip the first bolt (optional 1" cam placement in lower cracks). Leave your comfort zone as you blast through the crux roof. Haul yourself over the bulge with a thin flake above. Balancy moves on good, albeit small, holds lead up the exposed arête. The fun roof at the bottom combined with thin and airy moves up top make this route an area classic.

45 ft. 4 bolts, optional 1" piece. *Brad Singer, Steve Kravchuck, Dave Honeywell, David LePere, Nov. 2000.*

❻ Panamint Annie 5.7 ★

Slip a killer fingerlock into the crack just right of the roof on *Blackhawk Arête* to clear the difficult start. Follow the crack as it becomes a ramp and then turns vertical again. The heady finish through a notch feels harder than it is. Gear anchor.

45 ft. Gear to 2". *Brad Singer, David LePere, Nov. 2000.*

❼ Sliver 5.12b ★★

From the massive ledge, contemplate the difficulties of the improbable seam looming overhead. When you're good and ready, shove your fingertips into the thin seam to get a little bit of purchase. Scale the ever-so-slightly negative wall, edging on miniscule foot chips while the thin crack flares toward the top. Gear anchor.

25 ft. Thin gear to 2". *David LePere, Nov. 2000.*

Brandon Copp, *Blackhawk Arête*, 5.10b.
📷 Jacqueline Copp

Whosville

WHOSVILLE

Whosville is a remote little crag perched high on a hillside in the general vicinity of Blackhawk Pinnacle. The rock is somewhat gritty, yet the movement on both routes is fun. The wall basks in the sun and has a small natural rock arch at the top of a gully between the two climbs.

☀ **🚶 50 min**

Approach: As for Blackhawk Pinnacle, drive Highway 18 east past Baldwin Lake to Cactus Flats. Pass Cactus Flats/3N03 and locate the next paved pullout on the lefthand side of the road (7.0 miles from the intersection of highways 38 and 18 and 0.2 miles before the turn for Blackhawk Pinnacle). Park in this pullout or, alternatively, turn right onto an unmarked 4WD road and park after 100 feet at the rock barrier.

Either way, hike east on the closed 4WD road for 1.5 miles, or 30-40 minutes. The first half of the road is flat, then it descends into a small wash. Next, the road curls northeast for the last half mile to crest the shoulder of a small ridge, where the formation will be visible directly ahead (north) high on a hillside. Leave the road and continue cross-country up the steep hillside for the remaining 15 minutes to reach the crag.
[GPS: 34.32746, -116.79369]

❶ What's That? 5.10d ★★
Boulder past the high first bolt on minimal handholds to a little dish below a bulge. Clip a long runner on the 3rd bolt out left and continue climbing, sampling the unique features on the steep upper section. Varied and exciting!
40 ft. 5 bolts. Pat Brennan, John Cardmon, Nov. 2005.

❷ That's What 5.9 ★★
Challenging start from a skinny ledge as you coax the small features into allowing you passage through the slightly negative section. Once past the difficulties, bumble up ledges to the anchors.
40 ft. 4 bolts. Pat Brennan, John Cardmon, Nov. 2005.

ONYX SUMMIT CRAG

A unique, pyramid-shaped rock of excellent fine-grained granite in an easily accessible roadside setting. The crag sports a high concentration of quality routes, especially in the harder grades. Recent additions of easy and moderate climbs have helped make this a destination with a little something for everyone. The vast majority of climbs are bolted sport routes, predominately located on the south and east faces, with nearby trees providing shade at the base. Although this is one of the highest-elevation crags in the Big Bear area, the south-facing nature of the wall allows for climbing here from early spring until late fall.

5 min

Approach: Follow Highway 38 east from Big Bear. From the righthand turn to stay on Highway 38, it is 8.5 miles to where the road peaks at Onyx Summit. 0.2 miles before the Onyx Summit sign is a paved pullout on the left side of the road, just before the final hill. Park here and cross the road. Hike straight out from a small gravel area, picking up the faint climber's trail that crosses the drainage. Head up the hill on the other side next to a wire fence. 5-minute uphill approach.

If coming up Highway 38 from Redlands, the pullout is 23.7 miles from the Forest Falls turnoff. **[GPS: 34.19629, -116.72272]**

Onyx Approach

Palm Pilot

❶ Here Comes the Fun 5.10a ★★

Race up past a bulge and motor through the smooth face underneath the pyramid. Blast up the backside of the formation and surf the slab above.

45 ft. 5 bolts. Chris Miller, Reed Ames, Jorden Darr, Alex Brady, Sept. 2018.

Variation, 5.9, Triggernometry: A toprope variation that makes the climb a bit easier. Climb the lower face 10 feet left of the regular start, beginning atop a boulder.

❷ Skylarking 5.10b ★★

A linkup that combines the low crux and first 2 bolts of *Here Comes the Fun* with the exciting upper traverse of *Palm Pilot*.

55 ft. 8 bolts. Unknown.

❸ Palm Pilot 5.10b ★★★★

A beautiful line up the sharp left arête of the pyramid-shaped headwall. Begin this captivating route near a fence post. Tread lightly past a block that moves above the 3rd clip and ogle at the magnificent arête above. Dive headfirst into the excellent airy traverse with demanding footwork. Shared anchor with *Opiate*.

60 ft. 8 bolts. Chris Miller, May 2001.

Angela Hwangpo on *Palm Pilot*, 5.10b, previous page. 📷 Brandon Copp

Onyx Summit Center

4 Fun Pilot 5.7 ★★★
Fun, easy linkup that combines the first 3 bolts of *Palm Pilot* with the upper 3 of *Here Comes the Fun*.
55 ft. 6 bolts. Chris Miller, Reed Ames, Sept. 2018.

5 Branch Out! 5.9 ★
A short, bolted route that ends at mussy hooks on the midway ledge. Follow easy, blocky holds at first, ending with a perplexing pull around the left corner.
40 ft. 4 bolts. Reed Ames, Chris Miller, Aug. 2018.

6 Lost on the Horizon 5.8 ★★
An adventurous climb that takes the path of least resistance across the wall. Directly behind the large pine is a small crack that meanders up to the large midway ledge. Traverse the ledge, climb past a couple of bolts on the arête, and finally pop over to finish on *Sardonyx*. Bring lots of slings to reduce rope drag.
60 ft. Gear to 1", 4 bolts. Brad Singer, May 2000.

7 Opiate 5.11c ★★★
Start from a stack of cheater stones and struggle past 2 closely spaced bolts on slick, overhanging rock without much in the way of feet. Finish with tough crimping straight up the center of the headwall. Shared anchor.
60 ft. 9 bolts. Chris Miller, May 2001.

8 Cliptomania 5.11d ★★★
A hard, direct start to *Clip Art*. Reachy and tenuous, with a lot of grit needed for the big crux just past the flake. Join *Clip Art* for outstanding climbing on the beautiful arête. A tough line with a rewarding finish. Shared anchor.
60 ft. 8 bolts. Chris Miller, Aug. 1999.

9 Clip Art 5.10c ★★
The original, easier line to reach the upper arête. Start right and trend left on incuts across the slick face. Impeccable climbing on fantastic granite above, following the sharp arête to the peak of the pyramid. Shared anchor with *Opiate*.
60 ft. 7 bolts. Chris Miller, July 1999.

10 Sardonyx 5.10a ★★★
A relatively new route that starts on the first 2 bolts of *Clip Art* but stays right on the face to share the last bolt and anchors with *Big BM*. Fun, with great movement.
55 ft. 6 bolts. Chris Miller, Reed Ames, Aug. 2018.

11 Whose Line Is It Anyway? 5.10a ★★
Begin on the ramp with a dike left of the *Big BM* dihedral. Cross over *Big BM* at the 3rd bolt and progress through tricky terrain. Thin and balancy.
50 ft. 6 bolts.
Alex Brady, Reed Ames, Chris Miller, Jorden Darr, Sept. 2018.

12 Big BM 5.9 ★★
The nice crack system in the left-facing dihedral that passes a small roof and ends with a short section of face.
50 ft. Gear to 2", 1 bolt. Preston Sowell, 1991.

Onyx Summit Right

13 Freak on a Leash 5.12c ★★★

Unleash the beast on this improbable blank face! The formidable sequence to start has tormented many a rock jock and is bound to throw you for a loop. Go ballistic and hope for the best. The last 2 bolts and anchors are shared with *Nothing Could Be Finer*.

60 ft. 6 bolts. Eric Odenthal, Apr. 2001.

14 Nothing Could Be Finer 5.11a ★★

Or something like that. Best to use a little additional protection for this uniquely shaped and slightly dirty crack.

55 ft. 5 bolts, optional gear to 2". David LePere, Brad Singer, Ryan Crochiere, Eric Odenthal, Apr. 2001.

15 Endless Sky 5.8 ★★

A well-protected slab with ample friction and a bit of exposure. Mentally engaging, as the miniature holds lead over the void. Shared anchor with *Blue Sky Highway*.

55 ft. 7 bolts. Chris Miller, Reed Ames, Clint Oveson, Aug. 2018.

16 Endless Blue Sky 5.8 ★

Linkup of the first 5 bolts and thin crux of *Endless Sky* with the last 2 bolts of *Blue Sky Highway*. Step right at the big ledge before the final slab.

55 ft. 7 bolts. Unknown.

17 Blue Sky Highway 5.5 ★★

Super-chill low-angle slab climb.

55 ft. 6 bolts. Reed Ames, Chris Miller, Clint Oveson, Aug. 2018.

18 Skytower 5.5 ★

The inverse of *Endless Blue Sky*. Start on the first 5 bolts of *Blue Sky Highway* and step left across the ledge to the final 2 bolts of *Endless Sky*. Bring a few long runners for the transition.

55 ft. 7 bolts. Unknown.

19 Juniper Route 5.3

Easy climb on the right margin of the face, using the crack for protection. Shared anchor with *Blue Sky Highway*.

55 ft. Gear to 2". Unknown.

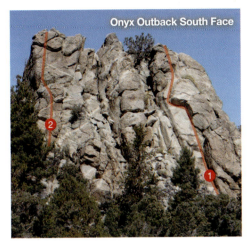
Onyx Outback South Face

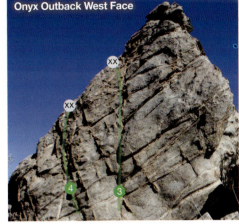
Onyx Outback West Face

ONYX OUTBACK

A peaceful crag with decent climbing in a beautiful alpine setting. The wall is broken into two main pillars, separated by a gully that can be used to descend. The easy trad climbs are south facing and the toprope routes sit in a corridor on the west face. This spot sits right on the edge of the mountains with magnificent views to the valleys below.

PM   🚶 **5 min**

Approach: The approach drive is very scenic and easily passable with a 2WD car. From Highway 38's righthand turn at the eastern edge of town, it is 8.5 miles to where the road peaks at Onyx Summit. Turn left at the crest of the road into a large paved pullout and the start of 1N01. Follow 1N01 for 1.9 miles to a fork in the road. Instead of going right to Onyx Peak, take the left spur and continue the scenic drive on 1N01 through juniper and pines for 2.0 miles. There is a good pullout for parking about 100 yards before the formation, in a big open area on the left. Park and walk down the road, then cut up the steep hillside to the wall. **[GPS: 34.19884, -116.69537]**

Routes listed right to left.

1 **Fifties Nifties** 5.4 ★★
Savor this laidback trad line that starts in a left-facing dihedral. Hug the bottom of a roof, traversing out to its left side, and continue to the summit. Build a gear anchor and descend via a gully in the middle of the south face.
55 ft. Gear to 4". Pat Brennan, Lori Brennan, Eric Tipton, Elaine Tipton, Aug. 2010.

2 **Four Over Fifty** 5.6
Discontinuous climbing with the roof being the only interesting feature. Ascend a small buttress, step across to reach disjointed cracks on the upper face, and progress past the roof. Build a gear anchor and descend via the gully.
55 ft. Gear to 4". Eric Tipton, Elaine Tipton, Pat Brennan, Lori Brennan, Aug. 2010.

3 **Green Light, Red Light** 5.10a ★★
A nifty toprope line located on the west face in a corridor. This lovely stretch of wall is checkered with crisscrossing ridges, creating a unique face of protruding features. Ascend the thin, positive edges along a seam.
35 ft. Eric Tipton, Aug. 2010.

4 **Slave to the Streetlight** 5.7 ★
Take the easiest line on the wall, marked by a nearby light-colored vertical streak. Angle left on good features to the bolted anchor without rap rings.
30 ft. Eric Tipton, Elaine Tipton, Pat Brennan, Lori Brennan, Aug. 2010.

8000-FOOT CRAG

This north-facing hunk of granite may not look like much, but the routes here climb great. The elevation and shadiness of the crag keep temps cool on all but the warmest of days. Due to the high concentration of bolts and somewhat indistinct lines, especially on the left side of the wall, some of the routes blur together. Take extra care to determine your intended line — it can be easy to get off route. *Out of Sight* (5.10b), *El Rayo* (5.10a trad), and *Princess Vicious* (5.11b) are the standouts here.

5 min

Approach: From the east end of Big Bear, turn right to stay on Highway 38. Follow Highway 38 for 8.5 miles to reach the Onyx Summit sign, then continue an additional 1.4 miles to Rainbow Lane and the Laurel Pines Camp. At this point, the crag will be on the left, visible from the road. **The owners of Laurel Pines Camp and Rainbow Lane have prohibited parking on their roads.** You may be towed or ticketed for parking there, in addition to endangering access for climbers. Please continue down the road an extra 0.25 miles and park in the large pullout on the left where the 8000-foot elevation sign is located. Walk back along the road to Rainbow Lane and drop down a faint climber's trail to reach the crag.

If coming up Highway 38 from Redlands, the pullout for the crag is 21.8 miles from the Forest Falls turnoff, at the 8000-foot elevation sign. **[GPS: 34.17295, -116.71806]**

---

❶ The Laughing Tiger 5.4 ★

On the far left end of the wall is a bush marking the start of this easy line. Proceed up behind the bush through a series of ledges on nice jugs to the shared anchor of *Fifty Shades*. *50 ft. 4 bolts. Matt Myers, June 2013.*

❷ Fifty Shades of Green 5.6 ★

Step right of *Laughing Tiger* to a cutout with orange lichen. Deal with the initial slab, utilizing the washboard features. Continue to the steep crux section. Surmount a cool overlap at the 5th bolt and finish at shiny anchors on a small turret. *55 ft. 6 bolts. Clint Oveson, Chris Miller, Aug. 2018.*

❸ Blurry 5.8 ★★

Long and moderate. Move through a brief vertical section, then trend right up a dirty gully. Punch over the overlap, run up a short slab, and conquer the enjoyable steep headwall. *70 ft. 7 bolts. Brad Singer, Ryan Crochiere, Oct. 2006.*

❹ Drift and Die 5.10a ★

Clip the awkward first bolt out left before scaling the ramp. A bit grungy above the 2nd bolt, but once you're through the easy ledges, the final steep headwall is fun. Shared anchor with *Blurry*. *70 ft. 7 bolts. Ryan Crochiere, Oct. 2006.* **Variation 5.11a:** Instead of scaling the ramp, hug the corner and climb this direct start past the first bolt.

❺ Out of Sight 5.10b ★★★

The best route at the crag owing to its excellent upper section. Saunter up the right face of a corner and over an easy, ribbed slab. Athletic moves on the prominent arête are the bread-and-butter of this line, and easier than they look. The direct start has boosted the popularity of this fine route which originally started from the midway ledge. *75 ft. 8 bolts. Preston Sowell, 1991; Direct Start: Chris Miller, 2001.*

❻ Community Service 5.10a ★

Begin right of a tree, liebacking through vertical terrain. Mediocre climbing follows, bounding up and over ledges. Note: The 4th bolt is in a loose block. *40 ft. 5 bolts. Brad Singer, Ryan Crochiere, Oct. 2006.*

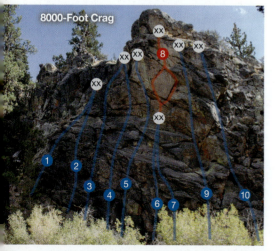
8000-Foot Crag

Ken Snyder on *Out of Sight*, 5.10b, opposite. 📷 Brandon Copp

❼ Keep Hope Alive 5.10b ★ □□

Typically done as an approach pitch to *El Rayo*, this route meanders through a variety of holds and ends at the midway ledge. Shares last 2 bolts and anchors with *Community Service*.

40 ft. 4 bolts. Brad Singer, Oct. 2006.

❽ El Rayo 5.10a ★★★ □□

Excellent crack climb on the upper face beginning from the anchors atop *Community Service* and *Keep Hope Alive* (can easily be done in a single pitch). Choose the left or right side of the diamond-shaped block, each with its own distinct challenges. Finish with more clean crack climbing up the final face, past a bolt. 2-bolt anchor without rap rings requires a walk off. Note: Be cautious of bats in these cracks; stick your hand in a slot and you might hear a squeak that'll make you shriek!

40 ft. Gear to 2", 1 bolt. Preston Sowell, 1991.

❾ Princess Vicious 5.11b ★★★ □□

This baby thrashes and gnashes with its tough opening sequence! The steep start on slick terrain near the orange paint streak has left many a climber scratching their head wondering what to do. Stick the dope technical moves and seize the large fang of rock. With the difficulties behind, fire up the back of a corner and fling yourself over an overhang.

80 ft. 8 bolts. Euan Cameron, May 2010.

❿ Talk to Me 5.11a ★★ □□

Ten feet right of the paint mark is a tough roof problem. Sack up for the cruxy roof (or bypass it with a hand crack on the right, which lowers the grade to 5.9). Balance up slab to a dirty black face.

80 ft. 10 bolts. Eric Odenthal, July 2006.

⓫ P.H.D. 5.10c ★★ □□

A recommended route with unique features. Start 30 feet right of *Talk to Me* — look for the beige-colored bolt hangers. Interesting climbing/sidepulling on opposing arêtes and blocks leads up a jumbled corner. Wedge into the flared dihedral that begs to spit you out. Grunt, grovel, and try not to flail too much as you inch through this section.

40 ft. 5 bolts. John Cardmon, Rob Stauder, Bryan Muramoto, Brad Singer, June 2006.

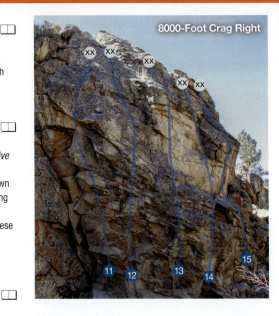

8000-Foot Crag Right

⓬ Funk Sole Brother 5.10c ★★ □□

The 3rd bolt had no hanger as of this writing, so best to TR this route if that's still the case. Float through nice underclings to pinches on a washboard section of wall, culminating in a short slab. A bit funky.

40 ft. 5 bolts (4 currently). Preston Sowell, 1991.

⓭ Funk Sole Sister 5.10b ★★ □□

Pumpy start on the steep, undercut wall. Groove through the funkiness, dance up the light-colored face, and keep stepping past the ledge to the big slab finish.

45 ft. 5 bolts. Preston Sowell, 1991.

⓮ Name of the Game 5.10b ★★ □□

Engage those biceps while blasting through strenuous moves on blocky features. Milk the rest in the middle while easily passing stair-steps. Fire directly up the overlap — or do the chump variation of bypassing it on the right.

40 ft. 4 bolts. Brad Singer, Bryan Muramoto, June 2006.

⓯ Trip Like I Do 5.10d □□

Weird bolt placements plague this miserable climb. Steep start leads to slab. Bypass the pathetic original anchors and head over the bulge to the new ones.

55 ft. 6 bolts. Preston Sowell, 1991.

COON CREEK ROCK

A south-facing roadside crag close to the Heart Bar Campground and numerous yellow-post campsites. This short wall doesn't get a lot of traffic but the rock is clean with nice horizontals. Although not a "destination" crag, it is a fine spot if you're camping in the area or traveling along Highway 38 — a nice little stop late in the day or done in conjunction with nearby 8000-Foot or Onyx Summit. Build a gear anchor for all climbs here on the large ledge with an easy walk-off. The top of the formation sits level with the road and the rock drops down beside a small creek.

1 min

Approach: As you drive east out of Big Bear, turn right to stay on Highway 38, heading toward Onyx Summit. Crest Onyx Summit and continue downhill past the 7000-foot elevation sign until you see the sign for Heart Bar Campground. Turn left here onto 1N02 (14.2 miles from the Highway 38 turnoff at the end of town). Pass Heart Bar Campground and the group equestrian camp. After 1.2 miles, you will reach a fork. Turn left to stay on 1N02 (Coon Creek Jump-Off). Continue down the road, passing many yellow-post campsites, with site #15 being the last, at 2.5 miles from Highway 38. At 2.7 miles, the top of the crag will come into view, level with the right side of the road. Park here and slide down the hill to reach the wall, or continue a bit further to park on an old road and hike back along the creek for 1-2 minutes. Either way, there's really no approach.

If coming up Highway 38 from Redlands, the turnoff for the Heart Bar Campground is 17.8 miles from the Forest Falls turnoff.
[GPS: 34.15396, -116.74605]

---

❶ Coonstock 5.9 ★
Gravitate up the slightly overhung left margin. Flow past numerous horizontals, reaching the top by jamming up a final diagonal crack.
25 ft. Gear to 3".
Pat Brennan, Lori Brennan, Jeff Brennan, Adam Brennan.

❷ Coondoggolin' 5.8 ★
Don your coonskin cap and take the crack straight up the gullet of the formation. A tough undercut start followed by a series of slopey bulges make this an exciting line. Good pro.
30 ft. Gear to 2.5".
Pat Brennan, Lori Brennan, Jeff Brennan, Adam Brennan.

❸ Star Gazers 5.6 ★
Neat little line that angles across the face. Start on big horns on the arête and continue up the broken corner system, culminating in a crack with a dike.
30 ft. Gear to 2.5".
Pat Brennan, Lori Brennan, Jeff Brennan, Adam Brennan.

❹ Raccoon 5.2
Ascends the manky east face. So easy and short it's really not worth doing.
25 ft. Gear to 3".
Pat Brennan, Lori Brennan, Jeff Brennan, Adam Brennan.

Coon Creek Rock

GRAPEVINE CANYON

GRAPEVINE **CANYON**

Grapevine Canyon lies on the northern flanks of the San Bernardino range, hovering in the transition zone between the mountains and the desert. It is best visited in spring and fall due to its lower elevation and warmer climate, and may be a good spot to seek out when the weather isn't ideal near the lake. There are numerous crags spread out over a 10-mile radius, with formations up to 100 feet tall. While it has an abundance of excellent lines, it was kept off the radar for many years — this is its first full treatment in print. Even the 4-star routes hardly see any traffic, and there is a vast amount of untapped potential for new route development.

The area was initially developed by Brian Elliott, Doug Odenthal, Joe Sheehy, and Cindy Elliott from 1989 to the mid 1990s. Doug Odenthal is credited with discovering the potential of the area. The group of friends spent countless weekends exploring and putting up bold new lines at a time when local ethics dictated that ascents should be ground-up. Bolts were hand-drilled on hooks and used sparingly, providing a more runout feel compared to today's standards. Most routes have 5/16" buttonheads placed in good-quality rock, with a sprinkling of 3/8" bolts. Additional route contributors at the time included Richard Kramer, Todd Burrill, Bill Odenthal, Dave Evans, and others.

The climbing at Grapevine Canyon is primarily technical face on tiny crystals, plus a substantial number of crack lines. The rock quality spans a wide range, from the bomber, fine-grained granite of Butt Rock to dismal walls coated in crumbly crystals. Often, a single face on a formation has decent rock, while the other sides don't. Route grades are old-school and stout, reminiscent of Joshua Tree, and typically feel a grade or two harder than those at Holcomb Valley Pinnacles. Many routes haven't been repeated, and the grades are as reported by the FA party.

Grapevine Canyon is a wild and remote area, containing a large population of wildlife. Coyotes, snakes, horned lizards, hares, deer, quail, owls, and more have made this place their home. Be more aware of critters since this place sees infrequent visitor traffic. Note that many hunters descend on this area during hunting season. Take care to be recognized, or better yet, avoid climbing during this time.

As a lesser-known climbing spot, Grapevine Canyon does not have much of a trail system. That said, it is recommended to walk along the well-marked OHV trails when possible instead of hiking cross-country to reach the crags. In general, these dirt bike trails are easier to follow and less impactful to the fragile desert environment, and typically lead fairly close to the rock formations. Be aware that oftentimes the most difficult part of the approach will be hiking around the base of the crag, as the vegetation tends to be thickest next to the wall. GPS coordinates can be extremely helpful for locating the right formation.

The Horse Springs Campground on Grapevine Canyon Road is the only Forest Service campground here. It has pit toilets and 11 first-come, first serve campsites with picnic tables but no running water. Additionally, the Oak Springs Ranch has a campground suitable for tents and

RVs, along with two cabins available to rent. The campground has drinking water, toilets, and an outdoor kitchen but no power. The closest town is Hesperia, to the northwest, which has grocery stores, restaurants, gas, automotive repair shops, camping supplies, etc. It is a good place to resupply, spend a rest day, or get your In-N-Out fix.

Approach: Grapevine Canyon has especially rough roads, where a high-clearance vehicle is mandatory and **4WD is strongly recommended**.

From Big Bear, the most direct route is to drive north from the town of Fawnskin on 3N14

(marked as Rim of the World Drive in Fawnskin and becoming the Coxey Truck Trail once out of town). Follow 3N14 for 6.7 miles to an intersection with 3N16 near the Big Pine Flat Campground. Continue straight through the intersection. At 12.2 miles total from Fawnskin, 3N14 intersects with 4N16, the Grapevine Canyon Road. **All mileages for the crags is given from this intersection.** This drive takes approximately 45 minutes to 1 hour on dirt roads.

For those coming directly from the LA basin or the high desert, it's quicker to approach via the town of Hesperia. From the I-15, take exit 143 for Main Street. Head east for just over 7 miles, all the way through town. Turn left at a stoplight onto Rock Springs Road. Drive 2.7 miles until you reach a stop sign (intersection with Kiowa Road). Continue straight onto Roundup Way. Drive this for 4.2 miles, past the point where the road becomes dirt. Turn right at the stop sign for Bowen Ranch Road. After 2.0 miles on Bowen Ranch Road, you will reach a Y-junction with the Coxey Truck Trail (3N14). Alternate approach directions for the crags are listed from this junction. Turn left onto 3N14 for all crags except Bubba Rocks and Zeppelin Dome.

Important Note: Do not attempt to follow GPS navigation to this area. The default route directs you in from the northeast corner on Grapevine Canyon Road (4N16), which has an extremely rough uphill section that is impassable for most vehicles.

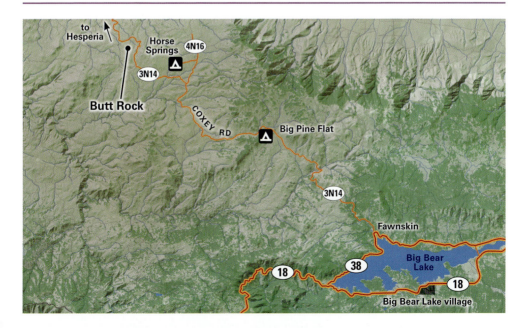

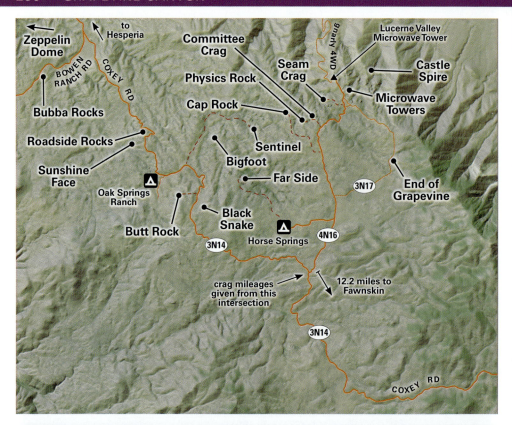

CLIMBING AREA	ELEVATION	HIKE	ROUTES	GRADE RANGE	CRAGS
THE FAR SIDE *Shady, densely packed corridors* **page 298**	5700 ft.	50 min	17	≤.5 .6 .7 .8 .9 .10 .11 .12	
CAP ROCK AREA *Must do: Canoe Slab, 11a* **page 302**	5600 ft.	40-45 min	21	≤.5 .6 .7 .8 .9 .10 .11 .12	
COMMITTEE CRAG *Crack-climbing destination* **page 307**	5700 ft.	5-10 min	10	≤.5 .6 .7 .8 .9 .10 .11 .12	
PHYSICS ROCK AND ENVIRONS *Neat sport climbing on edges* **page 310**	5700 ft.	15-20 min	18	≤.5 .6 .7 .8 .9 .10 .11 .12	

CLIMBING AREA	ELEVATION	HIKE	ROUTES	GRADE RANGE	CRAGS
SEAM CRAG AREA *Must do: Armageddon, 12a* page 314	5500 ft.	10-20 min	19	≤.5 .6 .7 .8 .9 .10 .11 .12	
CASTLE SPIRE *Phenomenal exposure* page 318	5300 ft.	40 min	2	≤.5 .6 .7 .8 .9 .10 .11 .12	
END OF GRAPEVINE *Secluded and gritty* page 319	6100 ft.	2 min	4	≤.5 .6 .7 .8 .9 .10 .11 .12	
MICROWAVE TOWERS *Roadside, fragile crystals* page 321	5650 ft.	2 min	12	≤.5 .6 .7 .8 .9 .10 .11 .12	
BUTT ROCK AREA *Crown jewel of Grapevine Canyon* page 324	5550 ft.	5-20 min	25	≤.5 .6 .7 .8 .9 .10 .11 .12+	AKA Gnome Dome
BLACK SNAKE AND THE HIDEOUT *Short climbs, minimal approach* page 330	5800 ft.	10 min	15	≤.5 .6 .7 .8 .9 .10 .11 .12	
WELCOME TO GRAPEVINE *Scattered lines* page 332	4700 ft. 5300 ft.	5-60 min	11	≤.5 .6 .7 .8 .9 .10 .11 .12	Bigfoot, Classic Crack, Sentinel, Sunshine Face, Roadside Rocks, Bushmaster
BUBBA ROCKS *Good rock, quality climbs* page 334	4150 ft.	2 min	10	≤.5 .6 .7 .8 .9 .10 .11 .12	
ZEPPELIN DOME *Tall, sweeping wall with fantastic routes* page 336	4250 ft.	10 min	8	≤.5 .6 .7 .8 .9 .10 .11 .12	

THE FAR SIDE

The Far Side is a large mass of rock with hidden corridors that are chock full of routes. While the approach is a decent hike, the crag is near the Horse Springs Campground, making it a nice spot to spend a day if you're also planning to camp. *Contortionist* (5.10d) is a splendid technical climb to do in Circus Corridor, while *Killer Crack* (5.10d) is the gear line to hit. Don't forget to try the lines on the summit block, which have excellent exposure and amazing views down to the desert floor. This area, with its corridors and northerly aspect, stays relatively cool and shaded, making it a good spot for warmer days.

50 min

Approach: From the intersection of 3N14 and 4N16, turn onto 4N16 and drive for 1.0 mile. Turn left onto 4N16A, following signs for the Horse Springs Campground, and take this road for 0.75 miles. While the campground isn't often busy, please be courteous and don't park in someone else's site.

Walk northwest from campsite #2 (near the information signs and toilet) and pick up a trail that leads through a gap in the barbed-wire fence. Follow this dirt bike trail as it parallels the fence line for a brief time before heading northwest. After following this path for close to 30 minutes (1.1 miles), you will reach a rocky outcropping and an overlook, where the formation is visible across a deep gully. Continue following the dirt bike trail around this gully and up a small rise (5-10 minutes more) to the northwest face of the wall. Bushwhack along the base to reach the climbs. Circus Corridor and Mordor sit at the far northeast end of the wall. **[GPS: 34.36369, -117.08176]**

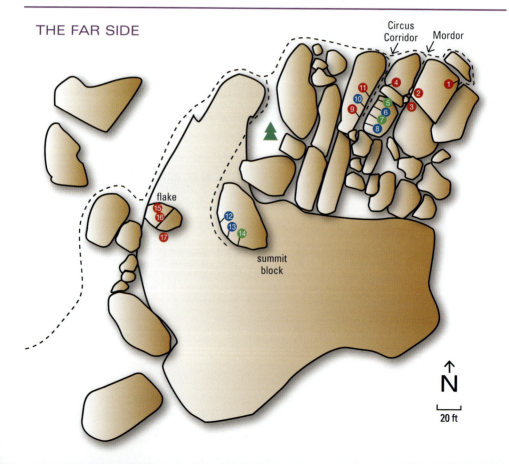

THE FAR SIDE

Killer Crack

① Killer Crack 5.10d ★★★

This magnificent crack is a lesser-known gem of Grapevine Canyon. Fight your way up the slightly overhanging fat-fist crack, savoring each constriction before heading back into battle. A physical undertaking that's not for the soft!

45 ft. Gear to 4".

Brian Elliott, Doug Odenthal, Joe Sheehy, Cindy Elliott, 1990s.

The next 2 routes are found in a neighboring corridor called Mordor.

② Mordor Crack 5.9 ★

The leftmost of the two crack lines in the dark corridor. Journey up this wide crack as it slants right before going straight up past where the walls of the corridor pinch together. No anchor — Class 5 downclimb.

70 ft. Gear to 5".

Brian Elliott, Doug Odenthal, Joe Sheehy, Cindy Elliott, 1990s.

③ Thin Man's Crack 5.9 ★

Deep in the corridor is this thin crack in a right-facing corner. No anchor — Class 5 downclimb.

70 ft. Gear to 3".

Brian Elliott, Doug Odenthal, Joe Sheehy, Cindy Elliott, 1990s.

The following 8 routes are located in Circus Corridor.

④ Side Show 5.7 ★

A mixed line up a corner next to a break in the wall. It is the first route encountered on the left side of Circus Corridor. Open with a bolt before popping in a cam beside a block. Continue up the easy but runout arête to anchors.

50 ft. Gear to 2", 2 bolts.

Brian Elliott, Doug Odenthal, Joe Sheehy, Cindy Elliott, 1990s.

⑤ Fortune Teller 5.10d ★★

A technical line that begins underneath a flake. Tenuous moves on the balancy slab gain a sloping rail. Shares anchors with *Lion Tamer*.

50 ft. Brian Elliott, Doug Odenthal, Joe Sheehy, Cindy Elliott, 1990s.

⑥ Lion Tamer 5.10a ★★

Tame the beast in the middle of the face by aggressively edging to a large flake. Mantel atop this feature and crimp to the wall's apex. Good climbing at the grade.

50 ft. 4 bolts.

Brian Elliott, Doug Odenthal, Joe Sheehy, Cindy Elliott, 1990s.

⑦ Getting Whacked 5.10a ★

Slender features are the name of the game on this short line that sure packs a punch. Figure out the best way through the dishes and small edges dotting the face between *Lion Tamer* and *Clowning*. Shared anchor with *Lion Tamer*.

45 ft.

Brian Elliott, Doug Odenthal, Joe Sheehy, Cindy Elliott, 1990s.

⑧ Clowning 5.7 ★★

Cling to edges on the right arête as you claw your way to the top. Quite nice. Shared anchor with *Lion Tamer*.

40 ft. 3 bolts.

Brian Elliott, Doug Odenthal, Joe Sheehy, Cindy Elliott, 1990s.

Circus Corridor

Elliot Warden climbs *It's Just a Jump to the Left*, 5.8, opposite.
📷 Brandon Copp

The Far Side

⑨ Circus Crack 5.10d ★

This is the textured crack at the back of the corridor on its right side. Actively work the wide section until it narrows to hands. Shared anchor with *Contortionist*.

50 ft. Gear to 3.5".

Brian Elliott, Doug Odenthal, Joe Sheehy, Cindy Elliott, 1990s.

⑩ Contortionist 5.10d ★★★

An exemplary exercise in the art of delicate edging. Master the dime edges, balancing on thin but positive incuts. Contort and dance from hold to hold throughout the remarkably sustained sequence.

50 ft. 5 bolts.

Brian Elliott, Doug Odenthal, Joe Sheehy, Cindy Elliott, 1990s.

⑪ Big Top 5.10b ★★★

Break out the big cams for this one! Shove body parts into this massive offwidth until you feel nice and secure. Employ masochistic circus tricks to move an inch. Repeat. Shared anchor with *Contortionist*.

50 ft. Gear to 6".

Brian Elliott, Doug Odenthal, Joe Sheehy, Cindy Elliott, 1990s.

Routes #12-14 are situated on the summit block. Approach these climbs from the left via a low-angle slab.

⑫ Time Warp 5.10c ★★

Yard through giant jugs, perform a tenuous traverse left to the blunt corner, then crimp crystals to the top. A spooky lead with cool position. Bolted anchor without rap rings.

40 ft. 4 bolts. Doug Odenthal, Kurt Lyons, 1990s.

⑬ It's Just a Jump to the Left 5.8 ★

An enjoyable line in a beautiful setting. Cruise up the less-than-vertical face on the right side of the summit block.

35 ft. 4 bolts. Doug Odenthal, Joe Sheehy, 1990s.

⑭ And Then a Step to the Right 5.9 ★

Toprope the orange face right of the previous route.

35 ft. Doug Odenthal, Joe Sheehy, 1990s.

⑮ Tickle Me 5.6

Plug up the left side of the thick flake that leans against the lower face to end below the summit block. Gear anchor.

70 ft. Gear to 5".

Brian Elliott, Doug Odenthal, Joe Sheehy, Cindy Elliott, 1990s.

⑯ Make Fun of Me 5.7

Ascend the right side of the flake, then worm across it following a diagonal crack. When this crack ends, finish up the flake's left side. Gear anchor.

70 ft. Gear to 5".

Brian Elliott, Doug Odenthal, Joe Sheehy, Cindy Elliott, 1990s.

⑰ Poke Me 5.8

Sprint up the right side of the fat flake all the way to the ledge. Gear anchor.

70 ft. Gear to 5".

Brian Elliott, Doug Odenthal, Joe Sheehy, Cindy Elliott, 1990s.

CAP ROCK AREA

The massive roof of Cap Rock is unmistakable, distinctly sitting on a ridge beside its two prominent companion formations. A wide variety of climbing can be found here: tall lines, short and powerful ones, sport climbs, traditional cracks, slab routes, offwidth, and everything in between. *Canoe Slab* (5.11a) is the highlight of the area, ascending a slab of rock that from its side profile looks like a Native American dugout canoe. Many of the routes here are high quality, yet some lack proper anchors. Installing anchors and rap rings atop these lines would help!

Approach: From the intersection of 3N14 and 4N16, turn onto 4N16 and drive for 1.9 miles. Park on the left near a BLM sign for Juniper Flats. Start by hiking west on JF3221, passing through a motorcycle gate after 500 feet where the path turns to the northwest. After 15 minutes (0.6 miles), the trail crests a large hill with 360-degree views of the area. Just down this hill is a Y-intersection with JF3219. Take the fork on the right and follow JF3219 for another 15 minutes (0.6 miles) to arrive at the east side of the crags. It is a lengthy hike, but the dirt bike trails are easy to follow.

Cap Rock Overview

Finger of God
Cap Rock
Gable Rock
Baby's Butt
Oden Wall
Canoe Slab

Finger of God
[GPS: 34.37798, -117.06989]

40 min

❶ Black Hole 5.11a ★★

Stem out of a nook, executing a unique set of moves on the lower features. Dial in the technical sequence needed to gain passage through thin seams and minute features, angling right across the face.

40 ft. 6 bolts.

Brian Elliott, Doug Odenthal, Joe Sheehy, Cindy Elliott, 1990s.

❷ Simulrap Tower 5.10b ★★

An adventurous climb on the tiny pillar behind the Finger of God. No anchor — carefully simulrap from the top.

40 ft. Gear to 4", 2 bolts.

Brian Elliott, Doug Odenthal, Joe Sheehy, Cindy Elliott, 1990s.

❸ Canoe Slab 5.11a ★★★★

This quintessential slab route is the centerpiece of the area. Airy exposure and panoramic landscape views complement outstanding movement on quality rock to provide a well-rounded experience. Boldly engage the attractive face, where a definite crux hits at the 4th bolt. Master this route with technical prowess and precision footwork.

55 ft. 7 bolts. Brian Elliott, Richard Kramer, Doug Odenthal, Joe Sheehy, Cindy Elliott, 1990.

Canoe Slab

❹ Sistine Chapel 5.10a ★★★

Begin from the north face and proceed along the coarse crack to a ledge. Gather your courage and confront the bolted face above, grasping crystals on the low-angle prow. Enjoy the final view from the tip of the Finger of God.

65 ft. Gear to 4.5", 3 bolts.

Brian Elliott, Doug Odenthal, Joe Sheehy, Cindy Elliott, 1989.

❺ First Route 5.6

A low-angle romp in a wide crack/gully.

50 ft. Wide gear.

Brian Elliott, Doug Odenthal, Joe Sheehy, Cindy Elliott, 1989.

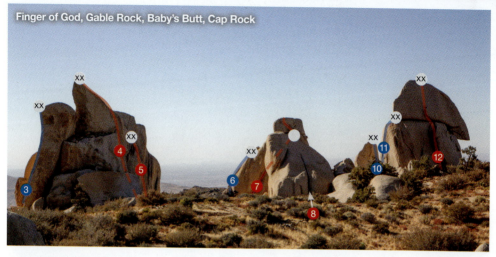

Finger of God, Gable Rock, Baby's Butt, Cap Rock

Gable Rock and Baby's Butt
[GPS: 34.37844, -117.06979]

40 min

6 Laissez Les Bon Temps Rouler 5.11c ★★
"Let the good times roll!" This invigorating line begins from a ledge. Grapple with a shallow, right-facing flake that peters out near the 3rd bolt. Smear on the insecure slab, where a slight run to the anchors adds spice.
50 ft. 4 bolts.

Brian Elliott, Doug Odenthal, Joe Sheehy, Cindy Elliott, 1990s.

7 Arc de Triomphe 5.8 ★★★
The obvious arching crack. Burrow down to reach the base, then slot hands securely and cruise happily along. Continue climbing past a horizontal to reach the summit. There is no fixed anchor however; one must downclimb the final crack and rappel from the fixed gear below. This outing would be much improved with the addition of a summit anchor.
60 ft. Gear to 4".

Brian Elliott, Doug Odenthal, Joe Sheehy, Cindy Elliott, 1989.

8 Baby's Butt 5.9 ★★
The conspicuous flaring offwidth with an unprotected finish. No anchors — exit right off the slab.
50 ft. Wide gear.

Brian Elliott, Doug Odenthal, Joe Sheehy, Cindy Elliott, 1990s.

9 Bush Crack 5.10a
On the northeast side of Gable. Avoid the bush in the rough crack. Head left underneath big flakes, wrapping around the formation. Same anchor situation as *Arc De Triomphe*.
55 ft. Gear to 3.5".

Brian Elliott, Doug Odenthal, Joe Sheehy, Cindy Elliott, 1990s.

Cap Rock
[GPS: 34.37873, -117.06979]

40 min

10 Dilithium Crystal 5.9 ★★★
A solid and sustained route on the freestanding pillar beside Cap Rock. Strenuously lieback the righthand arête, all the while wondering, "Will this crystal hold me?" and "How much weight can I put on this hold?" Sporty getting to the 3rd bolt!
40 ft. 4 bolts. *Brian Elliott, Chris Miller, 1990s.*

11 Sonic Separator 5.10d ★★★
Start from the same corridor as *Dilithium Crystal* and grapple with the technical southwest face of Cap Rock. At press time the bolted anchor needed rap rings. The FA party instead made the hairy traverse with extreme rope drag to wrap around the formation and ascend the upper portion of *Nothing but the Blues*.
45 ft. 4 bolts. *Brian Elliott, Chris Miller, 1990s.*

12 Nothing but the Blues 5.7 ★★
This is the easiest way to reach the summit of Cap Rock. Take the stack of flakes that lean against the east face up to a ledge. Push past another flake to a section of bolted slab that protects the summit.
60 ft. Gear to 5", 2 bolts.

Brian Elliott, Doug Odenthal, Joe Sheehy, Cindy Elliott, 1989.

Brian Elliott revisits *Dilithium Crystal*,
5.9, opposite. 📷 Brandon Copp

Stellar Eggs

no fixed anchor

13   14   15

Captain Crunch

XX   XX

16   11   10

Oden Wall

XX

17   18   19

The following 3 routes on the northeast face are in need of a dedicated anchor. Currently you must climb across the ledge and finish on Nothing but the Blues *to reach the summit anchors. Bring a large cam or 2 for the traverse.*

13 Hypercard Crack 5.10b
Wiggle in behind a tree and climb the gritty, right-facing flake.
40 ft. Gear to 4".
Brian Elliott, Doug Odenthal, Joe Sheehy, Cindy Elliott, 1990s.

14 Stellar Eggs 5.11c ★★
Wedge into a crack behind the tree. When it peters out, follow bolts up the egg-citing, lichen-crusted face.
45 ft. Gear to 2.5", 5 bolts.
Brian Elliott, Doug Odenthal, Joe Sheehy, Cindy Elliott, 1990s.

15 Green Lichen Route 5.8 ★
Breeze up a shallow channel underneath the overhanging cap. Cut left at the finish to reach the ledge.
45 ft. 5 bolts, gear anchor. Brian Elliott, Bill Odenthal, Doug Odenthal, Joe Sheehy, Cindy Elliott, 1990s.

16 Captain Crunch 5.10b ★★
Cast off from the leaning slab on the northwest face. Trend right past a good ledge and end by edging through the slick face. Invigorating! No bolted anchor — rappel from the fixed gear underneath the roof.
45 ft. 6 bolts. Brian Elliott, Todd Burrill, 1990s.

Oden Wall:
[GPS: 34.37945, -117.06950]

45 min

17 Great Oden's Raven 5.9+ ★
10 feet left of *Ripper* lies this arching offwidth. Shove your body into the crack until you feel some sense of security, then scoot awkwardly to the top. Gear anchor.
30 ft. Gear to 4.5".
Brian Elliott, Doug Odenthal, Joe Sheehy, Cindy Elliott, 1990s.

18 Ripper 5.10a ★★
The vertical finger crack in the middle of the northeast face. Best suited for those with thin fingers. Gear anchor.
35 ft. Gear to 3".
Brian Elliott, Doug Odenthal, Joe Sheehy, Cindy Elliott, 1990s.

19 Vikings Don't Cry 5.10a ★
A right-slanting crack that begins right of a bush. Fight back tears as this gritty hand crack rips your flesh. Gear anchor.
30 ft. Gear to 2.5".
Brian Elliott, Doug Odenthal, Joe Sheehy, Cindy Elliott, 1990s.

20 Crystal Delights 5.8
A simple hand crack around the corner from *Vikings*. Really poor rock. Gear anchor.
30 ft. Gear to 4".
Brian Elliott, Doug Odenthal, Joe Sheehy, Cindy Elliott, 1990s.

21 Eric the Red 5.8
Climb past rotten rock in a narrowing offwidth. Gear anchor.
30 ft. Wide gear.
Brian Elliott, Doug Odenthal, Joe Sheehy, Cindy Elliott, 1990s.

Doug Odenthal and Joe Sheehy, Physics Rock.
📷 Odenthal collection

`89 10 29`

COMMITTEE CRAG

This easily accessible crag is predominantly a crack-climbing destination with very few bolts. It is home to the excellent *Committee Crack* (5.10c), the first line to be climbed at Grapevine Canyon. All of the climbs here require gear anchors be built, with the descent located on the formation's north end.

Approach: From the intersection of 3N14 and 4N16, turn onto 4N16 and drive for 2.4 miles. Park on the left beside a barbed wire fence. Duck under the fence and walk along what used to be an old road for 5 minutes. The crag will be on the right-hand side; it's hard to miss.

Committee Crag:
[GPS: 34.37727, -117.06235]

 PM   5 min

Routes 1-4 are located on the main wall's west face and route 5 is on its east face.

❶ Stemfister 5.10a ★★

A brief moment in a flared corner reaches a crack that hooks left. Tear out into this arching crack and whiz past the left side of a small overhang.
45 ft. Gear to 3".
Brian Elliott, Doug Odenthal, Joe Sheehy, Cindy Elliott, 1989.

❷ Easy Route 5.6 ★

The easiest route on the wall is situated beside the hardest — funny how that works out sometimes! From a flake, make a heady step to the right, then easy face climbing in a channel while plugging gear in the crack to the left.
45 ft. Gear to 2".
Brian Elliott, Doug Odenthal, Joe Sheehy, Cindy Elliott, 1989.

❸ Aid Route 5.12a A0 ★★

Clip the low pin and hoist yourself (A0) onto the wall. Slick feet and minimal fingertip purchase in the thin seam characterize the next moves. Calm yourself as you try to wedge in a micro nut for protection. Will it hold a fall? I don't know. Climb up. Don't look down. Fiddle in a small cam if you can, then keep climbing. Cram in more small gear. At this point you may be crying. I know I was.
45 ft. RPs, TCUs, and thin gear to 0.75", 1 pin.
Brian Elliott, Doug Odenthal, Joe Sheehy, Cindy Elliott, 1990s.

Committee Crag

Three-Bolt Salad

Jacumba

4 Committee Crack 5.10c ★★★★

This instantly recognizable splitter is a magnificent right-leaning crack that widens ever so slightly throughout its length, from fingertips to hand-sized. Slip your mitts into this sucker and bust through the tough start. Reap the rewards of delightful hand-over-hand jams, better-than-average protection, and that wonderful feeling of a crack that's the perfect fit. This classic line was the first route to be put up at Grapevine Canyon and it was done "by committee" on the first ascent.

45 ft. Gear to 3".

Brian Elliott, Doug Odenthal, Joe Sheehy, Cindy Elliott, 1989.

5 East Committee Crack 5.10d ★

Short little crack on the backside. Sink in at least a knuckle on the lower part of the left-angling seam and propel yourself upward while the crack tapers. Crimp along the left or right seam of the "Y", depending on which looks the best. Build a gear anchor on the ledge, or eek out an extra 10' of climbing by bringing a wide piece to shove into the arching crack above.

20 ft. Thin gear to 0.75", optional 3-4" piece.

Brian Elliott, Doug Odenthal, Joe Sheehy, Cindy Elliott, 1990s.

Jacumba Tower:
[GPS: 34.37729, -117.06216]

  10 min

Routes 6-9 are situated on a rock mass to the east of Committee Crag.

6 Weird Route 5.10b ★

From a corridor, grovel underneath a giant leaning block. Past the block, pick up an incipient seam and follow this to the arête, finishing on the last bolt of *Three-Bolt Salad*.

45 ft. Gear to 4.5", 1 bolt. Brian Elliott, Doug Odenthal, Joe Sheehy, Cindy Elliott, 1990s.

7 Three-Bolt Salad 5.8+ ★★

Adjacent to *Weird Route* is this neat mixed line. Cling to a well-featured flake until it ends, then step left onto the face and clip the first bolt. Fluid movement on knobs gains the arête.

45 ft. Thin gear to 0.75" (TCUs or wires), 3 bolts.

Brian Elliott, Doug Odenthal, Joe Sheehy, Cindy Elliott, 1990s.

8 Jacumba 5.10c ★★★

Jacumba and *Faulty Tower* both begin from a ledge on the east side. Conquer this high-caliber crack that comes fully stocked with locks, jams, liebacks, and even a few face holds. Inch up underneath a V-shaped notch to start, then power through the overlap and haul ass on the clean arching crack above. Rad climbing on a lesser-known gem.

60 ft. Gear to 4".

Brian Elliott, Doug Odenthal, Joe Sheehy, Cindy Elliott, 1990s.

9 Faulty Tower 5.10d ★★

On the right side of the ledge is a large flake marking this climb's start. Continue along an obvious wide crack, meandering to the top.

60 ft. Gear to 5".

Brian Elliott, Doug Odenthal, Joe Sheehy, Cindy Elliott, 1990s.

Route 10 is on the south face of a satellite rock located 100 yards west of Committee Crag.

10 West Crack 5.8 ★

Take the challenging, thin crack halfway to reach a wider groove on a more well-featured part of the face.

30 ft. Gear to 3".

Brian Elliott, Doug Odenthal, Joe Sheehy, Cindy Elliott, 1990s.

Brian Elliott, *Committee Crack*, 5.10c, opposite. 📷 Brandon Copp

PHYSICS ROCK AND ENVIRONS

If you've never been out to Grapevine Canyon before and are looking for sport climbs that span a wide range of difficulty, this is the crag to visit. The numerous great routes here are all about edging and climbing on crystals. Don't miss *Nice Melons* (5.9+) and *Wook'n Pa Nub* (5.10a) for their unique, knobby features and old-school flavor! This area offers both sun and shade, as well as good rock, making it enjoyable no matter the season.

Approach: From Committee Crag, look southwest to locate this large hill with a collection of rocks covering its summit. Hike 0.2 miles cross-country out to the hill, staying on the southern edge of it. Physics Rock and Einstein Rock are most easily approached this way and can be found on the western side, whereas Nub Face and Shady Wall are on the northern slope.

PHYSICS ROCK AND ENVIRONS

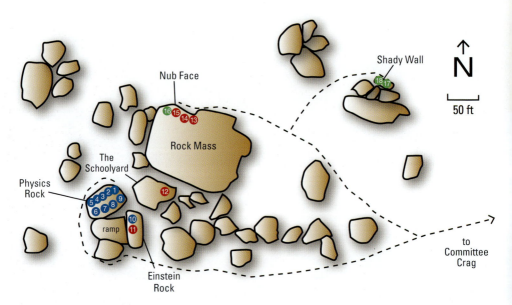

Physics Rock
[GPS: 34.37627, -117.06561]

15 min

① No Prisoners Direct 5.12a ★★
Have your game face on for this route! Fire up the steep face on thin flakes to reach a blank section guarding the anchor.
40 ft. 6 bolts. Brian Elliott, Dave Evans, 1990s.

② No Prisoners 5.11c ★★
Start as above, but after the 4th bolt, cut right to the arête.
40 ft. 6 bolts.
Brian Elliott, Doug Odenthal, Joe Sheehy, Cindy Elliott, 1990s.

③ Critical Mass 5.11a ★★★
An excellent face climb sporting just enough features in all the right places. Share the first bolt with *F=ma* and head directly up the left side of the west face on good knobs and edges. Shares anchors with *No Prisoners*.
40 ft. 5 bolts.
Brian Elliott, Doug Odenthal, Joe Sheehy, Cindy Elliott, 1990s.

④ F=ma 5.10b ★★
Head up and right, making liberal use of the good edges that punctuate the face. When you reach the singular gray xenolith, blast straight upward on thinning holds.
40 ft. 5 bolts.
Brian Elliott, Doug Odenthal, Joe Sheehy, Cindy Elliott, 1989.

Brigitte Ngo-Trinh, *No Prisoners Direct*, 5.12a, opposite. 📷 Kimmie Tu

Physics Rock

5 Inertia 5.10a ★★

The first route to be put up on Physics Rock. Gravitate past the opening 3 bolts shared with *F=ma* to the gray xenolith, then follow better edges out right for an easier ending. Share anchors with *F=ma*.

40 ft. 4 bolts.

Brian Elliott, Doug Odenthal, Joe Sheehy, Cindy Elliott, 1989.

6 Rampology 5.9 ★★

A unique traverse line that clips the first 2 bolts of *Newtonian Mechanics*, then abruptly cuts left. Shared anchor with *F=ma*.

40 ft. 4 bolts.

Brian Elliott, Doug Odenthal, Joe Sheehy, Cindy Elliott, 1990s.

Physics Rock & Einstein Rock

7 Newtonian Mechanics 5.10b ★★★★

Pick a crisp day to take on this technical endeavour, the best line on the face. This superb route with a distinct crux demands precision footwork and a problem-solving mindset. Delightful and outstanding for the grade. Shared anchor with *No Prisoners*.

40 ft. 4 bolts.

Brian Elliott, Doug Odenthal, Joe Sheehy, Cindy Elliott, 1989.

8 No Kissing Allowed 5.10a ★

A typical slab climb that shares anchors with *No Prisoners*. You'll have to ask the first ascensionists about the cute story behind the route name …

40 ft. 4 bolts.

Brian Elliott, Doug Odenthal, Joe Sheehy, Cindy Elliott, 1989.

9 Bolting Begins at 40 5.9 ★★

Decipher the slab moves, following bolts that trend right over the airy void before making their way back to the *No Prisoners* anchor. An enjoyable route put up on Doug Odenthal's 40th birthday.

35 ft. 4 bolts.

Brian Elliott, Doug Odenthal, Joe Sheehy, Cindy Elliott, 1989.

Einstein Rock:
[GPS: 34.37616, -117.06543]

15 min

10 Arête Dream 5.10a ★

A difficult move gains the wall, then ample friction and large features lead to the top. Share anchors with *Nasal Passage*.

35 ft. 3 bolts.

Brian Elliott, Doug Odenthal, Joe Sheehy, Cindy Elliott, 1990s.

11 Nasal Passage 5.10d ★★

An exciting crack line with liebacks, jams, and even a few face holds. Sink your mitts into the crack that splits the overhang and go ballistic as you make the difficult transition over the roof. Sniffle up the wide crack above.

50 ft. Gear to 5".

Brian Elliott, Doug Odenthal, Joe Sheehy, Cindy Elliott, 1990s.

The Schoolyard
[GPS: 34.37629, -117.06523]

AM   20 min

12 Playing Hooky 5.6 ★

Take the slightly flared finger crack up the well-featured face. Gear anchor.

30 ft. Gear to 1.5".

Brian Elliott, Doug Odenthal, Joe Sheehy, Cindy Elliott, 1989.

Nub Face
[GPS: 34.37672, -117.06522]

20 min

13 Toe Moss 5.8

Tread up the grungy slab/left-facing corner. Gear anchor.

50 ft. Gear to 3".

Brian Elliott, Doug Odenthal, Joe Sheehy, Cindy Elliott, 1989.

14 Nice Melons 5.9+ ★★★

An extremely fun route on magnificent knobs. Slide up under an arching roof, then pivot over onto the dark face. On the sketchy runout, as you wonder how the hell anyone could call this 5.9, take a deep breath and appreciate the beautiful landscape around you. Now quit your bitching and send! Gear anchor.

55 ft. 4 bolts, slings for knobs, gear to 3.5" for anchor.

Brian Elliott, Doug Odenthal, Joe Sheehy, Cindy Elliott, 1989.

Nub Face

Playing Hooky

Shady Wall

15 Wook'n Pa Nub 5.10a ★★★
Another don't-miss route with an old-school thrill! Heady, with large runs between bolts that force one to sling the unique protruding xenoliths as natural pro. Gear anchor; scramble off the ledge climber's left.
55 ft. 4 bolts, slings for knobs, gear to 3.5" for anchor.
Brian Elliott, Doug Odenthal, Joe Sheehy, Cindy Elliott, 1989.

16 No Knockers 5.10c ★
TR a line that is devoid of the wonderful features on the neighboring lines. Punch up to the 2nd bolt of *Wook'n Pa Nub*, then veer right and ascend the thin face. Gear anchor.
55 ft. Gear to 3.5" for anchor.
Brian Elliott, Doug Odenthal, Joe Sheehy, Cindy Elliott, 1989.

Shady Wall
[GPS: 34.37680, -117.06411]

15 min

17 Think Thin 5.10d ★
Good luck squeezing your sausage fingers inside this thin seam! Strenuously fingerlock and smear as you progress up the middle of this short black-and-white wall. Gear anchor.
25 ft. Brian Elliott, Doug Odenthal, Joe Sheehy, Cindy Elliott, 1990s.

18 This One Is For You 5.9
Muscle up the offwidth flare on the right margin of the wall. Gear anchor.
25 ft. Brian Elliott, Doug Odenthal, Joe Sheehy, Cindy Elliott, 1990s.

SEAM CRAG AREA

Unlike many of the other locations in Grapevine Canyon, this area has a vast array of large rocks nearby that make locating the walls with climbs a touch more challenging. Seam Crag is a big dome containing the majority of the routes in this area, and it might help to find this crag first before seeking out the satellite walls. The best routes here include the 5.11a crack-to-face testpiece *Nuclear Meltdown*, the overhanging splitter hand crack *Armageddon* (5.12a), and the flake-to-thin-face line *Lost Arrowhead Spire* (5.10d).

Approach: From the intersection of 3N14 and 4N16, turn onto 4N16 and drive 3.2 miles. Park on the left at a small rise. Start by hiking 200 feet southwest, following a dirt-bike trail. As that trail heads down and left, instead choose the faint climber's path on the right. Follow this west/northwest as it leads past a large jumble of rock formations (where the Toy Blocks are located) and over to the top of Seam Crag. To reach Armageddon Wall, continue hiking north as the trail winds downhill to the crag.

SEAM CRAG **AREA**

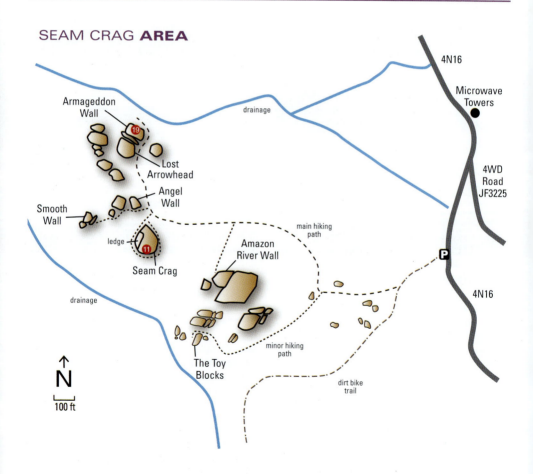

The Toy Blocks

Piranha Crack

The Toy Blocks
[GPS: 34.37968, -117.05889]

 PM   20 min

❶ Toy Blocks 5.10b
A short route on the west face. A thin start leads to a water gully to end between two rock stacks. Gear anchor. Simulrap, or downclimb the backside and rap off a boulder.
50 ft. Gear to 4", 3 bolts.
Brian Elliott, Doug Odenthal, Joe Sheehy, Cindy Elliott, 1990s.

Amazon River Wall
[GPS: 34.38039, -117.05866]

10 min

❷ Piranha Crack 5.8 ★★★
A flesh-eating hand and offwidth crack. Dive into the gritty offwidth and swim for your life. This river monster spits you out below a final 10-foot section of low-angle face. Gear belay from a large ledge.
70 ft. Wide gear.
Brian Elliott, Doug Odenthal, Joe Sheehy, Cindy Elliott, 1990s.

Seam Crag
[GPS: 34.38092, -117.05987]

15 min

❸ Bolt Fever 5.10d R ★
Exploit thin seams on the left side of the headstone-looking block. Gear anchor on the ledge in the middle of the wall.
45 ft. Thin gear to 1", 1 bolt.
Brian Elliott, Doug Odenthal, Joe Sheehy, Cindy Elliott, 1989.

❹ Ethics Breakdown 5.10c ★
Cram small gear behind a thin flake, then race past 2 bolts on the improbable face. Gear anchor.
45 ft. Thin gear to 1", 2 bolts.
Brian Elliott, Doug Odenthal, Joe Sheehy, Cindy Elliott, 1989.

❺ Approach Crack 5.8
As the name suggests, this crack is the easiest way to reach the midway ledge where routes #6-9 start. Gear anchor.
35 ft. Gear to 4".
Brian Elliott, Doug Odenthal, Joe Sheehy, Cindy Elliott, 1989.

The following 4 routes begin from a midway ledge:

❻ Traveling Companion 5.6 ★★
Grab a buddy and enjoy this smooth-sailing adventure over ledges in a right-facing dihedral. A nice easy climb with good exposure. Shared anchor with *Nuclear Meltdown*.
60 ft. Gear to 3".
Brian Elliott, Doug Odenthal, Joe Sheehy, Cindy Elliott, 1990s.

❼ Graceland 5.10b ★★★
The striking dihedral crack. Capitalize on the fabulous stemming opportunities, then cope with the blocky roof moves. Shared anchor with *Nuclear Meltdown*.
60 ft. Gear to 3".
Brian Elliott, Doug Odenthal, Joe Sheehy, Cindy Elliott, 1989.

❽ Rainy Day 5.10b ★★
A rainy day would sure put a damper on climbing this face-and-crack route. Shared anchor with *Nuclear Meltdown*.
60 ft. Gear to 2", 2 bolts.
Brian Elliott, Doug Odenthal, Joe Sheehy, Cindy Elliott, 1990s.

❾ Solar Power Arête 5.11a ★★
Power up the arête on the right, embracing thin features and balancy movement on the smooth face. Shared anchor with *Nuclear Meltdown*.
65 ft. Gear to 2", 4 bolts. *Brian Elliott, Doug Odenthal, Joe Sheehy, Cindy Elliott, 1990s.*

Seam Crag

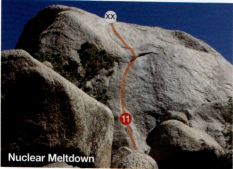

Nuclear Meltdown

10 Alternative Energy 5.10b ★★

Cautiously tiptoe along a fragile undercling flake to its apex. Delicately traverse right across the face past 2 bolts. Dance along additional flakes to the top. Shared anchor with *Nuclear Meltdown*.

95 ft. Gear to 4", 4 bolts.

Brian Elliott, Doug Odenthal, Joe Sheehy, Cindy Elliott, 1990s.

11 Nuclear Meltdown 5.11a ★★★★

Testpiece. This classic and sustained line demands a variety of techniques to succeed. Step up to the arching crack that dominates the southwest portion of the wall. An intense sequence leads to the top of the arch. Master the heady transition onto the blank face above, where holds seem nonexistent. You absolutely must give this daring and bold route a try! Bolted anchor without rap rings.

95 ft. Gear to 2.5", 4 bolts, 1 fixed pin.

Brian Elliott, Doug Odenthal, Joe Sheehy, Cindy Elliott, 1989.

12 Fistful of Crystals 5.10c ★

Fight the finger crack in a right-facing dihedral on the east face. Jam and smear on crumbly rock until the angle kicks back toward the top and the climbing improves. Shared anchor with *Nuclear Meltdown*.

60 ft. Gear to 2".

Brian Elliott, Doug Odenthal, Joe Sheehy, Cindy Elliott, 1990s.

Angel Wall
[GPS: 34.38131, -117.06010]

15 min

13 Grievous Angel 5.9 ★

Fluid climbing up a leaning hand crack on the squatty formation's southwest face. Gear anchor.

45 ft. Gear to 3".

Brian Elliott, Doug Odenthal, Joe Sheehy, Cindy Elliott, 1990s.

Smooth Face
[GPS: 34.38108, -117.06101]

15 min

14 Armed Conflict 5.10c ★★

Scramble across the ledge from the right to begin, or increase your mileage by ascending the 35-foot crack directly below (gear to 2"). Coax yourself left over the void, carefully choosing secure crystals and knobs to take you safely to the top.

35 ft. 4 bolts.

Brian Elliott, Doug Odenthal, Joe Sheehy, Cindy Elliott, 1990s.

Angel Wall

Smooth Face

variation

15 Ultimatum 5.11c ★★

Fingers of steel are a prerequisite for this thin encounter. Take it or leave it! Gracefully finesse up the face on bumps and edges. Shares anchors with *Armed Conflict*.

35 ft. 4 bolts.

Brian Elliott, Doug Odenthal, Joe Sheehy, Cindy Elliott, 1990s.

Lost Arrowhead
[GPS: 34.38202, -117.06030] 15 min

Lost Arrowhead

16 Left Arrowhead Spire 5.10d ★★★

A quick jaunt past 2 bolts on the lower face achieves the left side of the flake. Cruise to the top of this delicate finger and finish on the crystal-infused slab above. Gear anchor.

60 ft. Gear to 3.5", 4 bolts.

Brian Elliott, Doug Odenthal, Joe Sheehy, Cindy Elliott, 1989.

17 Lost Arrowhead Spire 5.10d ★★★

Hand traverse left to reach the slender flake, then shoot up its right side. Balance atop the pinnacle and brave the same upper slab as above. Gear anchor.

50 ft. Gear to 4", 2 bolts.

Brian Elliott, Doug Odenthal, Joe Sheehy, Cindy Elliott, 1989.

18 She's a Cutie 5.8 ★

Advance up the thin vertical crack system past horizontals and a triangular xenolith. Gear anchor.

30 ft. Gear to 2".

Brian Elliott, Doug Odenthal, Joe Sheehy, Cindy Elliott, 1989.

Armageddon Wall
[GPS: 34.38222, -117.06007] 15 min

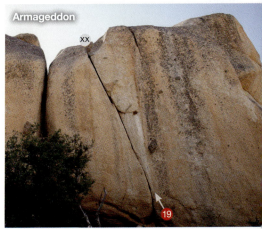

Armageddon

19 Armageddon 5.12a ★★★★

A crucible for hard crack climbing. Wage war as you fight to stay inside this savage overhanging crack. The steep line is unrelenting on blood-filled forearms. Suppress your internal instincts to bail on this grueling challenge.

55 ft. Gear to 3". Troy Mayr, early 1990s.

Castle Spire

CASTLE SPIRE

This massive tower perched at the top of a valley can be seen from the desert floor. The exposure here is phenomenal, culminating at the peak as the climbing gets technical and the formation narrows to a point. Bask in the morning sun or seek out afternoon shade depending on conditions.

AM · 40 min

Approach: From the intersection of 3N14 and 4N16, turn onto 4N16 and drive 3.2 miles. Take a sharp right onto a 4WD road marked JF3225. Drive this for 0.6 miles and locate a dirt-bike trail on the left. Pull off and park here.

Hike a short distance down the trail to a fork; turn left here onto a small ridge (don't take the right path down into a gully). Follow this trail north/northwest for just under a mile (30 minutes). The peak of the formation will come into view on the right. Leave the path and head downhill to its east face.

Alternatively, if you have a 4WD vehicle and want to park closer to the crag, instead drive 1.0 mile along JF3225 and then turn left onto an offshoot 4WD road. Take this to its terminus (approximately 1 mile) and park. Hike west across the final gully to the crag.
[GPS: 34.38732, -117.04745]

❶ Pigeon Roost 5.9+ ★★

The better line up the tall spire. Fly through the initial wide fist/lieback crack behind the lower buttress. Mellower climbing leads to the ridge, above which lies the crux. Be careful here, as the rock is sugary and the bolts are suspect. Rap off the west face. Less than a ropelength, but best done in multiple pitches to reduce rope drag.
170 ft. Gear to 5", 4 bolts.
Eric Tipton, Kevin Graves, Pat Brennan, Nov. 2005.

❷ Golden Eagle 5.9+ ★

Slip up a crack system on the north face to reach the ridge. Traverse across the ridge to share the final bolted section and anchors with *Pigeon Roost*. Best done in multiple pitches to reduce rope drag.
150 ft. Gear to 3", 4 bolts. Brad Singer, Dave Honeywell, Nov. 2005.

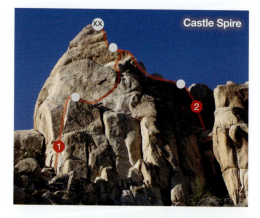

Castle Spire

End of Grapevine

END OF GRAPEVINE

A secluded, west-facing wall marked with streaks of orange, located on the outskirts of Grapevine Canyon. This area never sees traffic, so the routes are in need of exfoliation.

PM 2 min

Approach: From the intersection of 3N14 and 4N16, turn onto 4N16 and drive 3.2 miles. Take a sharp right onto a 4WD road marked JF3225. Drive along this for 1.4 miles until the crag is visible on the left. Hike briefly through brush to reach the wall.
[GPS: 34.36793, -117.04173]

❶ Raisin Crack 5.8 ★

Slink up the short hand crack on the left margin of the wall. It's good, just a bit gritty inside. Gear belay and rappel from anchors atop *Seedless*.
35 ft. Gear to 3". Kenn Kenaga, Eric Tipton, Pat Brennan, Nov. 2005.

❷ Grappa 5.6 ★★

Jump into this cool squeeze chimney with a nice wide crack in the back. Hasten through the brief vertical section until the angle eases. Gear belay. Rap from anchors atop *Seedless*.
35 ft. Gear to 5". Eric Tipton, Kenn Kenaga, Nov. 2005.

❸ Table Grapes 5.7

Just left of *Seedless* is a flake leaning against the wall. Lieback the right-facing dihedral on the flake and continue up the crack system above. Shares anchors with *Seedless*.
50 ft. Gear to 4". Pat Brennan, Kenn Kenaga, Eric Tipton, Nov. 2005.

❹ Seedless 5.10b ★★

Try your hand at this decent sport route that ascends the gritty face between orange streaks of lichen. Thin features and crystals are all you've got until the horizontal below the distinct block at the top of the formation.
50 ft. 5 bolts. Eric Tipton, Kenn Kenaga, Nov. 2005.

BRIAN ELLIOTT

Brian Elliott, Joe Sheehy, Doug Odenthal, and Cindy Elliott are responsible for the development of Grapevine Canyon. After Doug realized the climbing potential of the area in 1989, the group spent countless weekends establishing hundreds of routes. Brian was most often found on the sharp end, hand-drilling routes on lead. His bold first ascents of *Canoe Slab* (5.11a) and *Nuclear Meltdown* (5.11a) established classic area testpieces, and the incredible line *Vector Analysis* (5.11b) at Butt Rock is quite possibly the best arête climb in Southern California. Brian's favorite crag at Grapevine Canyon is Physics Rock, a spectacular block of granite that is home to numerous fantastic lines.

Brian grew up in Illinois and Ohio. While attending graduate school at the University of Toledo, he took a rock-climbing class that included a weekend at Seneca Rocks. Instantly, he was hooked! After obtaining a Masters in Geology, he moved to New Orleans, where he spent six years as a geologist for Gulf Oil. Weekends consisted of climbing on sandstone cliffs near Birmingham, Alabama, or canoeing in the Louisiana bayous. When the oil industry tanked, he moved to California, taking a job as a physics, chemistry, and environmental-science teacher at San Dimas High School. Brian claims this was the best thing that could have happened to him. The career fit his personality better — and it gave him a lot of time off to pursue climbing.

In California, Brian quickly got immersed in climbing. Joshua Tree became his home away from home, and he spent many weekends in the late '80s and early '90s staying at Todd Gordon's house. Brian liked runout routes, and the long multi-pitch lines of Red Rocks often drew him out to the Nevada desert.

When he, Doug, Joe, and Cindy began exploring Grapevine Canyon in 1989, Brian's focus shifted to new-route development. The ethics at the time dictated ground-up ascents, so Brian and his friends bolted all their routes on lead. While on a trip to El Gran Trono Blanco in Baja, however, Brian's bolt kit was stolen. He never replaced it, and the group closed the chapter of developing at Grapevine Canyon.

Brian's lifelong passion for climbing has taken him around the world in the pursuit of classic lines. He did his first big-wall climb with Todd Burrill in 1991 — *Triple Direct* on El Capitan. Brian's climbing résumé is impressive, including the *Direct Northwest Face* of Half Dome in Yosemite, *Moonlight Buttress* in Zion National Park, the *Pan American Route* on El Gran Trono Blanco, Lotus Flower Tower in Canada's Northwest Territories, and Naysa Peak in Pakistan. The past two years, Brian has spent more time climbing in Australia than in the U.S. *Kachoong* (5.10c) in Arapiles and *Pole Dancer* (5.11b) in Tasmania are two of his favorite routes down under, along with his first ascent of *Energizer* (5.12a) at Girraween National Park.

Brian has been married to his wife, Janice, for 24 years. In 2015, Brian retired after 29 years of teaching, which has allowed him to focus more time on his outdoor hobbies. Janice retired from teaching as well, and together they enjoy hiking with their dogs and birding. Brian has been an avid bird watcher for 40 years, and for him every trip is a bird-watching trip. No matter where he goes, Brian is always carrying a pair of binoculars. To him, birding is like a window in the world, an opportunity to observe the behaviors and habitats of beautiful creatures in truly unique places. In addition to bird watching, he is also passionate about canoeing Arctic rivers, taking month-long trips to explore the remote wilderness of Alaska and Canada. Ultimately, Brian hopes to maintain his fitness and still be climbing when he is 80!

First ascent of *Nothing but the Blues*, Cap Rock, 1989, page 304. 📷 Odenthal collection

MICROWAVE TOWERS

This area lies in the vicinity of the Lucerne Valley Microwave Repeater Tower and comprises multiple formations with routes strewn among them. The rock quality here is subpar, with crumbling crystals making the climbing sketchy. That aside, these crags do have roadside appeal! The lines to hit are *Microwave Tower #9* (5.11a) and *Microwave Tower #10* (5.10c), two tall and consistent routes on Tower B. No names or first-ascent information are known. There are a few other routes and formations here not described.

Approach: From the intersection of 3N14 and 4N16, turn onto 4N16 and drive for 3.3 miles. Park near the base of these crags that sit on the right side of the road. If you reach the actual microwave repeater tower, you've gone 0.3 miles too far.

Microwave Tower A
[GPS: 34.38296, -117.05456]

  1 min

1 Microwave Tower #1 5.8 ★
Mellow climbing in a wide channel. Close enough to the car for a beer-lay.
35 ft. 3 bolts. Unknown.

2 Microwave Tower #2 5.9+ ★
Marked by a large horizontal xenolith beneath the first bolt. The crux is the somewhat blank section below the crack.
40 ft. 4 bolts. Unknown.

3 Microwave Tower #3 5.11b ★★
Located on the prow of a detached portion of the wall. Slap up the sharp corner, cranking through the steep and blank middle section and passing horizontals near the top. Bolted anchor without rap rings.
50 ft. Unknown.

4 Microwave Tower #4 5.9 ★
On the east face. Chimney or stem the crack as it widens, then make a heady exit move on crumbly crystals to reach the anchors.
50 ft. 4 bolts. Unknown.

The following 4 routes are accessed from a tunnel to the left of Microwave Tower #9.

5 Microwave Tower #5 5.7
From inside the tunnel, exit the left side by scrambling up under wedged boulders to reach the base of this route. Weasel past plants while ascending this corner crack.
40 ft. Gear to 4". Unknown.

6 Microwave Tower #6 5.7
Slide and crawl across this slanted offwidth/ramp in the tunnel. More grovel than climb.
40 ft. 4 bolts. Unknown.

Microwave Towers Overview

Tower A

Tower B

7 Microwave Tower #7 5.7 ★★

Straightforward climbing in a full-body chimney. Bridge the gap and scoot along toward the last bolt of *Microwave Tower #6* and shared anchors. Great for honing your chimney technique!

45 ft. 5 bolts. Unknown.

8 Microwave Tower #8 5.9+ ★★

Exit the right side of the tunnel, scrambling up a short gully. Clip the first bolt that prevents the belayer from accidentally pulling out the lower gear. Make a committing move to reach the crack, stuff in gear, and swing around into the crack behind the flake. Sink in good jams and away you go!

35 ft. Gear to 3", 1 bolt. Unknown.

Microwave Tower B
[GPS: 34.38324, -117.05416]

2 min

9 Microwave Tower #9 5.11a R ★★★

Start this fantastic line from down in a pit/corridor. Hard liebacking and fingerlocking in the sharp lower crack give way to an off-fingers crack above the horizontal. The burly climbing ends at a ledge, where one must tiptoe on crystals up the final section of face. Note: This climb could use a bolt on the final face to be safely led. You can climb *Microwave Tower #10* and set up a TR on this route.

90 ft. Gear to 5". Unknown.

10 Microwave Tower #10 5.10c ★★★

This massive route is a fabulous introduction to the crystal climbing at Grapevine. Ascend the enjoyable alligator scales to start, then peer up at the blank-looking slab. Your mental fortitude will be tested as you make committing clips, pleading with the fragile crystals not to crumble. Grab the life-saving jug at the finish, clip the anchors, and breathe a happy sigh of relief!

85 ft. 10 bolts. Unknown.

11 Microwave Tower #11 5.9 ★★

Walk around the corner of the formation to locate this right-leaning crack that transitions from nice jams to a difficult offwidth. Wedge hands and a foot into this gritty man-eater as you flag the other foot on crystals. Turn the corner and gear belay from the large ledge.

50 ft. Gear to 4.5". Unknown.

Microwave Tower C
[GPS: 34.38324, -117.05373]

3 min

12 Microwave Tower #12 5.8+ ★

Not pictured, but located on the northwest face of the next formation to the east. Saunter up an easy gully to 2 closely spaced bolts. Rock over a fin and scale lichen-covered edges beside a corner. The rock quality on this one's a bit sub-par, and there's a small runout to the 5th bolt (optional gear placements).

95 ft. 6 bolts. Unknown.

Brad MacArthur on *Microwave Tower #10*, 5.10c, opposite. 📷 Brandon Copp

BUTT ROCK (AKA GNOME DOME) AREA

Butt Rock is the crown jewel of Grapevine Canyon. The rock here is impeccable, fine-grained granite that drastically contrasts with the crumbly stuff found at other Grapevine crags. Butt Rock is home to the area's hardest climbs, although you really can't go wrong with any of the spectacular routes on this massive dome. *Vector Analysis* (5.11b) is quite possibly the best arête climb of its grade in Southern California, whereas *Butt Crack* (AKA *Getting Small*, 5.10b) is a fabulous chimney-to-hand crack in a perfect dihedral. Try out *Chasm Spasm* (5.9) for a unique adventure within the depths of a hole in the dome! In addition, there are routes located on satellite crags, mostly shorter and more moderate, but with a few challenging 5.12 seams to work as well.

GNOME DOME **AREA**

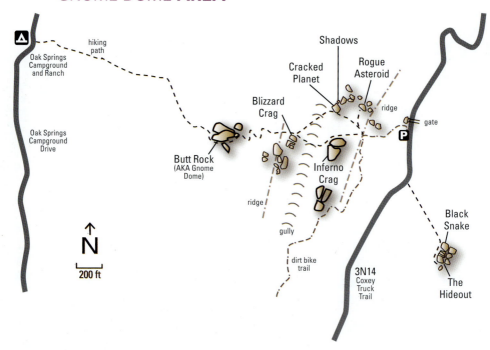

Approach: From the intersection of 3N14 and 4N16, drive north on 3N14 for 2.7 miles. Park in a small pullout on the left side of the road, just before a gate.

Alternatively, if driving from the direction of Hesperia, the parking pullout is located 4.3 miles south on 3N14 from the turn off of Bowen Ranch Road.

From the parking, hike 100 yards uphill on a dirt-bike trail to the crest of a small ridge. From here, the satellite crags are scattered to the west, within a gully. Butt Rock lies further away, situated 0.25 miles due west. To reach this formation, hike in and out of the gully to the top of another ridgeline. With the wall in view, drop down the backside of this ridge to the crag.

Beth Renn, *Vector Analysis*,
5.11b, next page.
📷 Greg Epperson

Butt Rock

Butt Rock
(AKA Gnome Dome)
[GPS: 34.35981, -117.09940]

20 min

1 Butt Rock #1 5.11b R ★★

A perplexing crux sequence on the opening slab demands your immediate attention. Skirt the midway roof to the left, plugging a piece of gear before committing to the runout upper face.

75 ft. Gear to 1", 5 bolts. Dave Tidwell, mid 1990s.

2 Knob Job 5.12a ★★★

Spectacular climbing on tiny bumps, knobs, and crystals passes through the improbable lower face. Crank the right side of the roof, then float up the balancy slab above. Surge upward on dark xenoliths, crossing over the thin white streak to reach the anchors. A safe but thrilling venture!

100 ft. 13 bolts. Louie Anderson, 2006.

3 Analysis Paralysis 5.13c ★★★

Gnarly and steep, this overhanging beast is not for the faint of heart. Burly moves along a thin seam in the shallow corner will test the best climbers' skill and endurance. Sucker your partner into hanging the draws.

70 ft. 11 bolts. Louie Anderson, 2006.

4 Butt Out of It 5.12c ★★

A bold line that requires a variety of creative techniques to succeed. Blast past the low bolts to a crack system that leads to the anchor.

70 ft. Gear to 2", 4 bolts, 1 pin.
Bill Leventhal, Erik Eriksson, mid 1990s.

5 Vector Analysis 5.11b ★★★★

This photogenic climb is truly a phenomenal route for those climbing at the grade. Keep your force vectors in line, pressing your feet precisely into the thin features as you work up the stunning arête. Technical edging, spectacular exposure on clean rock, and the sustained nature of the climb all perfectly combine to make this route magnificent.

70 ft. 7 bolts. Brian Elliott, 1990.

6 Gnome Dome Project 5.12a

Pioneered by Brian Elliott, Joe Sheehy, and Doug Odenthal, this exceptionally thin face route right of *Vector Analysis* remains for the next generation of hard climbers to equip. Shares anchors with *Vector Analysis*.

70 ft.

Knob Job

Fallen Traverse

The following 3 routes are hidden in a chasm that is accessed from the formation's summit. There is a separate bolt on top to help you safely reach Chasm Spasm's anchor with rap rings.

⑦ Butt Crack (AKA Getting Small) 5.10b ★★★★
The most obvious line in the area, a spectacular dihedral crack well worth jamming into. Zoom past a thin fin of rock and wiggle into the squeeze chimney protected by 3 bolts. As the crack narrows, stem, lieback, and jam in the nice clean corner for an exciting finish. One of the best 5.10s in the San Bernardinos! Brownie points if you forego the bolts and use 2x4s in the wide section as the first-ascent party did. Gear anchor.
75 ft. Gear to 4", 3 bolts. FA: (without bolts) Dwain Warren, Rodger Gorss, Roccko Spina, winter 1982.

⑧ Losing My Edge 5.13c/d ★★★★
Step on up to the extremely slick arête's south face to begin this superb climb. Nails hard, this ultra-sustained scare-a-thon is similar in character to *Vector Analysis*, on holds that are significantly smaller. Use any features that present themselves on the glassy face to reach a small rest stance above the 4th bolt. Here the route crosses over onto the east face. Employ your resilient fingers of steel to carry you past another ludicrous crimping sequence to the chains.
75 ft. 9 bolts. Chris Righter, 2006.

⑨ Fallen Traverse (Grade Unknown) ★★
A unique hand-traverse that goes right to left across the top of the massive fallen block lying behind *Analysis Paralysis*. In its current state, be extremely cautious of decking potential that could result from a nasty swing. To make it safe, this really could use a bolt between each of the current ones!
65 ft. 5 bolts. Unknown.

⑩ Chasm Spasm 5.9 ★★★
Rap into the hole, realizing that the only way out is to climb a route! Lead up the corner, passing 2 bolts on the left face. Embrace sustained liebacking on the steep flake/arête as you ascend toward the light. A well-protected climb that's pretty sweet and unique!
50 ft. 7 bolts. Louie Anderson, 2006.

⑪ Chasm Offwidth 5.9+ ★
The wide crack situated to the right of *Chasm Spasm*. While not quite as enjoyable as many routes at this crag, this offwidth provides a challenge for those who like this style of climbing. Gear anchor.
50 ft. Wide gear. Unknown.

⑫ Chasm Chimney 5.10b ★★
Dead center in the long passageway behind *Chasm Spasm* lies this full-body chimney. Wiggle and worm out of the tight lower section as the chimney widens. Place gear in horizontals between the bolts and maintain your cool as this bad boy keeps getting wider. No anchor — before climbing this you can build a gear anchor in the crack at the top of the dome and extend it with a 30- or 40-foot piece of cord, hanging it over the lip so that you can clip it from inside the chimney to protect the final mantel move.
60 ft. Gear to 1", 6 bolts. Dave Tidwell, mid 1990s.

Blizzard Crag

Blizzard Crag
[GPS: 34.35976, -117.09769]

AM 🚶 10 min

13 Slippery When White Out 5.10b ★
Take the steeper left side past a large gray spot. Shared anchor with *Snow Job*.
40 ft. 4 bolts. Brad Singer, Joe Sheehy, Eric Odenthal, Apr. 2004.

14 Snow Job 5.10b ★
Techy slab climbing on crystals leads past a bulge at the 3rd bolt. Stay on your toes for the slight run near the top.
40 ft. 4 bolts. B. King, Eric Odenthal, Brad Singer, Joe Sheehy, Doug Odenthal, S. Berghoff, Apr. 2004.

15 Leap Frog 5.10d ★★
Step through a delicate start, then leap past scattered xenoliths and miniscule edges to the *Snow Job* anchors.
40 ft. 4 bolts. Eric Odenthal, B. King, Apr. 2004.

16 Storm Watch 5.8
Reach high to a hand crack above the distinguishable rockhouse feature. A one-move-wonder route that becomes a walk in the park. 1-bolt anchor without a rap ring; rap from the *Snow Job* anchors.
35 ft. Gear to 4". Brad Singer, B. King, Joe Sheehy, Doug Odenthal, S. Berghoff, Eric Odenthal, Apr. 2004.

The next 3 routes can be found in a corridor behind the main low-angle face.

17 Fists of Flurry 5.9+ ★
Enter the corridor from the west end and identify this fist crack on the left (north) side. Same anchor situation as *Storm Watch*.
25 ft. Gear to 5". Brad Singer, Joe Sheehy, Apr. 2004.

18 Toad Licker 5.9 ★
The orange dihedral across from *Fists of Flurry* on the right (south) side of the corridor. The widening offwidth at the top makes for a gritty finish. Gear anchor.
25 ft. Gear to 5". Eric Odenthal, S. Berghoff, Apr. 2004.

19 Abominable Snow Jam 5.6 ★★
An uncommon full-body chimney climb inside the corridor. Set this up from the shared anchor on *Snow Job*. Quite enjoyable.
30 ft. Brad Singer, May 2004.

Inferno Crag
[GPS: 34.35963, -117.09684]

PM 🚶 10 min

20 Emotional Breakdown 5.11b ★★
A hard start catapults you from an undercling into a water channel. The crack spits you out onto a slick face that'll get you thinking.
40 ft. Gear to 4", 3 bolts. Brad Singer, Eric Odenthal, May 2004.

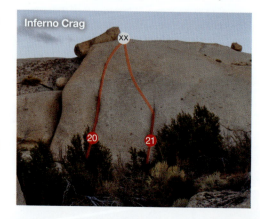

Inferno Crag

Vaginator

Shadows and Cracked Planet

Rogue Asteroid

㉑ Dehydration 5.10c ★★

Take a sip of water before tackling this wonder. Uneventful climbing in the crack lasts until it flares, at which point you exit left onto the face. Tech past 3 bolts to the shared anchor with *Emotional Breakdown*.

40 ft. Gear to 3", 4 bolts. Eric Odenthal, May 2004.

Cracked Planet
[GPS: 34.36047, -117.09658]

 5 min

㉒ Vaginator 5.10c ★★

Jam fists into a flaring crack on the southeast face that becomes an easier lieback as it widens. So-so climbing up a ramp empties into the suggestive feature 2/3 of the way up.

35 ft. Gear to 5". Brad Singer, Eric Odenthal, 2004.

㉓ Planet Dust 5.12d ★★★

A stellar left-leaning finger crack splits the blank northwest face. It's just wide enough for fingerlocks, while toes smear on the slick wall below. If your skills are up to par, go berserk on this heinous crack that's sure to make you scream!

40 ft. Unknown.

Shadows
[GPS: 34.36060, -117.09653]

 5 min

㉔ Shadows 5.9

Located on a small wall 100 feet left of *Planet Dust*. Ascend fragile flakes sprinkled on the slabby face to reach the peak.

25 ft. 3 bolts.

Eric Tipton, Pat Brennan, Sheila Romane, Lee Clark, Mar. 2007.

Rogue Asteroid
[GPS: 34.36041, -117.09594]

PM 5 min

㉕ Rogue Seam (Project)

Located on the west face. Start on a big xenolith and mash fingertips into this extremely thin seam. Hard is an understatement. Bolted anchor without rap rings.

25 ft.

BLACK SNAKE AND THE HIDEOUT

The prominent dark streak, or "black snake", on the foremost boulder is an easy landmark for identifying this compact collection of roadside rocks. The climbs here are generally well protected, and though they are on the shorter side, the approach is minimal. The Hideout is the upper pit with walls on three sides, a nice spot for a group to hang out and set multiple lines near one another.

Approach: From the intersection of 3N14 and 4N16, drive north on 3N14 for 2.7 miles. Park in the same pullout as for Butt Rock, on the left side of the road, just before a gate. The crag is visible to the east, 200 yards from the road.
    Alternatively, if driving from Hesperia, the parking pullout is located 4.3 miles south on 3N14 from the turn off of Bowen Ranch Road. **[GPS: 34.35749, -117.09373]**

❶ Unknown 5.12a ★
A sustained face climb on a short north-facing block. Attach yourself to the wall and pull through long reaches, powering through a blank section while trending right.
40 ft. 4 bolts. Unknown.

❷ Unknown 5.12b ★
Another fierce yet short-lived climb similar to its neighbor.
40 ft. 4 bolts. Unknown.

❸ There's a Snake in My Boot 5.7 ★
Ascend a ramp in the corridor to the left of *Rattler*, plugging gear into a crack where the ramp meets a boulder. As the crack tapers near the top, encounter a tricky crux.
30 ft. Gear to 2", 2 bolts. Unknown.

❹ Rattler 5.10b ★★★
Reach the splendid finger-to-hand crack by conquering its thought-provoking start. This clean crack will leave you wishing it was taller. You might need to take a second lap!
40 ft. Gear to 3". Unknown.

❺ Black Snake 5.12c ★★★
The first route encountered on the approach is this climb on the wall's namesake feature. Pass a lone bolt before finding yourself paralyzed and confused in the blank middle section.
35 ft. Unknown.

❻ Stick 'Em Up 5.10a ★
A short problem that is engaging the whole way up.
20 ft. 3 bolts. Brad Singer, Eric Odenthal, Doug Odenthal, Mar. 2004.

❼ Lookout 5.6
TR or solo this one-hit-wonder that takes the rounded arête to shared anchors with *Stick 'Em Up*.
20 ft. Eric Odenthal, Mar. 2004.

Black Snake and the Hideout

The Hideout

Unloaded 5.10b ★★

A neat mixed route. Climb out of a corridor via a good flake. When it diminishes, clip bolts while angling right.

40 ft. Gear to 1.5", 3 bolts. Eric Odenthal, Brad Singer, Mar. 2004.

Gun Sight 5.8 ★

Shimmy skyward from an offwidth section into a mediocre hand crack. Gear anchor.

40 ft. Gear to 4".

Eric Odenthal, Doug Odenthal, Brad Singer, Mar. 2004.

Desperado 5.11c ★★★

Reach high into the fist crack, then desperately flail up the difficult flaring crack. Fingerlock and fly up the better upper portion to finish on easy terrain. You may find this climb to be just as advertised. Gear anchor.

40 ft. Gear to 3". Unknown.

Rough Rider 5.10d ★★

Boulder up the right arête to a high first bolt. Keep steady as you climb the shallow concave corner.

40 ft. 3 bolts. Unknown.

Saddle Sore 5.9 ★

Start from the lowest point of the slab for full value. The first bolt has been chopped, leaving the initial moves onto the main block unprotected. Step high on the corner, then mantel onto a ledge and follow big holds to the chains.

40 ft. 3 bolts (2 currently).

Eric Odenthal, Brad Singer, Doug Odenthal, Mar. 2004.

Trap Shoot 5.9

Begin 5 feet right of the arching crack on a right-facing flake. (If you really want a challenge, slap up the slick, flaring crack on the left for the initial 20 feet.) Slip past a wedged block and exit through a notch. Gear anchor.

50 ft. Gear to 3". Unknown.

The Wedge 5.8+ ★

Take the left-facing flake/wide crack up the mellow face, passing a wedged block on the way. Gear anchor.

40 ft. Gear to 4". Unknown.

Tape Please 5.7 ★★

Good advice for this gritty, straight-in hand crack. Once wrapped, breeze up this fun line. Gear anchor.

40 ft. Gear to 3". Unknown.

BIGFOOT

A massive if slightly discontinuous wall that receives mostly shade on its northwest face. It has one main line that takes the path of least resistance to the highest point of the formation.

PM · 30 min

Approach: From the intersection of 3N14 and 4N16, drive north on 3N14 for 3.5 miles. Park in a pullout on the right beside a cattle guard.

Alternatively, if driving from Hesperia, the parking pullout is located 3.5 miles south on 3N14 from the turnoff of Bowen Ranch Road.

Walk along the road for 150 yards to reach a BLM sign and a dirt-bike trail on the right. Hike north on the trail (JF3221). After 5 minutes, stay right at a fork to continue hiking along JF3221. In another 15 minutes, this large formation will come into view on the hillside to the right. It is a short bushwhack/boulder hop to its base. **[GPS: 34.37328, -117.08988]**

❶ **Bigfoot North Face** 5.9 ★★
This adventurous line is one of the few multi-pitch outings in the San Bernardinos. It was originally done as 4 short pitches with little rope drag, but it is possible to do it in less. Begin in a gritty thin-hands/fingers crack (5.9). Pass a large boulder (possible first belay station) and encounter a dual crack system (5.6) that leads to a large ledge (2nd belay station). Choose the good hand/finger crack on the right (5.8) and climb to the base of the headwall block (possible 3rd belay station). Finish by shimmying up behind this leaning block (5.7) to a bolted rap station.
140 ft. Gear to 4". Eric Tipton, Pat Brennan, Nov. 2006.

❷ **Sasquatch Shuffle** 5.10c ★★
An alternate start. Stem the slick dihedral underneath a small roof. Shuffle left along the roof crack and meet up with the previous line where the 2nd short pitch begins. Finish as above.
150 ft. Gear to 4". Eric Tipton, Nov. 2006.

CLASSIC CRACK

This small formation is located approximately 200 yards southwest of the Bigfoot wall, and situated high on the same hillside. An excellent crack cuts across its northeast face.

AM · 25 min

Approach: When hiking out to Bigfoot along the dirt bike trail (JF3221), leave the path 5 minutes earlier to bushwhack across the gully on the right and up the hillside to this crag. **[GPS: 34.37185, -117.09068]**

❸ **Classic Crack** 5.11b ★★★★
Aptly if unimaginatively named, this stellar splitter will make you giddy the moment you lay eyes on it. Bomber locks and jams will feel like you could hang off of them forever. Follow the seam as it angles left across the face, culminating with a final grainy crescent. No anchors — sling a boulder to rappel.
45 ft. Gear to 2".
Brian Elliott, Doug Odenthal, Joe Sheehy, Cindy Elliott, 1990s.

Bigfoot

Classic Crack

SENTINEL

A tall, solitary pillar of granite. Make the long trek for *Brothers in Arms* (5.10d), an old-school route with a spectacular view from the top.

 PM 60 min

Approach: Continue hiking past Bigfoot along the JF3221 dirt-bike trail for an additional 10-15 minutes (1.25 miles total from 3N14) to a BLM map. Just past this sign is a fork in the road. Turn right and follow JF3221 uphill for 0.4 miles (10-15 minutes). As the path crests a ridge, the Sentinel will be visible in the distance to the east. A relatively easy bushwhack over ridges leads downhill to the formation.
[GPS: 34.37525, -117.08041]

Sentinel

❹ **Brothers in Arms** 5.10d ★★
Fight the tree encroaching on the base, passing a single bolt before a low-angle crack that leads to a bolted belay. Angle left past a bolt and optional gear to the blunt arête. The holds diminish on the imposing shield that looms overhead, delivering a race-the-clock scenario that's the definition of spicy. Crumbly rock and sketchy bolts on the upper portion!
110 ft. Gear to 4.5", 9 bolts. Doug Odenthal, Bill Odenthal, late 1980s.

SUNSHINE FACE

A sunny, south-facing wall that's a good stop for a few quick burns (including a sunburn!).

  3 min

Approach: From the intersection of 3N14 and 4N16, drive north on 3N14 for 4.6 miles. Turn left onto an OHV road and park in a turn-around circle after 150 feet.

Alternatively, if driving from Hesperia, the offshoot road is located 2.4 miles south on 3N14 from the turn off of Bowen Ranch Road.

Walk briefly west along the dirt road before heading downhill to the rock's south face.
[GPS: 34.37119, -117.11073]

Sunshine Face

❺ **SPF 57** 5.8 ★
Climb past 2 closely spaced bolts, then tech through thin edges to anchors that sit below the large block.
30 ft. 4 bolts.
Eric Tipton, Brad Singer, Kenn Kenaga, Pat Brennan, Nov. 2006.

❻ **SPF 59** 5.10c ★
Slip past the bush and slide into the crack in a dihedral. Eek out extra mileage by following the right side of the block over to shared anchors atop *Stingray*.
35 ft. Gear to 3". Eric Tipton, Pat Brennan, Brad Singer, Nov. 2006.

❼ **Stingray Left** 5.10b ★
A direct start. From behind a boulder, use a golf-ball-sized pocket and a seam to pull onto the vertical wall. Bump over the small roof and burn rubber on the slab above.
30 ft. 4 bolts.
Brad Singer, Eric Tipton, Kenn Kenaga, Pete Paredes, Nov. 2006.

❽ **Stingray Right** 5.7 ★
The easier start. Start from the right margin and traverse left across a xenolith to the first bolt.
30 ft. 4 bolts. Pat Brennan, Nov. 2006.

ROADSIDE ROCKS

The name says it all about this stack of boulders with just two mediocre lines. You might warm up here on your way in from Hesperia.

Approach: From the intersection of 3N14 and 4N16, drive north on 3N14 for 5.0 miles. Park beside the crag in a small pullout on the left.

Alternatively, if driving from Hesperia, the parking pullout is located 2.0 miles south on 3N14 from the turn off of Bowen Ranch Road.

The crack climb is easily accessible, but a bushwhack through dense vegetation and large boulders is required for *Roadside Ramp*.
[GPS: 34.37435, -117.10877]

❶ Roadside Crack 5.10b
Swim up the dirty offwidth/squeeze chimney using any and all body parts to conquer this beast.
45 ft. Wide gear. Unknown.

❷ Roadside Ramp 5.10b ★
Scale a ramp on the upper block. Face moves, then lieback a crack in the corner.
40 ft. 5 bolts. Unknown.

Roadside Rocks

Bushmaster

BUSHMASTER

A decent-sized formation with a single crack line on its west face.

Approach: Park as for Roadside Rocks, but instead hike north from the right side of the road. Duck under a fence atop a small embankment and head 200 yards downhill.
[GPS: 34.37599, -117.10724]

❸ Bushmaster 5.10a ★
Begin underneath the namesake bush that sits on a ledge 10 feet off the ground. Straddle the bush and pull yourself into the somewhat grainy finger/hand crack. Gear anchor.
40 ft. Gear to 3". Unknown.

BUBBA ROCKS

Bubba Rocks consists of one large dome plus a jumble of smaller boulders on its western side. The rock here is fine-grained and quite good, and the top of the dome is a tranquil spot to watch the sunset, where the mountains, the desert, and the rocks scattered atop the hillsides of Grapevine Canyon combine for spectacular, panoramic views.

Approach: From the intersection of 3N14 and 4N16, drive north on 3N14 for 7.0 miles. Turn left onto Bowen Ranch Road and drive 1.1 miles, passing Rock Springs Ranch. Turn left onto an unmarked road that heads uphill underneath the power lines. In 0.1 miles, the road ends; park beside the rocks.

Alternatively, if driving from of Hesperia, drive 3.1 miles south on Bowen Ranch Road from its intersection with Roundup Way to reach the left turn onto the unmarked road.
[GPS: 34.38609, -117.13647]

❹ Village Idiot 5.10b ★★★
A mixed line on the southeast side of the dome. Begin with a short crack right of an alcove, then continue past 3 bolts to reach the main event, a nice wide crack with a bit of flare. Fist-jam and surge upward before ending with an easier romp above.
65 ft. Gear to 4", 3 bolts. Jim Voss, Billy Holder, 2014.

5 Bubba Seam (Project)

Gnarly! Punch out a steep section to grapple with the thin diagonal seam. Fight for purchase in pods as the finger crack narrows. Saunter up the final slab to anchors. 5.12+ ? *65 ft.*

6 Broken Wing 5.9+ ★★

Easily seen from the parking area. A brief bout with an easy crack gains a massive ledge. Make heady moves off the ledge, grasping small holds on the thin face.

60 ft. Gear to 3", 2 bolts. Reed Ames, Kim Dang, May 2014.

7 Hubba Bubba 5.11a ★★★

Over on the west face is this cool route that rides the left arête of the taller pillar. Exploit the horizontal seams and watch your footwork on the slick face.

35 ft. 5 bolts. Jim Voss, Rich Hoover, 2014.

8 Bubbalicious 5.9 ★★

Toe hooks, heel hooks, and compression moves may help on the textured face of the tiny pillar. Short and sweet.

20 ft. 3 bolts. Jim Voss, Rich Hoover, 2014.

9 Bubba's Crack 5.11a ★★

The arching crack located 15 feet left of *Bubba Gump* that shares anchors with that route.

40 ft. Gear to 1". Reed Ames, July 2013.

10 Bubba Gump 5.10a ★

Place gear before the first bolt and set sail on a right-facing flake. Balance up the less-than-vertical face on decent edges. Plug more gear high in the horizontal and top out.

40 ft. Gear to 1", 3 bolts. Reed Ames, Dave Kosmal, July 2013.

11 Bubba Kush 5.9 ★★★

Slip through the tunnel right of *Bubba Gump* to arrive at the base of this rad chimney. Stem wide until the gap narrows, then scoot through to a short jaunt on the face.

40 ft. 4 bolts. Reed Ames, July 2013.

12 Bubba 5.12a ★★

A short yet stout line. Aggressively boulder through the steep opening sequence on decent edges. Confront the in-your-face crux as the holds thin.

30 ft. 4 bolts. Jim Voss, Billy Holder, 2014.

13 Powerline 5.11a ★★★

Step around the corner to find this blank arête. Grasp slender features on the face as you ascend the arête, eventually transitioning onto the opposite face inside the corridor. A fabulous route that's an excellent challenge.

50 ft. Reed Ames, 2014.

Village Idiot

Broken Wing

rap to set up #5

Bubba Kush

Zeppelin Dome South Face

ZEPPELIN DOME

This tall, sweeping wall is home to
a handful of fantastic routes. Each
seems to feature its own style of
climbing, with *Over the Hills and
Far Away* (5.10b) being the standout overall.
Please be extra respectful here, as there is a
private property line running very close to
the wall.

10 min

Approach: From the intersection of 3N14 and
4N16, drive north on 3N14 for 7.0 miles. Turn
right onto Bowen Ranch Road. After 1.6 miles,
turn left onto Valley View Road. Drive this for
0.4 miles until the road turns left and becomes
Juniper Flats Road. After 0.3 miles on Juniper
Flats Road, you will reach a BLM sign; go an
additional 1.6 miles past the sign, then turn left
at the tee to continue on Juniper Flats Road. In
another 0.3 miles, park on the right.

Alternatively, if driving from Hesperia, drive
0.4 miles south on Bowen Ranch Road from
its intersection with Roundup Way to reach the
right turn onto Valley View Road.

From the parking, hike through a gate in the
fence, heading east along a faint climbers' trail
marked with cairns. Merge with a dirt-bike trail,
pass a fence, and head downhill to the rock. You
will arrive at the top/back of the dome.
[GPS: 34.39616, -117.15408]

❶ Tangerine 5.10d ★
Set this up from the anchors of *In Through the Out Door* and
crimp through incut edges on the face left of that route.
60 ft. Jim Voss, Billy Holder.

❷ In Through the Out Door 5.11b ★★★
Toy with the groove and its rounded corners, toiling on the
textured rock that seems devoid of any other large features.
An outstanding and atypical climb.
60 ft. 7 bolts. Jim Voss, Billy Holder.

❸ Going to California 5.9 ★
Straightforward climbing on a left-trending ramp leads to
a final blank section with thought-provoking movement.
Shares anchors with *In Through the Out Door.*
60 ft. Jim Voss, Billy Holder.

Over the Hills and Far Away

4 Kashmir 5.10d ★★★

This spectacular and engaging route exploits the beautiful streak of plates on the south face. Dope movement and a plethora of tantalizing hold options add to the allure.
60 ft. 6 bolts. Jim Voss, Billy Holder, Rich Hoover.

5 Crunge 5.12a ★★

A sequential face climb that's very thin at the bottom and eases up higher.
60 ft. Jim Voss, Billy Holder.

6 Over the Hills and Far Away 5.10b ★★★★

Around on the north corner in a recess is this line that's an absolute must-do! Slip past a bit of moss and finesse up the light and dark face, encountering flakes and amazing edges that will keep your stoke high. A fantastic combination of great holds, mental challenge, and enjoyably fluid motion.
75 ft. 9 bolts. Jim Voss, Billy Holder.

7 Misty Mountain Hop 5.10c ★★★

Another rewarding route on the same splendid face. Groove through the moss maze in the beginning and transition to cleaner rock above. The remainder of the route is a long, magnificent stretch of sublime climbing on solid edges.
75 ft. 10 bolts. Jim Voss, Billy Holder.

8 Stairway to Heaven 5.11a ★★

Who doesn't love a long slab route? Located on the formation's east flank, this tall line is a 60m rope-stretcher that's good for the sole. Expect to fake it with your hands, especially when confronting the high crux. The slabby goodness lasts and lasts, just like the song it's named for.
100 ft. 13 bolts. FA (TR): Jim Voss, Billy Holder.

Joe De Luca goes full speed ahead on *Railroad Gin*, V0. 📷 Joe De Luca

BIG BEAR LAKE
BOULDERING

BIG BEAR LAKE
BOULDERING

There are vast amounts of boulders scattered on the hillsides and around many of the crags in the Big Bear lake area. This chapter is by no means a comprehensive bouldering guide, but instead a sampling from the more established bouldering areas to supplement your roped excursions or plant the seed for more extensive adventures. For a detailed bouldering guide containing hundreds of problems at the nearby Snow Valley Boulders, check out Matt Artz's book *Boulderfest! The Snow Valley Bouldering Guide*.

Shadow Winds Boulders

SHADOW WINDS BOULDERS

The Shadow Winds Boulders are really one formation, split into a left and right half. The boulders face primarily northeast, garnering a touch of morning sun and mostly shade in the afternoon. With 9 problems up to 15-20 feet in height, these are some of the bigger boulders in the region. The following problems were initially done by Craig Pearson, Julie Pearson, and Dean Goolsby.

From left to right, the problems on the left boulder are: V0, V0+, V1, V2 (sit start). From left to right, the problems on the right boulder are: V0, V0, V3, V3+, V1.

Approach: Drive 3.6 miles on Mill Creek Road (2N10) to the intersection with 2N86. Turn right and follow 2N86 for 0.4 miles. The boulders are on the left side of the road, a short 1-minute walk from the car.

LITTLE TIBET BOULDERING

Little Tibet is located on the south shore of Big Bear Lake near the Bluff Mesa Group Campground. It features many outstanding boulder problems on mostly high-quality rock. With a heavy concentration of boulders, unique rock features, and wide range of difficulty, Little Tibet is perhaps the premier bouldering area of the San Bernardino range.

Little Tibet is extensive with several sub-areas, each containing hundreds of boulder problems that would require a dedicated guidebook to detail. Serious development first began around 2010 by Joe and Carey De Luca, James Baker, Casey Ayotte, and friends. Much of the original field notes, pictures, and topo maps have been lost to time. The following is a brief introduction to some of the area's classics within close proximity to the campground. Further exploration will reward the adventurous climber with additional gems, but please tread lightly in this ecologically important area.

Approach: From the stoplight at the dam, drive 2.9 miles along the south shore of Big Bear Lake on Highway 18, then turn right onto Tulip Lane. Drive 0.4 miles and turn right onto Mill Creek Road (2N10). Take 2N10 for 3.6 miles to the intersection with 2N86. Turn right and follow 2N86 for 0.6 miles to a fork in the road. Turn left at the sign for the Bluff Mesa Group Campground and drive 2N86A for 0.25 miles until it dead-ends at the campground. Park and be respectful of campers.

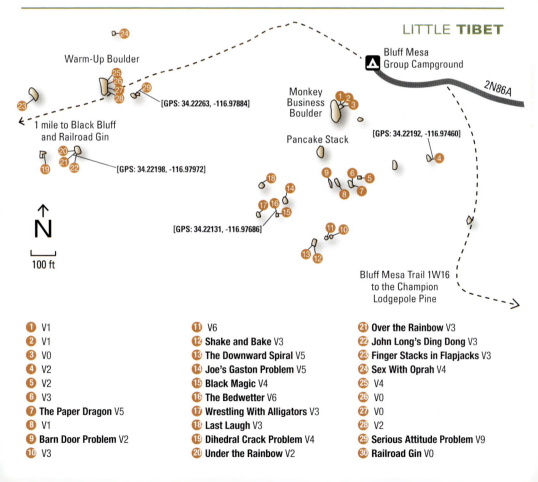

① V1	⑪ V6	㉑ **Over the Rainbow** V3
② V1	⑫ **Shake and Bake** V3	㉒ **John Long's Ding Dong** V3
③ V0	⑬ **The Downward Spiral** V5	㉓ **Finger Stacks in Flapjacks** V3
④ V2	⑭ **Joe's Gaston Problem** V5	㉔ **Sex With Oprah** V4
⑤ V2	⑮ **Black Magic** V4	㉕ V4
⑥ V3	⑯ **The Bedwetter** V6	㉖ V0
⑦ **The Paper Dragon** V5	⑰ **Wrestling With Alligators** V3	㉗ V0
⑧ V1	⑱ **Last Laugh** V3	㉘ V2
⑨ **Barn Door Problem** V2	⑲ **Dihedral Crack Problem** V4	㉙ **Serious Attitude Problem** V9
⑩ V3	⑳ **Under the Rainbow** V2	㉚ **Railroad Gin** V0

HOLCOMB VALLEY EAST SIDE BOULDERING

While Holcomb Valley Pinnacles is primarily known for its sport climbing, bouldering has been happening in and around the Pinnacles for quite some time. There is an abundance of boulders scattered throughout the forest, though most of the problems have never been documented. The boulders near the north or south parking areas are the most popular, since these are easy spots to get in a few laps at the end of a climbing day.

While an entire book could be dedicated to bouldering at Holcomb, the sampling of problems listed here focuses on a separate dedicated bouldering area east of HVP that features a high concentration of moderately graded problems. The rock quality is great, sporting the same weather-worn features that make climbing at the Pinnacles enjoyable. Most of the landings are fairly flat and the approaches are minimal, and it is easy to run a circuit of all of the boulders. Dino Banco is responsible for establishing the majority of the problems, although there is still much potential for future development.

Approach: From the stoplight at the dam, drive 9.0 miles on Highway 38 along Big Bear Lake's north shore. Turn left onto Van Dusen Canyon Road (3N09) and drive this for 3.8 miles to a tee. Turn right onto 3N16 and follow this for 1.4 miles, passing the Belleville log cabin. Turn left onto 3N32 and after 0.2 miles, take the first left. Stay right when the road forks and park beside the boulders.

1. Good Enough For a Dog V0
2. Warm-Up #1 V-Easy
3. Warm-Up #2 V-Easy
4. Warm-Up #3 V-Easy
5. Warm-Up #4 V-Easy
6. Warm-Up #5 V-Easy
7. Liquid Tips V3
8. The Bee's Knees V2
9. Falling Arch V2
10. Checkmate V2
11. Wanderer V2
12. The Main Squeeze V2
13. Stone Soul V2+
14. Man In Full V0
15. The Prow V-Easy
16. Bad Belly V4
17. Cindy's Memorial Boulder Problem V0
18. Activator #1 V0
19. Activator #2 V0
20. Activator #3 V0
21. The Ram V1
22. Crack Attack V2+
23. The Gullywag V0-
24. Ninkasi #1 V1-
25. Ninkasi #2 V0
26. My Green Desire V2+
27. Short but Sweet V-Easy
28. No Pain, No Gain V2
29. The Black Widow V3
30. The Arachnid V0
31. Spider Man V4
32. Beer Barfs V3
33. Beer For Free V1+
34. Beer For All V0-
35. A Beer by Any Name V2
36. Beer, It's What's For Dinner V3
37. No Corn in My Beer V1-
38. Beer Is Food Too V0-
39. Total Domination V3-
40. The Fall of Man V3
41. Patina #1 V-Easy
42. Patina #2 V-Easy
43. Patina #3 V-Easy
44. Patina #4 V0
45. Patina #5 V0
46. Sit-Down Crack V1-
47. Desperado V4
48. Cream Cheese V4
49. Free Spirit V2+
50. Free Spirit Variation V3+
51. Perpetuate Better Living V1+
52. Cracked V0+
53. The Scoop V0
54. Tin Can #1 V0-
55. Tin Can #2 V-Easy
56. Tin Can #3 V0-
57. Tin Can #4 V0+
58. Tin Can #5 V0
59. Tin Can #6 V0
60. Tin Can #7 V1
61. Queen of Patina V2

HOLCOMB VALLEY **EAST SIDE**

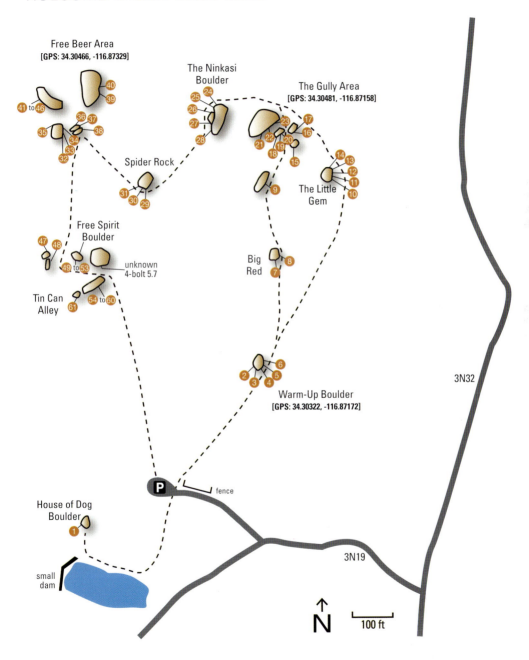

Free Beer Area
[GPS: 34.30466, -116.87329]

The Ninkasi
Boulder

The Gully Area
[GPS: 34.30481, -116.87158]

41 to 46

40
39

36 37
35   38
34
33
32

25 24
26
27
28

Spider Rock

23
22 17
21 16
20
19
18 15

14 13
12
11
10

The Little
Gem

31
30 29

9

Free Spirit
Boulder

47 48

49 to 53

unknown
4-bolt 5.7

Big
Red

8
7

Tin Can
Alley

61   54 to 60

6
2   5
3   4

Warm-Up Boulder
[GPS: 34.30322, -116.87172]

3N32

P

fence

House of Dog
Boulder

1

3N19

small
dam

N

100 ft

GRADED LIST OF TRAD CLIMBS

GRADED LIST OF SPORT CLIMBS

5.13c/d		
Losing My Edge	★★★★	327

5.13c		
Analysis Paralysis	★★★	326

5.13b		
4-Star 5.9	★★★	43

5.12d		
Screaming Trees	★★★★	229
Silk	★★★★	202
Crematorium	★★★	93

5.12c		
Under the Influence	★★★★	215
Fierce	★★★	229
Freak on a Leash	★★★	286
Joe's Dilemma	★★★	82
Shadowcaster	★★★	162
Harsh	★★	103

5.12b		
Reticent Arête	★★★	138
Prowler, The	★★	53
Everclear	★	101
Unknown	★	330

5.12a		
Incinerator, The	★★★★	93
King of the Castle	★★★★	168
Road Crew	★★★★	48
Trouser Trout	★★★★	163
Drug of Choice	★★★	81
Firewalker	★★★	198
Fish Out of Water	★★★	162
Green Planet	★★★	192
Knob Job	★★★	326
Lord, Have Mercy	★★★	158
Rumblefish	★★★	163
Showdown, The	★★★	85
Thor's Revenge	★★★	140
Alchemy	★★	230
Bass Assassin	★★	159
Bubba	★★	335
Check Your Fly	★★	164
Conklin Face	★★	175
No Prisoners Direct	★★	310
Sugar	★★	246
Unknown	★	330

5.11d		
Big-Mouth Fever	★★★★	163
Cliptomania	★★★	285
Nowhere to Go but Down	★★★	50
Point Blank	★★★	105
Public Hanging	★★★	68
Hammock Boys	★★	167
Hammock Boys Left	★★	167
Kremlin Wall	★★	168

5.11c		
Coriander and the...	★★★★★	141
Black and Tan	★★★	198
By Hook or Crook	★★★	137
Catch of the Day	★★★	162
Cling Plus	★★★	41
Duct Tape and Candy	★★★	132
Finger Crimping Good	★★★	81
Hangin' Judge, The	★★★	66
Opiate	★★★	285
Benchmark	★★	121
Final Conquest	★★	185
Firing Line	★★	86
Laissez Les Bon Temps Rouler	★★	304
No Prisoners	★★	310
Sleight of Hand	★★	122
Splash Dancer	★★	159
Tear the Roof Off the Sucker	★★	138
Ultimatum	★★	317
Night Shift	★	241

5.11b		
Migs Over Moscow	★★★★	226
Trout Fishing in America	★★★★	163
Vector Analysis	★★★★	326
China Doll	★★★	124
Holy Fingers	★★★	166
In Through the Out Door	★★★	336
Princess Vicious	★★★	290
Rusted Root	★★★	104
Slytherin	★★★	238
Trail of Tiers	★★★	53
Apollo	★★	158
Eyes Wide Shut	★★	180
Five O'Clock Shadow	★★	41
Gargoyle, The	★★	238
Mad Season	★★	68

5.11a			
Motherlode		★★	89
Peacemaker, The		★★	85
Ricochet		★★	265
Unforgiven		★★	70
Golden Gloves		★	89
Melon Factor, The		★	101

5.11a			
Arrogant Bastard		★★★★	114
Canoe Slab		★★★★	303
Lunar Eclipse		★★★★	50
Critical Mass		★★★	310
Hubba Bubba		★★★	335
Long Arm of the Law		★★★	92
Lost Highway		★★★	48
Out of Our Mines		★★★	90
Pistol Whipped		★★★	85
Black Bart		★★	90
Black Hole		★★	303
Catch and Release		★★	163
Chaps My Hide		★★	68
Gryffindor		★★	236
Highgrader		★★	92
Hy-Pro-Glo		★★	214
Lucky Cuss		★★	66
March of Dimes		★★	74
Nothing Could Be Finer		★★	286
Power Keg		★★	91
Redline		★★	269
Shout in the Dark		★★	198
Stairway to Heaven		★★	337
Stanley-Slip Bobber		★★	164
Stout		★★	124
Takes a Thief	R	★★	97
Talk to Me		★★	290
Unas, Slayer of the Gods		★★	175
Far Beyond Driven	R	★	70
Fresh Squeezed		★	275
Jedi Magic		★	40
Miso Horny		★	123

5.10d			
Coyotes in the Henhouse		★★★★	68
Doc's Holiday		★★★★	70
Roofs, The		★★★★	167
Angry Inch, The		★★★	47
Captain Hook		★★★	137

GRADED LIST OF TOPROPES

5.11b
Around the Influence	★★★	215
Fire in the Hole	★★	268
Microwave Tower #3	★★	321
Cat Nip	★	126
Soul Doubt	★	241

5.11a
Powerline	★★★	335
Color of Fear, The	★★	118
Fish Face	★★	164
Redman	★★	106
Bovine Eyes	★	75
King of the Blue Flame	★	184
Narcotic Prayer	★	81
Turn and Face the Music	★	61
Witching Hour	★	234

5.10d
Quartzite Quandary	★★★	269
Bait and Switch	★★	164
Fortune Teller	★★	299
Saddle Up	★★	101
Big Test, The	★	220
Black Sabbath	★	116
Boudica	★	124
Brainstorm	★	182
Hang 'Em High	★	85
Tangerine	★	336
Think Thin	★	313
Voodoo Jive	★	234

5.10c
Black Tower Headwall Left	★★	172
Coolie Crank	★★	75
No Knockers	★	313
Park Off the Curb	★	152
Percival's Face	★	174
Sitting Duck	★	265
Lofting Air Biscuit		184

5.10b
Merlin	★★	234
Pull Over to Pass	★★	152
Fracture, The	★	271
Pull My Finger	★	184
South American Cruise	★	243
Stinky Boy	★	184
Trembling Tips	★	271
Upper QB #2	★	269
Wings of Slack	★	44
Dihedral		185
Target Practice		266

5.10a
Get a Rope!	★★	67
Green Light, Red Light	★★	287
Exit Planet Dust	★	50
Getting Whacked	★	299
Gold Fever	★	103
Here's Mud in Your Eye	★	76
Litter Removal	★	152
Over the Band Gap	★	188
Pablo Cruise	★	51
Spectre, The	★	238
Triples	★	127
Eye of Newt		228
Free Be Free		203
Oxidation		189

5.9
Belleville	★★	90
Doubles	★★	127
Drawbridge, The	★★	170
Girls in the Middle	★★	136
And Then a Step to the...	★	301
Angler	★	162
Bonus	★	146
Bullseye	★	127
Crocs in the Moat	★	170

Going to California	★	336
Grain Scoop	★	54
Ground	★	182
I Like It Dirty but ...	★	174
Magnum Force		265
Saddle Tramp	★	74
Stupidest Lannister, The	★	97
Upper QB #4	★	269
Hairy Eyeball		60
Poke You With My Stick		202
Ripple		80
This One Is For You		313
Wrenched		181

5.8
After the Gold Rush	★★	84
A Thunder of Drums	★	80
Big Easy, The	★	139
Timeline	★	170
Upper QB #3		269

5.7
Rosy Cheeks	★	268
Sharkface	★	272
Slave to the Streetlight	★	287
Rust		189

5.6
Abominable Snow Jam	★★	328
El Gordo	★	119
Lakeview Arête	★	272
Lookout		330

5.5
Cali Gold	★★	84

5.4
Boy's Gotta Pee		152

5.2
Humbolt Hunt		254

GRADED LIST OF BOULDER PROBLEMS

INDEX

ABOUT THE AUTHOR

Brandon Copp grew up on a farm in the small town of Lawrenceville, Illinois. An avid outdoorsman from an early age, he was introduced to the sport of climbing through the Boy Scouts, and those experiences planted the seed. Brandon really cut his teeth climbing on the overhanging sport routes of the Red River Gorge, a place that became like a second home to him. He later moved to Boulder, Colorado, to pursue a Master's degree in aerospace engineering — or maybe it was the mountains that drew him there. In Boulder he rounded out his skills by adding traditional and ice climbing to his repertoire. After graduating, he moved west to California and discovered Holcomb Valley and Big Bear Lake, which quickly became his favorite local climbing area. He has laid eyes on every climb in this book, visiting over 200 crags in the process.

In addition to his Big Bear exploits, Brandon has climbed at various destinations around the world including Australia, New Zealand, Canada, Bolivia, and Norway. Rock climbing has been his biggest passion for 20+ years, but he also enjoys skiing, scuba diving, hiking, curling, and traveling. He currently lives in Huntington Beach, California, with his wife, Jackie, and dog, Jackson. On any given day you might find him tinkering on a woodworking project, wandering the woods well after sunset because there's always just "one more climb" he wants to do, or telling long-winded stories around a campfire with a glass of scotch in hand.